THE ENCYCLOPEDIA OF
TRADING STRATEGIES

Other Books in The Irwin Trader's Edge Series

Techinical Analysis for the Trading Professional
  by Constance Brown   (0-07-012062-5)
Agricuktural Futures and Options
  by Richard Duncan   (0-07-134922-7)
The Options Edge by William Gallacher   (0-07-038296-4)
The Art of the Trade by R. E. McMaster   (0-07-045542-2)

THE ENCYCLOPEDIA OF TRADING STRATEGIES

JEFFREY OWEN KATZ, Ph.D.
DONNA L. McCORMICK

McGraw-Hill

New York   San Francisco   Washington, D.C.   Auckland   Bogotá
Caracas   Lisbon   London   Madrid   Mexico City   Milan
Montreal   New Delhi   San Juan   Singapore
Sydney   Tokyo   Toronto

Library of Congress Cataloging-in-Publication Data

Katz, Jeffrey (Jeffrey Owen)
    The encyclopedia of trading strategies / by Jeffrey Katz and Donna McCormick.
       p.   cm.
    Includes bibliographical references and index.
    ISBN 0-07-058099-5
    1. Commodity futures. I. McCormick, Donna (Donna L.)
HG6046.K33   2000
332.64'421—dc21   99-045943
                                               CIP

McGraw-Hill

A Division of The McGraw-Hill Companies

   9 BKM BKM   0 9 8

ISBN-13: 978-0-07-058099-2

ISBN-10: 0-07-058099-5

The authors would like to thank the sponsoring editor for this book, Stephen Isaacs, the editing supervisor, John M. Morriss, and the production supervisor, Elizabeth J. Strange. It was set in Times Roman per the IPROF design specs by Joanne Morbit and Paul Scozzari of McGraw-Hill's Professional Book Group Desktop Publishing Unit.

McGraw-Hill books are available at special quantity discounts to use as premiums and sales promotions, or for use in corporate training programs. For more information, please write to the Director of Special Sales, Professional Publishing, McGraw-Hill, 2 Penn Plaza, New York, NY 10121-2298. Or contact your local bookstore.

To Rosalyn Anker Katz

With our thanks for your love and support

TRADEMARKS AND SERVICE MARKS

Company and product names associated with listings in this book should be considered as trademarks or service marks of the company indicated. The use of a registered trademark is not permitted for commercial purposes without the permission of the company named. In some cases, products of one company are offered by other companies and are presented in a number of different listings in this book. It is virtually impossible to identify every trademark or service mark for every product and every use, but we would like to highlight the following:

Visual Basic, Visual C++, and Excel are trademarks of Microsoft Corp.

NAG function library is a service mark of Numerical Algorithms Group, Ltd.

Numerical Recipes in C (book and software) is a service mark of Numerical Recipes Software.

TradeStation, SuperCharts, and SystemWriter Plus are trademarks of Omega Research.

Evolver is a trademark of Palisade Corporation.

Master Chartist is a trademark of Robert Slade, Inc.

TS-Evolve and TradeCycles (MESA) are trademarks of Ruggiero Associates.

Divergengine is a service mark of Ruggiero Associates.

C++ Builder, Delphi, and Borland Database Engine are trademarks of Borland.

CQG for Windows is a trademark of CQG, Inc.

Metastock is a trademark of Equis International.

technical analysis function library is a service mark of FM Labs.

Excalibur is a trademark of Futures Truth.

MATLAB is a trademark of The MathWorks, Inc.

MESA96 is a trademark of Mesa.

CONTENTS

PREFACE   xiii

INTRODUCTION   xv
What Is a Complete Mechanical Trading System? • What Are Good Entries and Exits? • The Scientific Approach to System Development • Tools and Materials Needed for the Scientific Approach

PART I

Tools of the Trade
Introduction   1

Chapter 1

Data   3

Types of Data • Data Time Frames • Data Quality • Data Sources and Vendors

Chapter 2

Simulators   13

Types of Simulators • Programming the Simulator • Simulator Output (*performance summary reports; trade-by-trade reports*) • Simulator Performance (*speed; capacity; power*) • Reliability of Simulators • Choosing the Right Simulator • Simulators Used in This Book

Chapter 3

Optimizers and Optimization   29

What Optimizers Do • How Optimizers Are Used • Types of Optimization (*implicit optimizers; brute force optimizers; user-guided optimization; genetic optimizers; optimization by simulated annealing; analytic optimizers; linear programming*) • How to Fail with Optimization (*small samples; large parameter sets; no verification*) • How to Succeed with Optimization (*large, representative samples; few rules and parameters; verification of results*) • Alternatives to Traditional Optimization • Optimizer Tools and Information • Which Optimizer Is for You?

Chapter 4

Statistics   51

Why Use Statistics to Evaluate Trading Systems? • Sampling • Optimization and Curve-Fitting • Sample Size and Representativeness • Evaluating a System Statistically • Example 1: Evaluating the Out-of-Sample Test (*what if the distribution is not normal? what if there is serial dependence? what if the markets change?*) • Example 2: Evaluating the In-Sample Tests • Interpreting the Example Statistics (*optimization results; verification results*) • Other Statistical Techniques and Their Use (*genetically evolved systems; multiple regression; monte carlo simulations; out-of-sample testing; walk-forward testing*) • Conclusion

PART II

The Study of Entries

Introduction   71

What Constitutes a Good Entry? • Orders Used in Entries (*stop orders; limit orders; market orders; selecting appropriate orders*) • Entry Techniques Covered in This Book (*breakouts and moving averages; oscillators; seasonality; lunar and solar phenomena; cycles and rhythms; neural networks; genetically evolved entry rules*) • Standardized Exits • Equalization of Dollar Volatility • Basic Test Portfolio and Platform

Chapter 5

Breakout Models   83

Kinds of Breakouts • Characteristics of Breakouts • Testing Breakout Models • Channel Breakout Entries (*close only channel breakouts; highest high/lowest low breakouts*) • Volatility Breakout Entries • Volatility Breakout Variations (*long positions only; currencies only; adx trend filter*) • Summary Analyses (*breakout types; entry orders; interactions; restrictions and filters; analysis by market*) • Conclusion • What Have We Learned?

Chapter 6

Moving Average Models   109

What is a Moving Average? • Purpose of a Moving Average • The Issue of Lag • Types of Moving Averages • Types of Moving Average Entry Models • Characteristics of Moving Average Entries • Orders Used to Effect Entries • Test Methodology • Tests of Trend-Following Models • Tests of Counter-Trend Models • Conclusion • What Have We Learned?

Chapter 7

Oscillator-Based Entries   133

What Is an Oscillator? • Kinds of Oscillators • Generating Entries with Oscillators • Characteristics of Oscillator Entries • Test Methodology • Test Results (*tests of overbought/oversold models; tests of signal line models; tests of divergence models; summary analyses*) • Conclusion • What Have We Learned?

Chapter 8

Seasonality   153

What Is Seasonality? • Generating Seasonal Entries • Characteristics of Seasonal Entries • Orders Used to Effect Seasonal Entries • Test Methodology • Test Results (*test of the basic crossover model; tests of the basic momentum model; tests of the crossover model with confirmation; tests of the crossover model with confirmation and inversions; summary analyses*) • Conclusion • What Have We Learned?

Chapter 9

Lunar and Solar Rhythms   179

Legitimacy or Lunacy? • Lunar Cycles and Trading (*generating lunar entries; lunar test methodology; lunar test results; tests of the basic crossover model; tests of the basic momentum model; tests of the crossover model with confirmation; tests of the crossover model with confirmation and inversions; summary analyses; conclusion*) • Solar Activity and Trading (*generating solar entries; solar test results; conclusion*) • What Have We Learned?

Chapter 10

Cycle-Based Entries   203

Cycle Detection Using MESA • Detecting Cycles Using Filter Banks (*butterworth filters; wavelet-based filters*) • Generating Cycle Entries Using Filter Banks • Characteristics of Cycle-Based Entries • Test Methodology • Test Results • Conclusion • What Have We Learned?

Chapter 11

Neural Networks   227

What Are Neural Networks? (*feed-forward neural networks*) • Neural Networks in Trading • Forecasting with Neural Networks • Generating Entries with Neural Predictions • Reverse Slow %K Model (*code for the reverse slow %k model; test methodology for the reverse slow %k model; training results for the reverse slow %k model*) • Turning Point Models (*code for the turning point models; test methodology*

for the turning point models; training results for the turning point models) • Trading
Results for All Models *(trading results for the reverse slow %k model; trading results
for the bottom turning point model; trading results for the top turning point model)* •
Summary Analyses • Conclusion • What Have We Learned?

Chapter 12

Genetic Algorithms   257

What Are Genetic Algorithms? • Evolving Rule-Based Entry Models • Evolving an
Entry Model *(the rule templates)* • Test Methodology *(code for evolving an entry
model)* • Test Results *(solutions evolved for long entries; solutions evolved for short
entries; test results for the standard portfolio; market-by-market test results; equity
curves; the rules for the solutions tested)* • Conclusion • What Have We Learned?

PART III

The Study of Exits

Introduction   281

The Importance of the Exit • Goals of a Good Exit Strategy • Kinds of Exits
Employed in an Exit Strategy *(money management exits; trailing exits; profit target
exits; time-based exits; volatility exits; barrier exits; signal exits)* • Considerations
When Exiting the Market *(gunning; trade-offs with protective stops; slippage;
contrarian trading; conclusion)* • Testing Exit Strategies • Standard Entries for Testing
Exits *(the random entry model)*

Chapter 13

The Standard Exit Strategy   293

What is the Standard Exit Strategy? • Characteristics of the Standard Exit • Purpose of
Testing the SES • Tests of the Original SES *(test results)* • Tests of the Modified SES
(test results) • Conclusion • What Have We Learned?

Chapter 14

Improvements on the Standard Exit   309

Purpose of the Tests • Tests of the Fixed Stop and Profit Target • Tests of Dynamic
Stops *(test of the highest high/lowest low stop; test of the dynamic atr-based stop; test
of the modified exponential moving average dynamic stop)* • Tests of the Profit Target •
Test of the Extended Time Limit • Market-By-Market Results for the Best Exit •
Conclusion • What Have We Learned?

Chapter 15

Adding Artificial Intelligence to Exits   335

Test Methodology for the Neural Exit Component • Results of the Neural Exit Test (*baseline results; neural exit portfolio results; neural exit market-by-market results*) • Test Methodology for the Genetic Exit Component (*top 10 solutions with baseline exit; results of rule-based exits for longs and shorts; market-by-market results of rule-based exits for longs; market-by-market results of rule-based exits for shorts*) • Conclusion • What Have We Learned?

Conclusion   353

The Big Picture • Points of Light • Looking into the Light

Notice   362

Companion Software Available

Appendix   363

References and Suggested Reading

INDEX   367

In this book is the knowledge needed to become a more successful trader of commodities. As a comprehensive reference and system developer's guide, the book explains many popular techniques and puts them to the test, and explores innovative ways to take profits out of the market and to gain an extra edge. As well, the book provides better methods for controlling risk, and gives insight into which methods perform poorly and could devastate capital. Even the basics are covered: information on how to acquire and screen data, how to properly back-test systems using trading simulators, how to safely perform optimization, how to estimate and compensate for curve-fitting, and even how to assess the results using inferential statistics. This book demonstrates why the surest way to success in trading is through use of a good, mechanized trading system.

For all but a few traders, system trading yields more profitable results than discretionary trading. Discretionary trading involves subjective decisions that frequently become emotional and lead to losses. Affect, uncertainty, greed, and fear easily displace reason and knowledge as the driving forces behind the trades. Moreover, it is hard to test and verify a discretionary trading model. System-based trading, in contrast, is objective. Emotions are out of the picture. Through programmed logic and assumptions, mechanized systems express the trader's reason and knowledge. Best of all, such systems are easily tested: Bad systems can be rejected or modified, and good ones can be improved. This book contains solid information that can be of great help when designing, building, and testing a profitable mechanical trading system. While the emphasis is on an in-depth, critical analysis of the various factors purported to contribute to winning systems, the essential elements of a complete, mechanical trading system are also dissected and explained.

To be complete, all mechanical trading systems must have an entry method and an exit method. The entry method must detect opportunities to enter the market at points that are likely to yield trades with a good risk-to-reward ratio. The exit method must protect against excessive loss of capital when a trade goes wrong or when the market turns, as well as effectively capture profits when the market moves favorably. A considerable amount of space is devoted to the systematic back-testing and evaluation of exit systems, methods, and strategies. Even the trader who already has a trading strategy or system that provides acceptable exits is likely to discover something that can be used to improve the system, increase profits, and reduce risk exposure.

Also included in these pages are trading simulations on entire portfolios of tradables. As is demonstrated, running analyses on portfolios is straightforward, if not easy to accomplish. The ease of computing equity growth curves, maximum drawdowns, risk-to-reward ratios, returns on accounts, numbers of trades, and all the other related kinds of information useful in assessing a trading system on a whole portfolio of commodities or stocks at once is made evident. The process of conducting portfolio-wide walk-forward and other forms of testing and optimization is also described. For example, instruction is provided on how to search for a set of parameters that, when plugged into a system used to trade each of a set of commodities, yields the best total net profit with the lowest drawdown (or perhaps the best Sharpe Ratio, or any other measure of portfolio performance desired) for that *entire* set of commodities. Small institutional traders (CTAs) wishing to run a system on multiple tradables, as a means of diversification, risk reduction, and liquidity enhancement, should find this discussion especially useful.

Finally, to keep all aspects of the systems and components being tested objective and completely mechanical, we have drawn upon our academic and scientific research backgrounds to apply the scientific method to the study of entry and exit techniques. In addition, when appropriate, statistics are used to assess the significance of the results of the investigations. This approach should provide the most rigorous information possible about what constitutes a valid and useful component in a successful trading strategy.

So that everyone will benefit from the investigations, the exact logic behind every entry or exit strategy is discussed in detail. For those wishing to replicate and expand the studies contained herein, extensive source code is also provided in the text, as well as on a CD-ROM (see offer at back of book).

Since a basic trading system is always composed of two components, this book naturally includes the following two parts: "The Study of Entries" and "The Study of Exits." Discussions of particular technologies that may be used in generating entries or exits, e.g., neural networks, are handled within the context of developing particular entry or exit strategies. The "Introduction" contains lessons on the fundamental issues surrounding the implementation of the scientific approach to trading system development. The first part of this book, "Tools of the Trade," contains basic information, necessary for all system traders. The "Conclusion" provides a summary of the research findings, with suggestions on how to best apply the knowledge and for future research. The "Appendix" contains references and suggested reading.

Finally, we would like to point out that this book is a continuation and elaboration of a series of articles we published as Contributing Writers to *Technical Analysis of Stocks and Commodities* from 1996, onward.

Jeffrey Owen Katz, Ph.D., and Donna L. McCormick

There is one thing that most traders have in common: They have taken on the challenge of forecasting and trading the financial markets, of searching for those small islands of lucrative inefficiency in a vast sea of efficient market behavior. For one of the authors, Jeffrey Katz, this challenge was initially a means to indulge an obsession with mathematics. Over a decade ago, he developed a model that provided entry signals for the Standard & Poor's 500 (S&P 500) and OEX. While these signals were, at that time, about 80% accurate, Katz found himself second-guessing them. Moreover, he had to rely on his own subjective determinations of such critical factors as what kind of order to use for entry, when to exit, and where to place stops. These determinations, the essence of discretionary trading, were often driven more by the emotions of fear and avarice than by reason and knowledge. As a result, he churned and vacillated, made bad decisions, and lost more often than won. For Katz, like for most traders, discretionary trading did not work.

If discretionary trading did not work, then what did? Perhaps system trading was the answer. Katz decided to develop a completely automated trading system in the form of a computer program that could generate buy, sell, stop, and other necessary orders without human judgment or intervention. A good mechanical system, logic suggested, would avoid the problems associated with discretionary trading, if the discipline to follow it could be mustered. Such a system would provide explicit and well-defined entries, "normal" or profitable exits, and "abnormal" or money management exits designed to control losses on bad trades.

A fully automated system would also make it possible to conduct historical tests, unbiased by hindsight, and to do such tests on large quantities of data. Thorough testing was the only way to determine whether a system really worked and would be profitable to trade, Katz reasoned. Due to familiarity with the data series, valid tests could not be performed by eye. If Katz looked at a chart and "believed" a given formation signaled a good place to enter the market, he could not trust that belief because he had already seen what happened after the formation occurred. Moreover, if charts of previous years were examined to find other examples of the formation, attempts to identify the pattern by "eyeballing" would be biased. On the other hand, if the pattern to be tested could be formally defined and explicitly coded, the computer could then objectively do all the work: It would run the code on many years of historical data, look for the specified formation, and evaluate (without hindsight) the behavior of the market *after* each instance. In this way, the computer could indicate whether he was indeed correct in his hypothesis that a given formation was a profitable one. Exit rules could also be evaluated objectively.

Finally, a well-defined mechanical trading system would allow such things as commissions, slippage, impossible fills, and markets that moved before he could to be factored in. This would help avoid unpleasant shocks when moving from computer simulations to real-world trading. One of the problems Katz had in his earlier trading attempt was failing to consider the high transaction costs involved in trading OEX options. Through complete mechanization, he could ensure that the system tests would include all such factors. In this way, potential surprises could be eliminated, and a very realistic assessment could be obtained of how any system or system element would perform. System trading might, he thought, be the key to greater success in the markets.

WHAT IS A COMPLETE, MECHANICAL TRADING SYSTEM?

One of the problems with Katz's early trading was that his "system" only provided entry signals, leaving the determination of exits to subjective judgment; it was not, therefore, a complete, mechanical trading system. A complete, mechanical trading system, one that can be tested and deployed in a totally objective fashion, without requiring human judgment, must provide both *entries* and *exits*. To be truly complete, a mechanical system must explicitly provide the following information:

1. When and how, and possibly at what price, to enter the market
2. When and how, and possibly at what price, to exit the market with a loss
3. When and how, and possibly at what price, to exit the market with a profit

The entry signals of a mechanical trading system can be as simple as explicit orders to buy or sell at the next day's open. The orders might be slightly more elaborate, e.g., to enter tomorrow (or on the next bar) using either a limit or stop. Then again, very complex contingent orders, which are executed during certain periods only if specified conditions are met, may be required–for example, orders to buy or sell the market on a stop if the market gaps up or down more than so many points at the open.

A trading system's exits may also be implemented using any of a range of orders, from the simple to the complex. Exiting a bad trade at a loss is frequently achieved using a *money management stop*, which terminates the trade that has gone wrong before the loss becomes seriously damaging. A money management stop, which is simply a stop order employed to prevent runaway losses, performs one of the functions that must be achieved in some manner by a system's exit strategy; the function is that of risk control. Exiting on a profit may be accomplished in any of several different ways, including by the use of *profit targets*, which are simply limit orders placed in such a way that they end the trade once the market moves a certain amount in the trader's favor; *trailing stops*, which are stop orders used to exit with a profit when the market begins to reverse direction; and a wide variety of other orders or combinations of orders.

In Katz's early trading attempts, the only signals available were of probable direction or turning points. These signals were responded to by placing buy-at-market or sell-at-market orders, orders that are often associated with poor fills and lots of slippage. Although the signals were often accurate, not every turning point was caught. Therefore, Katz could not simply reverse his position at each signal. Separate exits were necessary. The software Katz was using only served as a partially mechanical entry model; i.e., it did not provide exit signals. As such, it was not a complete mechanical trading system that provided both entries and exits. Since there were no mechanically generated exit signals, all exits had to be determined subjectively, which was one of the factors responsible for his trading problems at that time. Another factor that contributed to his lack of success was the inability to properly assess, in a rigorous and objective manner, the behavior of the trading regime over a sufficiently long period of historical data. He had been flying blind! Without having a complete system, that is, exits as well as entries, not to mention good system-testing software, how could such things as net profitability, maximum drawdown, or the Sharpe Ratio be estimated, the historical equity curve be studied, and other important characteristics of the system (such as the likelihood of its being profitable in the future) be investigated? To do these things, it became clear—a system was needed that completed the full circle, providing complete "round-turns," each consisting of an entry followed by an exit.

WHAT ARE GOOD ENTRIES AND EXITS?

Given a mechanical trading system that contains an entry model to generate entry orders and an exit model to generate exit orders (including those required for money management), how are the entries and exits evaluated to determine whether they are good? In other words, what constitutes a good entry or exit?

Notice we used the terms entry *orders* and exit *orders*, not entry or exit *signals*. Why? Because "signals" are too ambiguous. Does a buy "signal" mean that one should buy at the open of the next bar, or buy using a stop or limit order? And if so, at what price? In response to a "signal" to exit a long position, does the exit occur at the close, on a profit target, or perhaps on a money management stop? Each of these orders will have different consequences in terms of the results achieved. To determine whether an entry or exit method works, it must produce more than mere *signals*; it must, at some point, issue highly specific entry and exit *orders*. A fully specified entry or exit order may easily be tested to determine its quality or effectiveness.

In a broad sense, a *good entry order* is one that causes the trader to enter the market at a point where there is relatively low risk and a fairly high degree of potential reward. A trader's Nirvana would be a system that generated entry orders to buy or sell on a limit at the most extreme price of every turning point. Even if the exits were only merely acceptable, none of the trades would have more than one or two ticks of *adverse excursion* (the largest unrealized loss to occur within a trade), and in every case, the market would be entered at the best obtainable price. In an imperfect world, however, entries will never be that good, but they can be such that, when accompanied by reasonable effective exits, adverse excursion is kept to acceptable levels and satisfying risk-reward ratios are obtained.

What constitutes an *effective exit*? An effective exit must quickly extricate the trader from the market when a trade has gone wrong. It is essential to preserve capital from excessive erosion by losing trades; an exit must achieve this, however, without cutting too many potentially profitable trades short by converting them into small losses. A superior exit should be able to hold a trade for as long as it takes to capture a significant chunk of any large move; i.e., it should be capable of riding a sizable move to its conclusion. However, riding a sizable move to conclusion is not a critical issue if the exit strategy is combined with an entry formula that allows for reentry into sustained trends and other substantial market movements.

In reality, it is almost impossible, and certainly unwise, to discuss entries and exits independently. To back-test a trading system, both entries and exits must be present so that complete round-turns will occur. If the market is entered, but never exited, how can any completed trades to evaluate be obtained? An entry method and an exit method are required before a testable system can exist. However, it would be very useful to study a variety of entry strategies and make some assessment regarding how each performs independent of the exits. Likewise, it would be advantageous to examine exits, testing different techniques, without having to deal with entries as well. In general, it is best to manipulate a minimum number of entities at a time, and measure the effects of those manipulations, while either ignoring or holding everything else constant. Is this not the very essence of the scientific, experimental method that has achieved so much in other fields? But how can such isolation and control be achieved, allowing entries and exits to be separately, and scientifically, studied?

THE SCIENTIFIC APPROACH TO SYSTEM DEVELOPMENT

This book is intended to accomplish a systematic and detailed analysis of the individual components that make up a complete trading system. We are proposing nothing less than a scientific study of entries, exits, and other trading system elements. The basic substance of the scientific approach as applied herein is as follows:

> **1.** The object of study, in this case a trading system (or one or more of its elements), must be either directly or indirectly observable, preferably without dependence on subjective judgment, something easily achieved

with proper testing and simulation software when working with complete mechanical trading systems.

2. An orderly means for assessing the behavior of the object of study must be available, which, in the case of trading systems, is back-testing over long periods of historical data, together with, if appropriate, the application of various models of statistical inference, the aim of the latter being to provide a fix or reckoning of how likely a system is to hold up in the future and on different samples of data.

3. A method for making the investigative task tractable by holding most parameters and system components fixed while focusing upon the effects of manipulating only one or two critical elements at a time.

The structure of this book reflects the scientific approach in many ways. Trading systems are dissected into entry and exit models. Standardized methods for exploring these components independently are discussed and implemented, leading to separate sections on entries and exits. Objective tests and simulations are run, and statistical analyses are performed. Results are presented in a consistent manner that permits direct comparison. This is "old hat" to any practicing scientist.

Many traders might be surprised to discover that they, like practicing scientists, have a working knowledge of the scientific method, albeit in different guise! Books for traders often discuss "paper trading" or historical back-testing, or present results based on these techniques. However, this book is going to be more consistent and rigorous in its application of the scientific approach to the problem of how to successfully trade the markets. For instance, few books in which historical tests of trading systems appear offer statistical analyses to assess validity and to estimate the likelihood of future profits. In contrast, this book includes a detailed tutorial on the application of inferential statistics to the evaluation of trading system performance.

Similarly, few pundits test their entries and exits independently of one another. There are some neat tricks that allow specific system components to be tested in isolation. One such trick is to have a set of standard entry and exit strategies that remain fixed as the particular entry, exit, or other element under study is varied. For example, when studying entry models, a standardized exit strategy will be repeatedly employed, without change, as a variety of entry models are tested and tweaked. Likewise, for the study of exits, a standardized entry technique will be employed. The rather shocking entry technique involves the use of a random number generator to generate random long and short entries into various markets! Most traders would panic at the idea of trading a system with entries based on the fall of the die; nevertheless, such entries are excellent in making a harsh test for an exit strategy. An exit strategy that can pull profits out of randomly entered trades is worth knowing about and can, amazingly, be readily achieved, at least for the S&P 500 (Katz and McCormick, March 1998, April 1998). The tests will be done in a way that allows meaningful comparisons to be made between different entry and exit methods.

To summarize, the core elements of the scientific approach are:

1. The isolation of system elements

2. The use of standardized tests that allow valid comparisons

3. The statistical assessment of results

TOOLS AND MATERIALS NEEDED FOR THE SCIENTIFIC APPROACH

Before applying the scientific approach to the study of the markets, a number of things must be considered. First, a universe of reliable market data on which to perform back-testing and statistical analyses must be available. Since this book is focused on commodities trading, the market data used as the basis for our universe on an end-of-day time frame will be a subset of the diverse set of markets supplied by Pinnacle Data Corporation; these include the agriculturals, metals, energy resources, bonds, currencies, and market indices. Intraday time-frame trading is not addressed in this book, although it is one of our primary areas of interest that may be pursued in a subsequent volume. In addition to standard pricing data, explorations into the effects of various exogenous factors on the markets sometimes require unusual data. For example, data on sunspot activity (solar radiation may influence a number of markets, especially agricultural ones) was obtained from the Royal Observatory of Belgium.

Not only is a universe of data needed, but it is necessary to simulate one or more trading accounts to perform back-testing. Such a task requires the use of a *trading simulator*, a software package that allows simulated trading accounts to be created and manipulated on a computer. The C++ Trading Simulator from Scientific Consultant Services is the one used most extensively in this book because it was designed to handle portfolio simulations and is familiar to the authors. Other programs, like Omega Research's TradeStation or SystemWriter Plus, also offer basic trading simulation and system testing, as well as assorted charting capabilities. To satisfy the broadest range of readership, we occasionally employ these products, and even Microsoft's Excel spreadsheet, in our analyses.

Another important consideration is the *optimization of model parameters*. When running tests, it is often necessary to adjust the parameters of some component (e.g., an entry model, an exit model, or some piece thereof) to discover the best set of parameters and/or to see how the behavior of the model changes as its parameters change. Several kinds of model parameter optimizations may be conducted. In *manual optimization*, the user of the simulator specifies a parameter that is to be manipulated and the range through which that parameter is to be stepped; the user may wish to simultaneously manipulate two or more parameters in this manner, generating output in the form of a table that shows how the parameters interact to affect the outcome. Another method is *brute force optimization*, which comes in several varieties: The most common form is stepping every parameter through every possible value. If there are many parameters, each having many possible values, running this kind of optimization may take years. Brute force optimization can, however, be a workable approach if the number of parameters, and values through which they must be stepped, is small. Other forms of brute force optimization are not as complete, or as likely to find the global optimum, but can be run much more quickly. Finally, for heavy-duty optimization (and, if naïvely applied, truly impressive curve-fitting) there are *genetic algorithms*. An appropriate genetic algorithm (GA) can quickly find a good solution, if not a global optimum, even when large numbers of parameters are involved, each having large numbers of values through which it must be stepped. A genetic optimizer is an important tool in the arsenal of any trading system developer, but it must be used cautiously, with an ever-present eye to the danger of curve-fitting. In the investigations presented in this book, the statistical assessment techniques, out-of-sample tests, and such other aspects of the analyses as the focus on entire portfolios provide protection against the curve-fitting demon, regardless of the optimization method employed.

Jeffrey Owen Katz, Ph.D., and Donna F. McCormick

PART I

Tools of the Trade

Introduction

To objectively study the behavior of mechanical trading systems, various experimental materials and certain tools are needed.

To study the behavior of a given entry or exit method, a simulation should be done using that method on a portion of a given market's past performance; that requires *data*. Clean, historical data for the market on which a method is being tested is the starting point.

Once the data is available, software is needed to simulate a trading account. Such software should allow various kinds of trading orders to be posted and should emulate the behavior of trading a real account over the historical period of interest. Software of this kind is called a *trading simulator*.

The model (whether an entry model, an exit model, or a complete system) may have a number of parameters that have to be adjusted to obtain the best results from the system and its elements, or a number of features to be turned on or off. Here is where an *optimizer* plays its part, and a choice must be made among the several types of optimizers available.

The simulations and optimizations will produce a plethora of results. The system may have taken hundreds or thousands of trades, each with its own profit/loss, maximum adverse excursion, and maximum favorable excursion. Also generated will be simulated equity curves, risk-to-reward ratios, profit factors, and other information provided by the trading simulator about the simulated trading account(s). A way to assess the significance of these results is needed. Is the apparent profitability of the trades a result of excessive optimization? Could the system have been profitable due to chance alone, or might it really be a valid trading strategy? If the system is valid, is it likely to hold up as well in the future, when actually being traded, as in the past? Questions such as these require the basic machinery provided by *inferential statistics*.

In the next several chapters, we will cover data, simulators, optimizers, and statistics. These items will be used throughout this book when examining entry and exit methods and when attempting to integrate entries and exits into complete trading systems.

CHAPTER 1

Data

$\mathbf{A}$ determination of what works, and what does not, cannot be made in the realm of commodities trading without quality data for use in tests and simulations. Several types of data may be needed by the trader interested in developing a profitable commodities trading system. At the very least, the trader will require historical pricing data for the commodities of interest.

TYPES OF DATA

Commodities pricing data is available for individual or continuous contracts. *Individual contract data* consists of quotations for individual commodities contracts. At any given time, there may be several contracts actively trading. Most speculators trade the *front-month* contracts, those that are most liquid and closest to expiration, but are not yet past first notice date. As each contract nears expiration, or passes first notice date, the trader "rolls over" any open position into the next contract. Working with individual contracts, therefore, can add a great deal of complexity to simulations and tests. Not only must trades directly generated by the trading system be dealt with, but the system developer must also correctly handle rollovers and the selection of appropriate contracts.

To make system testing easier and more practical, the *continuous contract* was invented. A continuous contract consists of appropriate individual contracts strung together, end to end, to form a single, continuous data series. Some data massaging usually takes place when putting together a continuous contract; the purpose is to close the gaps that occur at rollover, when one contract ends and another begins. Simple *back-adjustment* appears to be the most reasonable and popular gap-closing method (Schwager, 1992). Back-adjustment involves nothing more than the subtraction of constants, chosen to close the gaps, from all contracts in a series other than the most recent. Since the only operation performed on a contract's prices is the subtraction of a constant, all linear price relationships (e.g., price changes over time, volatility levels, and ranges) are preserved. Account simulations performed using back-adjusted continuous contracts yield results that need correction only for rollover costs. Once corrected for rollover, simulated trades will produce profits and losses identical to those derived from simulations performed using individual contracts. However, if trading decisions depend upon information involving absolute levels, percentages, or ratios of prices, then additional data series (beyond back-adjusted continuous contracts) will be required before tests can be conducted.

End-of-day pricing data, whether in the form of individual or continuous contracts, consists of a series of daily *quotations*. Each quotation, "bar," or data point typically contains seven fields of information: date, open, high, low, close, volume, and open interest. Volume and open interest are normally unavailable until after the close of the following day; when testing trading methods, use only past values of these two variables or the outcome may be a fabulous, but essentially untradable, system! The open, high, low, and close (sometimes referred to as the *settlement price*) are available each day shortly after the market closes.

Intraday pricing data consists either of a series of fixed-interval bars or of individual ticks. The data fields for fixed-interval bars are date, time, open, high, low, close, and tick volume. *Tick volume* differs from the volume reported for end-of-day data series: For intraday data, it is the number of ticks that occur in the period making up the bar, regardless of the number of contracts involved in the transactions reflected in those ticks. Only date, time, and price information are reported for individual ticks; volume is not. Intraday tick data is easily converted into data with fixed-interval bars using readily available software. Conversion software is frequently provided by the data vendor at no extra cost to the consumer.

In addition to commodities pricing data, other kinds of data may be of value. For instance, long-term historical data on sunspot activity, obtained from the Royal Observatory of Belgium, is used in the chapter on lunar and solar influences. Temperature and rainfall data have a bearing on agricultural markets. Various economic time series that cover every aspect of the economy, from inflation to housing starts, may improve the odds of trading commodities successfully. Do not forget to examine reports and measures that reflect sentiment, such as the Commitment of Traders (COT) releases, bullish and bearish consensus surveys, and put-call ratios. Nonquantitative forms of sentiment data, such as news headlines, may also be acquired and quantified for use in systematic tests. Nothing should be ignored. Mining unusual data often uncovers interesting and profitable discoveries. It is often the case that the more esoteric or arcane the data, and the more difficult it is to obtain, the greater its value!

DATA TIME FRAMES

Data may be used in its natural time frame or may need to be processed into a different time frame. Depending on the time frame being traded and on the nature of the trading system, individual ticks, 5-minute bars, 20-minute bars, or daily, weekly, fortnightly (bimonthly), monthly, quarterly, or even yearly data may be necessary. A data source usually has a natural time frame. For example, when collecting intraday data, the natural time frame is the *tick*. The tick is an elastic time frame: Sometimes ticks come fast and furious, other times sporadically with long intervals between them. The day is the natural time frame for end-of-day pricing data. For other kinds of data, the natural time frame may be bimonthly, as is the case for the Commitment of Traders releases; or it may be quarterly, typical of company earnings reports.

Although going from longer to shorter time frames is impossible (resolution that is not there cannot be created), conversions from shorter to longer can be readily achieved with appropriate processing. For example, it is quite easy to create a series consisting of 1-minute bars from a series of ticks. The conversion is usually handled automatically by the simulation, testing, or charting software; by simple utility programs; or by special software provided by the data vendor. If the data was pulled from the Internet by way of ftp (file transfer protocol), or using a standard web browser, it may be necessary to write a small program or script to convert the downloaded data to the desired time frame, and then to save it in a format acceptable to other software packages.

What time frame is the best? It all depends on the trader. For those attracted to rapid feedback, plenty of action, tight stops, overnight security, and many small profits, a short, intraday time frame is an ideal choice. On an intraday time frame, many small trades can be taken during a typical day. The numerous trades hasten the learning process. It will not take the day trader long to discover what works, and what does not, when trading on a short, intraday time frame. In addition, by closing out all positions at the end of the trading day, a day trader can completely sidestep overnight risk. Another desirable characteristic of a short time frame is that it often permits the use of tight stops, which can keep the losses small on losing trades. Finally, the statistically inclined will be enamored by the fact that representative data samples containing hundreds of thousands of data points, and thousands of trades, are readily obtained when working with a short time frame. Large data samples lessen the dangers of curve-fitting, lead to more stable statistics, and increase the likelihood that predictive models will perform in the future as they have in the past.

On the downside, the day trader working with a short time frame needs a real-time data feed, historical tick data, fast hardware containing abundant memory, specialized software, and a substantial amount of time to commit to actually trading. The need for fast hardware with plenty of memory arises for two reasons: (1) System tests will involve incredibly large numbers of data points and trades; and (2) the real-time software that collects the data, runs the system, and draws the charts must keep up with a heavy flow of ticks without missing a beat. Both a database of historical tick data and software able to handle sizable data sets are necessary for system development and testing. A real-time feed is required for actual trading. Although fast hardware and mammoth memory can now be purchased at discount prices, adequate software does not come cheap. Historical tick data is likely to be costly, and a real-time data feed entails a substantial and recurring expense.

In contrast, data costs and the commitment of time to trading are minimal for those operating on an end-of-day (or longer) time frame. Free data is available on the Internet to anyone willing to perform cleanup and formatting. Software costs are also likely to be lower than for the day trader. The end-of-day trader needs less time to actually trade: The system can be run after the markets close and trading orders are communicated to the broker before the markets open in the morning; perhaps a total of 15 minutes is spent on the whole process, leaving more time for system development and leisure activities.

Another benefit of a longer time frame is the ability to easily diversify by simultaneously trading several markets. Because few markets offer the high levels of volatility and liquidity required for day trading, and because there is a limit on how many things a single individual can attend to at once, the day trader may only be able to diversify across systems. The end-of-day trader, on the other hand, has a much wider choice of markets to trade and can trade at a more relaxed pace, making diversification across markets more practical than for intraday counterparts. Diversification is a great way to reduce risk relative to reward. Longer time frame trading has another desirable feature: the ability to capture large profits from strong, sustained trends; these are the profits that can take a $50,000 account to over a million in less than a year. Finally, the system developer working with longer time frames will find more exogenous variables with potential predictive utility to explore.

A longer time frame, however, is not all bliss. The trader must accept delayed feedback, tolerate wider stops, and be able to cope with overnight risk. Holding overnight positions may even result in high levels of anxiety, perhaps full-blown insomnia. Statistical issues can become significant for the system developer due to the smaller sample sizes involved when working with daily, weekly, or monthly data. One work-around for small sample size is to develop and test systems on complete portfolios, rather than on individual commodities.

Which time frame is best? It all depends on you, the trader! Profitable trading can be done on many time frames. The hope is that this discussion has clarified some of the issues and trade-offs involved in choosing correctly.

DATA QUALITY

Data quality varies from excellent to awful. Since bad data can wreak havoc with all forms of analysis, lead to misleading results, and waste precious time, only use the best data that can be found when running tests and trading simulations. Some forecasting models, including those based on neural networks, can be exceedingly sensitive to a few errant data points; in such cases, the need for clean, error-free data is extremely important. Time spent finding good data, and then giving it a final scrubbing, is time well spent.

Data errors take many forms, some more innocuous than others. In real-time trading, for example, ticks are occasionally received that have extremely deviant, if not obviously impossible, prices. The S&P 500 may appear to be trading at 952.00 one moment and at 250.50 the next! Is this the ultimate market crash? No—a few seconds later, another tick will come along, indicating the S&P 500 is again trading at 952.00 or thereabouts. What happened? A bad tick, a "noise spike," occurred in the data. This kind of data error, if not detected and eliminated, can skew the results produced by almost any mechanical trading model. Although anything but innocuous, such errors are obvious, are easy to detect (even automatically), and are readily corrected or otherwise handled. More innocuous, albeit less obvious and harder to find, are the common, small errors in the settling price, and other numbers reported by the exchanges, that are frequently passed on to the consumer by the data vendor. Better data vendors repeatedly check their data and post corrections as such errors are detected. For example, on an almost daily basis, Pinnacle Data posts error corrections that are handled automatically by its software. Many of these common, small errors are not seriously damaging to software-based trading simulations, but one never knows for sure.

Depending on the sensitivity of the trading or forecasting model being analyzed, and on such other factors as the availability of data-checking software, it may be worthwhile to run miscellaneous statistical scans to highlight suspicious data points. There are many ways to flag these data points, or *outliers*, as they are sometimes referred to by statisticians. Missing, extra, and logically inconsistent data points are also occasionally seen; they should be noted and corrected. As an example of data checking, two data sets were run through a utility program that scans for missing data points, outliers, and logical inconsistencies. The results appear in Tables 1-1 and 1-2, respectively.

Table 1-1 shows the output produced by the data-checking program when it was used on Pinnacle Data Corporation's (800-724-4903) end-of-day, continuous-contract data for the S&P 500 futures. The utility found no illogical prices or volumes in this data set; there were no observed instances of a high that was less than the close, a low that was greater than the open, a volume that was less than zero, or of any cognate data faux pas. Two data points (bars) with suspiciously high ranges, however, were noted by the software: One bar with unusual range occurred on 10/19/87 (or 871019 in the report). The other was dated 10/13/89. The abnormal range observed on 10/19/87 does not reflect an error, just the normal volatility associated with a major crash like that of Black Monday; nor is a data error responsible for the aberrant range seen on 10/13/89, which appeared due to the so-called anniversary effect. Since these statistically aberrant data points were not errors, corrections were unnecessary.

Nonetheless, the presence of such data points should emphasize the fact that market events involving exceptional ranges do occur and must be managed adequately by a trading system. All ranges shown in Table 1-1 are standardized ranges, computed by dividing a bar's range by the average range over the last 20 bars. As is common with market data, the distribution of the standardized range had a longer tail than would be

TABLE 1-1

Output from Data-Checking Utility for End-of-Day S&P 500
Continuous-Contract Futures Data from Pinnacle

```
CHECK OF 7-FIELD EOD DATA FILE: /data/sp.lng
DATE RANGE: 830103 TO 980521
TOTAL NUMBER OF BARS: 4014

BARS WITH ILLOGICAL PRICES OR VOLUMES
    DATE       OPEN        HIGH        LOW        CLOSE       VOLUME      OPENINT
COUNT=0

BARS WITH EXCESSIVE HIGH-LOW RANGE
    DATE       OPEN        HIGH        LOW        CLOSE       VOLUME      OPENINT   RANGE
   871019    424.400     429.400     358.400     361.900     162022      172178      10
   891013    496.100     497.550     466.950     466.950      62514      125604      10
COUNT=2

DISTRIBUTION OF RANGES
            RANGE             COUNT
              1                3838
              2                 128
              3                  11
              4                   6
              5                   5
              6                   1
              7                   0
              8                   0
              9                   0
             10                   2

BARS WITH DEVIANT CLOSES
    DATE       OPEN        HIGH        LOW        CLOSE       VOLUME      OPENINT    DEV
   860911    413.450     413.450     401.550     402.350     151300      120864       8
   871019    424.400     429.400     358.400     361.900     162022      172178      10
   891013    496.100     497.550     466.950     466.950      62514      125604      10
   911115    507.450     507.450     488.250     492.750      65533      151861       8
   971027    960.400     966.300     896.400     896.400      85146      201015       8
COUNT=5

DISTRIBUTION OF DEVIANCES
           REL_DEV            COUNT
              1                3439
              2                 352
              3                 122
              4                  48
              5                  16
              6                   9
              7                   0
              8                   3
              9                   0
             10                   2

BARS WITH DUPLICATE OR OUT-OF-ORDER DATES
    DATE       OPEN        HIGH        LOW        CLOSE       VOLUME      OPENINT    ERR
COUNT=0

DATES OF MISSING AND WEEKEND BARS
            DATE              ERROR
COUNT=0
```

expected given a normally distributed underlying process. Nevertheless, the events of 10/19/87 and 10/13/89 appear to be statistically exceptional: The distribution of all other range data declined, in an orderly fashion, to zero at a standardized value of 7, well below the range of 10 seen for the critical bars.

The data-checking utility also flagged 5 bars as having exceptionally deviant closing prices. As with range, deviance has been defined in terms of a distribution, using a standardized close-to-close price measure. In this instance, the standardized measure was computed by dividing the absolute value of the difference between each closing price and its predecessor by the average of the preceding 20 such absolute values. When the 5 flagged (and most deviant) bars were omitted, the same distributional behavior that characterized the range was observed: a long-tailed distribution of close-to-close price change that fell off, in an orderly fashion, to zero at 7 standardized units. Standardized close-to-close deviance scores (*DEV*) of 8 were noted for 3 of the aberrant bars, and scores of 10 were observed for the remaining 2 bars. Examination of the flagged data points again suggests that unusual market activity, rather than data error, was responsible for their statistical deviance. It is not surprising that the 2 most deviant data points were the same ones noted earlier for their abnormally high range. Finally, the data-checking software did not find any missing bars, bars falling on weekends, or bars with duplicate or out-of-order dates. The only outliers detected appear to be the result of bizarre market conditions, not corrupted data. Overall, the S&P 500 data series appears to be squeaky-clean. This was expected: In our experience, Pinnacle Data Corporation (the source of the data) supplies data of very high quality.

As an example of how bad data quality can get, and the kinds of errors that can be expected when dealing with low-quality data, another data set was analyzed with the same data-checking utility. This data, obtained from an acquaintance, was for Apple Computer (AAPL). The data-checking results appear in Table 1-2.

In this data set, unlike in the previous one, 2 bars were flagged for having outright logical inconsistencies. One logically invalid data point had an opening price of zero, which was also lower than the low, while the other bar had a high price that was lower than the closing price. Another data point was detected as having an excessive range, which may or may not be a data error. In addition, several bars evidenced extreme closing price deviance, perhaps reflecting uncorrected stock splits. There were no duplicate or out-of-order dates, but quite a few data points were missing. In this instance, the missing data points were holidays and, therefore, only reflect differences in data handling; for a variety of reasons, we usually fill holidays with data from previous bars. Considering that the data series extended only from 1/2/97 through 11/6/98 (in contrast to the S&P 500, which ran from 1/3/83 to 5/21/98), it is distressing that several serious errors, including logical violations, were detected by a rather simple scan.

The implication of this exercise is that data should be purchased only from a

TABLE 1-2

Output from Data-Checking Utility for Apple Computer, Symbol AAPL

```
CHECK OF 7-FIELD EOD DATA FILE: ../techstks/aapl.dat
DATE RANGE: 970102 TO 981106
TOTAL NUMBER OF BARS: 468

BARS WITH ILLOGICAL PRICES OR VOLUMES
    DATE        OPEN        HIGH         LOW       CLOSE        VOLUME      OPENINT
    981019      0.000*      38.063      35.875     37.500       4248000       0
    981030      36.500      36.500*     36.250     37.125       2836100       0
COUNT=2

BARS WITH EXCESSIVE HIGH-LOW RANGE
    DATE        OPEN        HIGH         LOW       CLOSE        VOLUME      OPENINT    RANGE
    980106      15.938      20.000      14.750     18.938      16191000       0          7
COUNT=1

DISTRIBUTION OF RANGES
            RANGE            COUNT
              1               407
              2                29
              3                 6
              4                 1
              5                 1
              6                 0
              7                 1
              8                 0
              9                 0
             10                 0

BARS WITH DEVIANT CLOSES
    DATE        OPEN        HIGH         LOW       CLOSE        VOLUME      OPENINT    DEV
    970806      25.250      27.750      25.000     26.313      37430000       0         10
    980102      13.625      16.250      13.500     16.250       6411700       0         10
    980106      15.938      20.000      14.750     18.938      16191000       0          7
COUNT=3

DISTRIBUTION OF DEVIANCES
           REL_DEV            COUNT
              1               380
              2                40
              3                12
              4                 5
              5                 2
              6                 3
              7                 1
              8                 0
              9                 0
             10                 2

BARS WITH DUPLICATE OR OUT-OF-ORDER DATES
    DATE        OPEN        HIGH         LOW       CLOSE        VOLUME      OPENINT     ERR
COUNT=0

DATES OF MISSING AND WEEKEND BARS
            DATE             ERROR
            970217          MISSING
            970328          MISSING
            970526          MISSING
            970704          MISSING
            970901          MISSING
            971127          MISSING
            971225          MISSING
            980101          MISSING
            980119          MISSING
            980216          MISSING
            980410          MISSING
            980525          MISSING
            980703          MISSING
            980907          MISSING
COUNT=14
```

reputable vendor who takes data quality seriously; this will save time and ensure reliable, error-free data for system development, testing, and trading. In addition, all data should be scanned for errors to avoid disturbing surprises. For an in-depth discussion of data quality, which includes coverage of how data is produced, transmitted, received, and stored, see Jurik (1999).

DATA SOURCES AND VENDORS

Today there are a great many sources from which data may be acquired. Data may be purchased from value-added vendors, downloaded from any of several exchanges, and extracted from a wide variety of databases accessible over the Internet and on compact discs.

Value-added vendors, such as Tick Data and Pinnacle, whose data have been used extensively in this work, can supply the trader with relatively clean data in easy-to-use form. They also provide convenient update services and, at least in the case of Pinnacle, error corrections that are handled automatically by the downloading software, which makes the task of maintaining a reliable, up-to-date database very straightforward. Popular suppliers of end-of-day commodities data include Pinnacle Data Corporation (800-724-4903), Prophet Financial Systems (650-322-4183), Commodities Systems Incorporated (CSI, 800-274-4727), and Technical Tools (800-231-8005). Intraday historical data, which are needed for testing short time frame systems, may be purchased from Tick Data (800-822-8425) and Genesis Financial Data Services (800-621-2628). Day traders should also look into Data Transmission Network (DTN, 800-485-4000), Data Broadcasting Corporation (DBC, 800-367-4670), Bonneville Market Information (BMI, 800-532-3400), and FutureSource-Bridge (800-621-2628); these data distributors can provide the fast, real-time data feeds necessary for successful day trading. For additional information on data sources, consult Marder (1999). For a comparative review of end-of-day data, see Knight (1999).

Data need not always be acquired from a commercial vendor. Sometimes it can be obtained directly from the originator. For instance, various exchanges occasionally furnish data directly to the public. Options data can currently be downloaded over the Internet from the Chicago Board of Trade (CBOT). When a new contract is introduced and the exchange wants to encourage traders, it will often release a kit containing data and other information of interest. Sometimes this is the only way to acquire certain kinds of data cheaply and easily.

Finally, a vast, mind-boggling array of databases may be accessed using an Internet web browser or ftp client. These days almost everything is on-line. For example, the Federal Reserve maintains files containing all kinds of economic time series and business cycle indicators. NASA is a great source for solar and astronomical data. Climate and geophysical data may be downloaded from the National Climatic Data Center (NCDC) and the National Geophysical Data Center (NGDC), respectively.

For the ardent net-surfer, there is an overwhelming abundance of data in a staggering variety of formats. Therein, however, lies another problem: A certain level of skill is required in the art of the search, as is perhaps some basic programming or scripting experience, as well as the time and effort to find, tidy up, and reformat the data. Since "time is money," it is generally best to rely on a reputable, value-added data vendor for basic pricing data, and to employ the Internet and other sources for data that is more specialized or difficult to acquire.

Additional sources of data also include databases available through libraries and on compact discs. ProQuest and other periodical databases offer full text retrieval capabilities and can frequently be found at the public library. Bring a floppy disk along and copy any data of interest. Finally, do not forget newspapers such as *Investor's Business Daily, Barron's*, and the *Wall Street Journal*; these can be excellent sources for certain kinds of information and are available on microfilm from many libraries.

In general, it is best to maintain data in a standard text-based (ASCII) format. Such a format has the virtue of being simple, portable across most operating systems and hardware platforms, and easily read by all types of software, from text editors to charting packages.

CHAPTER 2

Simulators

No savvy trader would trade a system with a real account and risk real money without first observing its behavior on paper. A *trading simulator* is a software application or component that allows the user to simulate, using historical data, a trading account that is traded with a user-specified set of trading rules. The user's trading rules are written into a small program that automates a rigorous "paper-trading" process on a substantial amount of historical data. In this way, the trading simulator allows the trader to gain insight into how the system might perform when traded in a real account. The *raison d'être* of a trading simulator is that it makes it possible to efficiently back-test, or paper-trade, a system to determine whether the system works and, if so, how well.

TYPES OF SIMULATORS

There are two major forms of trading simulators. One form is the integrated, easy-to-use software application that provides some basic historical analysis and simulation along with data collection and charting. The other form is the specialized software component or class library that can be incorporated into user-written software to provide system testing and evaluation functionality. Software components and class libraries offer open architecture, advanced features, and high levels of performance, but require programming expertise and such additional elements as graphics, report generation, and data management to be useful. Integrated applications packages, although generally offering less powerful simulation and testing capabilities, are much more accessible to the novice.

PROGRAMMING THE SIMULATOR

Regardless of whether an integrated or component-based simulator is employed, the trading logic of the user's system must be programmed into it using some computer language. The language used may be either a generic programming language, such as C++ or FORTRAN, or a proprietary scripting language. Without the aid of a formal language, it would be impossible to express a system's trading rules with the precision required for an accurate simulation. The need for programming of some kind should not be looked upon as a necessary evil. Programming can actually benefit the trader by encouraging an explicit and disciplined expression of trading ideas.

For an example of how trading logic is programmed into a simulator, consider TradeStation, a popular integrated product from Omega Research that contains an interpreter for a basic system writing language (called Easy Language) with historical simulation capabilities. Omega's Easy Language is a proprietary, trading-specific language based on Pascal (a generic programming language). What does a simple trading system look like when programmed in Easy Language? The following code implements a simple moving-average crossover system:

```
{ Simple moving average crossover system in Easy Language}
Inputs: Len(4);                        {length parameter }
If (Close > Average(Close, Len)) And
   (Close[1] <= Average(Close, Len)[1]) Then
    Buy("A") 1 Contract At Market;     {buys at open of next bar}
If (Close <= Average(Close, Len)) And
   (Close[1] > Average(Close, Len)[1]) Then
    Sell("B") 1 Contract At Market;    {sells at open of next bar
```

This system goes long one contract at tomorrow's open when the close crosses above its moving average, and goes short one contract when the close crosses below the moving average. Each order is given a name or identifier: A for the buy; B for the sell. The length of the moving average (Len) may be set by the user or optimized by the software.

Below is the same system programmed in C++ using Scientific Consultant Services' component-based C-Trader toolkit, which includes the C++ Trading Simulator:

```
// simple moving-average crossover system in C++
len = parms[1];                        // length parameter
if (cls[cb] > Average(cls, len, cb) &&
    cls[cb-1] <= Average(cls, len, cb-1))
        ts.buyopen(`A', 1);            // buys at open of next bar
if (cls[cb] <= Average(cls, len, cb) &&
    cls[cb-1] > Average(cls, len, cb-1))
        ts.sellopen(`B', 1);          // sells at open of next bar
```

Except for syntax and naming conventions, the differences between the C++ and Easy Language implementations are small. Most significant are the explicit references to the current bar (cb) and to a particular simulated trading account or simulator class instance (ts) in the C++ implementation. In C++, it is possible to explicitly declare and reference any number of simulated accounts; this becomes important when working with portfolios and *metasystems* (systems that trade the accounts of other systems), and when developing models that incorporate an implicit walk-forward adaptation.

SIMULATOR OUTPUT

All good trading simulators generate output containing a wealth of information about the performance of the user's simulated account. Expect to obtain data on gross and net profit, number of winning and losing trades, worst-case drawdown, and related system characteristics, from even the most basic simulators. Better simulators provide figures for maximum run-up, average favorable and adverse excursion, inferential statistics, and more, not to mention highly detailed analyses of individual trades. An extraordinary simulator might also include in its output some measure of risk relative to reward, such as the annualized risk-to-reward ratio (ARRR) or the *Sharpe Ratio,* an important and well-known measure used to compare the performances of different portfolios, systems, or funds (Sharpe, 1994).

The output from a trading simulator is typically presented to the user in the form of one or more reports. Two basic kinds of reports are available from most trading simulators: the performance summary and the trade-by-trade, or "detail," report. The information contained in these reports can help the trader evaluate a system's "trading style" and determine whether the system is worthy of real-money trading.

Other kinds of reports may also be generated, and the information from the simulator may be formatted in a way that can easily be run into a spreadsheet for further analysis. Almost all the tables and charts that appear in this book were produced in this manner: The output from the simulator was written to a file that would be read by Excel, where the information was further processed and formatted for presentation.

Performance Summary Reports

As an illustration of the appearance of performance summary reports, two have been prepared using the same moving-average crossover system employed to illustrate simulator programming. Both the TradeStation (Table 2-1) and C-Trader (Table 2-2) implementations of this system were run using their respective target software applications. In each instance, the length parameter (controls the period of the moving average) was set to 4.

Most performance summary reports break down information into data applicable to long positions, short positions, and all positions combined. In addition, they contain numbers reflecting reward, risk, and trading style. Reward factors include the profit on all winning trades taken together, on the largest winning trade, and on the average winning trade. Reported risk factors include the accumulated loss on all

TABLE 2-1

Performance Summary Generated by TradeStation for the Moving-Average Crossover System

```
BOOK_CH5  SP.LNG-Daily   01/01/91 - 01/01/96
        Performance Summary:  All Trades

Total net profit       $ -15625.00    Open position P/L      $       75.00
Gross profit           $ 280350.00    Gross loss             $-295975.00

Total # of trades             362     Percent profitable            40%
Number winning trades         146     Number losing trades          216

Largest winning trade  $  14800.00    Largest losing trade   $   -5750.00
Average winning trade  $   1920.21    Average losing trade   $   -1370.25
Ratio avg win/avg loss        1.40    Avg trade(win & loss)  $     -43.16

Max consec. winners             6     Max consec. losers             10
Avg # bars in winners           5     Avg # bars in losers            2

Max intraday drawdown  $ -50650.00
Profit factor                 0.95    Max # contracts held            1
Account size required  $  50650.00    Return on account            -31%


        Performance Summary:  Long Trades

Total net profit       $  42300.00    Open position P/L      $        0.00
Gross profit           $ 173075.00    Gross loss             $-130775.00

Total # of trades             181     Percent profitable            48%
Number winning trades          87     Number losing trades           94

Largest winning trade  $  14800.00    Largest losing trade   $   -5750.00
Average winning trade  $   1989.37    Average losing trade   $   -1391.22
Ratio avg win/avg loss        1.43    Avg trade(win & loss)  $     233.70

Max consec. winners             9     Max consec. losers              7
Avg # bars in winners           5     Avg # bars in losers            2

Max intraday drawdown  $ -17225.00
Profit factor                 1.32    Max # contracts held            1
Account size required  $  17225.00    Return on account            246%


        Performance Summary:  Short Trades

Total net profit       $ -57925.00    Open position P/L      $       75.00
Gross profit           $ 107275.00    Gross loss             $-165200.00

Total # of trades             181     Percent profitable            33%
Number winning trades          59     Number losing trades          122

Largest winning trade  $   8125.00    Largest losing trade   $   -5675.00
Average winning trade  $   1818.22    Average losing trade   $   -1354.10
Ratio avg win/avg loss        1.34    Avg trade(win & loss)  $    -320.03

Max consec. winners             3     Max consec. losers             10
Avg # bars in winners           5     Avg # bars in losers            2

Max intraday drawdown  $ -65625.00
Profit factor                 0.65    Max # contracts held            1
Account size required  $  65625.00    Return on account            -88%
```

TABLE 2-2

Performance Summary Generated Using the C-Trader Toolkit for the
Moving-Average Crossover System

```
SUMMARY FOR SYMBOL SP
IN SAMPLE: 910601 TO 960101   OUT OF SAMPLE: 960101 TO 970108   TESTS: 1
```

DESCRIPTION	ALL_IS	LONG_IS	SHORT_IS	ALL_OS	LONG_OS	SHORT_OS
NumTrades	362	181	181	71	35	36
NumWinners	138	83	55	33	17	16
NumLosers	216	94	122	38	18	20
MaxConsecWinners	6	7	3	4	5	3
MaxConsecLosers	10	7	10	6	4	4
TotalBars	1562	834	728	337	195	142
BarsWinners	843	529	314	210	140	70
BarsLosers	698	295	403	127	55	72
AvgBars	4	4	4	4	5	3
AvgBarsWin	6	6	5	6	8	4
AvgBarsLose	3	3	3	3	3	3
PctWinners	38	45	30	46	48	44
NetProfit	-15625	42300	-57925	35800	45975	-10175
NetWinners	280350	173075	107275	156875	111225	45650
NetLosers	-295975	-130775	-165200	-121075	-65250	-55825
MaxEquity	8575	44600	4025	47175	49875	12425
MinEquity	-43125	-12675	-62650	-22350	-14300	-20425
MaxRunnup	40300	57200	18775	68075	62725	28675
MaxDrawdown	-50650	-17225	-65625	-28875	-17600	-20425
TradeStdDev	2262	2444	2026	5634	7108	3498
TradeAvgPL	-43	233	-320	504	1313	-282
AvgWinner	2031	2085	1950	4753	6542	2853
AvgFavExc	2205	2195	2215	5149	5573	4736
AvgLoser	-1370	-1391	-1354	-3186	-3625	-2791
AvgAdvExc	-1439	-1450	-1427	-2921	-3416	-2440
LargestWinner	14800	14800	8125	23150	23150	8600
MaxFavExc	16950	16950	15375	29050	29050	20075
LargestLoser	-5750	-5750	-5675	-8300	-8300	-5450
MaxAdvExc	-8500	-8500	-5675	-10125	-10125	-8250
AvgWLRat*100	148	149	144	149	180	102
PftFactor*100	94	132	64	129	170	81
AnnualRet$	-3404	9217	-12622	35032	44988	-9956
AnnualRet%	-7	31	-37	120	251	-49
Sharpe*100	-18	0	0	40	0	0
T-Stat*100	-36	129	-213	76	112	-49
T-Prob*10000	7160	1974	340	4469	2682	6211
OCProb*10000	7160	1974	340	4469	2682	6211

```
--IS--------------------------------------------------------------OOS--------
*******                                                        :
       *                                                       :        *
                                                       *       :       **
     *                                                         :        *
    * *                                          *     *    *  :  *   * **
   *   *                                 *                     :
  *  *                              **    *   *          * *:   *
 *   **                           *   *     *          * *:
                                      *               *
           *  **                                        * :
         * *    *  **       * * ***        * *          * :    **
        * * ** *    *   *    *          **
         *  *         *  *** *                          *
                        **
--ACCOUNT EQUITY------------------------------------------------:-------------
```

losing trades, the loss on the largest losing trade, the loss on the average losing
trade, and the maximum drawdown sustained by the simulated account. Both
reward and risk factors are reflected in the net profit (or loss) resulting from all
trades taken by the system, the profit (or loss) on the average trade, the ratio of the
average winner to the average loser, the profit factor (gross profit divided by gross
loss), and the overall return (whether annualized or not) on the simulated account.

Such style factors as the total number of trades, the number of winning trades, the number of losing trades, the percentage of profitable trades, the maximum numbers of consecutive winners and losers, and the average numbers of bars in winners and losers also appear in performance summary reports. Reward, risk, and style are critical aspects of system performance that these reports address.

Although all address the issues of reward, risk and trading style, there are a number of differences between various performance summary reports. Least significant are differences in formatting. Some reports, in an effort to cram as much information as possible into a limited amount of space, round dollar values to the nearest whole integer, scale up certain values by some factor of 10 to avoid the need for decimals, and arrange their output in a tabular, spreadsheet-like format. Other reports use less cryptic descriptors, do not round dollar values or rescale numbers, and format their output to resemble more traditional reports.

Somewhat more significant than differences in formatting are the variations between performance summary reports that result from the definitions and assumptions made in various calculations. For instance, the number of winning trades may differ slightly between reports because of how winners are defined. Some simulators count as a winner any trade in which the *P/L* (profit/loss) figure is greater than or equal to zero, whereas others count as winners only trades for which the *P/L* is strictly greater than zero. This difference in calculation also affects figures for the average winning trade and for the ratio of the average winner to the average loser. Likewise, the average number of bars in a trade may be greater or fewer, depending on how they are counted. Some simulators include the entry bar in all bar counts; others do not. Return-on-account figures may also differ, depending, for instance, on whether or not they are annualized.

Differences in content between performance summary reports may even be more significant. Some only break down their performance analyses into long positions, short positions, and all trades combined. Others break them down into in-sample and out-of-sample trades, as well. The additional breakdown makes it easy to see whether a system optimized on one sample of data (the in-sample set) shows similar behavior on another sample (the out-of-sample data) used for verification; out-of-sample tests are imperative for optimized systems. Other important information, such as the total bar counts, maximum run-up (the converse of drawdown), adverse and favorable excursion numbers, peak equity, lowest equity, annualized return in dollars, trade variability (expressed as a standard deviation), and the annualized risk-to-reward ratio (a variant of the Sharpe Ratio), are present in some reports. The calculation of inferential statistics, such as the t-statistic and its associated probability, either for a single test or corrected for multiple tests or optimizations, is also a desirable feature. Statistical items, such as t-tests and probabilities, are important since they help reveal whether a system's performance reflects the capture of a valid market inefficiency or is merely due to chance or excessive curve-fitting. Many additional, possibly useful statistics can also be *cal-*

culated, some of them on the basis of the information present in performance summaries. Among these statistics (Stendahl, 1999) are net positive outliers, net negative outliers, select net profit (calculated after the removal of outlier trades), loss ratio (greatest loss divided by net profit), run-up–to–drawdown ratio, longest flat period, and buy-and-hold return (useful as a baseline). Finally, some reports also contain a text-based plot of account equity as a function of time.

To the degree that history repeats itself, a clear image of the past seems like an excellent foundation from which to envision a likely future. A good performance summary provides a panoramic view of a trading method's historical behavior. Figures on return and risk show how well the system traded on test data from the historical period under study. The Sharpe Ratio, or annualized risk to reward, measures return on a risk- or stability-adjusted scale. T-tests and related statistics may be used to determine whether a system's performance derives from some real market inefficiency or is an artifact of chance, multiple tests, or inappropriate optimization. Performance due to real market inefficiency may persist for a time, while that due to artifact is unlikely to recur in the future. In short, a good performance summary aids in capturing profitable market phenomena likely to persist; the capture of persistent market inefficiency is, of course, the basis for any sustained success as a trader.

This wraps up the discussion of one kind of report obtainable within most trading simulation environments. Next we consider the other type of output that most simulators provide: the trade-by-trade report.

Trade-by-Trade Reports

Illustrative trade-by-trade reports were prepared using the simulators contained in TradeStation (Table 2-3) and in the C-Trader toolkit (Table 2-4). Both reports pertain to the same simple moving-average crossover system used in various ways throughout this discussion. Since hundreds of trades were taken by this system, the original reports are quite lengthy. Consequently, large blocks of trades have been edited out and ellipses inserted where the deletions were made. Because these reports are presented merely for illustration, such deletions were considered acceptable.

In contrast to a performance report, which provides an overall evaluation of a trading system's behavior, a *detail* or *trade-by-trade* report contains detailed information on each trade taken in the simulated account. A minimal detail report contains each trade's entry and exit dates (and times, if the simulation involves intraday data), the prices at which these entries and exits occurred, the positions held (in numbers of contracts, long or short), and the profit or loss resulting from each trade. A more comprehensive trade-by-trade report might also provide information on the type of order responsible for each entry or exit (e.g., stop, limit, or market), where in the bar the order was executed (at the open, the close, or in

TABLE 2-3

Trade-by-Trade Report Generated by TradeStation for the Moving-
Average Crossover System

```
BOOK_CH5   SP.LNG-Daily  910103  -  960103

Date        Type    Cnts    Price Signal Name     Entry P/L       Cumulative
...
03/13/91    Sell    1       511.75      B
03/14/91    SExit   1       516.75      A        $  -2500.00    $  -2500.00
03/14/91    Buy     1       516.75      A
03/18/91    LExit   1       511.95      B        $  -2400.00    $  -4900.00
03/18/91    Sell    1       511.95      B
03/25/91    SExit   1       507.45      A        $   2250.00    $  -2650.00
03/25/91    Buy     1       507.45      A
03/29/91    LExit   1       517.10      B        $   4825.00    $   2175.00
03/29/91    Sell    1       517.10      B
04/03/91    SExit   1       519.85      A        $  -1375.00    $    800.00
04/03/91    Buy     1       519.85      A
04/08/91    LExit   1       514.60      B        $  -2625.00    $  -1825.00
04/08/91    Sell    1       514.60      B
04/09/91    SExit   1       517.75      A        $  -1575.00    $  -3400.00
04/09/91    Buy     1       517.75      A
04/10/91    LExit   1       513.15      B        $  -2300.00    $  -5700.00
04/10/91    Sell    1       513.15      B
04/12/91    SExit   1       519.35      A        $  -3100.00    $  -8800.00
04/12/91    Buy     1       519.35      A
04/22/91    LExit   1       523.10      B        $   1875.00    $  -6925.00
04/22/91    Sell    1       523.10      B
05/02/91    SExit   1       519.65      A        $   1725.00    $  -5200.00
...
```

between), the number of bars each trade was held, the account equity at the start
of each trade, the maximum favorable and adverse excursions within each trade,
and the account equity on exit from each trade.

Most trade-by-trade reports contain the date (and time, if applicable) each
trade was entered, whether a buy or sell was involved (that is, a long or short position established), the number of contracts in the transaction, the date the trade
was exited, the profit or loss on the trade, and the cumulative profit or loss on all
trades up to and including the trade under consideration. Reports also provide the
name of the order on which the trade was entered and the name of the exit order.
A better trade-by-trade report might include the fields for *maximum favorable
excursion* (the greatest unrealized profit to occur during each trade), the *maximum adverse excursion* (the largest unrealized loss), and the number of bars each
trade was held.

As with the performance summaries, there are differences between various
trade-by-trade reports with respect to the ways they are formatted and in the
assumptions underlying the computations on which they are based.

While the performance summary provides a picture of the whole forest, a good
trade-by-trade report focuses on the trees. In a good trade-by-trade report, each trade
is scrutinized in detail: What was the worst paper loss sustained in this trade? What
would the profit have been with a perfect exit? What was the actual profit (or loss)

TABLE 2-4

Trade-by-Trade Report Generated Using the C-Trader Toolkit for the Moving-Average Crossover System

TRADE-BY-TRADE FOR SYMBOL: SP

ENTRY DATE	POS	ENTRY PRICE	ORDER TYPE	WHEN	ENTRY : ID :	EXIT DATE	EXIT PRICE	WHEN	ORDER TYPE	EXIT : ID :	TRADE BARS	TRADE P/L	MFE	MAE	CUM
IN_SAMPLE_TRADES															
...															
910527	-1	492.150	M	O	B :	910528	492.150	O	M	A :	2	0	500	1250	0
910528	1	492.150	M	O	A :	910607	501.250	O	M	B :	11	4550	6900	500	4550
910607	-1	501.250	M	O	B :	910613	495.300	O	M	A :	7	2975	4025	400	7525
910613	1	495.300	M	O	A :	910614	492.200	O	M	B :	2	-1550	0	3100	5975
910614	-1	492.200	M	O	B :	910618	496.900	O	M	A :	5	-2350	525	2825	3625
910618	1	496.900	M	O	A :	910620	491.800	O	M	B :	3	-2550	400	2550	1075
910620	-1	491.800	M	O	B :	910625	490.650	O	M	A :	6	575	1650	500	1650
...															
951225	1	691.500	M	O	A :	960101	692.600	O	M	B :	8	550	1725	325	-15625
OUT_OF_SAMPLE_TRADES															
960101	-1	692.600	M	O	B :	960104	700.700	O	M	A :	4	-4050	1200	4050	-19675
960104	1	700.700	M	O	A :	960108	691.600	O	M	B :	5	-4550	1675	5100	-24225
960108	-1	691.600	M	O	B :	960110	697.600	O	M	A :	3	-3000	1450	3000	-27225
960110	1	697.600	M	O	A :	960111	681.000	O	M	B :	2	-8300	0	8800	-35525
960111	-1	681.000	M	O	B :	960118	683.000	O	M	A :	8	-1000	4300	2325	-36525
960118	1	683.000	M	O	A :	960216	729.300	O	M	B :	30	23150	29050	1450	-13375
960216	-1	729.300	M	O	B :	960223	727.500	O	M	A :	8	900	8400	1875	-12475
960223	1	727.500	M	O	A :	960228	724.750	O	M	B :	6	-1375	5725	2750	-13850
960228	-1	724.750	M	O	B :	960305	722.900	O	M	A :	7	925	8125	2525	-12925
960305	1	722.900	M	O	A :	960308	725.900	O	M	B :	4	1500	4475	1275	-11425
960308	-1	725.900	M	O	B :	960311	716.150	O	M	A :	4	4875	4875	1300	-6550

on the trade? Has the trading been fairly consistent? Are recent trades worse than those of the past? Or are they better? How might some of the worst trades be characterized in a way to improve the trading system? These are the kinds of questions that cannot be answered by a distant panoramic view of the forest (a summary report), but they can be answered with a good trade-by-trade or detail report. In addition, a properly formatted detail report can be loaded into a spreadsheet for further analysis. Spreadsheets are convenient for sorting and displaying data. They make it easy, for instance, to draw histograms. Histograms can be very useful in decisions regarding the placement of stops (Sweeney, 1993). Histograms can show how much of the potential profit in the trades is being captured by the system's exit strategy and is also helpful in designing profit targets. Finally, a detailed examination of the worst and best trades may generate ideas for improving the system under study.

SIMULATOR PERFORMANCE

Trading simulators vary dramatically in such aspects of performance as speed, capacity, and power. Speed is important when there is a need to carry out many tests or perform complex optimizations, genetic or otherwise. It is also essential when developing systems on complete portfolios or using long, intraday data series involving thousands of trades and hundreds of thousands of data points. In some instances, speed may determine whether certain explorations can even be attempted. Some problems are simply not practical to study unless the analyses can be accomplished in a reasonable length of time. Simulator capacity involves problem size restrictions regarding the number of bars on which a simulation may be performed and the quantity of system code the simulator can handle. Finally, the power a simulator gives the user to express and test complex trading ideas, and to run tests and even system optimizations on complete portfolios, can be significant to the serious, professional trader. A fairly powerful simulator is required, for example, to run many of the trading models examined in this book.

Speed

The most significant determinant of simulation processing speed is the nature of the scripting or programming language used by the simulator, that is, whether the language is compiled or interpreted. Modern optimizing compilers for generic languages, such as C++, FORTRAN, and Pascal/Delphi, translate the user-written source code into highly efficient machine code that the processor can execute directly at full bore; this makes simulator toolkits that use such languages and compilers remarkably fast. On the other hand, proprietary, interpreted languages, such as Microsoft's Visual Basic for Applications and Omega's Easy Language, must be translated and fed to the processor line by line. Simulators that employ interpreted languages can be quite sluggish, especially

FIGURE 2-1

Histogram of adverse excursions.

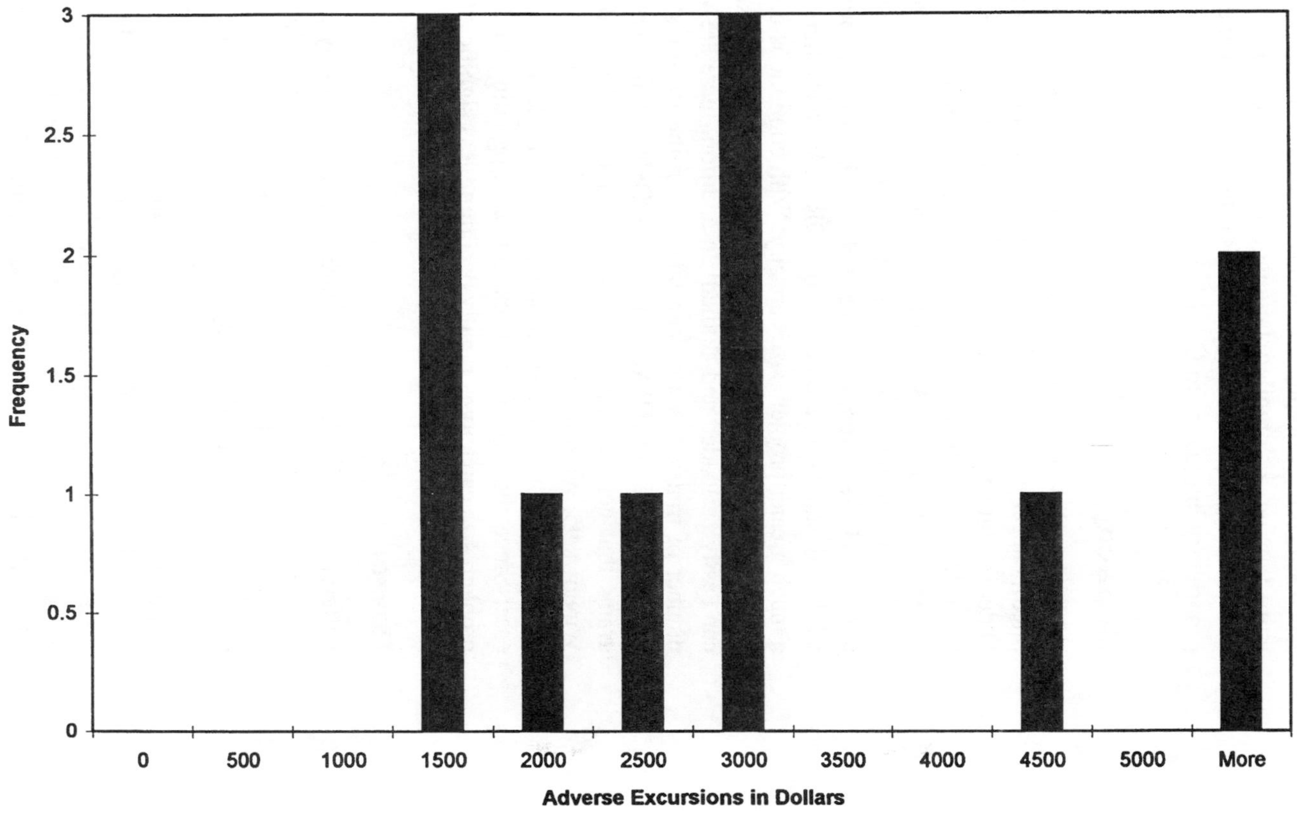

when executing complex or "loopy" source code. Just how much speed can be gained using a compiled language over an interpreted one? We have heard claims of systems running about 50 times faster since they were converted from proprietary languages to C++!

Capacity

While speed is primarily a function of language handling (interpreted versus compiled), capacity is mostly determined by whether 16-bit or 32-bit software is used. Older, 16-bit software is often subject to the dreaded 64K limit. In practical terms, this means that only about 15,000 bars of data (about 4 days of ticks, or 7 weeks of 1-minute bars on the S&P 500) can be loaded for system testing. In addition, as the system code is embellished, expect to receive a message to the effect that the system is too large to verify. Modern C++ or FORTRAN products, on the other hand, work with standard 32-bit C++ or FORTRAN compilers. Consequently, they have a much greater problem size capacity: With continuous-contract data on a machine with sufficient memory, every single tick of the S&P 500 since its inception in 1983 can easily be loaded and studied! In addition, there are virtually no limits on the number of trades a system can take, or on the system's size and complexity. All modern C++, FORTRAN, and Pascal/Delphi compilers are now full 32-bit programs that generate code for, and run under, 32-bit operating systems, such as Windows 95, Windows NT, or LINUX/UNIX. Any simulator that works with such a compiler should be able to handle large problems and enormous data sets with ease. Since most software packages are upgrading to 32-bit status, the issue of problem size capacity is rapidly becoming less significant than it once was.

Power

Differences in simulator power are attributable mostly to language and to design. Consider language first: In this case, it is not whether the language is compiled or interpreted, as was the case for speed, but rather its expressive power. Can the most elaborate and unusual trading ideas be expressed with precision and grace? In some languages they can; in others they cannot. It is unfortunate that the most powerful languages have steep learning curves. However, if one can climb the curve, a language like C++ makes it possible to do almost anything imaginable. Your word processor, spreadsheet, web browser, and even operating system were all probably written in C++ or its predecessor, C. Languages like C++ and Object Pascal (the basis of Borland's Delphi) are also extensible and can easily be customized for the purpose of trading system development by the use of appropriate libraries and add-on components. Visual Basic and Easy Language, although not as powerful as general-purpose, object-oriented languages like C++ or Object Pascal, have gentler learning curves and are still quite capable as languages go. Much less powerful, and not really adequate for the advanced system developer, are the macro-like languages embedded in popular charting packages, e.g., Equis International's MetaStock. The rule of thumb is the more powerful the language, the more powerful the simulator.

Design issues are also a consideration in a simulator's power. Extendability and modularity are especially important. Simulators that employ C++ or Object Pascal (Borland's Delphi) as their native language are incredibly extensible and can be highly modular, because such general-purpose, object-oriented languages are themselves highly extensible and modular; they were designed to be so from the ground up. Class libraries permit the definition of new data types and operators. Components can provide encapsulated functionality, such as charting and database management. Even old-fashioned function libraries (like the Numerical Algorithms Group library, the International Mathematics and Statistics Library and the Numerical Recipes library) are available to satisfy a variety of needs. Easy Language, too, is highly extensible and modular: Modules called *User Functions can be created in Easy Language, and functions written in other languages (including C++)* can be called (if they are placed in a dynamic link library, or DLL). Macrolike languages, on the other hand, are not as flexible, greatly limiting their usefulness to the advanced system developer. In our view, the ability to access modules written in other languages is absolutely crucial: Different languages have different expressive foci, and even with a powerful language like C++, it sometimes makes sense to write one or more modules in another language such as Prolog (a language designed for writing expert systems).

One additional design issue, unrelated to the language employed, is relevant when discussing simulator power: whether a simulator can work with whole portfolios as well as with individual tradables. Many products are not designed to perform simulations and optimizations on whole portfolios at once, although sometimes add-ons are available that make it possible to generate portfolio performance analyses after the fact. On the other hand, an appropriately designed simulator can make multiple-account or portfolio simulations and system optimizations straightforward.

RELIABILITY OF SIMULATORS

Trading simulators vary in their reliability and trustworthiness. No complex software, and that includes trading simulation software, is completely bug-free. This is true even for reputable vendors with great products. Other problems pertain to the assumptions made regarding ambiguous situations in which any of several orders could be executed in any of several sequences during a bar. Some of these items, e.g., the so-called bouncing tick (Ruggiero, 1998), can make it seem like the best system ever had been discovered when, in fact, it could bankrupt any trader. It seems better that a simulator makes worst-case assumptions in ambiguous situations; this way, when actual trading begins, there is greater likelihood of having a pleasant, rather than an unpleasant, surprise. All of this boils down to the fact that when choosing a simulator, select one that has been carefully debugged, that has a proven track record of reliability, and in which the assumptions and handling of ambiguous situations are explicitly stated. In addition, learn the simulator's quirks and how to work around them.

CHOOSING THE RIGHT SIMULATOR

If you are serious about developing sophisticated trading systems, need to work with large portfolios, or wish to perform tests using individual contracts or options, then buckle down, climb the learning curve, and go for an advanced simulator that employs a generic programming language such as the C++ or Object Pascal. Such a simulator will have an open architecture that provides access to an incredible selection of add-ons and libraries: technical analysis libraries, such as those from FM Labs (609-261-7357) and Scientific Consultant Services (516-696-3333); and general numerical algorithm libraries, such as Numerical Recipes (800-872-7423), Numerical Algorithms Group (NAG) (44-1865-511-245), and International Mathematics and Statistics Library (IMSL), which cover statistics, linear algebra, spectral analysis, differential equations, and other mathematics. Even neural network and genetic algorithm libraries are readily available. Advanced simulators that employ generic programming languages also open up a world of third-party components and graphical controls which cover everything from sophisticated charting and data display to advanced database management, and which are compatible with Borland's C++ Builder and Delphi, as well as with Microsoft's Visual Basic and Visual C++.

If your needs are somewhat less stringent, choose a complete, integrated solution. Make sure the simulation language permits procedures residing in DLLs to be called when necessary. Be wary of products that are primarily charting tools with limited programming capabilities if your intention is to develop, back-test, and trade mechanical systems that go significantly beyond traditional or "canned" indicators.

SIMULATORS USED IN THIS BOOK

We personally prefer simulators built using modern, object-oriented programming practices. One reason for our choice is that an object-oriented simulator makes it easy to create as many simulation instances or simulated accounts as might be desired. This is especially useful when simulating the behavior of a trading system on an entire portfolio of tradables (as is done in most tests in this book), rather than on a single instrument. An object-oriented simulator also comes in handy when building adaptive, self-optimizing systems where it is sometimes necessary to implement internal simulations. In addition, such software makes the construction of *metasystems* (systems that trade in or out of the equity curves of other systems) a simple matter. Asset allocation models, for instance, may be treated as metasystems that dynamically allocate capital to individual trading systems or accounts. A good object-oriented simulator can generate the portfolio equity curves and other information needed to create and back-test asset allocation models operating on top of multiple trading systems. For these reasons, and such others as familiarity, most tests carried out in this book have been performed using the C-Trader toolkit. Do not be alarmed. It is not necessary to have any expertise in $C++$ or modern software practices to benefit from this book. The logic of every system or system element examined will be explained in great detail in the text.

CHAPTER 3

Optimizers and Optimization

It would be nice to develop trading systems without giving a thought to optimization. Realistically, however, the development of a profitable trading strategy is a trial-and-error activity in which some form of optimization always plays a role. There is always an optimizer around somewhere — if not visible on the table, then lurking in the shadows.

An *optimizer* is simply an entity or algorithm that attempts to find the best possible solution to a problem; *optimization* is the search process by which that solution is discovered. An optimizer may be a self-contained software component, perhaps implemented as a C++ class, Delphi object, or ActiveX control. Powerful, sophisticated optimizers often take the form of software components designed to be integrated into user-written programs. Less sophisticated optimizers, such as those found in high-end simulation and charting packages, are usually simple algorithms implemented with a few lines of programming code. Since any entity or algorithm that performs optimization is an optimizer, optimizers need not be associated with computers or machines at all; an optimizer may be a person engaged in problem-solving activities. The human brain is one of the most powerful heuristic optimizers on earth!

WHAT OPTIMIZERS DO

Optimizers exist to find the best possible solution to a problem. What is meant by *the best possible solution to a problem*? Before attempting to define that phrase, let us first consider what constitutes a *solution*. In trading, a solution is a particular set of trading rules and perhaps system parameters.

All trading systems have at least two rules (an entry rule and an exit rule), and most have one or more parameters. *Rules* express the logic of the trading system, and generally appear as "if-then" clauses in whatever language the trading system has been written. *Parameters* determine the behavior of the logic expressed in the rules; they can include lengths of moving averages, connection weights in neural networks, thresholds used in comparisons, values that determine placements for stops and profit targets, and other similar items. The simple moving-average crossover system, used in the previous chapter to illustrate various trading simulators, had two rules: one for the buy order and one for the sell order. It also had a single parameter, the length of the moving average. Rules and parameters completely define a trading system and determine its performance. To obtain the best performance from a trading system, parameters may need to be adjusted and rules juggled.

There is no doubt that some rule and parameter combinations define systems that trade well, just as others specify systems that trade poorly; i.e., solutions differ in their quality. The goodness of a solution or trading model, in terms of how well it performs when measured against some standard, is often called *fitness*. The converse of fitness, the inadequacy of a solution, is frequently referred to as *cost*.

In practice, fitness is evaluated by a *fitness function*, a block of programming code that calculates a single number that reflects the relative desirability of any solution. A fitness function can be written to appraise fitness howsoever the trader desires. For example, fitness might be interpreted as net profit penalized for excessive drawdown. A *cost function* works in exactly the same way, but higher numbers signify worse solutions. The sum of the squared errors, commonly computed when working with linear regression or neural network models, is a cost function.

The *best possible solution to a problem* can now be defined: It is that particular solution that has the greatest fitness or the least cost. Optimizers endeavor to find the best possible solution to a problem by maximizing fitness, as measured by a fitness function, or minimizing cost, as computed by a cost function.

The best possible solution to a problem may be discovered in any number of ways. Sometimes problems can be solved by simple trial-and-error, especially when guided by human insight into the problem being worked. Alternatively, sophisticated procedures and algorithms may be necessary. For example, simulating the process of evolution (as genetic optimizers do) is a very powerful way to discover or evolve high-quality solutions to complex problems. In some cases, the best problem solver is an analytic (calculus-based) procedure, such as a conjugate gradient. Analytic optimization is an efficient approach for problems with smooth (differentiable) fitness surfaces, such as those encountered in training neural networks, developing multiple linear regression models, or computing simple-structure factor rotations.

HOW OPTIMIZERS ARE USED

Optimizers are wonderful tools that can be used in a myriad of ways. They help shape the aircraft we fly, design the cars we drive, and even select delivery routes for our mail. Traders sometimes use optimizers to discover rule combinations that trade profitably. In Part II, we will demonstrate how a genetic optimizer can evolve profitable rule-based entry models. More commonly, traders call upon optimizers to determine the most appropriate values for system parameters; almost any kind of optimizer, except perhaps an analytic optimizer, may be employed for this purpose. Various kinds of optimizers, including powerful genetic algorithms, are effective for training or evolving neural or fuzzy logic networks. Asset allocation problems yield to appropriate optimization strategies. Sometimes it seems as if the only limit on how optimizers may be employed is the user's imagination, and therein lies a danger: It is easy to be seduced into "optimizer abuse" by the great and alluring power of this tool. The correct and incorrect applications of optimizers are discussed later in this chapter.

TYPES OF OPTIMIZERS

There are many kinds of optimizers, each with its own special strengths and weaknesses, advantages and disadvantages. Optimizers can be classified along such dimensions as human versus machine, complex versus simple, special purpose versus general purpose, and analytic versus stochastic. All optimizers—regardless of kind, efficiency, or reliability—execute a search for the best of many potential solutions to a formally specified problem.

Implicit Optimizers

A mouse cannot be used to click on a button that says "optimize." There is no special command to enter. In fact, there is no special software or even machine in sight. Does this mean there is no optimizer? No. Even when there is no optimizer apparent, and it seems as though no optimization is going on, there is. It is known as *implicit optimization* and works as follows: The trader tests a set of rules based upon some ideas regarding the market. Performance of the system is poor, and so the trader reworks the ideas, modifies the system's rules, and runs another simulation. Better performance is observed. The trader repeats this process a few times, each time making changes based on what has been learned along the way. Eventually, the trader builds a system worthy of being traded with real money. Was this system an optimized one? Since no parameters were ever explicitly adjusted and no rules were ever rearranged by the software, it appears as if the trader has succeeded in creating an unoptimized system. However, more than one solution from a set of many possible solutions was tested and the best solution was selected for use in trading or further study. This means that the system was optimized after all! Any form of problem solving in which more than one solution is examined and the best is chosen constitutes de facto optimization. The trader has a powerful brain that employed mental problem-solving algorithms, e.g., heuristically guided trial-and-error ones, which are exceptionally potent optimizers.

This means that optimization is always present; optimizers are always at work. There is no escape!

Brute Force Optimizers

A *brute force optimizer* searches for the best possible solution by systematically testing all potential solutions, i.e., all definable combinations of rules, parameters, or both. Because every possible combination must be tested, brute force optimization can be very slow. Lack of speed becomes a serious issue as the number of combinations to be examined grows. Consequently, brute force optimization is subject to the law of "combinatorial explosion." Just how slow is brute force optimization? Consider a case where there are four parameters to optimize and where each parameter can take on any of 50 values. Brute force optimization would require that 50^4 (about 6 million) tests or simulations be conducted before the optimal parameter set could be determined; if one simulation was executed every 1.62 seconds (typical for TradeStation), the optimization process would take about 4 months to complete. This approach is not very practical, especially when many systems need to be tested and optimized, when there are many parameters, when the parameters can take on many values, or when you have a life. Nevertheless, brute force optimization is useful and effective. If properly done, it will always find the best possible solution. Brute force is a good choice for small problems where combinatorial explosion is not an issue and solutions can be found in minutes, rather than days or years.

Only a small amount of programming code is needed to implement brute force optimization. Simple loop constructs are commonly employed. Parameters to be optimized are stepped from a start value to a stop value by some increment using a For loop (C, C++, Basic, Pascal/Delphi) or a Do loop (FORTRAN). A brute force optimizer for two parameters, when coded in a modern dialect of Basic, might appear as follows:

```
BestFitness = -1.0E30
For Parm1 = Parm1Start To Parm1Stop By Parm1Incr
    For Parm2 = Parm2Start To Parm2Stop2 By Parm2Incr
            RunSystem(Parm1, Parm2, GlobalData)
            CurrentFitness = CalcFitness(GlobalData)
            WriteProgressLine(GlobalData)
            If CurrentFitness > BestFitness Then
                    CurrentFitness = BestFitness
                    BestParm1 = Parm1
                    BestParm2 = Parm2
            End If
    Next Parm2
Next Parm1
```

Because brute force optimizers are conceptually simple and easy to program, they are often built into the more advanced software packages that are available for traders.

As a practical illustration of brute force optimization, TradeStation was used to optimize the moving averages in a dual moving-average crossover system. Optimization was for net profit, the only trading system characteristic that Trade-Station can optimize without the aid of add-on products. The Easy Language code for the dual moving-average trading model appears below:

```
{ Dual moving-average crossover system in Easy Language }
Inputs: LenA(4), LenB(10);
If (Average(Close, LenA) > Average(Close, LenB)) And
    (Average(Close, LenA)[1] <= Average(Close, LenB)[1]) Then
        Buy("A") 1 Contract At Market;
If (Average(Close, LenA) <= Average(Close, LenB)) And
    (Average(Close, LenA)[1] > Average(Close, LenB)[1]) Then
        Sell("B") 1 Contract At Market;
```

The system was optimized by stepping the length of the first moving average (*LenA*) from 2 to 10 in increments of 2. The length of the second moving average (*LenB*) was advanced from 2 to 50 with the same increments. Increments were set greater than 1 so that fewer than 200 combinations would need to be tested (TradeStation can only save data on a maximum of 200 optimization runs). Since not all possible combinations of values for the two parameters were explored, the optimization was less thorough than it could have been; the best solution may have been missed in the search. Notwithstanding, the optimization required 125 tests, which took 3 minutes and 24 seconds to complete on 5 years of historical, end-of-day data, using an Intel 486 machine running at 66 megahertz. The results generated by the optimization were loaded into an Excel spreadsheet and sorted for net profit. Table 3-1 presents various performance measures for the top 25 solutions.

In the table, *LENA* represents the period of the shorter moving average, *LENB* the period of the longer moving average, *NetPrft* the total net profit, *L:NetPrft* the net profit for long positions, *S:NetPrft* the net profit for short positions, *PFact* the profit factor, *ROA* the total (unannualized) return-on-account, *MaxDD* the maximum drawdown, *#Trds* the total number of trades taken, and *%Prft* the percentage of profitable trades.

Since optimization is a problem-solving search procedure, it frequently results in surprising discoveries. The optimization performed on the dual moving-average crossover system was no exception to the rule. Conventional trading wisdom says that "the trend is your friend." However, having a second moving average that is faster than the first, the most profitable solutions in Table 3-1 trade against the trend. These profitable countertrend solutions might not have been discovered without the search performed by the optimization procedure.

TABLE 3-1

Top 25 Solutions Found Using Brute Force Optimization
in TradeStation

LENA	LENB	NetPrft	L:NetPrft	S:NetPrft	PFact	ROA	MaxDD	#Trds	%Prft
10	6	145125	123325	21800	2.11	596.61	-24325	153	67
10	4	140225	120075	20150	2.06	646.20	-21700	155	70
6	4	130575	116175	14400	1.67	627.76	-20800	261	63
8	6	123825	112350	11475	1.67	547.90	-22600	211	64
8	4	117875	108725	9150	1.75	474.82	-24825	187	68
10	8	94125	98475	-4350	1.55	267.40	-35200	181	60
10	2	89675	95875	-6200	1.56	345.24	-25975	187	70
8	2	57825	79800	-21975	1.31	140.86	-41050	211	64
6	2	54075	77850	-23775	1.25	226.26	-23900	244	62
10	22	49925	76000	-26075	1.61	188.57	-26475	53	47
4	2	26575	64100	-37525	1.09	54.88	-48425	344	61
10	24	22775	61950	-39175	1.24	60.90	-37400	57	44
8	22	22675	62225	-39550	1.21	50.59	-44825	65	40
10	38	17075	54975	-37900	1.20	35.39	-48250	42	38
10	20	13975	57875	-43900	1.12	36.97	-37800	73	42
8	34	13475	51975	-38500	1.16	27.13	-49675	50	40
10	14	12225	55875	-43650	1.08	25.47	-48000	123	45
10	36	8075	50475	-42400	1.09	14.93	-54075	46	33
10	40	6625	49750	-43125	1.07	11.06	-59875	40	33
10	18	6025	53900	-47875	1.05	15.63	-38550	85	41
6	24	5425	53250	-47825	1.05	9.60	-56525	67	36
2	2	0	0	0	100.00	0.00	0	0	0
4	4	0	0	0	100.00	0.00	0	0	0
6	6	0	0	0	100.00	0.00	0	0	0
8	8	0	0	0	100.00	0.00	0	0	0

User-Guided Optimization

User-guided optimization is carried out by a partnership between the computer and
an intelligent user. Like brute force optimization, the user-guided variety involves
stepping through potential solutions to a problem (*solution space*) in search of the
best possible solution. However, where brute force demanded a sweeping search for
the best solution, user-guided optimization attempts a selective hunt in which only
certain regions of solution space are investigated. The hope is that, with intelligent
guidance, the optimization process can rapidly zero in on the optimal solution to
the problem at hand without having to probe every blind alley.

The same tools employed for brute force optimization can generally
be used for user-guided optimization. Instead of instructing the software to perform
a single, global optimization by stepping every parameter through every possible
(or reasonable) value, a series of partial optimizations are executed. Each partial
optimization entails a small number of tests. Perhaps a single parameter is marched
through a sequence of values, or all parameters are stepped through a range of values using large increments to create a coarse search grid. After each partial optimization, the results are studied and another partial optimization is carried out. The
process is expected to converge to the desired solution.

Successful user-guided optimization calls for skill, domain knowledge, or both, on the part of the person guiding the optimization process. Given adequate skill and experience, not to mention a tractable problem, user-guided optimization can be extremely efficient and dramatically faster than brute force methods. The speed and efficiency derive from the addition of intelligence to the search process: Zones with a high probability of paying off can be recognized and carefully examined, while time-consuming investigations of regions unlikely to yield good results can be avoided.

User-guided optimization is most appropriate when ballpark results have already been established by other means, when the problem is familiar or well understood, or when only a small number of parameters need to be manipulated. As a means of "polishing" an existing solution, user guided-optimization is an excellent choice. It is also useful for studying model sensitivity to changes in rules or parameter values.

Genetic Optimizers

Imagine something powerful enough to solve all the problems inherent in the creation of a human being. That something surely represents the ultimate in problem solving and optimization. What is it? It is the familiar process of evolution. *Genetic optimizers* endeavor to harness some of that incredible problem-solving power through a crude simulation of the evolutionary process. In terms of overall performance and the variety of problems that may be solved, there is no general-purpose optimizer more powerful than a properly crafted genetic one.

Genetic optimizers are *Stochastic* optimizers in the sense that they take advantage of random chance in their operation. It may not seem believable that tossing dice can be a great way to solve problems, but, done correctly, it can be! In addition to randomness, genetic optimizers employ selection and recombination. The clever integration of random chance, selection, and recombination is responsible for the genetic optimizer's great power. A full discussion of genetic algorithms, which are the basis for genetic optimizers, appears in Part II.

Genetic optimizers have many highly desirable characteristics. One such characteristic is speed, especially when faced with combinatorial explosion. A genetic optimizer can easily be many orders of magnitude faster than a brute force optimizer when there are a multiplicity of rules, or parameters that have many possible values, to manipulate. This is because, like user-guided optimization, genetic optimization can focus on important regions of solution space while mostly ignoring blind alleys. In contrast to user-guided optimization, the benefit of a selective search is achieved without the need for human intervention.

Genetic optimizers can swiftly solve complex problems, and they are also more immune than other kinds of optimizers to the effects of local maxima in the fitness surface or, equivalently, local minima in the cost surface. Analytic methods are worst in that they almost always walk right to the top of the nearest hill or bottom of the nearest valley, without regard to whether higher hills or lower valleys exist elsewhere. In contrast, a good genetic optimizer often locates the globally best solution—quite an impressive feat when accomplished for cantankerous fitness surfaces, such as those associated with matrices of neural connection weights.

Another characteristic of genetic optimization is that it works well with fitness surfaces marked by discontinuities, flat regions, and other troublesome irregularities. Genetic optimization shares this characteristic with brute force, user-guided, annealing-based, and other nonanalytic optimization methods. Solutions that maximize such items as net profit, return on investment, the Sharpe Ratio, and others that define difficult, nonanalytic fitness landscapes can be found using a genetic optimizer. Genetic optimizers shine with difficult fitness functions that lie beyond the purview of analytic methods. This does not mean that they cannot be used to solve problems having more tractable fitness surfaces: Perhaps slower than the analytic methods, they have the virtue of being more resistant to the traps set by local optima.

Overall, genetic optimizers are the optimizers of choice when there are many parameters or rules to adapt, when a global solution is desired, or when arbitrarily complex (and not necessarily differentiable or continuous) fitness or cost functions must be handled. Although special-purpose optimizers can outperform genetic optimizers on specific kinds of problems, for general-purpose optimization, genetic optimizers are among the most powerful tools available.

What does a genetic optimizer look like in action? The dual moving-average crossover system discussed earlier was translated to C11 so that the genetic optimizer in the C-Trader toolkit could be used to solve for the two system parameters, *LenA* and *LenB*. *LenA*, the period of the first moving average, was examined over the range of 2 through 50, as was *LenB*, the period of the second moving average. Optimization was for net profit so that the results would be directly comparable with those produced earlier by brute force optimization. Below is the C11 code for the crossover system:

```
static void Model (float *parms, float *dt, float *opn,
   float *hi, float *lo, float *cls, float *vol, float *oi,
   int nb, TRDSIM &ts, float *eqcls) {
      // Function implements trading model to be tested and
      // has following arguments:
      // parms     - vector [1..MAXPRM] of parameters
      // dt        - vector [1..nb] of dates in YYMMDD form
      // opn       - vector [1..nb] of opening prices
      // hi        - vector [1..nb] of high prices
      // lo        - vector [1..nb] of low prices
      // cls       - vector [1..nb] of closing prices
      // vol       - vector [1..nb] of volume numbers
```

```
// oi      - vector [1..nb] of open interest numbers
// nb      - number of bars in data series
// ts      - trading simulator class instance
// eqcls   - vector [1..nb] of closing equity levels

// declare local variables and macro functions
static int cb, LenA, LenB;
static float MavgA[MAXBAR+1], MavgB[MAXBAR+1];
#define CrossesAbove(a,b)  ((a[cb]>=b[cb])&&(a[cb-1]<b[cb-1]))
#define CrossesBelow(a,b)  ((a[cb]<b[cb])&&(a[cb-1]>=b[cb-1]))

// clear simulated account and flush any pending orders
ts.clear();

// calculate moving averages using series (vector) functions
LenA = parms[1];
LenB = parms[2];
AverageS(MavgA, cls, LenA, nb);     // First moving average
AverageS(MavgB, cls, LenB, nb);     // Second moving average

// step through bars (days) to simulate actual trading
for(cb = 1; cb <= nb; cb++) {
    // take no trades in lookback period
    if(dt[cb] < 910302) { eqcls[cb] = 0.0; continue; }

    // execute pending orders and save closing equity
    ts.update(opn[cb], hi[cb], lo[cb], cls[cb], cb);
    eqcls[cb] = ts.currentequity(EQ_CLOSETOTAL);

    // dual moving-average crossover system trading rules
    if(CrossesAbove(MavgA, MavgB)) ts.buyopen('A', 1);
    if(CrossesBelow(MavgA, MavgB)) ts.sellopen('B', 1);
}
}
```

To solve for the best parameters, brute force optimization would require that 2,041 tests be performed; in TradeStation, that works out to about 56 minutes of computing time, extrapolating from the earlier illustration in which a small subset of the current solution space was examined. Only 1 minute of running time was required by the genetic optimizer; in an attempt to put it at a significant disadvantage, it was prematurely stopped after performing only 133 tests.

The output from the genetic optimizer appears in Table 3-2. In this table, *P1* represents the period of the faster moving average, *P2* the period of the slower moving average, *NET* the total net profit, *NETLNG* the net profit for long positions, *NETSHT* the net profit for short positions, *PFAC* the profit factor, *ROA%* the annualized return on account, *DRAW* the maximum drawdown, *TRDS* the number of trades taken by the system, *WIN%* the percentage of winning trades, *AVGT* the profit or loss resulting from the average trade, and *FIT* the fitness of the solution (which, in this instance, is merely the total net profit). As with the brute force data in Table 3-1, the genetic data have been sorted by net profit (fitness) and only the 25 best solutions were presented.

TABLE 3-2

Top 25 Solutions Found Using Genetic Optimization in C-Trader Toolkit

P1	P2	NET	NETLNG	NETSHT	PFAC	ROA%	DRAW	TRDS	WIN%	AVGT	FIT
10	5	172725	136325	36400	2.39	817.6	21125	155	70	1114	172725
11	5	163475	132625	30850	2.33	762.1	21450	148	72	1104	163475
12	4	156975	129250	27725	2.23	816.5	19225	137	77	1145	156975
10	4	138875	120075	18800	2.04	637.0	21800	156	68	890	138875
49	3	138475	85600	52875	5.28	190.5	72700	73	87	1896	138475
50	3	138125	85425	52700	5.36	190.0	72700	73	87	1892	138125
13	4	134825	116525	18300	2.02	614.9	21925	131	72	1029	134825
47	4	132375	82550	49825	5.29	176.4	75050	65	87	2036	132375
48	3	130225	81375	48850	5.04	177.6	73325	71	85	1834	130225
50	2	130175	81350	48825	4.94	175.0	74375	85	85	1531	130175
49	4	126150	80275	45875	5.38	173.4	72750	65	87	1940	126150
11	6	125225	113500	11725	1.93	410.9	30475	146	63	857	125225
13	3	119325	109300	10025	1.96	592.2	20150	136	72	877	119325
12	2	117275	109400	7875	1.84	481.6	24350	163	71	719	117275
45	23	113300	73475	39825	7.16	157.2	72075	31	87	3654	113300
50	22	111200	72425	38775	6.59	154.3	72075	31	83	3587	111200
44	23	110525	71825	38700	7.02	151.6	72900	31	87	3565	110525
48	22	108750	71200	37550	6.63	150.9	72075	31	87	3508	108750
11	7	106125	101875	4250	1.68	332.2	31950	144	63	736	106125
50	21	103150	68850	34300	6.18	141.5	72900	29	82	3556	103150
46	23	102700	68175	34525	5.29	142.5	72075	31	80	3312	102700
45	2	102650	95700	6950	2.26	168.6	60900	93	84	1103	102650
46	22	101425	67275	34150	6.3	139.1	72900	31	83	3271	101425
50	23	100150	66275	33875	5.1	137.0	73100	31	80	3230	100150
17	3	98925	101550	-2625	1.82	384.5	25725	114	74	867	98925

Comparison of the brute force and genetic optimization results (Tables 3-1 and 3-2, respectively) reveals that the genetic optimizer isolated a solution with a greater net profit ($172,725) than did the brute force optimizer ($145,125). This is no surprise since a larger solution space, not decimated by increments, was explored. The surprise is that the better solution was found so quickly, despite the handicap of a prematurely stopped evolutionary process. Results like these demonstrate the incredible effectiveness of genetic optimization.

Optimization by Simulated Annealing

Optimizers based on *annealing* mimic the thermodynamic process by which liquids freeze and metals anneal. Starting out at a high temperature, the atoms of a liquid or molten metal bounce rapidly about in a random fashion. Slowly cooled, they arrange themselves into an orderly configuration—a crystal—that represents a minimal energy state for the system. Simulated in software, this thermodynamic process readily solves large-scale optimization problems.

As with genetic opimization, optimization by *simulated annealing* is a very powerful Stochastic technique, modeled upon a natural phenomenon, that can find globally optimal solutions and handle ill-behaved fitness functions. Simulated annealing has effectively solved significant combinatorial problems, including the famous "traveling salesman problem," and the problem of how best to arrange the millions of circuit elements found on modern integrated circuit chips, such as those that power computers. Methods based on simulated annealing should not be construed as limited to combinatorial optimization; they can readily be adapted to the optimization of real-valued parameters. Consequently, optimizers based on simulated annealing are applicable to a wide variety of problems, including those faced by traders.

Since genetic optimizers perform so well, we have experienced little need to explore optimizers based on simulated annealing. In addition, there have been a few reports suggesting that, in many cases, annealing algorithms do not perform as well as genetic algorithms. Because of these reasons, we have not provided examples of simulated annealing and have little more to say about the method.

Analytic Optimizers

Analysis (as in "real analysis" or "complex analysis") is an extension of classical college calculus. *Analytic optimizers* involve the well-developed machinery of analysis, specifically differential calculus and the study of analytic functions, in the solution of practical problems. In some instances, analytic methods can yield a direct (noniterative) solution to an optimization problem. This happens to be the case for multiple regression, where solutions can be obtained with a few matrix calculations. In multiple regression, the goal is to find a set of regression weights that minimize the sum of the squared prediction errors. In other cases, iterative techniques must be used. The connection weights in a neural network, for example, cannot be directly determined. They must be estimated using an iterative procedure, such as back-propagation.

Many iterative techniques used to solve multivariate optimization problems (those involving several variables or parameters) employ some variation on the theme of *steepest ascent*. In its most basic form, optimization by steepest ascent works as follows: A point in the domain of the fitness function (that is, a set of parameter values) is chosen by some means. The gradient vector at that point is evaluated by computing the derivatives of the fitness function with respect to each of the variables or parameters; this defines the direction in *n*-dimensional parameter space for which a fixed amount of movement will produce the greatest increase in fitness. A small step is taken up the hill in fitness space, along the direction of the gradient. The gradient is then recomputed at this new point, and another, perhaps smaller, step is taken. The process is repeated until convergence occurs.

A real-world implementation of steepest ascent optimization has to specify how the step size will be determined at each iteration, and how the direction defined by the gradient will be adjusted for better overall convergence of the optimization process. Naive implementations assume that there is an analytic fitness surface (one that can be approximated locally by a convergent power series) having hills that must be climbed. More sophisticated implementations go further, commonly assuming that the fitness function can be well approximated locally by a quadratic form. If a fitness function satisfies this assumption, then much faster convergence to a solution can be achieved. However, when the fitness surface has many irregularly shaped hills and valleys, quadratic forms often fail to provide a good approximation. In such cases, the more sophisticated methods break down entirely or their performance seriously degrades.

Worse than degraded performance is the problem of local solutions. Almost all analytic methods, whether elementary or sophisticated, are easily trapped by local maxima; they generally fail to locate the globally best solution when there are many hills and valleys in the fitness surface. Least-squares, neural network predictive modeling gives rise to fitness surfaces that, although clearly analytic, are full of bumps, troughs, and other irregularities that lead standard analytic techniques (including back-propagation, a variant on steepest ascent) astray. Local maxima and other hazards that accompany such fitness surfaces can, however, be sidestepped by cleverly marrying a genetic algorithm with an analytic one. For fitness surfaces amenable to analytic optimization, such a combined algorithm can provide the best of both worlds: fast, accurate solutions that are also likely to be globally optimal.

Some fitness surfaces are simply not amenable to analytic optimization. More specifically, analytic methods cannot be used when the fitness surface has flat areas or discontinuities in the region of parameter space where a solution is to be sought. Flat areas imply null gradients, hence the absence of a preferred direction in which to take a step. At points of discontinuity, the gradient is not defined; again, a stepping direction cannot be determined. Even if a method does not explicitly use gradient information, such information is employed implicitly by the optimization algorithm. Unfortunately, many fitness functions of interest to traders—including, for instance, all functions that involve net profit, drawdown, percentage of winning trades, risk-to-reward ratios, and other like items—have plateaus and discontinuities. They are, therefore, not tractable using analytic methods.

Although the discussion has centered on the maximization of fitness, everything said applies as well to the minimization of cost. Any maximization technique can be used for minimization, and vice versa: Multiply a fitness function by -1 to obtain an equivalent cost function; multiply a cost function by -1 and a fitness function is the result. If a minimization algorithm takes your fancy, but a maximization is required, use this trick to avoid having to recode the optimization algorithm.

Linear Programming

The techniques of *linear programming* are designed for optimization problems involving linear cost or fitness functions, and linear constraints on the parameters or input variables. Linear programming is typically used to solve resource allocation problems. In the world of trading, one use of linear programming might be to allocate capital among a set of investments to maximize net profit. If risk-adjusted profit is to be optimized, linear programming methods cannot be used: Risk-adjusted profit is not a linear function of the amount of capital allocated to each of the investments; in such instances, other techniques (e.g., genetic algorithms) must be employed. Linear programming methods are rarely useful in the development of trading systems. They are mentioned here only to inform readers of their existence.

HOW TO FAIL WITH OPTIMIZATION

Most traders do not seek failure, at least not consciously. However, knowledge of the way failure is achieved can be of great benefit when seeking to avoid it. Failure with an optimizer is easy to accomplish by following a few key rules. First, be sure to use a small data sample when running simulations: The smaller the sample, the greater the likelihood it will poorly represent the data on which the trading model will actually be traded. Next, make sure the trading system has a large number of parameters and rules to optimize: For a given data sample, the greater the number of variables that must be estimated, the easier it will be to obtain spurious results. It would also be beneficial to employ only a single sample on which to run tests; annoying out-of-sample data sets have no place in the rose-colored world of the ardent loser. Finally, do avoid the headache of inferential statistics. Follow these rules and failure is guaranteed.

What shape will failure take? Most likely, system performance will look great in tests, but terrible in real-time trading. Neural network developers call this phenomenon "poor generalization"; traders are acquainted with it through the experience of margin calls and a serious loss of trading capital. One consequence of such a failure-laden outcome is the formation of a popular misconception: that all optimization is dangerous and to be feared.

In actual fact, optimizers are not dangerous and not all optimization should be feared. Only bad optimization is dangerous and frightening. Optimization of large parameter sets on small samples, without out-of-sample tests or inferential statistics, is simply a bad practice that invites unhappy results for a variety of reasons.

Small Samples

Consider the impact of small samples on the optimization process. Small samples of market data are unlikely to be representative of the universe from which they are drawn; consequently, they will probably differ significantly from other samples obtained from the same universe. Applied to a small development sample, an optimizer will faithfully discover the best possible solution. The best solution for the development sample, however, may turn out to be a dreadful solution for the later sample on which genuine trades will be taken. Failure ensues, not because optimization has found a bad solution, but because it has found a good solution to the wrong problem!

Optimization on inadequate samples is also good at spawning solutions that represent only mathematical artifact. As the number of data points declines to the number of free (adjustable) parameters, most models (trading, regression, or otherwise) will attain a perfect fit to even random data. The principle involved is the same one responsible for the fact that a line, which is a two-parameter model, can always be drawn through any two distinct points, but cannot always be made to intersect three arbitrary points. In statistics, this is known as the *degrees-of-freedom* issue; there are as many degrees of freedom as there are data points beyond that which can be fitted perfectly for purely mathematical reasons. Even when there are enough data points to avoid a totally artifact-determined solution, some part of the model fitness obtained through optimization will be of an artifact-determined nature, a by-product of the process.

For multiple regression models, a formula is available that can be used to estimate how much "shrinkage" would occur in the multiple correlation coefficient (a measure of model fitness) if the artifact-determined component were removed. The *shrinkage correction formula*, which shows the relationship between the number of parameters (regression coefficients) being optimized, sample size, and decreased levels of apparent fitness (correlation) in tests on new samples, is shown below in FORTRAN-style notation:

```
RC = SQRT ( 1. - ( (N - 1.) / (N - P) ) * (1. - R**2) )
```

In this equation, *N* represents the number of data points, *P* the number of model parameters, *R* the multiple correlation coefficient determined for the sample by the regression (optimization) procedure, and *RC* the shrinkage-corrected multiple correlation coefficient. The inverse formula, one that estimates the optimization-inflated correlation (*R*) given the true correlation (*RC*) existing in the population from which the data were sampled, appears below:

```
R = SQRT ( 1. - ( (N - P) / (N - 1.) ) * (1. - RC**2) )
```

These formulas, although legitimate only for linear regression, are not bad for estimating how well a fully trained neural network model—which is nothing more than a particular kind of nonlinear regression—will generalize. When working with neural networks, let *P* represent the total number of connection weights in the model. In addition, make sure that simple correlations are used when working with these formulas; if a neural network or regression package reports the squared multiple correlation, take the square root.

Large Parameter Sets

An excessive number of free parameters or rules will impact an optimization effort in a manner similar to an insufficient number of data points. As the number of elements undergoing optimization rises, a model's ability to capitalize on idiosyncrasies in the development sample increases along with the proportion of the model's fitness that can be attributed to mathematical artifact. The result of optimizing a large number of variables—whether rules, parameters, or both—will be a model that performs well on the development data, but poorly on out-of-sample test data and in actual trading.

It is not the absolute number of free parameters that should be of concern, but the number of parameters relative to the number of data points. The shrinkage formula discussed in the context of small samples is also heuristically relevant here: It illustrates how the relationship between the number of data points and the number of parameters affects the outcome. When there are too many parameters, given the number of data points, mathematical artifacts and capitalization on chance (curve-fitting, in the bad sense) become reasons for failure.

No Verification

One of the better ways to get into trouble is by failing to verify model performance using out-of-sample tests or inferential statistics. Without such tests, the spurious solutions resulting from small samples and large parameter sets, not to mention other less obvious causes, will go undetected. The trading system that appears to be ideal on the development sample will be put "on-line," and devastating losses will follow. Developing systems without subjecting them to out-of-sample and statistical tests is like flying blind, without a safety belt, in an uninspected aircraft.

HOW TO SUCCEED WITH OPTIMIZATION

Four steps can be taken to avoid failure and increase the odds of achieving successful optimization. As a first step, optimize on the largest possible representative sample and make sure many simulated trades are available for analysis. The second step is to keep the number of free parameters or rules small, especially in relation to sample size. A third step involves running tests on out-of-sample data, that is, data not used or even seen during the optimization process. As a fourth and final step, it may be worthwhile to statistically assess the results.

Large, Representative Samples

As suggested earlier, failure is often a consequence of presenting an optimizer with the wrong problem to solve. Conversely, success is likely when the optimizer is presented with the right problem. The conclusion is that trading models should be optimized on data from the near future, the data that will actually be traded; do that and watch the profits roll in. The catch is where to find tomorrow's data today.

Since the future has not yet happened, it is impossible to present the optimizer with precisely the problem that needs to be solved. Consequently, it is necessary to attempt the next-best alternative: to present the optimizer with a broader problem, the solution to which should be as applicable as possible to the actual, but impossible-to-solve, problem. One way to accomplish this is with a data sample that, even though not drawn from the future, embodies many characteristics that might appear in future samples. Such a data sample should include bull and bear markets, trending and nontrending periods, and even crashes. In addition, the data in the sample should be as recent as possible so that it will reflect current patterns of market behavior. This is what is meant by a *representative sample*.

As well as representative, the sample should be large. Large samples make it harder for optimizers to uncover spurious or artifact-determined solutions. *Shrinkage*, the expected decline in performance on unoptimized data, is reduced when large samples are employed in the optimization process.

Sometimes, however, a trade-off must be made between the sample's size and the extent to which it is representative. As one goes farther back in history to bolster a sample, the data may become less representative of current market conditions. In some instances, there is a clear transition point beyond which the data become much less representative: For example, the S&P 500 futures began trading in 1983, effecting a structural change in the general market. Trade-offs become much less of an issue when working with intraday data on short time frames, where tens of thousands or even hundreds of thousands of bars of data can be gathered without going back beyond the recent past.

Finally, when running simulations and optimizations, pay attention to the number of trades a system takes. Like large data samples, it is highly desirable that simulations and tests involve numerous trades. Chance or artifact can easily be responsible for any profits produced by a system that takes only a few trades, regardless of the number of data points used in the test!

Few Rules and Parameters

To achieve success, limit the number of free rules and parameters, especially when working with small data samples. For a given sample size, the fewer the rules or parameters to optimize, the greater the likelihood that a trading system will maintain its performance in out-of-sample tests and real-time trading. Although several dozen parameters may be acceptable when working with several thousand trades taken on 100,000 1-minute bars (about 1 year for the S&P 500 futures), even two or three parameters may be excessive when developing a system using a few years of end-of-day data. If a particular model requires many parameters, then significant effort should be put into assembling a mammoth sample (the legendary Gann supposedly went back over 1,000 years in his study of wheat prices). An alternative that sometimes works is optimizing a trading model on a whole portfolio, using the same rules and parameters across all markets—a technique used extensively in this book.

Verification of Results

After optimizing the rules and parameters of a trading system to obtain good behavior on the development or in-sample data, but before risking any real money, it is essential to verify the system's performance in some manner. Verification of system performance is important because it gives the trader a chance to veto failure and embrace success: Systems that fail the test of verification can be discarded; ones that pass can be traded with confidence. Verification is the single most critical step on the road to success with optimization or, in fact, with any other method of discovering a trading model that really works.

To ensure success, verify any trading solution using out-of-sample tests or inferential statistics, preferably both. Discard any solution that fails to be profitable in an out-of-sample test: It is likely to fail again when the rubber hits the road. Compute inferential statistics on all tests, both in-sample and out-of-sample. These statistics reveal the probability that the performance observed in a sample reflects something real that will hold up in other samples and in real-time trading. Inferential statistics work by making probability inferences based on the distribution of profitability in a system's trades or returns. Be sure to use statistics that are corrected for multiple tests when analyzing in-sample optimization results. Out-of-sample tests should be analyzed with standard, uncorrected statistics. Such statistics appear in some of the performance reports that are displayed in the chapter on simulators. The use of statistics to evaluate trading systems is covered in depth in the following chapter. Develop a working knowledge of statistics; it will make you a better trader.

Some suggest checking a model for sensitivity to small changes in parameter values. A model highly tolerant of such changes is more "robust" than a model not as tolerant, it is said. Do not pay too much attention to these claims. In truth, parameter tolerance cannot be relied upon as a gauge of model robustness. Many extremely robust models are highly sensitive to the values of certain parameters. The only true arbiters of system robustness are statistical and, especially, out-of-sample tests.

ALTERNATIVES TO TRADITIONAL OPTIMIZATION

There are two major alternatives to traditional optimization: walk-forward optimization and self-adaptive systems. Both of these techniques have the advantage that any tests carried out are, from start to finish, effectively out-of-sample.

Examine the performance data, run some inferential statistics, plot the equity curve, and the system is ready to be traded. Everything is clean and mathematically unimpeachable. Corrections for shrinkage or multiple tests, worries over excessive curve-fitting, and many of the other concerns that plague traditional optimization methodologies can be forgotten. Moreover, with today's modern computer technology, walk-forward and self-adaptive models are practical and not even difficult to implement.

The principle behind *walk-forward optimization* (also known as *walk-forward testing*) is to emulate the steps involved in actually trading a system that requires periodic optimization. It works like this: Optimize the system on the data points *1* through *M*. Then simulate trading on data points *M* + *1* through *M* + *K*. Reoptimize the system on data points *K* + *1* through *K* + *M*. Then simulate trading on points (*K* + *M*) + *1* through (*K* + *M*) + *K*. Advance through the data series in this fashion until no more data points are left to analyze. As should be evident, the system is optimized on a sample of historical data and then traded. After some period of time, the system is reoptimized and trading is resumed. The sequence of events guarantees that the data on which trades take place is always in the future relative to the optimization process; all trades occur on what is, essentially, out-of-sample data. In walk-forward testing, *M* is the look-back or optimization window and *K* the reoptimization interval.

Self-adaptive systems work in a similar manner, except that the optimization or adaptive process is part of the system, rather than the test environment. As each bar or data point comes along, a self-adaptive system updates its internal state (its parameters or rules) and then makes decisions concerning actions required on the next bar or data point. When the next bar arrives, the decided-upon actions are carried out and the process repeats. Internal updates, which are how the system learns about or adapts to the market, need not occur on every single bar. They can be performed at fixed intervals or whenever deemed necessary by the model.

The trader planning to work with self-adapting systems will need a powerful, component-based development platform that employs a strong language, such as C++, Object Pascal, or Visual Basic, and that provides good access to third-party libraries and software components. Components are designed to be incorporated into user-written software, including the special-purpose software that constitutes an adaptive system. The more components that are available, the less work there is to do. At the very least, a trader venturing into self-adaptive systems should have at hand genetic optimizer and trading simulator components that can be easily embedded within a trading model. Adaptive systems will be demonstrated in later chapters, showing how this technique works in practice.

There is no doubt that walk-forward optimization and adaptive systems will become more popular over time as the markets become more efficient and difficult to trade, and as commercial software packages become available that place these techniques within reach of the average trader.

OPTIMIZER TOOLS AND INFORMATION

Aerodynamics, electronics, chemistry, biochemistry, planning, and business are just a few of the fields in which optimization plays a role. Because optimization is of interest to so many problem-solving areas, research goes on everywhere, information is abundant, and optimization tools proliferate. Where can this information be found? What tools and products are available?

Brute force optimizers are usually buried in software packages aimed primarily at tasks other than optimization; they are usually not available on their own. In the world of trading, products like TradeStation and SuperCharts from Omega Research (800-292-3453), Excalibur from Futures Truth (828-697-0273), and MetaStock from Equis International (800-882-3040) have built-in brute force optimizers. If you write your own software, brute force optimization is so trivial to implement using in-line programming code that the use of special libraries or components is superfluous. Products and code able to carry out brute force optimization may also serve well for user-guided optimization.

Although sometimes appearing as built-in tools in specialized programs, genetic optimizers are more often distributed in the form of class libraries or software components, add-ons to various application packages, or stand-alone research instruments. As an example of a class library written with the component paradigm in mind, consider OptEvolve, the C++ genetic optimizer from Scientific Consultant Services (516-696-3333): This general-purpose genetic optimizer implements several algorithms, including differential evolution, and is sold in the form of highly portable C++ code that can be used in UNIX/LINUX, DOS, and Windows environments. TS-Evolve, available from Ruggiero Associates (800-211-9785), gives users of TradeStation the ability to perform full-blown genetic optimizations. The Evolver, which can be purchased from Palisade Corporation (800-432-7475), is a general-purpose genetic optimizer for Microsoft's Excel spreadsheet; it comes with a dynamic link library (DLL) that can provide genetic optimization services to user programs written in any language able to call DLL functions. GENESIS, a stand-alone instrument aimed at the research community, was written by John Grefenstette of the Naval Research Laboratory; the product is available in the form of generic C source code. While genetic optimizers can occasionally be found in modeling tools for chemists and in other specialized products, they do not yet form a native part of popular software packages designed for traders.

Information about genetic optimization is readily available. Genetic algorithms are discussed in many books, magazines, and journals and on Internet newsgroups. A good overview of the field of genetic optimization can be found in the *Handbook of Genetic Algorithms* (Davis, 1991). Price and Storm (1997) described an algorithm for "differential evolution," which has been shown to be an exceptionally powerful technique for optimization problems involving real-valued parameters. Genetic algorithms are currently the focus of many academic journals and conference proceedings. Lively discussions on all aspects of genetic optimization take place in several Internet newsgroups of which comp.ai.genetic is the most noteworthy.

A basic exposition of simulated annealing can be found in *Numerical Recipes in C* (Press et al., 1992), as can C functions implementing optimizers for both combinatorial and real-valued problems. *Neural, Novel & Hybrid Algorithms for Time Series Prediction* (Masters, 1995) also discusses annealing-based optimization and contains relevant C++ code on the included CD-ROM. Like genetic optimization, simulated annealing is the focus of many research studies, conference presentations, journal articles, and Internet newsgroup discussions.

Algorithms and code for conjugate gradient and variable metric optimization, two fairly sophisticated analytic methods, can be found in *Numerical Recipes in C* (Press et al., 1992) and *Numerical Recipes* (Press et al., 1986). Masters (1995) provides an assortment of analytic optimization procedures in C++ (on the CD-ROM that comes with his book), as well as a good discussion of the subject. Additional procedures for analytic optimization are available in the IMSL and the NAG library (from Visual Numerics, Inc., and Numerical Algorithms Group, respectively) and in the optimization toolbox for MATLAB (a general-purpose mathematical package from The MathWorks, 508-647-7000, that has gained popularity in the financial engineering community). Finally, Microsoft's Excel spreadsheet contains a built-in analytic optimizer—the Solver—that employs conjugate gradient or Newtonian methods.

As a source of general information about optimization applied to trading system development, consult *Design, Testing and Optimization of Trading Systems* by Robert Pardo (1992). Among other things, this book shows the reader how to optimize profitably, how to avoid undesirable curve-fitting, and how to carry out walk-forward tests.

WHICH OPTIMIZER IS FOR YOU?

At the very least, you should have available an optimizer that is designed to make both brute force and user-guided optimization easy to carry out. Such an optimizer is already at hand if you use either TradeStation or Excalibur for system development tasks. On the other hand, if you develop your systems in Excel, Visual Basic, C++, or Delphi, you will have to create your own brute force optimizer. As demonstrated earlier, a brute force optimizer is simple to implement. For many problems, brute force or user-guided optimization is the best approach.

If your system development efforts require something beyond brute force, a genetic optimizer is a great second choice. Armed with both brute force and genetic optimizers, you will be able to solve virtually any problem imaginable. In our own efforts, we hardly ever reach for any other kind of optimization tool! TradeStation users will probably want TS-Evolve from Ruggiero Associates. The

Evolver product from Palisade Corporation is a good choice for Excel and Visual Basic users. If you develop systems in C++ or Delphi, select the C++ Genetic Optimizer from Scientific Consultant Services, Inc. A genetic optimizer is the Swiss Army knife of the optimizer world: Even problems more efficiently solved using such other techniques as analytic optimization will yield, albeit more slowly, to a good genetic optimizer.

Finally, if you want to explore analytic optimization or simulated annealing, we suggest *Numerical Recipes in C* (Press et al., 1992) and Masters (1995) as good sources of both information and code. Excel users can try out the built-in Solver tool.

CHAPTER 4

Statistics

Many trading system developers have little familiarity with inferential statistics. This is a rather perplexing state of affairs since statistics are essential to assessing the behavior of trading systems. How, for example, can one judge whether an apparent edge in the trades produced by a system is real or an artifact of sampling or chance? Think of it—the next sample may not merely be another test, but an actual trading exercise. If the system's "edge" was due to chance, trading capital could quickly be depleted. Consider optimization: Has the system been tweaked into great profitability, or has the developer only succeeded in the nasty art of curve-fitting? We have encountered many system developers who refuse to use any optimization strategy whatsoever because of their irrational fear of curve-fitting, not knowing that the right statistics can help detect such phenomena. In short, inferential statistics can help a trader evaluate the likelihood that a system is capturing a real inefficiency and will perform as profitably in the future as it has in the past. In this book, we have presented the results of statistical analyses whenever doing so seemed useful and appropriate.

Among the kinds of inferential statistics that are most useful to traders are t-tests, correlational statistics, and such nonparametric statistics as the runs test.

T-tests are useful for determining the probability that the mean or sum of any series of independent values (derived from a sampling process) is greater or less than some other such mean, is a fixed number, or falls within a certain band. For example, t-tests can reveal the probability that the total profits from a series of trades, each with its individual profit/loss figure, could be greater than some threshold as a result of chance or sampling. These tests are also useful for evaluating samples of returns, e.g., the daily or monthly returns of a portfolio over a period of years. Finally, t-tests can help to set the boundaries of likely future performance (assuming no structural change in the market), making possible such statements as "the probability that the average profit will be between x and y in the future is greater than 95%."

Correlational statistics help determine the degree of relationship between different variables. When applied inferentially, they may also be used to assess whether any relationships found are "statistically significant," and not merely due to chance. Such statistics aid in setting confidence intervals or boundaries on the "true" (population) correlation, given the observed correlation for a specific sample. Correlational statistics are essential when searching for predictive variables to include in a neural network or regression-based trading model.

Correlational statistics, as well as such nonparametric statistics as the *runs test*, are useful in assessing serial dependence or serial correlation. For instance, do profitable trades come in streaks or runs that are then followed by periods of unprofitable trading? The runs test can help determine whether this is actually occurring. If there is serial dependence in a system, it is useful to know it because the system can then be revised to make use of the serial dependence. For example, if a system has clearly defined streaks of winning and losing, a metasystem can be developed. The metasystem would take every trade after a winning trade until the first losing trade comes along, then stop trading until a winning trade is hit, at which point it would again begin taking trades. If there really are runs, this strategy, or something similar, could greatly improve a system's behavior.

WHY USE STATISTICS TO EVALUATE TRADING SYSTEMS?

It is very important to determine whether any observed profits are real (not artifacts of testing), and what the likelihood is that the system producing them will continue to yield profits in the future when it is used in actual trading. While out-of-sample testing can provide some indication of whether a system will hold up on new (future) data, statistical methods can provide additional information and estimates of probability. Statistics can help determine whether a system's performance is due to chance alone or if the trading model has some real validity. Statistical calculations can even be adjusted for a known degree of curve-fitting, thereby providing estimates of whether a chance pattern, present in the data sample being used to develop the system, has been curve-fitted or whether a pattern present in the population (and hence one that would probably be present in future samples drawn from the market being examined) has been modeled.

It should be noted that statistics generally make certain theoretical assumptions about the data samples and populations to which they may be appropriately applied. These assumptions are often violated when dealing with trading models. Some violations have little practical effect and may be ignored, while others may be worked around. By using additional statistics, the more serious violations can sometimes be detected, avoided, or compensated for; at the very least, they can be understood. In short, we are fully aware of these violations and will discuss our acts of hubris and their ramifications after a foundation for understanding the issues has been laid.

SAMPLING

Fundamental to statistics and, therefore, important to understand, is the act of *sampling*, which is the extraction of a number of data points or trades (a *sample*) from a larger, abstractly defined set of data points or trades (a *population*). The central idea behind statistical analysis is the use of samples to make inferences about the populations from which they are drawn. When dealing with trading models, the populations will most often be defined as all raw data (past, present, and future) for a given tradable (e.g., all 5-minute bars on all futures on the S&P 500), all trades (past, present, and future) taken by a specified system on a given tradable, or all yearly, monthly, or even daily returns. All quarterly earnings (past, present, and future) of IBM is another example of a population. A sample could be the specific historical data used in developing or testing a system, the simulated trades taken, or monthly returns generated by the system on that data.

When creating a trading system, the developer usually draws a sample of data from the population being modeled. For example, to develop an S&P 500 system based on the hypothesis "If yesterday's close is greater than the close three days ago, then the market will rise tomorrow," the developer draws a sample of end-of-day price data from the S&P 500 that extends back, e.g., 5 years. The hope is that the data sample drawn from the S&P 500 is *representative* of that market, i.e., will accurately reflect the actual, typical behavior of that market (the population from which the sample was drawn), so that the system being developed will perform as well in the future (on a previously unseen sample of population data) as it did in the past (on the sample used as development data). To help determine whether the system will hold up, developers sometimes test systems on one or more *out-of-sample* periods, i.e., on additional samples of data that have not been used to develop or optimize the trading model. In our example, the S&P 500 developer might use 5 years of data—e.g., 1991 through 1995—to develop and tweak the system, and reserve the data from 1996 as the out-of-sample period on which to test the system. Reserving one or more sets of out-of-sample data is strongly recommended.

One problem with drawing data samples from financial populations arises from the complex and variable nature of the markets; today's market may not be tomorrow's. Sometimes the variations are very noticeable and their causes are easily discerned, e.g., when the S&P 500 changed in 1983 as a result of the introduction of futures and options. In such instances, the change may be construed as having created two distinct populations: the S&P 500 prior to 1983 and the S&P 500 after 1983. A sample drawn from the earlier period would almost certainly

not be representative of the population defined by the later period because it was
drawn from a different population! This is, of course, an extreme case. More
often, structural market variations are due to subtle influences that are sometimes
impossible to identify, especially before the fact. In some cases, the market may
still be fundamentally the same, but it may be going through different phases;
each sample drawn might inadvertently be taken from a different phase and be
representative of that phase alone, not of the market as a whole. How can it be
determined that the population from which a sample is drawn for the purpose of
system development is the same as the population on which the system will be
traded? Short of hopping into a time machine and sampling the future, there is no
reliable way to tell if tomorrow will be the day the market undergoes a system-
killing metamorphosis! Multiple out-of-sample tests, conducted over a long period of time, may provide some assurance that a system will hold up, since they
may show that the market has not changed substantially across several sampling
periods. Given a representative sample, statistics can help make accurate inferences about the population from which the sample was drawn. Statistics cannot,
however, reveal whether tomorrow's market will have changed in some fundamental manner.

OPTIMIZATION AND CURVE-FITTING

Another issue found in trading system development is *optimization*, i.e., improving the performance of a system by adjusting its parameters until the system performs its best on what the developer hopes is a representative sample. When the
system fails to hold up in the future (or on out-of-sample data), the optimization
process is pejoratively called *curve-fitting*. However, there is good curve-fitting
and bad curve-fitting. *Good curve-fitting* is when a model can be fit to the entire
relevant population (or, at least, to a sufficiently large sample thereof), suggesting
that valid characteristics of the entire population have been captured in the model.
Bad curve-fitting occurs when the system only fits chance characteristics, those
that are not necessarily representative of the population from which the sample
was drawn.

Developers are correct to fear bad curve-fitting, i.e., the situation in which
parameter values are adapted to the particular sample on which the system was
optimized, not to the population as a whole. If the sample was small or was not
representative of the population from which it was drawn, it is likely that the system will look good on that one sample but fail miserably on another, or worse, lose
money in real-time trading. However, as the sample gets larger, the chance of this
happening becomes smaller: Bad curve-fitting declines and good curve-fitting
increases. All the statistics discussed reflect this, even the ones that specifically
concern optimization. It is true that the more combinations of things optimized,
the greater the likelihood good performance may be obtained by chance alone.

However, if the statistical result was sufficiently good, or the sample on which it was based large enough to reduce the probability that the outcome was due to chance, the result might still be very real and significant, even if many parameters were optimized.

Some have argued that size does not matter, i.e., that sample size and the number of trades studied have little or nothing to do with the risk of overoptimization, and that a large sample does not mitigate curve-fitting. This is patently untrue, both intuitively and mathematically. Anyone would have less confidence in a system that took only three or four trades over a 10-year period than in one that took over 1,000 reasonably profitable trades. Think of a linear regression model in which a straight line is being fit to a number of points. If there are only two points, it is easy to fit the line perfectly every time, regardless of where the points are located. If there are three points, it is harder. If there is a scatterplot of points, it is going to be harder still, unless those points reveal some real characteristic of the population that involves a linear relationship.

The linear regression example demonstrates that bad curve-fitting does become more difficult as the sample size gets larger. Consider two trading systems: One system had a profit per trade of $100, it took 2 trades, and the standard deviation was $100 per trade; the other system took 1,000 trades, with similar means and standard deviations. When evaluated statistically, the system with 1,000 trades will be a lot more "statistically significant" than the one with the 2 trades.

In multiple linear regression models, as the number of regression parameters (*beta weights*) being estimated is increased relative to the sample size, the amount of curve-fitting increases and statistical significance lessens for the same degree of model fit. In other words, the greater the degree of curve-fitting, the harder it is to get statistical significance. The exception is if the improvement in fit when adding regressors is sufficient to compensate for the loss in significance due to the additional parameters being estimated. In fact, an estimate of *shrinkage* (the degree to which the multiple correlation can be expected to shrink when computed using out-of-sample data) can even be calculated given sample size and number of regressors: Shrinkage increases with regressors and decreases with sample size. In short, there is mathematical evidence that curve-fitting to chance characteristics of a sample, with concomitant poor generalization, is more likely if the sample is small relative to the number of parameters being fit by the model. In fact, as n (the sample size) goes to infinity, the probability that the curve-fitting (achieved by optimizing a set of parameters) is nonrepresentative of the population goes to zero. The larger the number of parameters being optimized, the larger the sample required. In the language of statistics, the parameters being estimated use up the available "degrees of freedom."

All this leads to the conclusion that the larger the sample, the more likely its "curves" are representative of characteristics of the market as a whole. A small sample almost certainly will be nonrepresentative of the market: It is unlikely that its curves will reflect those of the entire market that persist over time. Any model built using a small sample will be capitalizing purely on the chance of sampling. Whether curve-fitting is "good" or "bad" depends on if it was done to chance or to real market patterns, which, in turn, largely depends on the size and representativeness of the sample. Statistics are useful because they make it possible to take curve-fitting into account when evaluating a system.

When dealing with neural networks, concerns about overtraining or *generalization* are tantamount to concerns about bad curve-fitting. If the sample is large enough and representative, curve-fitting some real characteristic of the market is more likely, which may be good because the model should fit the market. On the other hand, if the sample is small, the model will almost certainly be fit to peculiar characteristics of the sample and not to the behavior of the market generally. In neural networks, the concern about whether the neural network will generalize is the same as the concern about whether other kinds of systems will hold up in the future. To a great extent, generalization depends on the size of the sample on which the neural network is trained. The larger the sample, or the smaller the number of connection weights (parameters) being estimated, the more likely the network will generalize. Again, this can be demonstrated mathematically by examining simple cases.

As was the case with regression, an estimate of shrinkage (the opposite of generalization) may be computed when developing neural networks. In a very real sense, a neural network is actually a multiple regression, albeit, nonlinear, and the correlation of a neural net's output with the target may be construed as a multiple correlation coefficient. The multiple correlation obtained between a net's output and the target may be corrected for shrinkage to obtain some idea of how the net might perform on out-of-sample data. Such shrinkage-corrected multiple correlations should routinely be computed as a means of determining whether a network has merely curve-fit the data or has discovered something useful. The formula for correcting a multiple correlation for shrinkage is as follows:

```
RC = SQRT(1.0 - ( (N - 1.0) / (N - P) ) * (1.0 - R*R) )
```

A FORTRAN-style expression was used for reasons of typesetting. In this formula, *SQRT* represents the square root operator; *N* is the number of data points or, in the case of neural networks, facts; *P* is the number of regression coefficients or, in the case of neural networks, connection weights; *R* represents the uncorrected multiple correlation; and *RC* is the multiple correlation corrected for shrinkage. Although this formula is strictly applicable only to linear multiple regression (for which it was originally developed), it works well with neural networks and may be used to estimate how much performance was inflated on the in-sample data due to curve-fitting. The formula expresses a relationship between sample size, number of parameters, and deterioration of results. The statistical correction embodied in the shrinkage formula is used in the chapter on neural network entry models.

SAMPLE SIZE AND REPRESENTATIVENESS

Although, for statistical reasons, the system developer should seek the largest sample possible, there is a trade-off between sample size and representativeness when dealing with the financial markets. Larger samples mean samples that go farther back in time, which is a problem because the market of years ago may be fundamentally different from the market of today—remember the S&P 500 in 1983? This means that a larger sample may sometimes be a less representative sample, or one that confounds several distinct populations of data! Therefore, keep in mind that, although the goal is to have the largest sample possible, it is equally important to try to make sure the period from which the sample is drawn is still representative of the market being predicted.

EVALUATING A SYSTEM STATISTICALLY

Now that some of the basics are out of the way, let us look at how statistics are used when developing and evaluating a trading system. The examples below employ a system that was optimized on one sample of data (the in-sample data) and then run (tested) on another sample of data (the out-of-sample data). The out-of-sample evaluation of this system will be discussed before the in-sample one because the statistical analysis was simpler for the former (which is equivalent to the evaluation of an unoptimized trading system) in that no corrections for multiple tests or optimization were required. The system is a lunar model that trades the S&P 500; it was published in an article we wrote (see Katz with McCormick, June 1997). The TradeStation code for this system is shown below:

```
DefineDLLFunc:"SCSIWA.DLL",LONG,"SA_MoonPhaseDate",LONG,LONG;
Inputs: L1(0);
Vars: FullMoonDate(0), NewMoonDate(0), Trend(0);

{ Function returns date of the next full or new moon }
FullMoonDate = SA_MoonPhaseDate (Date[5], 2);
NewMoonDate = SA_MoonPhaseDate (Date[5], 0);

Value1 = 0;
If (Date < FullMoonDate) And (Date Tomorrow >= FullMoonDate)
      Then Value1 = 1; { Moon full tonight or tomorrow }
Value2 = 0;
If (Date < NewMoonDate) And (Date Tomorrow >= NewMoonDate)
      Then Value2 = 1; { Moon new tonight or tomorrow }

If Value1[L1] > 0 Then Buy At Market;
If Value2[L1] > 0 Then Sell At Market;
```

Example 1: Evaluating the Out-of-Sample Test

Evaluating an optimized system on a set of out-of-sample data that was never used during the optimization process is identical to evaluating an unoptimized system. In both cases, one test is run without adjusting any parameters. Table 4-1 illustrates the use of statistics to evaluate an unoptimized system: It contains the out-of-sample or verification results together with a variety of statistics. Remember, in this test, a fresh set of data was used; this data was not used as the basis for adjustments in the system's parameters.

The parameters of the trading model have already been set. A sample of data was drawn from a period in the past, in this specific case, 1/1/95 through 1/1/97; this is the out-of-sample or verification data. The model was then run on this out-of-sample data, and it generated simulated trades. Forty-seven trades were taken. This set of trades can itself be considered a sample of trades, one drawn from the population of all trades that the system took in the past or will take in the future; i.e., it is a sample of trades taken from the universe or population of all trades for that system. At this point, some inference must be made regarding the average profit per trade in the population as a whole, based on the sample of trades. Could the performance obtained in the sample be due to chance alone? To find the answer, the system must be statistically evaluated.

To begin statistically evaluating this system, the sample mean (average) for *n* (the number of trades or *sample size*) must first be calculated. The *mean* is simply the sum of the profit/loss figures for the trades generated divided by *n* (in this case, 47). The sample mean was $974.47 per trade. The *standard deviation* (the variability in the trade profit/loss figures) is then computed by subtracting the sample mean from each of the profit/loss numbers for all 47 trades in the sample; this results in 47 (*n*) deviations. Each of the deviations is then squared, and then all squared deviations are added together. The sum of the squared deviations is divided by *n* − *1* (in this case, 46). By taking the square root of the resultant number (the *mean squared deviation*), the *sample standard deviation* is obtained. Using the sample standard deviation, the expected *standard deviation of the mean* is computed: The sample standard deviation (in this case, $6,091.10) is divided by the square root of the sample size. For this example, the expected standard deviation of the mean was $888.48.

To determine the likelihood that the observed profitability is due to chance alone, a simple *t-test* is calculated. Since the sample profitability is being compared with no profitability, zero is subtracted from the sample mean trade profit/loss (computed earlier). The resultant number is then divided by the sample standard deviation to obtain the value of the t-statistic, which in this case worked out to be 1.0968. Finally the probability of getting such a large t-statistic by chance alone (under the assumption that the system was not profitable in the population from which the sample was drawn) is calculated: The *cumulative t-distribution* for that t-statistic is computed with the appropriate degrees of freedom, which in this case was *n* − *1*, or 46.

TABLE 4-1

Trades from the S&P 500 Data Sample on Which the Lunar Model Was Verified

Entry Date	Exit Date	Profit/Loss	Cumulative	Statistical Analyses of Mean Profit/Loss	
950207	950221	650	88825		
950221	950223	-2500	86325	Sample Size	47.0000
950309	950323	6025	92350	Sample Mean	974.4681
950323	950324	-2500	89850	Sample Standard Deviation	6091.1029
950407	950419	-2500	87350	Expected SD of Mean	888.4787
950421	950424	-2500	84850		
950509	950518	-2500	82350	T Statistic (P/L > 0)	1.0968
950523	950524	-2500	79850	Probability (Significance)	0.1392
950606	950609	-2500	77350		
950620	950622	-2500	74850	Serial Correlation (lag=1)	0.2120
950704	950719	4400	79250	Associated T Statistic	1.4391
950719	950725	-2500	76750	Probability (Significance)	0.1572
950803	950818	2575	79325		
950818	950901	25	79350	Number Of Wins	16.0000
950901	950918	10475	89825	Percentage of Wins	0.3404
950918	950929	-2500	87325	Upper 99% Bound	0.5319
951002	951003	-2500	84825	Lower 99% Bound	0.1702
951017	951018	-2550	82275		
951031	951114	3150	85425		
951114	951116	-2500	82925		
951129	951214	6750	89675		
951214	951228	5250	94925		
951228	960109	-2500	92425		
960112	960117	-2500	89925		
960129	960213	18700	108625		
960213	960213	-2500	106125		
960227	960227	-2500	103625		

Additional rows follow but are not shown in the table.

(Microsoft's Excel spreadsheet provides a function to obtain probabilities based on the t-distribution. *Numerical Recipes in C* provides the incomplete beta function, which is very easily used to calculate probabilities based on a variety of distributions, including Student's t.) The cumulative t-distribution calculation yields a figure that represents the probability that the results obtained from the trading system were due to chance. Since this figure was small, it is unlikely that the results were due to capitalization on random features of the sample. The smaller the number, the more likely the system performed the way it did for reasons other than chance. In this instance, the probability was 0.1392; i.e., if a system with a true (population) profit

FIGURE 4-1

Frequency and Cumulative Distribution for In-Sample Trades

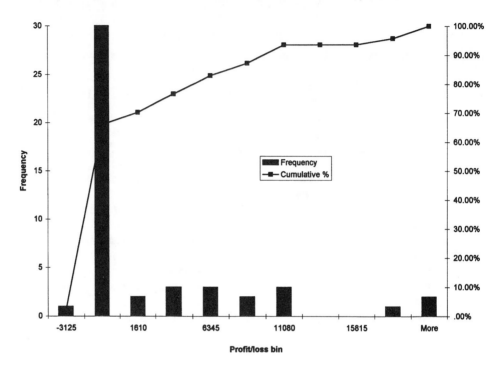

of $0 was repeatedly tested on independent samples, only about 14% of the time would it show a profit as high as that actually observed.

Although the t-test was, in this example, calculated for a sample of trade profit/loss figures, it could just as easily have been computed for a sample of daily returns. Daily returns were employed in this way to calculate the probabilities referred to in discussions of the substantitive tests that appear in later chapters. In fact, the annualized risk-to-reward ratio (*ARRR*) that appears in many of the tables and discussions is nothing more than a rescaled t-statistic based on daily returns.

Finally, a *confidence interval* on the probability of winning is estimated. In the example, there were 16 wins in a sample of 47 trades, which yielded a percentage of wins equal to 0.3404. Using a particular inverse of the cumulative binomial distribution, upper 99% and lower 99% boundaries are calculated. There is a 99% probability that the percentage of wins in the population as a whole is between 0.1702 and 0.5319. In Excel, the CRITBINOM function may be used in the calculation of confidence intervals on percentages.

The various statistics and probabilities computed above should provide the system developer with important information regarding the behavior of the trading model—that is, if the assumptions of normality and independence are met and if the sample is representative. Most likely, however, the assumptions underlying the t-tests and other statistics are violated; market data deviates seriously from the normal distribution, and trades are usually not independent. In addition, the sample might not be representative. Does this mean that the statistical evaluation just discussed is worthless? Let's consider the cases.

What if the Distribution Is Not Normal?   An assumption in the t-test is that the underlying distribution of the data is normal. However, the distribution of profit/loss figures of a trading system is anything but normal, especially if there are stops and profit targets, as can be seen in Figure 4-1, which shows the distribution of profits and losses for trades taken by the lunar system. Think of it for a moment. Rarely will a profit greater than the profit target occur. In fact, a lot of trades are going to bunch up with a profit equal to that of the profit target. Other trades are going to bunch up where the stop loss is set, with losses equal to that; and there will be trades that will fall somewhere in between, depending on the exit method. The shape of the distribution will not be that of the bell curve that describes the normal distribution. This is a violation of one of the assumptions underlying the t-test. In this case, however, the *Central Limit Theorem* comes to the rescue. It states that as the number of cases in the sample increases, the distribution of the sample mean approaches normal. By the time there is a sample size of 10, the errors resulting from the violation of the normality assumption will be small, and with sample sizes greater than 20 or 30, they will have little practical significance for inferences regarding the mean. Consequently, many statistics can be applied with reasonable assurance that the results will be meaningful, as long as the sample size is adequate, as was the case in the example above, which had an *n* of 47.

What if There Is Serial Dependence?   A more serious violation, which makes the above-described application of the t-test not quite cricket, is *serial dependence*, which is when cases constituting a sample (e.g., trades) are not statistically independent of one another. Trades come from a time series. When a series of trades that occurred over a given span of dates is used as a sample, it is not quite a *random sample*. A truly random sample would mean that the 100 trades were randomly taken from the period when the contract for the market started (e.g., 1983 for the S&P 500) to far into the future; such a sample would not only be less likely to suffer from serial dependence, but be more representative of the population from which it was drawn. However, when developing trading systems, sampling is usually done from one narrow point in time; consequently, each trade may be correlated with those adjacent to it and so would not be independent.

The practical effect of this statistically is to reduce the *effective* sample size. When trying to make inferences, if there is substantial serial dependence, it may be as if the sample contained only half or even one-fourth of the actual number of trades or data points observed. To top it off, the extent of serial dependence cannot definitively be determined. A rough "guestimate," however, can be made. One such guestimate may be obtained by computing a simple lag/lead *serial correlation*: A correlation is computed between the profit and loss for Trade i and the profit and loss for Trade $i + 1$, with i ranging from 1 to $n - 1$. In the example, the serial correlation was 0.2120, not very high, but a lower number would be preferable. An associated t-statistic may then be calculated along with a statistical significance for the correlation. In the current case, these statistics reveal that if there really were no serial correlation in the population, a correlation as large as the one obtained from the sample would only occur in about 16% of such tests.

Serial dependence is a serious problem. If there is a substantial amount of it, it would need to be compensated for by treating the sample as if it were smaller than it actually is. Another way to deal with the effect of serial dependence is to draw a random sample of trades from a larger sample of trades computed over a longer period of time. This would also tend to make the sample of trades more representative of the population.

What if the Markets Change?   When developing trading systems, a third assumption of the t-test may be inadvertently violated. There are no precautions that can be taken to prevent it from happening or to compensate for its occurrence. The reason is that the population from which the development or verification sample was drawn may be different from the population from which future trades may be taken. This would happen if the market underwent some real structural or other change. As mentioned before, the population of trades of a system operating on the S&P 500 before 1983 would be different from the population after that year since, in 1983, the options and futures started trading on the S&P 500 and the market changed. This sort of thing can devastate any method of evaluating a trading system. No matter how much a system is back-tested, if the market changes before trading begins, the trades will not be taken from the same market for which the system was developed and tested; the system will fall apart. All systems, even currently profitable ones, will eventually succumb to market change. Regardless of the market, change is inevitable. It is just a question of when it will happen. Despite this grim fact, the use of statistics to evaluate systems remains essential, because if the market does not change substantially shortly after trading of the system commences, or if the change is not sufficient to grossly affect the system's performance, then a reasonable estimate of expected probabilities and returns can be calculated.

Example 2: Evaluating the In-Sample Tests

How can a system that has been fit to a data sample by the repeated adjustment of parameters (i.e., an optimized system) be evaluated? Traders frequently optimize systems to obtain good results. In this instance, the use of statistics is more important than ever since the results can be analyzed, compensating for the multiplicity of tests being performed as part of the process of optimization. Table 4-2 contains the profit/loss figures and a variety of statistics for the in-sample trades (those taken on the data sample used to optimize the system). The system was optimized on data from 1/1/90 through 1/2/95.

Most of the statistics in Table 4-2 are identical to those in Table 4-1, which was associated with Example 1. Two additional statistics (that differ from those in the first example) are labeled "Optimization Tests Run" and "Adjusted for Optimization." The first statistic is simply the number of different parameter combinations tried, i.e., the total number of times the system was run on the data, each time using a different set of parameters. Since the lunar system parameter, $L1$, was stepped from 1 to 20 in increments of 1, 20 tests were performed; consequently, there were 20 t-statistics, one for each test. The number of tests run is used to make an adjustment to the probability or significance obtained from the best t-statistic

TABLE 4-2

Trades from the S&P 500 Data Sample on Which the Lunar Model Was Optimized

Entry Date	Exit Date	Profit/Loss	Cumulative	Statistical Analyses of Mean Profit/Loss	
900417	900501	5750	5750		
900501	900516	11700	17450	Sample Size	118.0000
900516	900522	-2500	14950	Sample Mean	740.9664
900531	900615	150	15100	Sample Standard Deviation	3811.3550
900615	900702	2300	17400	Expected SD of Mean	350.8637
900702	900716	4550	21950		
900716	900731	6675	28625	t-Statistic (P/L > 0)	2.1118
900731	900802	-2500	26125	Probability (Significance)	0.0184
900814	900828	9500	35625	Optimization Tests Run	20.0000
900828	900911	575	36200	Adjusted for Optimization	0.3104
900911	900926	7225	43425		
900926	900926	-2500	40925	Serial Correlation (lag=1)	0.0479
901010	901019	-2875	38050	Associated t-Statistic	0.5139
901026	901029	-2500	35550	Probability (Significance)	0.6083
901109	901112	-2700	32850		
901126	901211	8125	40975	Number of Wins	58.0000
901211	901225	-875	40100	Percentage of Wins	0.4915
901225	910102	-2500	37600	Upper 99% Bound	0.6102
910108	910109	-2500	35100	Lower 99% Bound	0.3729
910122	910206	9850	44950	(Bounds not corrected for optimization)	
910206	910206	-2500	42450		
910221	910308	4550	47000		
910308	910322	5250	52250		
910322	910409	5600	57850		
910409	910416	-2500	55350		
910423	910425	-2500	52850		
910507	910521	3800	56650		

Additional rows follow but are not shown in the table.

computed on the sample: Take 1, and subtract from it the statistical significance obtained for the best-performing test. Take the resultant number and raise it to the mth power (where m = the number of tests run). Then subtract that number from 1. This provides the probability of finding, in a sample of m tests (in this case, 20), at least one t-statistic as good as the one actually obtained for the optimized solution. The uncorrected probability that the profits observed for the best solution were due to chance was less than 2%, a fairly significant result. Once adjusted for multiple tests, i.e., optimization, the statistical significance does not appear anywhere near as good. Results at the level of those observed could have been obtained for such an optimized system 31% of the time by chance alone. However, things are not quite as bad as they seem. The adjustment was extremely conservative and assumed that every test was completely independent of every other test. In actual fact, there will be a high serial correlation between most tests since, in many trading systems, small changes in the parameters produce relatively small changes in the results. This is exactly like serial dependence in data samples: It reduces the effective population size, in this case, the effective number of tests run. Because many of the tests are correlated, the 20 actual tests probably correspond to about 5 to 10 independent tests. If the serial dependence among tests is considered, the adjusted-for-optimization probability would most likely be around 0.15, instead of the 0.3104 actually calculated. The nature and extent of serial dependence in the multiple tests are never known, and therefore, a less conservative adjustment for optimization cannot be directly calculated, only roughly reckoned.

Under certain circumstances, such as in multiple regression models, there are exact mathematical formulas for calculating statistics that incorporate the fact that parameters are being fit, i.e., that optimization is occurring, making corrections for optimization unnecessary.

Interpreting the Example Statistics

In Example 1, the verification test was presented. The in-sample optimization run was presented in Example 2. In the discussion of results, we are returning to the natural order in which the tests were run, i.e., optimization first, verification second.

Optimization Results.   Table 4-2 shows the results for the in-sample period. Over the 5 years of data on which the system was optimized, there were 118 trades (n = 118), the mean or average trade yielded about $740.97, and the trades were highly variable, with a sample standard deviation of around ±$3,811; i.e., there were many trades that lost several thousand dollars, as well as trades that made many thousands. The degree of profitability can easily be seen by looking at the profit/loss column, which contains many $2,500 losses (the stop got hit) and a significant number of wins, many greater than $5,000, some even greater than $10,000. The expected standard deviation of the mean suggests that if samples of this kind were repeatedly taken, the mean would vary only about one-tenth as much as the individual trades, and that many of the samples would have mean profitabilities in the range of $740 ± $350.

The t-statistic for the best-performing system from the set of optimization runs was 2.1118, which has a statistical significance of 0.0184. This was a fairly strong result. If only one test had been run (no optimizing), this good a result would have been obtained (by chance alone) only twice in 100 tests, indicating that the system is probably capturing some real market inefficiency and has some chance of holding up. However, be warned: This analysis was for the best of 20 sets of parameter values tested. If corrected for the fact that 20 combinations of parameter values were tested, the adjusted statistical significance would only be about 0.31, not very good; the performance of the system could easily have been due to chance. Therefore, although the system may hold up, it could also, rather easily, fail.

The serial correlation between trades was only 0.0479, a value small enough in the present context, with a significance of only 0.6083. These results strongly suggest that there was no meaningful serial correlation between trades and that the statistical analyses discussed above are likely to be correct.

There were 58 winning trades in the sample, which represents about a 49% win rate. The upper 99% confidence boundary was approximately 61% and the lower 99% confidence boundary was approximately 37%, suggesting that the true percentage of wins in the population has a 99% likelihood of being found between those two values. In truth, the confidence region should have been broadened by correcting for optimization; this was not done because we were not very concerned about the percentage of wins.

Verification Results.   Table 4-1, presented earlier, contains the data and statistics for the out-of-sample test for the model. Since all parameters were already fixed, and only one test was conducted, there was no need to consider optimization or its consequences in any manner. In the period from 1/1/95 to 1/1/97, there were 47 trades. The average trade in this sample yielded about $974, which is a greater average profit per trade than in the optimization sample! The system apparently did maintain profitable behavior.

At slightly over $6,000, the sample standard deviation was almost double that of the standard deviation in the optimization sample. Consequently, the standard deviation of the sample mean was around $890, a fairly large standard error of estimate; together with the small sample size, this yielded a lower t-statistic than found in the optimization sample and, therefore, a lowered statistical significance of only about 14%. These results were neither very good nor very bad: There is better than an 80% chance that the system is capitalizing on some real (non-chance) market inefficiency. The serial correlation in the test sample, however, was quite a bit higher than in the optimization sample and was significant, with a probability of 0.1572; i.e., as large a serial correlation as this would only be expected about 16% of the time by chance alone, if no true (population) serial correlation was present. Consequently, the t-test on the profit/loss figures has likely overstated the statistical significance to some degree (maybe between 20 and 30%). If the sample size was adjusted downward the right amount, the t-test probability would most likely be around 0.18, instead of the 0.1392 that was calculated. The confidence interval for the percentage of wins in the population ranged from about 17% to about 53%.

Overall, the assessment is that the system is probably going to hold up in the future, but not with a high degree of certainty. Considering there were two independent tests—one showing about a 31% probability (corrected for optimization) that the profits were due to chance, the other showing a statistical significance of approximately 14% (corrected to 18% due to the serial correlation), there is a good chance that the average population trade is profitable and, consequently, that the system will remain profitable in the future.

OTHER STATISTICAL TECHNIQUES AND THEIR USE

The following section is intended only to acquaint the reader with some other statistical techniques that are available. We strongly suggest that a more thorough study be undertaken by those serious about developing and evaluating trading systems.

Genetically Evolved Systems

We develop many systems using genetic algorithms. A popular *fitness function* (criterion used to determine whether a model is producing the desired outcome) is the total net profit of the system. However, net profit is not the best measure of system quality! A system that only trades the major crashes on the S&P 500 will yield a very high total net profit with a very high percentage of winning trades. But who knows if such a system would hold up? Intuitively, if the system only took two or three trades in 10 years, the probability seems very low that it would continue to perform well in the future or even take any more trades. Part of the problem is that net profit does not consider the number of trades taken or their variability.

An alternative fitness function that avoids some of the problems associated with net profit is the t-statistic or its associated probability. When using the t-statistic as a fitness function, instead of merely trying to evolve the most profitable systems, the intention is to genetically evolve systems that have the greatest likelihood of being profitable in the future or, equivalently, that have the least likelihood of being profitable merely due to chance or curve-fitting. This approach works fairly well. The t-statistic factors in profitability, sample size, and number of trades taken. All things being equal, the greater the number of trades a system takes, the greater the t-statistic and the more likely it will hold up in the future. Likewise, systems that produce more consistently profitable trades with less variation are more desirable than systems that produce wildly varying trades and will yield higher t-statistic values. The t-statistic incorporates many of the features that define the quality of a trading model into one number that can be maximized by a genetic algorithm.

Multiple Regression

Another statistical technique frequently used is multiple regression. Consider intermarket analysis: The purpose of intermarket analysis is to find measures of behaviors in other markets that are predictive of the future behavior of the market being studied. Running various regressions is an appropriate technique for analyzing such potential relationships; moreover, there are excellent statistics to use for testing and setting confidence intervals on the correlations and regression (beta) weights generated by the analyses. Due to lack of space and the limited scope of this chapter, no examples are presented, but the reader is referred to Myers (1986), a good basic text on multiple regression.

A problem with most textbooks on multiple regression analysis (including the one just mentioned) is that they do not deal with the issue of serial correlation in time series data, and its effect on the statistical inferences that can be made from regression analyses using such data. The reader will need to take the effects of serial correlation into account: Serial correlation in a data sample has the effect of reducing the effective sample size, and statistics can be adjusted (at least in a rough-and-ready manner) based on this effect. Another trick that can be used in some cases is to perform some transformations on the original data series to make the time series more "stationary" and to remove the unwanted serial correlations.

Monte Carlo Simulations

One powerful, unique approach to making statistical inferences is known as the *Monte Carlo Simulation*, which involves repeated tests on synthetic data that are constructed to have the properties of samples taken from a random population. Except for randomness, the synthetic data are constructed to have the basic characteristics of the population from which the real sample was drawn and about which inferences must be made. This is a very powerful method. The beauty of Monte Carlo Simulations is that they can be performed in a way that avoids the dangers of assumptions (such as that of the normal distribution) being violated, which would lead to untrustworthy results.

Out-of-Sample Testing

Another way to evaluate a system is to perform *out-of-sample testing*. Several time periods are reserved to test a model that has been developed or optimized on some other time period. Out-of-sample testing helps determine how the model behaves on data it had not seen during optimization or development. This approach is strongly recommended. In fact, in the examples discussed above, both in-sample and out-of-sample tests were analyzed. No corrections to the statistics for the process of optimization are necessary in out-of-sample testing. Out-of-sample and multiple-sample tests may also provide some information on whether the market has changed its behavior over various periods of time.

Walk-Forward Testing

In *walk-forward testing*, a system is optimized on several years of data and then traded the next year. The system is then reoptimized on several more years of data, moving the window forward to include the year just traded. The system is then traded for another year. This process is repeated again and again, "walking forward" through the data series. Although very computationally intensive, this is an excellent way to study and test a trading system. In a sense, even though optimization is occurring, all trades are taken on what is essentially out-of-sample test data. All the statistics discussed above, such as the t-tests, can be used on walk-forward test results in a simple manner that does not require any corrections for optimization. In addition, the tests will very closely simulate the process that occurs during real trading—first optimization occurs, next the system is traded on data not used during the optimization, and then every so often the system is reoptimized to update it. Sophisticated developers can build the optimization process into the system, producing what might be called an "adaptive" trading model. Meyers (1997) wrote an article illustrating the process of walk-forward testing.

CONCLUSION

In the course of developing trading systems, statistics help the trader quickly reject models exhibiting behavior that could have been due to chance or to excessive curve-fitting on an inadequately sized sample. Probabilities can be estimated, and if it is found that there is only a very small probability that a model's performance could be due to chance alone, then the trader can feel more confident when actually trading the model.

There are many ways for the trader to use and calculate statistics. The central theme is the attempt to make inferences about a population on the basis of samples drawn from that population.

Keep in mind that when using statistics on the kinds of data faced by traders, certain assumptions will be violated. For practical purposes, some of the violations may not be too critical; thanks to the Central Limit Theorem, data that are not normally distributed can usually be analyzed adequately for most needs. Other violations that are more serious (e.g., ones involving serial dependence) do need to be taken into account, but rough-and-ready rules may be used to reckon corrections to the probabilities. The bottom line: It is better to operate with some information, even knowing that some assumptions may be violated, than to operate blindly.

We have glossed over many of the details, definitions, and reasons behind the statistics discussed above. Again, the intention was merely to acquaint the reader with some of the more frequently used applications. We suggest that any committed trader obtain and study some good basic texts on statistical techniques.

PART II

The Study of Entries
Introduction

In this section, various entry methods are systematically evaluated. The focus is on which techniques provide good entries and which do not. A good entry is important because it can reduce exposure to risk and increase the likelihood that a trade will be profitable. Although it is sometimes possible to make a profit with a bad entry (given a sufficiently good exit), a good entry gets the trade started on the right foot.

WHAT CONSTITUTES A GOOD ENTRY?

A *good entry* is one that initiates a trade at a point of low potential risk and high potential reward. A point of low risk is usually a point from which there is little adverse excursion before the market begins to move in the trade's favor. Entries that yield small adverse excursions on successful trades are desirable because they permit fairly tight stops to be set, thereby minimizing risk. A good entry should also have a high probability of being followed quickly by favorable movement in the market. Trades that languish before finally taking off tie up money that might be better used elsewhere; not only do such trades increase market exposure, but they waste margin and lead to "margin-inefficient" trading or portfolios. Perfect entries would involve buying the exact lows of bottoming points and selling the exact highs of topping points. Such entries hardly ever occur in the real world and are not necessary for successful trading. For trading success it is merely necessary that entries, when coupled with reasonable exits, produce trading systems that have good overall performance characteristics.

ORDERS USED IN ENTRIES

Entries may be executed using any of several kinds of orders, including stop orders, limit orders, and market orders.

Stop Orders

A *stop order* enters a market that is already moving in the direction of the trade. A buy or sell is triggered when the market rises above a buy stop or falls below a sell stop; this characteristic often results in stop orders being used with trend-following entry models. A nice feature of a stop order is that the market must be moving in a favorable direction at the time of entry. Because of this, the order itself can act as a confirming "filter" of the signals generated by the entry model. If a particular entry happens to be a good one, momentum will cause the trade to quickly turn profitable with hardly any adverse excursion.

On the negative side, an entry executed on a stop order may experience considerable slippage, especially in fast moves, and the market will be bought high or sold low. Consider the case in which prices begin to move rapidly in favor of a trade: Buying or selling into such movement is like jumping onto an accelerating train and is likely to result in large amounts of slippage; the faster the move, the greater the slippage. *Slippage* is the difference between the price at which the stop is set and the price at which it is actually filled. Because slippage eats into the profit generated by the trade, it is undesirable. The most unpleasant situation is when the entry order gets filled far past the stop, just as the market begins to reverse! Because buying or selling takes place on a stop, the market entry occurs significantly into any move and at a relatively poor price.

Limit Orders

In contrast to a stop order, a *limit order* results in entry when the market moves against the direction of the trade. A limit order is an order to buy or to sell at a specified price or better. For a buy limit to be filled, the market must move below the limit price; for a sell order, the market must move above the limit price. At least in the short term, buying or selling takes place against the trend. The countertrend nature of a limit order and the fact that the market may never move to where the order can be filled are the primary disadvantages. However, when working with predictive, countertrend entry models, the countertrend nature of the limit order may not be a disadvantage at all. The advantage of a limit order is that there is no slippage and that entry takes place at a good, known price.

Market Orders

A *market order* is a simple order to buy or sell at the prevailing market price. One positive feature of a market order is that it will be executed quickly after being placed; indeed, many exchanges require market orders to be filled within a few minutes at most. Stop or limit orders, on the other hand, may sit for some time before market activity triggers a fill. Another benefit is guaranteed execution: After placing a market order, entry into the trade will definitely take place. The drawback to the market order is that slippage may occur. However, in contrast to the stop order, the slippage can go either way—sometimes in the trade's favor, sometimes against it—depending on market movement and execution delay.

Selecting Appropriate Orders

Determining which kind of order to use for an entry must include not only consideration of the advantages and disadvantages of the various kinds of orders, but also the nature of the model that generates the entry signals and its theory regarding market behavior.

If the entry model predicts turning points slightly into the future, a limit order may be the most appropriate, especially if the entry model provides some indication of the price at which the turning point will occur. If the entry model contains specification of price, as do systems based on critical retracement levels, entry on a limit (with a tight money management exit stop) is definitely the way to go: A bounce from the retracement level can be expected, and the limit order will enter at or near the retracement level, resulting in a trade that either quickly turns profitable (if the market has responded to the critical level as expected) or is stopped out with a very small loss.

If the entry model requires some kind of confirmation before entry that the market is moving in the appropriate direction, a stop order might be the best choice. For example, a breakout system can be naturally married to a stop-based entry. If the market moves in a favorable direction and passes the breakout threshold price (the same price at which the entry stop is set), entry will occur automatically, and it will be possible to capture any ensuing move. If the breakout price is not penetrated, the stop will not be triggered and no entry will take place. In this example, the entry order actually becomes part of the entry model or system.

Market orders are most useful when the entry model only provides timing information and when the cost (in terms of slippage and delay) of confirming the entry with a stop order is too great relative to the expected per-trade profit. A market order is also appropriate when the timing provided by the system is critical. For some models, it would make sense to place a stop or a limit order and then, if the order is not filled within a specified period of time, to cancel the order and replace it with a market order.

When developing an entry model, it is often worthwhile to examine various entry orders to determine which are most manageable and which perform best. The original entry model will probably need modification to make such tests possible, but the outcome may prove worth the trouble. Examples of various entry systems tested using these three types of orders (entry at open, on limit, and on stop) appear throughout the study of entries.

ENTRY TECHNIQUES COVERED IN THIS BOOK

This part of the book explores entry techniques that range from trend-following to countertrend, from endogenous to exogenous, from traditional to exotic, and from simple to complex. Since there are an infinite number of entry models, spatial limitations forced us to narrow our focus and discuss only a subset of the possibilities. We attempted to cover popular methods that are frequently discussed, some of which have been around for decades, but for which there is little objective, supportive evidence. We will systematically put these models to the test to see how well they work. We have also tried to expand upon some of our earlier, published studies of entry models in which readers (primarily of *Technical Analysis of Stocks and Commodities*) have expressed great interest.

Breakouts and Moving Averages

Traditional trend-following entry models that employ breakouts and moving averages are examined in Chapters 5 and 6, respectively. *Breakout entries* are simple and intuitively appealing: The market is bought when prices break above an upper band or threshold. It is sold short when prices break below a lower band or threshold. Operating this way, breakout entries are certain to get the trader on-board any large market movement or trend. The trend-following entries that underlie many popular trading systems are breakout entries. Breakout models differ from one another mainly in how the threshold bands are computed and the actual entry is achieved.

Like breakouts, *moving averages* are alluring in their simplicity and are extremely popular among technical traders. Entries may be generated using moving averages in any of several ways: The market may be entered when prices cross over a moving average, when a faster moving average crosses a slower one, when the slope of a moving average changes direction, or when prices pull back to a moving-average line as they might to lines of support or resistance. Additional variety is introduced by the fact that there are simple moving averages, exponential moving averages, and triangular moving averages, to mention only a few. Since the entry models of many trading systems employ some variation of breakouts or moving averages, it seems important to explore these techniques in great detail.

Oscillators

Oscillators are indicators that tend to fluctuate quasi-cyclically within a limited range. They are very popular among technical traders and appear in most charting packages. Entry models based on oscillators are "endogenous" in nature (they do not require anything but market data) and are fairly simple to implement, characteristics they share with breakout and moving-average models. However, breakout and moving-average models tend to enter the market late, often too late, because they are designed to respond to, rather than anticipate, market behavior. In contrast, oscillators anticipate prices by identifying turning points so that entry can occur before, rather than after, the market moves. Since they attempt to anticipate prices, oscillators characteristically generate countertrend entries.

Entries are commonly signaled by divergence between an oscillator and price. *Divergence* is seen when prices form a lower low but the oscillator forms a higher low, signaling a buy; or when prices form a higher high but the oscillator forms a lower high, signaling the time to sell short.

A *signal line* is another way to generate entries. It is calculated by taking a moving average of the oscillator. The trader buys when the oscillator crosses above the signal line and sells short when it crosses below. Although typically used in "trading range" markets for countertrend entries, an oscillator is sometimes employed in a trend-following manner: Long or short positions might be entered when the Stochastic oscillator climbs above 80 or drops below 20, respectively. Entry models that employ such classic oscillators as Lane's Stochastic, Williams's RSI, and Appel's MACD are studied in Chapter 7.

Seasonality

Chapter 8 deals with seasonality, which is construed in different ways by different traders. For our purposes, *seasonality* is defined as cyclic or recurrent phenomena that are consistently linked to the calendar, specifically, market behavior affected by the time of the year or tied to particular dates. Because they are predictive (providing trading signals weeks, months, or years ahead), these models are countertrend in nature. Of the many ways to time entries that use seasonal rhythms, two basic approaches will be examined: momentum and crossover. The addition of several rules for handling confirmations and inversions will also be tested to determine whether they would produce results better than the basic models.

Lunar and Solar Phenomena

Do lunar and solar events influence the markets? Is it possible for an entry model to capitalize on the price movements induced by such influences? The moon's role in the instigation of tides is undisputed. Phases of the moon correlate with rainfall and with certain biological rhythms, and they influence when farmers plant crops. Solar phenomena, such as solar flares and sunspots, are also known to impact events on earth. During periods of high solar activity, magnetic storms occur that can disrupt power distribution systems, causing serious blackouts. To assume that solar and lunar phenomena influence the markets is not at all unreasonable; but how might these influences be used to generate predictive, countertrend entries?

Consider the lunar rhythm: It is not hard to define a model that enters the market a specified number of days before or after either the full or new moon. The same applies to solar activity: An entry can be signaled when the sunspot count rises above some threshold or falls below another threshold. Alternatively, moving averages of solar activity can be computed and crossovers of these moving averages used to time market entries. Lunar cycles, sunspots, and other planetary rhythms may have a real, albeit small, impact on the markets, an impact that might be profitable with a properly constructed entry model. Whether lunar and solar phenomena actually affect the markets sufficiently to be taken advantage of by an astute trader is a question for an empirical investigation, such as that reported in Chapter 9.

Cycles and Rhythms

Chapter 10 explores *cycles* and rhythms as a means of timing entries into the market. The idea behind the use of cycles to time the market is fundamentally simple: Extrapolate observed cycles into the future, and endeavor to buy the cycle lows and sell short the cycle highs. If the cycles are sufficiently persistent and accurately extrapolated, excellent countertrend entries should be the result. If not, the entries are likely to be poor.

For a very long time, traders have engaged in visual cycle analysis using charts, drawing tools, and, more recently, charting programs. Although cycles can be analyzed visually, it is not very difficult to implement cycle recognition and analysis algorithms in software. Many kinds of algorithms are useful in cycle analysis—everything from counting the bars between tops or bottoms, to fast Fourier transforms (FFTs) and maximum entropy spectral analyses (MESAs). Getting such algorithms to work well, however, can be quite a challenge; but having reliable software for cycle analysis makes it possible to build objective, cycle-based entry models and to test them on historical data using a trading simulator.

Whether detected visually or by some mathematical algorithm, market cycles come in many forms. Some cycles are *exogenous*, i.e., induced by external phenomena, whether natural or cultural. Seasonal rhythms, anniversary effects, and cycles tied to periodic events (e.g., presidential elections and earnings reports) fall into the exogenous category; these cycles are best analyzed with methods that take the timing of the driving events into account. Other cycles are *endogenous*; i.e., their external driving forces are not apparent, and nothing other than price data is needed to analyze them. The 3-day cycle occasionally observed in the S&P 500 is an example of an endogenous cycle, as is an 8-minute cycle observed by the authors in S&P 500 tick data. Programs based on band-pass filters (Katz and McCormick, May 1997) and maximum entropy (e.g., MESA96 and TradeCycles) are good at finding endogenous cycles.

We have already discussed the exogenous seasonal cycles, as well as lunar and solar rhythms. In Chapter 10, endogenous cycles are explored using a sophisticated wavelet-based, band-pass filter model.

Neural Networks

As discussed in Chapter 11, *neural network* technology is a form of artificial intelligence (or AI) that arose from endeavors to emulate the kind of information processing and decision making that occurs in living organisms. Neural networks (or "nets") are components that learn and that are useful for pattern recognition, classification, and prediction. They can cope with probability estimates in uncertain situations and with "fuzzy" patterns, i.e., those recognizable by eye but difficult to define using precise rules. Nets can be used to directly detect turning points or forecast price changes, in an effort to obtain good, predictive, countertrend entry models. They can also vet entry signals generated by other models. In addition, neural network technology can help integrate information from both endogenous sources, such as past prices, and exogenous sources, such as sentiment data, seasonal data, and intermarket variables, in a way that benefits the trader. Neural networks can even be trained to recognize visually detected patterns in charts, and then serve as pattern-recognition blocks within traditional rule-based systems (Katz and McCormick, November 1997).

Genetically Evolved Entry Rules

Chapter 12 elaborates a study (Katz and McCormick, December 1996) demonstrating that genetic evolution can be used to create stable and profitable rule-based entry models. The process involves putting together a set of model fragments, or "rule templates," and allowing a genetic algorithm (GA) to combine and complete these fragments to achieve profitable entries. The way the methodology can discover surprising combinations of rules that consider both endogenous and exogenous variables, traditional indicators, and even nontraditional elements (e.g., neural networks) in making high-performance entry decisions will be examined. Evolutionary model building is one of the most advanced, cutting-edge, and unusual techniques available to the trading system developer.

STANDARDIZED EXITS

To study entries on their own, and to do so in a way that permits valid comparisons of different strategies, it is essential to implement a *standardized exit* that will be held constant across various tests; this is an aspect of the scientific method that was discussed earlier. The scientific method involves an effort to hold everything, except that which is under study, constant in order to obtain reliable information about the element being manipulated.

The standardized exit, used for testing entry models in the following chapters, incorporates the three functions necessary in any exit model: getting out with a profit when the market moves sufficiently in the trade's favor, getting out with a limited loss when the market moves against the trade, and getting out from a languishing market after a limited time to conserve margin and reduce exposure. The standard exit is realized using a combination of a *stop order*, a *limit order*, and a *market order*.

Stop and limit orders are placed when a trade is entered. If either order is filled within a specified interval, the trade is complete, the remaining order is canceled, and no additional orders are placed. If, after the allotted interval, neither the stop nor limit orders are filled, they are canceled and a market order is placed to force an immediate exit from the trade. The stop order, called a *money management* stop, serves to close out a losing position with a small, manageable loss. Taking a profit is accomplished with the limit order, also called a *profit target*. Positions that go nowhere are closed out by the market order. More elaborate exit strategies are discussed in "Part III: The Study of Exits," where the entries are standardized.

Money management stops and profit target limits for the standardized exits are computed using *volatility units*, rather than fixed dollar amounts, so that they will have reasonably consistent meaning across eras and markets. Because, e.g., a $1,000 stop would be considered tight on today's S&P 500 (yet loose on wheat), fixed-dollar-amount stops cannot be used when different eras and markets are being studied. Volatility units are like standard deviations, providing a uniform scale of measurement. A stop, placed a certain number of volatility units away from the current price, will have a consistent probability of being triggered in a given amount of time, regardless of the market. Use of standardized measures permits meaningful comparisons across markets and times.

EQUALIZATION OF DOLLAR VOLATILITY

Just as exits must be held constant across entry models, risk and reward potential, as determined by *dollar volatility* (different from raw volatility, mentioned above), must be equalized across markets and eras. This is done by adjusting the number of contracts traded. Equalization of risk and reward potential is important because it makes it easier to compare the performance of different entry methods over commodities and time periods. Equalization is essential for portfolio simulations, where each market should contribute in roughly equal measure to the performance of the whole portfolio. The issue of dollar volatility equalization arises because some markets move significantly more in dollars per unit time than others. Most traders are aware that markets vary greatly in size, as reflected in differing margin requirements, as well as in dollar volatility. The S&P 500, for example, is recognized as a "big" contract, wheat as a "small" one; many contracts of wheat would have to be traded to achieve the same bang as a single S&P 500 contract. Table II-1 shows, broken down by year and market, the dollar volatility of a single contract

TABLE II-1

Dollar Volatilities (First Line) and Number of Contracts Equivalent to 10 New S&P 500s on 12/31/1998 (Second Line) Broken Down by Market and Year

NAME	SYMB	1991	1992	1993	1994	1995	1996	1997	1998
S&P_INDEX	SP	1163.50	948.37	823.50	1124.37	1125.25	1989.00	4169.50	2836.50
		24	30	34	25	25	14	7	10
NYSE_INDEX	YX	625.50	509.75	452.50	613.75	558.00	967.87	1985.62	2651.00
		45	56	63	46	51	29	14	11
T_BONDS	US	348.13	342.97	434.22	510.00	439.84	475.63	368.59	469.84
		81	83	65	56	64	60	77	60
T_BILLS_90_DAYS	TB	82.87	82.38	50.25	95.25	72.38	54.63	49.12	75.50
		342	344	564	298	392	519	577	376
TEN_YEAR_NOTES	TY	235.31	302.34	257.50	352.50	274.22	283.59	204.70	276.41
		121	94	110	80	103	100	139	103
BRITISH_POUND	BP	642.88	697.81	534.69	329.56	359.75	268.62	377.69	338.81
		44	41	53	86	79	106	75	84
DEUTSCHEMARK	DM	467.37	501.69	387.00	336.37	476.00	247.88	332.31	282.06
		61	57	73	84	60	114	85	101
SWISS_FRANC	SF	530.38	661.56	491.44	438.50	668.75	387.87	426.94	418.12
		53	43	58	65	42	73	66	68
JAPANESE_YEN	JY	413.50	389.88	616.56	531.00	872.25	408.19	588.50	806.06
		69	73	46	53	33	69	48	35
CANADIAN_DOLLAR	CD	108.00	184.20	200.90	138.75	175.25	93.05	143.50	190.80
		263	154	141	204	162	305	198	149
EURODOLLARS_3M	ED	84.38	97.00	44.13	98.00	69.75	49.87	39.12	56.75
		336	292	643	289	407	569	725	500
CRUDE_LIGHT	CL	213.25	161.80	179.80	214.65	150.10	344.85	232.00	252.60
		133	175	158	132	189	82	122	112
HEATING_OIL_#2	HO	269.05	244.21	200.80	239.78	180.62	374.91	258.57	237.97
		105	116	141	118	157	76	110	119
UNLEADED_GASOL	HU	278.63	236.17	205.07	282.70	214.05	377.03	294.57	271.19
		102	120	138	100	133	75	96	105
GOLD	GC	143.55	123.90	252.10	141.35	97.45	84.60	179.40	166.25
		198	229	113	201	291	335	158	171
SILVER	SI	173.97	113.75	324.12	271.25	289.95	196.72	269.15	310.52
		163	249	88	105	98	144	105	91
PLATINUM	PL	137.00	128.73	148.40	131.53	135.45	74.93	212.12	185.53
		207	220	191	216	209	379	134	153
PALLADIUM	PA	86.30	74.28	128.83	102.18	121.14	97.65	307.82	567.27
		329	382	220	278	234	290	92	50

TABLE II-1

Dollar Volatilities (First Line) and Number of Contracts Equivalent to
10 New S&P 500s on 12/31/1998 (Second Line) Broken Down by
Market and Year (Continued)

NAME	SYMB	1991	1992	1993	1994	1995	1996	1997	1998
FEEDER_CATTLE	FC	201.13	143.94	160.00	220.62	180.69	256.31	223.69	271.00
		141	197	177	129	157	111	127	105
LIVE_CATTLE	LC	151.35	123.35	149.65	188.35	177.60	179.90	154.35	196.65
		187	230	190	151	160	158	184	144
LIVE_HOGS	LH	139.00	132.20	173.15	168.80	170.30	241.15	218.20	278.30
		204	215	164	168	167	118	130	102
PORK_BELLIES	PB	294.20	241.45	332.15	283.75	305.40	556.30	462.35	532.15
		96	117	85	100	93	51	61	53
SOYBEANS	S	286.37	194.88	262.81	262.19	249.19	381.31	404.31	244.25
		99	146	108	108	114	74	70	116
SOYBEAN_MEAL	SM	172.60	103.80	148.70	137.25	151.95	241.50	294.40	182.55
		164	273	191	207	187	117	96	155
SOYBEAN_OIL	BO	132.99	99.81	130.08	166.92	134.46	129.78	125.94	126.57
		213	284	218	170	211	219	225	224
CORN	C	108.19	91.94	94.31	98.56	106.50	234.62	150.06	115.56
		262	309	301	288	266	121	189	245
OATS	O	79.69	89.56	80.50	76.69	100.56	186.50	86.38	72.81
		356	317	352	370	282	152	328	390
CHICAGO_WHEAT	W	157.31	151.94	137.06	162.50	228.00	330.13	207.94	150.56
		180	187	207	175	124	86	136	188
KANSAS_WHEAT	KW	140.94	146.06	125.31	151.37	221.81	336.87	227.31	142.00
		201	194	226	187	128	84	125	200
MINNESOTA_WHEA	MW	123.06	141.44	157.81	166.69	226.50	318.50	210.19	167.38
		230	201	180	170	125	89	135	169
COFFEE	KC	295.22	352.97	472.13	1648.31	849.28	607.97	1905.94	731.53
		96	80	60	17	33	47	15	39
COCOA	CC	145.55	158.35	128.60	186.55	120.95	122.55	182.65	147.30
		195	179	221	152	235	231	155	193
SUGAR_#11	SB	145.38	124.99	193.42	151.09	139.61	108.08	92.96	139.33
		195	227	147	188	203	262	305	204
ORANGE_JUICE	JO	217.46	206.70	260.74	251.10	189.79	208.91	164.81	219.60
		130	137	109	113	149	136	172	129
COTTON_#2	CT	351.12	291.05	254.65	351.75	619.22	332.50	201.30	332.05
		81	97	111	81	46	85	141	85
RANDOM_LUMBER	LB	317.84	338.40	1021.52	924.96	713.60	900.16	681.68	593.44
		89	84	28	31	40	32	42	48

and the number of contracts that would have to be traded to equal the dollar volatility of 10 new S&P 500 contracts at the end of 1998.

For the current studies, the average daily volatility is computed by taking a 200-day moving average of the absolute value of the difference between the current close and the previous one. The average daily volatility is then multiplied by the dollar value of a point, yielding the desired average daily dollar volatility. The dollar value of a point can be obtained by dividing the dollar value of a *tick* (a market's minimum move) by the size of a tick (as a decimal number). For the new S&P 500 contract, this works out to a value of $250 per point (tick value/tick size = $25/0.10). To obtain the number of contracts of a target market that would have to be traded to equal the dollar volatility of 10 new S&P 500 contracts on 12/31/1998, the dollar volatility of the new S&P 500 is divided by the dollar volatility of the target market; the result is multiplied by 10 and rounded to the nearest positive integer.

All the simulations reported in this book assume that trading always involves the same amount of dollar volatility. There is no compounding; trade size is not increased with growth in account equity. Equity curves, therefore, reflect returns from an almost constant investment in terms of risk exposure. A *constant-investment model* avoids the serious problems that arise when a compounded-investment approach is used in simulations with such margin-based instruments as futures. With margin-based securities, it is difficult to define return except in absolute dollar amounts or in relationship to margin requirements or risk; simple ratios cannot be used. In addition, system equity may occasionally dip below zero, creating problems with the computation of logarithms and further obscuring the meaning of ratios. However, given a constant investment (in terms of volatility exposure), monthly returns measured in dollars will have consistent significance over time, t-tests on average dollar return values will be valid (the annualized risk-to-reward ratio used to assess performance in the tests that follow is actually a rescaled t-statistic), and it will be easy to see if a system is getting better or worse over time, even if there are periods of negative equity. The use of a fixed-investment model, although carried out more rigorously here by maintaining constant risk, rather than a constant number of contracts, is in accord with what has appeared in other books concerned with futures trading. This does not mean that a constant dollar volatility portfolio must always be traded. *Optimal f* and other reinvestment strategies can greatly improve overall returns; they just make simulations much more difficult to interpret. In any case, such strategies can readily and most appropriately be tested after the fact using equity and trade-by-trade data generated by a fixed-investment simulation.

BASIC TEST PORTFOLIO AND PLATFORM

A *standard portfolio* of futures markets is employed for all tests of entry methods reported in this section. The reason for a standard portfolio is the same as that for a fixed-exit strategy or dollar volatility equalization: to ensure that test results will be valid, comparable, and consistent in meaning. All price series were obtained from Pinnacle Data in the form of continuous contracts, linked and back-adjusted as suggested by Schwager (1992). The standard portfolio is composed of the following markets (also see Table II-1): the stock indices (S&P 500, NYFE), interest rate markets (T-Bonds, 90-day T-Bills, 10-Year Notes), currencies (British Pound, Deutschemark, Swiss Franc, Japanese Yen, Canadian Dollar, Eurodollars), energy or oil markets (Light Crude, #2 Heating Oil, Unleaded Gasoline), metals (Gold, Silver, Platinum, Palladium), livestock (Feeder Cattle, Live Cattle, Live Hogs, Pork Bellies), traditional agriculturals (Soybeans, Soybean Meal Soybean Oil, Corn, Oats, Wheat), and other miscellaneous commodities (Coffee, Cocoa, Sugar, Orange Juice, #2 Cotton, Random Lumber). Selection of markets was aimed at creating a high level of diversity and a good balance of market types. While the stock index bond, currency, metal, energy, livestock, and grain markets all have representation, several markets (e.g., the Nikkei Index and Natural Gas) would have improved the balance of the portfolio, but were not included due to the lack of a sufficient history. In the chapters that follow, entry models are tested both on the complete standard portfolio and on the individual markets that compose it. Since a good system should be able to trade a variety of markets with the same parameters, the systems were not optimized for individual markets, only for the entire portfolio. Given the number of data points available, optimizing on specific markets could lead to undesirable curve-fitting.

Unless otherwise noted, quotes from August 1, 1985, through December 31, 1994, are treated as in-sample or optimization data, while those from January 1, 1995, through February 1, 1999, are used for out-of-sample verification. The number of contracts traded is adjusted to achieve a constant effective dollar volatility across all markets and time periods; in this way, each market and time period is more comparable with other markets and periods, and contributes about equally to the complete portfolio in terms of potential risk and reward. All tests use the same standardized exit technique to allow meaningful performance comparisons between entry methods.

CHAPTER 5

Breakout Models

A *breakout model* enters the market long when prices break above an upper band or threshold, and enters short when they drop below a lower band or threshold. Entry models based on breakouts range from the simple to the complex, differing primarily in how the placement of the bands or thresholds is determined, and in how entry is achieved.

KINDS OF BREAKOUTS

Breakout models are very popular and come in many forms. One of the oldest is the *simple trendline breakout* used by chartists. The chartist draws a descending trend-line that serves as the upper threshold: When prices break above the trendline, a long position is established; if the market has been rising, and prices break below an ascending trendline, a short entry is taken. Support and resistance lines, drawn using Gann angles or Fibonacci retracements, can also serve as breakout thresholds.

Historically, *channel breakout models*, employing support and resistance levels determined by previous highs and lows, followed chart-based methods. The trader buys when prices rise above the highest of the last *n* bars (the upper channel), and sells when prices fall below the lowest of the last *n* bars (the lower channel). Channel breakouts are easily mechanized and appeal to traders wishing to avoid the subjectivity of drawing trendlines or Gann angles on charts.

More contemporary and sophisticated than channel breakouts are *volatility breakout models* where the points through which the market must move to trigger long or short positions are based on *volatility bands*. Volatility bands are placed a certain distance above and below some measure of current value (e.g., the most recent closing price), the distance determined by recent market volatility: As volatility increases, the bands expand and move farther away from the current price; as it declines, the bands contract, coming closer to the market. The central idea is statistical: If the market moves in a given direction more than expected from normal jitter (as reflected in the volatility measurement), then some force may have impinged, instigating a real trend worth trading. Many $3,000 systems sold since the late 1980s employed some variation on volatility breakouts.

Breakout models also differ in how and when they enter the market. Entry can occur at the open or the close, requiring only a simple market order. Entry inside the bar is accomplished with stops placed at the breakout thresholds. A more sophisticated way to implement a breakout entry is to buy or sell on a limit, attempting to enter the market on a small pull-back, after the initial breakout, to control slippage and achieve entry at a better price.

CHARACTERISTICS OF BREAKOUTS

Breakouts are intuitively appealing. To get from one place to another, the market must cross all intervening points. Large moves always begin with small moves. Breakout systems enter the market on small moves, when the market crosses one of the intermediate points on the way to its destination; they buy into movement. Breakout models are, consequently, trend-following. Another positive characteristic of breakout models is that, because they buy or sell into momentum, trades quickly become profitable. Sometimes a very tight stop-loss can be set, an approach that can only be properly tested with intraday, tick-level data. The intention would be to enter on a breakout and to then set a very tight stop loss, assuming momentum at the breakout will carry the market sufficiently beyond the stop-loss to prevent it from being triggered by normal market fluctuations; the next step would be to exit with a quick profit, or ratchet the protective stop to break-even or better. Whether a profit can be taken before prices reverse depends on the nature of the market and whether momentum is strong enough to carry prices into the profit zone.

On the downside, like many trend-following models, breakouts enter the market late—sometimes too late, after a move is mostly over. In addition, small moves can trigger market entries, but never become the large moves necessary for profitable trading. Since breakout systems buy or sell into trends, they are prone to sizeable slippage; however, if well-designed and working according to theory, occasional strong trends should yield highly profitable trades that make up for the more frequent (but smaller) losers. However, the consensus is that, although their performance might have been excellent before massive computational power became inexpensive and widespread, simple breakout methods no longer work well. As breakout systems were developed, back-tested, and put on-line, the markets may have become increasingly efficient with respect to them. The result is that the markets' current noise level around the prices where breakout thresholds are often set may be causing many breakout systems to generate an excessive number of bad entries; this is especially likely in active, volatile markets, e.g., the S&P 500 and T-Bonds. Finally, it is easy to encounter severe slippage (relative to the size of a typical trade) when trying to implement trading strategies using breakout entries on an intraday time frame; for longer term trading, however, breakout entry strategies may perform acceptably.

A well-designed breakout model attempts to circumvent the problem of market noise to the maximum extent possible. This may be accomplished by placing the thresholds at points unlikely to be reached by movements that merely represent random or nontrending market activity, but that are likely to be reached if the market has developed a significant and potentially profitable trend. If the bands are placed too close to the current price level, a large number of false breakouts (leading to whipsaw trades) will occur: Market noise will keep triggering entries, first in one direction, then in the other. Because such movements do not constitute real trends with ample follow-through, little profit will be made; instead, much heat (in the form of commissions and slippage) will be generated and dissipate the trader's capital. If the bands are set too wide, too far away from the prevailing price, the system will take few trades and entry into the market will be late in the course of any move; the occasional large profit from a powerful trend will be wiped out by the losses that occur on market reversals. When the thresholds are set appropriately (whether on the basis of trendlines, volatility bands, or support and resistance), breakout entry models can, theoretically, be quite effective: Frequent, small losses, occurring because of an absence of follow-through on noise-triggered entries, should be compensated for by the substantial profits that accrue on major thrusts.

To reduce false breakouts and whipsaws, breakout systems are sometimes married to indicators, like Welles Wilder's "directional movement index" (1978), that supposedly ascertain whether the market is in a trending or nontrending mode. If the market is not trending, entries generated by the breakouts are ignored; if it is, they are taken. If popular trend indicators really work, marrying one to a breakout system (or any other trend-following model) should make the trader rich: Whipsaw trades should be eliminated, while trades that enter into strong trends should yield ample profits. The problem is that trend indicators do not function well, or tend to lag the market enough to make them less than ideal.

TESTING BREAKOUT MODELS

Tests are carried out on several different breakout models, trading a diversified portfolio of commodities, to determine how well breakout entries perform. Do they still work? Did they ever? Breakout models supposedly work best on commodities with persistent trends, traditionally, the currencies. With appropriate filtering, perhaps these models can handle a wider range of markets. The investigations below should provide some of the answers. The standard portfolio and exit strategy were used in all tests (see "Introduction" to Part II for details).

CHANNEL BREAKOUT ENTRIES

The initial tests address several variations of the channel breakout entry. First examined are close-only channel breakout models, in which the price channels or bands are determined using only closing prices. A model involving breakouts that occur beyond the highest high or lowest low will also be studied. In these models, the price channels approach the traditional notion of support and resistance.

Close-Only Channel Breakouts

Test 1: Close-Only Channel Breakout with Entry on Market Order at Next Open, No Transaction Costs.   The rules are: "If the current position is either short or flat and the market closes above the highest close of the last *n* days, then buy tomorrow's open." Likewise, "If the current position is either long or flat and the market closes below the lowest close of the preceding *n* days, then sell (go short at) tomorrow's open." The channel breakout entry model has only one parameter, the look-back (*n*). The number of contracts to buy or sell (*ncontracts*) was chosen to produce, for the market being traded, an effective dollar volatility approximately equal to that of two new S&P 500 contracts at the end of 1998.

Exits occur either when a breakout entry reverses an existing position or when the standard exit closes out the trade, i.e., when a money management stop is triggered, a profit target is hit, or the position has been open more than a specified number of days (bars), whichever comes first. The money management stop is computed as the entry price plus (for short positions) or minus (for long positions) some multiple (a parameter, *mmstp*) of the 50-bar average true range. Profit target limits are at the entry price plus (long) or minus (short) another multiple (*ptlim*) of the same average true range. Finally, an "exit at close" order (a form of market order) is posted when a position has been held for more than a specified number of days (*maxhold*). All exit orders are "close-only," i.e., executed only at the close; this restriction avoids ambiguous simulations when testing entries with intrabar limits or stops. Were exits not restricted to the close, such cases would involve the posting of multiple intrabar orders. Simulations become indeterminate and results untrustworthy when multiple intrabar orders are issued: The course of prices throughout the period represented by the bar, and hence the sequence of order executions, is unknown.

The *average true range* (a measure of volatility) is calculated as the mean of the true range of each of a specified number of previous bars (in this case, 50). The true range is the highest of the day's high minus the day's low, the day's high minus the previous day's close, or the previous day's close minus the day's low.

Below is a C++ implementation of the close-only channel breakout entry model mated with the standard exit strategy. When calculating the number of contracts, no correction is explicitly made for the S&P 500 split. The new contract is treated as identical to the old one, both by the simulator and by the code. All simulations are, nevertheless, correct under the assumption that the trader (not the simulator) trades two new contracts for every old contract: The simulator is instructed to sell half as many new contracts as it should, but treats these contracts as twice their current size. Limit-locked days are detected by range checking: A zero range (high equal to the low) suggests poor liquidity, and a possibly limit-locked market. Although this detection scheme is not ideal, simulations using it resemble results obtained in actual trading. Compiling the information from the exchanges needed to identify limit-locked days would have been almost impossible; therefore, the zero-range method is used. The code allows re-entry into persistent trends as long as new highs or lows are made.

```
static void Model (float *parms, float *dt, float *opn, float *hi,
float *lo, float *cls, float *vol, float *oi, float *dlrv, int nb,
TRDSIM &ts, float *eqcls) {

    // Implements the trading model to be tested.
    // parms   - vector [1..MAXPRM] of parameters
    // dt      - vector [1..nb] of dates in YYMMDD form
    // opn     - vector [1..nb] of opening prices
    // hi      - vector [1..nb] of high prices
    // lo      - vector [1..nb] of low prices
    // cls     - vector [1..nb] of closing prices
    // vol     - vector [1..nb] of volumes
    // oi      - vector [1..nb] of open interest numbers
    // dlrv    - vector [1..nb] of average dollar volatilities
    // nb      - number of bars in data series
    // ts      - trading simulator class instance
    // eqcls   - vector [1..nb] of closing equity levels

    // declare local scratch variables
    static int cb, n, ncontracts, maxhold;
    static float mmstp, ptlim, atr;

    // copy parameters to local variables for easier reference
    n = parms[1];        // channel width parameter
    maxhold = 10;        // maximum holding period
    ptlim = 4.0;         // profit target in volatility units
    mmstp = 1.0;         // stop loss in volatility units

    // file = x09mod01.c
    // set transaction costs to zero for this test only
    ts.commission(0.0);
    ts.slippage(0.0);
```

```
// step through bars (days) to simulate actual trading
for(cb = 1; cb <= nb-1; cb++) {

    // take no trades before the in-sample period
    // ... same as TradeStation's MaxBarsBack setting
    if(dt[cb] < IS_DATE) { eqcls[cb] = 0.0;  continue; }

    // execute any pending orders and store closing equity
    ts.update(opn[cb], hi[cb], lo[cb], cls[cb], cb);
    eqcls[cb] = ts.currentequity(EQ_CLOSETOTAL);

    // calculate number of contracts to trade
    // ... we want to trade the dollar volatility equivalent
    // ... of 2 new S&P-500 contracts as of 12/31/98
    ncontracts = RoundToInteger(5673.0 / dlrv[cb]);
    if(ncontracts < 1) ncontracts = 1;

    // avoid placing orders on potentially limit-locked days
    if(hi[cb+1] == lo[cb+1]) continue;

    // file = x09mod01.c
    // close-only channel breakout with entry on next open
    if(cls[cb]>Highest(cls,n,cb-1) && ts.position()<=0) {
        ts.buyopen('1', ncontracts);
    }
    else if(cls[cb]<Lowest(cls,n,cb-1) && ts.position()>=0) {
        ts.sellopen('2', ncontracts);
    }

    // instruct simulator to employ standard exit strategy
    atr = AvgTrueRange(hi, lo, cls, 50, cb);
    ts.stdexitcls('X', ptlim*atr, mmstp*atr, maxhold);

} // process next bar
}
```

The code was compiled and linked with the development shell and associated libraries; in TradeStation™, this is called "verifying" a system. Using development shell commands, the look-back parameter was brute-force optimized. The best solution (in terms of the risk-to-reward ratio) was then verified on out-of-sample data. Optimization involved stepping the entry model look-back (n) from 5 to 100, in increments of 5. The stop-loss parameter (*mmstp*) was fixed at 1 (representing 1 volatility, or average true range, unit), the profit target (*pflim*) at 4 (4 units), and the maximum holding period (*maxdays*) at 10 days. These values are used for the standard exit parameters in all tests of entry methods, unless otherwise specified. To provide a sense of scale when considering the stop-loss and profit target used in the standard exit, the S&P 500 at the end of 1998 had an average true range of 17.83 points, or about $4,457 for one new contract. For the first test, slippage and commissions were set to zero.

For such a simple system, the results are surprisingly good: an annual return of 76% against maximum drawdown. All look-back parameter values were profitable; the best in terms of risk-to-reward ratio was 80 days. A t-test for daily returns (calculated using the risk-to-reward ratio) reveals the probability is far less than one in one-thousand that chance explains the performance; when corrected for the number of tests in the optimization, this probability is still under one in one-hundred. As expected given these statistics, profits continued out-of-sample. Greater net profits were observed from long trades (buys), relative to short ones (sells), perhaps due to false breakouts on the short side occasioned by the constant decay in futures prices as contracts neared expiration. Another explanation is that commodity prices are usually more driven by crises and shortages than by excess supply. As with many breakout systems, the percentage of winners was small (43%), with large profits from the occasional trend compensating for frequent small losses. Some may find it hard to accept a system that takes many losing trades while waiting for the big winners that make it all worthwhile.

Portfolio equity for the best in-sample look-back rose steadily both in- and out-of-sample; overoptimization was not an issue. The equity curve suggests a gradual increase in market efficiency over time, i.e., these systems worked better in the past. However, the simple channel breakout can still extract good money from the markets. Or can it? Remember Test 1 was executed without transaction costs. The next simulation includes slippage and commissions.

Test 2: Close-Only Channel Breakout with Entry at Next Open, Transaction Costs Assumed.   This test is the same as the previous one except that slippage (three ticks) and commissions ($15 per round turn) are now considered. While this breakout model was profitable without transaction costs, it traded miserably when realistic costs were assumed. Even the best in-sample solution had negative returns (losses); as might be expected, losses continued in the out-of-sample period. Why should relatively small commission and slippage costs so devastate profits when, without such costs, the average trade makes thousands of dollars? Because, for many markets, trades involve multiple contracts, and slippage and commissions occur on a per-contract basis. Again, long trades and longer look-backs were associated with higher profits. The model was mildly profitable in the 1980s, but lost money thereafter. Considering the profitable results of the previous test, it seems the model became progressively more unable to overcome the costs of trading. When simple computerized breakout systems became the rage in the late 1980s, they possibly caused the markets to become more efficient.

Table 5-1 shows the portfolio performance of the close-only channel break-out system broken down by sample and market (*SYM*). (For information about the various markets and their symbols, see Table II-1 in the "Introduction" to Part II.) *NETL* = the total net profit on long trades, in thousands of dollars; *NETS* = the total net profit on short trades, in thousands of dollars; *ROA%* = annualized return-on-account; *PROB* = associated probability or statistical significance; *AVTR* = average profit/loss per trade.

Trend-following methods, such as breakouts, supposedly work well on the currencies. This test confirms that supposition: Positive returns were observed both in-sample and out-of-sample for several currencies. Many positive returns were also evidenced in both samples for members of the Oil complex, Coffee, and Lumber. The profitable performance of the stock indices (S&P 500 and NYFE) is probably due to the raging bull of the 1990s. About 10 trades were taken in each market every year. The percentage of wins was similar to that seen in Test 1 (about 40%).

Test 3: Close-Only Channel Breakout with Entry on Limit on Next Bar, Transaction Costs Assumed. To improve model performance by controlling slippage and obtaining entries at more favorable prices, a limit order was used to enter the market the next day at a specified price or better. Believing that the market would retrace at least 50% of the breakout bar (*cb*) before moving on, the limit price (*limprice*) was set to the midpoint of that bar. Since most of the code remains unchanged, only significantly altered blocks are presented:

```
// file = x09mod03.c
// close-only channel breakout with entry next bar on limit
limprice = 0.5 * (hi[cb] + lo[cb]);
if(cls[cb]>Highest(cls,n,cb-1) && ts.position()<=0) {
    ts.buylimit('1', limprice, ncontracts);
}
else if(cls[cb]<Lowest(cls,n,cb-1) && ts.position()>=0) {
    ts.selllimit('2', limprice, ncontracts);
}

// instruct simulator to employ standard exit strategy
atr = AvgTrueRange(hi, lo, cls, 50, cb);
ts.stdexitcls('X', ptlim*atr, mmstp*atr, maxhold);
```

Trade entry took place inside the bar on a limit. If inside-the-bar profit target and stop-loss orders were used, problems would have arisen. Posting multiple intra-bar orders can lead to invalid simulations: The sequence in which such orders are filled cannot be specified with end-of-day data, but they can still strongly affect the outcome. This is why the standard exit employs orders restricted to the close.

TABLE 5-1

Performance Statistics for Close-Only Channel Breakout with Entry at Open for All Markets in the Standard Portfolio

| SYM | IN-SAMPLE RESULTS | | | | | OUT-OF-SAMPLE RESULTS | | | | |
	NETL	NETS	ROA%	PROB	AVTR	NETL	NETS	ROA%	PROB	AVTR
SP	-255	85	-4.7	0.720	-2071	142	-55	21.4	0.281	1628
YX	-346	-58	-7.5	0.896	-4763	268	-66	50.8	0.107	3881
US	108	-82	1.0	0.449	313	191	-59	28.9	0.175	3072
TB	-258	-150	-7.6	0.960	-3970	-111	-62	-18.2	0.852	-4696
TY	71	-23	2.5	0.408	543	-13	-83	-7.4	0.735	-2097
BP	240	-116	8.1	0.271	1346	-69	-67	-15.3	0.887	-5277
DM	172	-56	5.0	0.295	1114	91	63	30.0	0.115	4207
SF	-36	-40	-5.1	0.641	-734	25	129	26.6	0.139	4309
JY	419	-18	33.3	0.033	4178	17	84	17.5	0.279	1927
CD	-53	61	0.4	0.497	83	14	154	33.1	0.107	4813
ED	-109	-212	-6.7	0.889	-2976	-139	-122	-21.2	0.939	-7725
CL	303	-31	19.6	0.161	2565	100	8	25.8	0.256	2488
HO	66	77	7.9	0.257	1664	101	126	53.7	0.058	5168
HU	103	87	7.5	0.191	2352	-124	40	-8.6	0.739	-1908
GC	-209	-109	-8.7	0.925	-4253	26	26	9.4	0.364	1137
SI	-55	-344	-6.3	0.932	-4488	-138	-74	-17.2	0.942	-7118
PL	-85	-93	-5.6	0.814	-2486	0	-53	-8.7	0.656	-1526
PA	124	140	13.8	0.131	3499	102	-144	-5.0	0.588	-936
FC	63	159	18.0	0.125	2656	-55	7	-6.8	0.634	-1371
LC	-23	-100	-4.6	0.726	-1332	-121	-93	-18.7	0.968	-5250
LH	105	-109	-0.2	0.507	-38	-106	146	5.6	0.383	1061
PB	78	-104	-1.3	0.557	-258	-39	-26	-15.1	0.704	-1812
S	94	-50	2.0	0.430	527	-150	-86	-23.2	0.928	-6418
SM	422	-34	20.1	0.044	5547	8	-46	-7.3	0.620	-926
BO	0	40	1.6	0.375	425	-121	-1	-16.0	0.879	-3429
C	54	-280	-5.7	0.836	-2476	-31	39	1.1	0.481	157
O	229	-314	-2.3	0.653	-975	-121	0	-14.7	0.798	-2636
W	-152	-147	-7.4	0.937	-3414	22	0	4.0	0.412	567
KW	99	-171	-2.3	0.621	-783	222	-1	69.2	0.082	4921
MW	-114	38	-1.8	0.614	-835	118	44	38.9	0.137	4194
KC	448	170	40.9	0.028	6451	103	-73	4.1	0.429	818
CC	2	-374	-9.0	0.968	-3501	-201	-102	-20.5	0.994	-7431
SB	-37	-198	-5.7	0.854	-2749	-318	23	-16.4	0.981	-7195
JO	208	-23	14.7	0.207	2104	-181	-117	-23.3	0.996	-8069
CT	110	-49	4.4	0.347	496	0	-80	-10.3	0.717	-1932
LB	423	21	29.4	0.019	5552	66	-39	4.8	0.299	729

As before, the look-back parameter was stepped from 5 to 100, in increments of 5, and the solution with the best risk-to-reward ratio (and t-test probability) was selected. Commissions, slippage, exit parameters, and the ability to reenter a continuing trend (albeit on a pullback), remain unchanged.

With a best look-back of 80 (same as in Test 1), this model returned about 33% annually during the in-sample period. The probability that these returns were due to chance is less than 5% when not corrected, or 61% when corrected for 20 optimization runs. Although profitable in-sample, the statistics suggest the model may fail in the future; indeed, out-of-sample returns were negative. As in Tests 1 and 2, trades lasted about seven bars and long trades were more profitable than short ones. The percentage of winners was 42%. Although the limit entry did not eliminate the damaging impact of transaction costs, performance improved. The limit order did not seriously reduce the number of trades or cause many profitable trends to be missed; the market pulled back after most breakouts, allowing entry at more favorable prices. That a somewhat arbitrary, almost certainly suboptimal, limit entry strategy could so improve performance is highly encouraging. The equity curve again shows that this kind of system once worked but no longer does.

Table 5-2 shows that, with few exceptions, there were positive returns for the currencies and oils, both in-sample and out-of-sample, consistent with findings in earlier tests. Coffee continued to trade well on both samples, and the S&P 500 remained profitable in the verification sample.

Conclusion   A limit-based entry can significantly improve the overall performance of a breakout model. Substantial benefit is obtained even with a fairly crude choice for the limit price. It is interesting that the markets to benefit most from the use of a limit order for entry were not necessarily those with the lowest dollar volatilities and implied transaction costs, as had been expected. Certain markets, like the S&P 500 and Eurodollars, just seem to respond well to limit entries, while others, such as Cocoa and Live Cattle, do not.

HIGHEST HIGH / LOWEST LOW BREAKOUTS

Would placing the thresholds further from current prices reduce whipsaws, increase winning trades, and improve breakout performance? More stringent breakout levels are readily obtained by replacing the highest and lowest close from the previous model with the highest high and lowest low (HHLL) in the current model. Defined this way, breakout thresholds now represent traditional levels of support and resistance: Breakouts occur when previous highs or lows are "taken out" by the market. One possible way to further reduce spurious breakouts is by requiring the market to close beyond the bands, not merely to penetrate them at some point inside the bar. Speeding up system response by using a stop order for entry, or reducing transaction costs by entering on a pullback with a limit order, might also improve performance.

Test 4: Close-Only HHLL Breakout with Entry at Open of Next Bar.   This breakout buys at tomorrow's open when today's close breaks above the highest high of the last *n* days, and sells at tomorrow's open when today's close drops below the lowest low. The look-back (*n*) is the only model parameter. The beau-

TABLE 5-2

Performance Statistics for Close-Only Channel Breakout with Entry at Limit for All Markets in the Standard Portfolio

SYM	IN-SAMPLE RESULTS					OUT-OF-SAMPLE RESULTS				
	NETL	NETS	ROA%	PROB	AVTR	NETL	NETS	ROA%	PROB	AVTR
SP	-130	-175	-7.8	0.908	-4078	196	-10	66.3	0.111	3788
YX	-185	-176	-8.0	0.938	-4955	233	-84	42.4	0.146	3473
US	295	67	35.0	0.027	4962	10	-32	-3.1	0.572	-572
TB	-140	-24	-5.0	0.766	-1819	-217	-91	-22.6	0.997	-8835
TY	43	59	5.8	0.306	1231	91	-85	0.6	0.483	148
BP	352	-124	16.2	0.129	2366	-25	-96	-15.9	0.833	-4892
DM	202	-17	9.9	0.193	1963	83	81	32.9	0.097	4841
SF	36	-17	1.0	0.467	178	48	176	50.1	0.042	7025
JY	309	93	44.9	0.038	4525	72	109	45.2	0.152	3514
CD	112	110	14.2	0.159	2477	51	110	37.0	0.131	4276
ED	123	152	15.3	0.113	3001	-22	-106	-14.9	0.808	-4292
CL	196	-226	-1.2	0.547	-293	198	-19	28.0	0.131	4050
HO	77	-44	1.5	0.441	381	76	137	57.0	0.074	5339
HU	51	208	11.1	0.114	3565	-41	-18	-6.4	0.647	-1578
GC	-184	-27	-6.1	0.851	-3200	45	144	46.4	0.127	4626
SI	7	-189	-5.6	0.775	-2278	-92	-41	-15.8	0.827	-4470
PL	31	-98	-2.4	0.629	-965	-74	66	-1.6	0.527	-262
PA	194	109	16.8	0.082	4164	-18	-136	-16.8	0.820	-3987
FC	113	123	18.4	0.098	3048	-88	44	-4.7	0.629	-1328
LC	-82	24	-2.2	0.623	-665	-159	-93	-21.9	0.980	-7227
LH	284	-77	12.2	0.153	2277	-1	35	8.7	0.401	903
PB	88	101	14.4	0.140	2087	-42	-24	-12.3	0.702	-1908
S	325	-93	9.1	0.169	2906	-214	-102	-23.1	0.980	-8337
SM	364	-129	9.0	0.135	3405	28	-18	2.8	0.467	262
BO	11	255	16.0	0.082	3001	-84	-39	-18.3	0.891	-3350
C	41	-15	1.3	0.455	307	97	10	18.0	0.268	2233
O	129	-163	-1.7	0.572	-425	-126	-34	-14.1	0.874	-3431
W	-69	-129	-5.3	0.861	-2427	-66	65	0.0	0.464	-4
KW	-97	-42	-3.6	0.766	-1703	131	75	72.4	0.084	4807
MW	95	-182	-2.3	0.653	-971	0	4	0.9	0.486	121
KC	261	315	61.3	0.021	7121	118	-4	26.0	0.229	3689
CC	66	-141	-3.0	0.648	-789	-115	-129	-19.8	0.981	-6811
SB	137	-113	1.0	0.454	322	-196	61	-11.8	0.829	-3541
JO	110	-46	3.1	0.380	748	-93	-103	-20.9	0.913	-6567
CT	284	93	30.5	0.035	3572	-65	9	-9.1	0.637	-1456
LB	346	-26	20.0	0.055	4265	56	-59	-0.8	0.400	-88

ty of this model, besides its simplicity, is that no important trend will be missed, and tomorrow's trades are fully known after today's close.

```
// file = x09mod04.c
// HHLL channel breakout system with entry next bar on open
if(cls[cb]>Highest(hi,n,cb-1) && ts.position()<=0) {
    ts.buyopen('1', ncontracts);
}
else if(cls[cb]<Lowest(lo,n,cb-1) && ts.position()>=0) {
```

```
    ts.sellopen('2', ncontracts);
}

// instruct simulator to employ standard exit strategy
atr = AvgTrueRange(hi, lo, cls, 50, cb);
ts.stdexitcls('X', ptlim*atr, mmstp*atr, maxhold);
```

Look-backs from 5 to 100 were tested in steps of 5. On the in-sample data, the model was profitable for only four of the look-backs. The best results were obtained with a look-back of 85, where in-sample returns were a mere 1.2% annually. Given these returns and the associated statistics, it is no surprise that this model lost 15.9% annually out-of-sample. Winners occurred about 39% of the time, and long trades were more profitable than short ones in-sample. As in all previous breakout simulations, the HHLL breakout performed best on the currencies, the oils, and Coffee; it performed worst on metals, livestock, and grains. Equity shows a model that never performed well, but that now performs disastrously.

The results were slightly better than those for the close-only breakout with a similar entry at the open; they were not better enough to overcome transaction costs. In the close-only model, a limit order reduced the cost of failed breakouts and, thereby, improved performance. Because costs are higher with the HHLL breakout, due to the more stringent breakout thresholds, a limit entry may provide a greater boost to performance. A limit entry for a breakout model also sidesteps the flurry of orders that often hit the market when entry stops, placed at breakout thresholds, are triggered. Entries at such times are likely to occur at unfavorable prices. However, more sophisticated traders will undoubtedly "fade" the movements induced by the entry stops placed by more naïve traders, driving prices back. An appropriate limit order may be able to enter on the resultant pullback at a good price. If the breakout represents the start of a trend, the market is likely to resume its movement, yielding a profitable trade; if not, the market will have less distance to retrace from the price at entry, meaning a smaller loss. Even though the HHLL breakout appears only marginally better than the close-only breakout thus far, the verdict is not yet in; a limit entry may produce great improvement.

The annualized return-on-account is used as an index of performance in these discussions and the risk-to-reward ratio is rarely mentioned, even though the probability statistic (a t-statistic) is computed using that measure. The risk-to-reward ratio and return-on-account are very highly correlated with one another: They are almost interchangeable as indicators of model efficacy. Since it is easier to understand, the annualized return-on-account is referred to more often.

Test 5: Close-Only HHLL Breakout with Entry on Limit on Next Bar.   For the close-only channel breakout, use of a limit order for entry greatly improved performance. Perhaps a limit entry could similarly benefit the HHLL breakout model.

For the sake of consistency with the model examined in Test 3, the limit price is set to the mid-point of the breakout bar.

```
// file = x09mod05.c
// HHLL channel breakout system with entry next bar on limit
limprice = 0.5 * (hi[cb] + lo[cb]);
if(cls[cb]>Highest(hi,n,cb-1) && ts.position()<=0) {
    ts.buylimit('1', limprice, ncontracts);
}
else if(cls[cb]<Lowest(lo,n,cb-1) && ts.position()>=0) {
    ts.selllimit('2', limprice, ncontracts);
}

// instruct simulator to employ standard exit strategy
atr = AvgTrueRange(hi, lo, cls, 50, cb);
ts.stdexitcls('X', ptlim*atr, mmstp*atr, maxhold);
```

The look-back parameter was stepped through the same range as in previous tests. All look-backs produced positive returns. The best in-sample results were with a look-back of 85, which yielded a return of 36.2% annually; the probability is less than 2% (33% when corrected for multiple tests) that this was due to chance. In-sample, long positions again yielded greater profits than short positions. Surprisingly, out-of-sample, the short side produced a small profit, while the long side resulted in a loss! With a return of -2.3%, out-of-sample performance was poor, but not as bad as for many other systems tested. In-sample, there were 43% wins and the average trade produced an $1,558 profit; out-of-sample, 41% were winners and the average trade lost $912.

The equity curve in Figure 5-1 may seem to contradict the negative out-of-sample returns, but the trend in the out-of-sample data was up and on par with the trend in the latter half of the in-sample period. The apparent contradiction results from a bump in the equity curve at the start of the out-of-sample period. Nevertheless, the HHLL breakout with entry on a limit (together with the standard exit) is not a system that one would want to trade after June 1988: The return was too low relative to the risk represented by the fluctuation of equity above and below the least-squares polynomial trendline (also shown in Figure 5-1).

All currencies and oils had positive in-sample results. Strong out-of-sample returns were seen for the Swiss Franc, Canadian Dollar, and Deutschemark, as well as for Heating Oil and Light Crude; small losses were observed for the British Pound, Eurodollar, and Unleaded Gasoline. Coffee was profitable in both samples.

Test 6: Close-Only HHLL Breakout with Entry on Stop on Next Bar. This model buys on a stop at a level of resistance defined by recent highs, and sells on a stop at support as defined by recent lows. Because the occurrence of a breakout

FIGURE 5-1

Equity Curve for HHLL Breakout, Entry at Limit

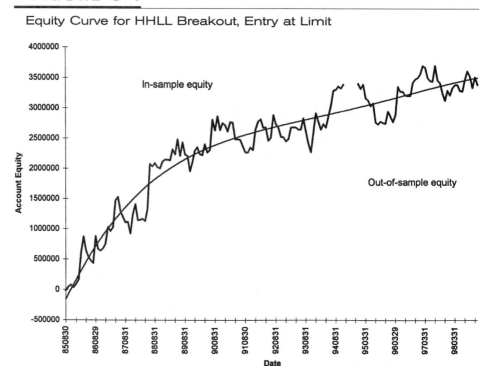

is decided on the entry bar by the stop itself, the highest high and lowest low are calculated for bars up to and including the current bar. The relative position of the close, with respect to the breakout thresholds, is used to avoid posting multiple intrabar orders. If the close is nearer to the upper threshold, then the buy stop is posted; if the close is closer to the lower threshold, the sell stop is posted. Both orders are never posted together. By implementing the HHLL breakout with stop orders, a faster response to breakout conditions is achieved; there is no need to wait for the next bar after a signal is given to enter the market. Entry, therefore, occurs earlier in the course of any market movement and no move will ever be missed, as might happen with a limit while waiting for a pull-back that never takes place. However, the reduced lag or response time may come at a cost: entry at a less favorable price. There is greater potential for slippage, when buying into momentum on a stop, and entry takes place at the breakout price, rather than at a better price on a retracement.

The look-back parameter was optimized as usual. The best in-sample look-back was 95, with look-backs of 65 through 100 being profitable. Annual returns were 8.7%. Although the results were better than those for Test 4, they were not as good as for Test 5. Faster response bought some advantage, but not as much as waiting for a retracement where entry can occur at a more favorable price. The percentage of winning trades was 41% and the average trade yielded a $430 profit. Out-of-sample, the picture was much worse, as might be expected given the low returns and poor statistics on the in-sample data. This model lost an average of $798 per trade. About 37% of the trades were winners. The model made most of its profits before June 1988, and lost money after January 1992.

All currencies, except Eurodollars, had positive returns in the optimization period. In the verification period, the Japanese Yen, Canadian Dollar, and Deutschemark, had solid returns in the 30% to 50% range. The model also generated moderate returns on the oils. Coffee traded well, with a 21.2% return in-sample and a 61.8% return out-of-sample. Random Lumber also had positive returns in both samples.

VOLATILITY BREAKOUT ENTRIES

The next three tests evaluate volatility breakout entry models, in which the trader buys when prices rise above an upper volatility band, and sells short when they fall below a lower volatility band. *Volatility bands* are bands placed above and below current prices. When volatility increases, the bands expand; when it decreases, they contract. The balance point around which the bands are drawn may be the most recent closing price, a moving average, or some other measure of current value.

Test 7: Volatility Breakout with Entry at Next Open.   This model buys at tomorrow's open when today's close pushes above the upper volatility band, and sells short at the next open when the close drops below the lower volatility band. The volatility bands are determined by adding to (for the upper band) and subtracting from (for the lower band) the estimate of current value a multiple (*bw*) of the *atrlen*-bar average true range (a measure of volatility). The estimate of value is a *malen*-bar exponential moving average of the closing price. If the moving average length (*malen*) is one, this estimate degrades to the closing price on the breakout or "signal" bar.

Because the volatility breakout model has three parameters, genetic optimization was chosen for the current test. Using genetic optimization, the bandwidth parameter (*bw*) was evaluated over a range of 1.5 to 4.5, with a grid size (increment) of 0.1; the period of the average true range (*atrlen*) was studied over a range of 5 to 50, with a grid size of 1; and the moving average length (*malen*) was examined over a range of 1 to 25, also with a unit grid size. The genetic optimization was allowed to run for 100 generations. As in all previous tests, the highest attainable risk-to-reward ratio (or, equivalently, the lowest attainable probability that any profits were due to chance) on the in-sample or optimization data was sought.

The best in-sample performance was obtained with a bandwidth of 3.8, a moving average length of 5, and an average true range of 20 bars. With these parameters, the annualized return was 27.4%. There was a probability of 5.6% (99.7%

when corrected for 100 tests or generations) that chance produced the observed return. Almost every combination of parameters examined generated profits on the long side and losses on the short side. The average trade for the best parameter set was held for 6 bars and yielded a profit of $4,675. Only 240 trades were present in the optimization period, about 45% of which were winners. Compared to previous tests, the smaller number of trades, and the higher percentage of winners, are explained by breakout thresholds placed further from current price levels. The average trade lost $7,371 in the verification sample and only 25% of the 112 trades were profitable. Both long positions and short positions lost about the same amount.

Almost all gain in equity occurred from August 1987 to December 1988, and then from December 1992 to August 1993. Equity declined from October 1985 through July 1986, from August 1989 through May 1992, and from May 1995 to December 1998.

Excessive optimization may have contributed to deteriorated performance in the verification sample. Nevertheless, given the number of parameters and parameter combinations tested, a good entry model should have generated a greater in-sample return than was seen and better statistics, capable of withstanding correction for multiple tests without total loss of significance. In other words, excessive optimization may not be the central issue: Despite optimization, this model generated poor in-sample returns and undesirably few trades. Like the others, this model may simply have worked better in the past.

As before, currencies were generally profitable. Oddly, the oil complex, which traded profitably in most earlier tests, became a serious loser in this one. Coffee and Lumber traded well in-sample, but poorly out-of-sample, the reverse of previous findings. Some of these results might be due to the model's limited number of trades.

Test 8: Volatility Breakout with Entry on Limit. This model attempts to establish a long position on the next bar using a limit order when the close of the current bar is greater than the current price level plus a multiple of the average true range. It attempts to establish a short position on the next bar using a limit order when the close of the current bar is less than the current price level minus the same multiple of the average true range. The current price level is determined by an exponential moving average of length *malen* calculated for the close. The multiplier for the average true range is referred to as *bw*, and the period of the average true range as *atrlen*. Price for the limit order to be posted on the next bar is set to the midpoint price of the current or breakout bar. Optimization was carried out exactly as in Test 7.

For all parameter combinations, long positions were more profitable (or lost less) than short positions. The best in-sample results were achieved with a bandwidth of 3.7, a moving average length of 22, and a period of 41 for the average true range measure of volatility; these parameter values produced a 48.3% annualized return. Results this good should occur less than twice in one-thousand experiments; corrected for multiple tests (100 generations), the probability is less than 13% that the observed profitability was due to chance. On the in-sample data, 1,244 trades were taken, the average trade lasted 7 days, yielded $3,616, and was a winner 45% of the time. Both long and short trades were profitable.

Given the statistics, there was a fair probability that the model would continue to be profitable out-of-sample; however, this was not the case. The model lost heavily in the out-of-sample period. Equity rose rather steadily from the beginning of the sample until August 1990, drifted slowly lower until May 1992, rose at a good pace until June 1995, then declined. These results primarily reflect the decreasing ability of simple breakout models to capture profits from the markets.

All currencies had positive in-sample returns and all, except the British Pound and Canadian Dollar, were profitable out-of-sample—confirmation that breakout systems perform best on these markets, perhaps because of their trendiness. Curiously, the currency markets with the greatest returns in-sample are not necessarily those with the largest returns out-of-sample. This implies that it is desirable to trade a complete basket of currencies, without selection based on historical performance, when using a breakout system. Although this model performed poorly on oils, it produced stunning returns on Coffee (both samples yielded greater than 65% annually) and Lumber (greater than 29%).

Test 9: Volatility Breakout with Entry on Stop.   This model enters immediately at the point of breakout, on a stop which forms part of the entry model. The advantage is that entry takes place without delay; the disadvantage is that it may occur at a less favorable price than might have been possible later, on a limit, after the clusters of stops that are often found around popular breakout thresholds have been taken out. To avoid multiple intrabar orders, only the stop for the band nearest the most recent closing price is posted; this rule was used in Test 6. The volatility breakout model buys on a stop when prices move above the upper volatility band, and sells short when they move below the lower volatility band.

The optimum values for the three model parameters were found with the aid of the genetic optimizer built into the C-Trader toolkit from Scientific Consultant Services, Inc. The smallest risk-to-reward ratio occurred with a bandwidth of 8.3, a moving average length of 11, and an average true range of 21 bars. Despite optimization, this solution returned only 11.6% annually. There were 1,465 trades taken; 40% were winners. The average trade lasted 6 days and took $931 out of the market. Only long positions were profitable across parameter combinations.

Both long and short trades lost heavily in the verification sample. There were 610 trades, of which only 29% were winners. The equity curve and other simulation data suggested that deterioration in the out-of-sample period was much greater for the volatility breakout model with a stop entry than with entry on a limit, or even at the open using a market order.

Can excessive optimization explain the rapid decay in the out-of-sample period? No. Optimization may have merely boosted overall in-sample performance from terrible to poor, without providing improved out-of-sample performance. Optimization does this with models that lack real validity, capitalizing on chance more than usual. The greater a model's real power, the more helpful and less destructive the process of optimization. As previously, the detrimental effects of curve-fitting are not the entire story: Performance declined well before the out-of-sample period was reached. The worsened out-of-sample performance can as easily be attributed to a continued gain in market efficiency relative to this model as it can to excessive optimization.

The model generated in-sample profits for the British Pound, Deutschemark, Swiss Franc, and Japanese Yen; out-of-sample, profits were generated for all of these markets except the British Pound. If all currencies (except the Canadian Dollar and Eurodollar) were traded, good profits would have been obtained in both samples. The Eurodollar lost heavily due to the greater slippage and less favorable prices obtained when using a stop for entry; the Eurodollar has low dollar volatility and, consequently, a large number of contracts must be traded, which magnifies transaction costs. In both samples, Heating Oil was profitable, but other members of the oil group lost money. The out-of-sample deterioration in certain markets, when comparison is to entry on a limit, suggests that it is now more difficult to enter on a stop at an acceptable price.

VOLATILITY BREAKOUT VARIATIONS

Would restricting breakout models to long positions improve their performance? How about trading only the traditionally trendy currencies? Would benefit be derived from a trend indicator to filter out whipsaws? What would happen without re-entries into existing, possibly stale, trends? The last question was answered by an unreported test in which entries took place only on breakout reversals. The results were so bad that no additional tests were completed, analyzed, or reported. The first three questions, however, are addressed below.

Long Positions Only

In the preceding tests, the long side almost always performed better than the short side, at least on in-sample data. What if one of the previously tested models was modified to trade only long positions? Test 10 answers that question.

Test 10: Volatility Breakout with Limit Entry Trading Only Long Positions.   The best in-sample model (Test 8) was modified to trade only long positions. A genetic algorithm optimized the model parameters. Band-width (*bw*) was optimized from 1.5

to 4.5, with a grid of 0.1; the period of the average true range (*atrlen*) from 5 to 50, with a grid of 1; and the length of the moving average (*malen*) from 1 to 25, with a grid of 1. Optimization was halted after 100 generations.

In-sample, the model performed well. The best parameter values were: bandwidth, 2.6; moving average length, 15; and average true range period, 18. The best parameters produced an annualized return of 53.0%, and a risk-to-reward ratio of 1.17 ($p < 0.0002$; $p < 0.02$, corrected). There were 1,263 trades, 48% profitable (a higher percentage than in any earlier test). The average trade lasted 7 days, with a $4,100 profit after slippage and commissions. Even suboptimal parameter values were profitable, e.g., the worst parameters produced a 15.5% return!

Out-of-sample, despite the high levels of statistical significance and the robustness of the model (under variations in parameter values when tested on in-sample data), the model performed very poorly: There were only 35% wins and a loss of -14.6% annually. This cannot be attributed to in-sample curve-fitting as all in-sample parameter combinations were profitable. Suboptimal parameters should have meant diminished, but still profitable, out-of-sample performance. Additional tests revealed that no parameter set could make this model profitable in the out-of-sample period! This finding rules out excessive optimization as the cause for out-of-sample deterioration. Seemingly, in recent years, there has been a change in the markets that affects the ability of volatility breakout models to produce profits, even when restricted to long positions. The equity curve demonstrated that the model had most of its gains prior to June 1988. The remainder of the optimization and all of the verification periods evidenced the deterioration.

As before, most currencies traded fairly well in both samples. The average currency trade yielded $5,591 in-sample and $1,723 out-of-sample. If a basket of oils were traded, profits would be seen in both samples. Coffee was also profitable in both samples.

Overall, this system is not one to trade today, although it might have made a fortune in the past; however, there may still be some life in the currency, oil, and Coffee markets.

Currencies Only

The currency markets are believed to have good trends, making them ideal for such trend-following systems as breakouts. This belief seems confirmed by the tests above, including Test 10. Test 11 restricts the model to the currencies.

Test 11: Volatility Breakout with Limit Entry Trading Only Currencies.   This model is identical to the previous one, except that the restriction to long trades was removed and a new restriction to trading only currencies was established. No optimization was conducted because of the small number of markets and, consequently, data points and trades; instead, the best parameters from Test 8 were used here.

This is the first test where a breakout produced clearly profitable results in both samples with realistic transaction costs included in the simulation! In-sample, the model returned 36.2% annually. Out-of-sample, the return was lower (17.7%), but still good. There were 268 trades, 48% wins, with an average profit per trade (in-sample) of $3,977. Out-of-sample, the model took 102 trades, won 43%, and averaged $2,106 per trade.

The equity curve in Figure 5-2 confirms the encouraging results. Almost all equity was gained in five thrusts, each lasting up to a few months. This model is potentially tradeable, especially if the standard exit was replaced with a more effective one.

ADX Trend Filter

One problem with breakouts is the tendency to generate numerous whipsaw trades in which the breakout threshold is crossed, but a real trend never develops. One possible solution is to use a trend indicator to filter signals generated by raw breakouts; many traders do this with the ADX, a popular trend indicator. Test 12 examines whether Wilder's ADX is beneficial.

FIGURE 5-2

Equity Curve for HHLL Breakout, Entry on Limit, Currencies Only

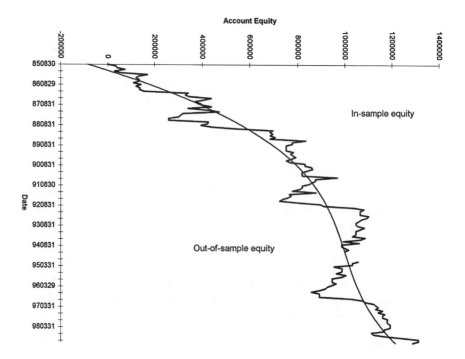

Test 12: Volatility Breakout with Limit Entry and Trend Filter.   The same
model from Tests 10 and 11 is used; instead of restriction to long positions or
currencies, the signals are "filtered" for trending conditions using the Average
Directional Movement index (or ADX; Wilder, 1978). By not entering trend-
less markets, whipsaws and languishing trades, and the resultant erosion of
capital, can hopefully be reduced. The ADX was implemented to filter breakouts as suggested by White (1993). Trending conditions exist as long as the
18-bar ADX makes a new 6-bar high, and entries are taken only when trends
exist.

```
// file = x09mod12.c
// volatility breakout model with entry on limit
// and 18-bar ADX trend filter
band_width = bw * atr[cb-1];
center_price = xmavg[cb-1];
upper_band = center_price + band_width;
lower_band = center_price - band_width;
limprice = 0.5 * (hi[cb] + lo[cb]);
trending = adx[cb] > Highest(adx, 6, cb-1);
if(trending && cls[cb] > upper_band &&
   ts.position() <= 0) {
      ts.buylimit('1', limprice, ncontracts);
}
else if(trending && cls[cb] < lower_band &&
   ts.position() >= 0) {
      ts.selllimit('2', limprice, ncontracts);
}

// instruct simulator to employ standard exit strategy
tmp = exitatr[cb];
ts.stdexitcls('X', ptlim*tmp, mmstp*tmp, maxhold);
```

As in previous tests, a genetic algorithm optimized the parameters. All 100
parameter combinations except one produced positive returns in-sample; 88
returned greater than 20%, demonstrating the model's tolerance of parameter variation. The best parameters were: bandwidth, 2.6; moving average length, 8; and
average true range period, 34. With these parameters the in-sample return was
68.3%; the probability that such a high return would result from chance was less
than one in two-thousand, or about one in twenty-nine instances when corrected
for optimization. There were 872 trades and 47% wins. The average trade generated about $4,500 in profit. Out-of-sample the average trade lost $2,415 and only
36% of all trades taken (373) were winners. The return was -20.9%, one of the
worst out-of-sample performances. The ADX appears to have helped more in the
past than in current times.

Most currencies, Heating Oil, Coffee, Lumber, and 10-Year Notes were profitable out-of-sample. The S&P500, Kansas Wheat, and Comex Gold were profitable out-of-sample, but lost money in-sample. The pattern is typical of what has been observed with breakout systems, i.e., the currencies, oils, and Coffee tend to be consistently profitable.

SUMMARY ANALYSES

Table 5-3 summarizes breakout results broken down by model, sample, and order type. *ARRR* = the annualized risk-to-reward ratio, *ROA* = the annualized return on account, and *AVTR* = the average trade's profit or loss.

Breakout Types

In the optimization sample (1985 to 1995), volatility breakouts worked best, the highest-high/lowest-low breakout fell in-between, and the close-only breakout did worst; this pattern was consistent across all three order types. In the verification period (1995 through 1998), the highest-high/lowest-low continued to do slightly better than the close-only, but the volatility model performed much worse. For reasons discussed earlier, optimization cannot account for the relatively dramatic deterioration of the volatility breakout in recent years. Perhaps the volatility breakout deteriorated more because of its early popularity. Even the best breakout models, however, do poorly in recent years.

When broken down by model, three distinct periods were observed in the averaged equity curves. From August 1985 through June 1988, all models were about equally profitable. From June 1988 to July 1994, the HHLL and close-only models were flat and choppy. The volatility model showed a substantial gain from August 1992 through July 1994. From July 1994 until December 1998, the HHLL and close-only breakouts were choppy and slightly down, with the HHLL model somewhat less down than the close-only model; equity for the volatility model declined significantly.

Entry Orders

Both in- and out-of-sample, and across all models, the limit order provided the greatest edge; the stop and market-at-open orders did poorly. The benefit of the limit order for entering the market undoubtedly stemmed from its ability to obtain entries at more favorable prices. The dramatic impact of transaction costs and unfavorable entry prices is evident in Tests 1 and 2. Surprisingly, the limit order even worked with a trend-following methodology like breakouts. It might be expected that too many good trends would be missed while waiting to enter on a limit; however, the market pulls back (even after valid breakouts) with

TABLE 5-3

Summary of Breakout Entry Results Arranged for Easy Comparison

		In-sample performance				Out-of-sample performance		
		Entry on Open	Entry on Limit	Entry on Stop		Entry on Open	Entry on Limit	Entry on Stop
Close-only	ARRR	-0.02	0.54			-0.33	-0.14	
channel breakout	ROA	-1.1	32.6			-13.5	-10.0	
	AVTR	-60	1066			-671	-299	
HHLL breakout	ARRR	0.04	0.66	0.22		-0.41	-0.01	-0.44
	ROA	1.2	36.3	8.7		-15.9	-2.1	-15.5
	AVTR	82	1558	430		-912	-72	-798
Volatility breakout	ARRR	0.51	0.96	0.28		-1.20	-0.58	-1.74
	ROA	27.4	48.3	11.6		-20.5	-16.9	-22.7
	AVTR	4675	3616	931		-7371	-2094	-5272
Volatility breakout	ARRR		1.17				-0.48	
longs only	ROA		53.0				-14.6	
	AVTR		4100				-1640	
Volatility breakout	ARRR		0.61				0.34	
currencies only	ROA		36.3				17.7	
	AVTR		3977				2106	
Volatility breakout	ARRR		1.09				-0.60	
with ADX trend	ROA		68.3				-20.0	
filter	AVTR		4570				-2415	

enough frequency to enter on a limit at a better price without missing too many good trends.

The same three periods, evident when average equity was broken down by breakout type, appeared when entry orders were analyzed. For the limit and stop entries, equity surged strongly from August 1985 to June 1988. Equity increased, but to a lesser extent, with a stop order. For entry at the open and on a stop, equity was choppy and down-trending from June 1988 to July 1994, when the limit order modestly gained. From July 1994 to December 1998, equity for entry at the open mildly declined, the stop evidenced a serious decline, and the limit had no consistent movement. The stop did better than average during the first period and much worse than average during the third; more decay in performance over time occurred with a stop order than with the other orders. In all periods, the limit order performed best.

When equity was analyzed for all models and order types combined, most of its gains were in the first period, which covered less than the first third of the in-sample period. By the end of this period, more than 70% of the peak equity had already accumulated. In the second period, equity drifted up a little. In the third period, equity declined, at first gradually and then, after July 1997, at a faster pace.

Interactions

Interactions seemed strongest between breakout types and time. The most notable was between volatility breakouts (versus the others) and time (in-sample versus out-of-sample). Volatility breakouts performed best early on, but later became the worst. The volatility breakout with stop entry deteriorated more in recent years than it did with entry on a limit, perhaps due to the common use of stops for entry in trend-following models. Finally, the highest-high/lowest-low breakout sometimes favored a stop, while the volatility model never did.

Restrictions and Filters

Restricting trades to long positions greatly improved the performance of the volatility breakout in-sample, and improved it to some extent out-of-sample. Breakout models do better on the long side than on the short one. The ADX trend filter had a smaller benefit in-sample and provided no benefit out-of-sample.

Restricting trading to currencies produced lessened in-sample performance, but dramatic improvements out-of-sample. The gain was so great that the model actually profited out-of-sample, which cannot be said for any of the other combinations tested! The currencies were not affected by the rising efficiency other markets had to simple breakout systems, perhaps because the currency markets are huge and driven by powerful fundamental forces. The poorer in-sample performance can be explained by the reduced number of markets traded.

Analysis by Market

Net profit and annual return were averaged for each market over all tests. The calculated numbers contained no surprises. Positive returns were seen in both samples for the Deutschemark, Swiss Franc, Japanese Yen, and Canadian Dollar, and for Light Crude and Heating Oil. Trading a basket of all six currencies, all three oils, or both, would have been profitable in both samples. Although no other market group demonstrated consistent profitability, some individual markets did. In order of minimum net profit, Coffee, Live Hogs, and Random Lumber had positive returns.

The S&P 500, NYFE, Comex Gold, Corn, and the wheats had positive out-of-sample returns with in-sample losses. The index markets' profitability may have resulted from the strong trends that developed out-of-sample. Positive in-sample returns, associated with out-of-sample losses, were somewhat more common; T-Bonds, 10-Year Notes, Palladium, Feeder Cattle, Pork Bellies, Soybeans, Soybean Meal, Bean Oil, Oats, Orange Juice, and Cotton had this pattern. T-Bills, Silver, Platinum, Live Cattle, Cocoa, and Sugar lost in both samples. A correlation of 0.15 between net in-sample and net out-of-sample profits implies markets that traded well in the optimization period tended to trade well in the verification period.

CONCLUSION

No technique, except restricting the model to the currencies, improved results enough to overcome transaction costs in the out-of-sample period. Of course, many techniques and combinations were not tested (e.g., the long-only restriction was tested only with the volatility breakout and not with the HHLL breakout, a better out-of-sample performer), although they might have been effective. In both samples, all models evidenced deterioration over time that cannot be attributed to overoptimization. Breakout models of the kind studied here no longer work, even though they once may have. This accords with the belief that there are fewer and fewer good trends to ride. Traders complain the markets are getting noisier and more countertrending, making it harder to succeed with trend-following methods. No wonder the countertrend limit entry works best!

Overall, simple breakout models follow the aforementioned pattern and do not work very well in today's efficient markets. However, with the right combination of model, entry order, and markets, breakouts can yield at least moderate profits. There are many variations on breakout models, many trend filters beyond the ADX, and many additional ways to improve trend-following systems that have not been examined. Hopefully, however, we have provided you with a good overview of popular breakout techniques and a solid foundation on which to begin your own investigations.

WHAT HAVE WE LEARNED?

- If possible, use a limit order to enter the market. The markets are noisy and usually give the patient trader an opportunity to enter at a better price; this is the single most important thing one can do to improve a system's profitability. Controlling transaction costs with limit orders can make a huge difference in the performance of a breakout model. Even an unsophisticated limit entry, such as the one used in the tests, can greatly improve trading results. A more sophisticated limit entry strategy could undoubtedly provide some very substantial benefits to this kind of trading system.

- Focus on support and resistance, fundamental verities of technical analysis that are unlikely to be "traded away." The highest-high/lowest-low breakout held up better in the tests than other models, even though it did not always produce the greatest returns. Stay away from popular volatility breakouts unless they implement some special twist that enables them to hold up, despite wide use.

■ Choose "trendy" markets to trade when using such trend-following models as breakouts. In the world of commodities, the currencies traditionally are good for trend-following systems. The tests suggest that the oils and Coffee are also amenable to breakout trading. Do not rely on indicators like the ADX for trendiness determination.

■ Use something better than the standard exit to close open positions. Better exit strategies are available, as will be demonstrated in Part III. A good exit can go a long way toward making a trading system profitable.

CHAPTER 6

Moving Average Models

Moving averages are included in many technical analysis software packages and written about in many publications. So popular are moving averages that in 1998, 5 of the 12 issues of *Technical Analysis of Stocks and Commodities* contained articles about them. Newspapers often show a 50-day moving average on stock charts, and a 20-day moving average on commodities charts.

WHAT IS A MOVING AVERAGE?

To help understand moving averages, it is first necessary to discuss *time series*, i.e., series of data points that are chronologically ordered. The daily closing prices for a commodity are one example: They form a string of "data points" or "bars" that follow one another in time. In a given series, a sample of consecutive data points may be referred to as a "time window." If the data points (e.g., closing prices) in a given time window were added together, and the sum divided by the number of data points in the sample, an "average" would result. A *moving average* is when this averaging process is repeated over and over as the sampling period is advanced, one data point at a time, through the series. The averages themselves form a new time series, a set of values ordered by time. The new series is referred to as "the moving average of the original or underlying time series" (in this case, the moving average of the close). The type of moving average just described is known as a *simple moving average*, since the average was computed by simply summing the data points in the time window, giving each point equal weight, and then dividing by the number of data points summed.

PURPOSE OF A MOVING AVERAGE

A moving average is used to reduce unwanted noise in a time series so that the underlying behavior, unmasked by interference, can be more clearly perceived; it serves as a *data smoother*. As a smoothing agent, a moving average is a rudimentary *low-pass filter*, i.e., a filter that permits low frequency activity to pass through unimpeded while blocking higher frequency activity. In the time domain, high frequency activity appears as rapid up-and-down jiggles, i.e., noise, and low frequency activity appears as more gradual trends or undulations. Ehlers (1989) discusses the relationship between moving averages and low-pass filters. He provides equations and compares several formal low-pass filters with various moving averages for their usefulness. Moving averages may be used to smooth any time series, not just prices.

THE ISSUE OF LAG

Besides their ability to decrease the amount of noise in a time series, moving averages are versatile, easy to understand, and readily calculated. However, as with any well-damped low-pass filter or real-time data smoothing procedure, reduced noise comes at a cost: *lag*. Although smoothed data may contain less noise and, therefore, be easier to analyze, there will be a delay, or "lag," before events in the original time series appear in the smoothed series. Such delay can be a problem when a speedy response to events is essential, as is the case for traders.

Sometimes lag is not an issue, e.g., when a moving average of one time series is predictive of another series. This occurs when the predictor series leads the series to be predicted enough to compensate for the lag engendered by the moving average. It is then possible to benefit from noise reduction without the cost of delay. Such a scenario occurs when analyzing solar phenomena and seasonal tendencies. Also, lag may not be a serious problem in models that enter when prices cross a moving average line: In fact, the price must lead the moving average for such models to work. Lag is more problematic with models that use the slope or turning points in the average to make trading decisions. In such cases, lag means a delayed response, which, in turn, will probably lead to unprofitable trades.

A variety of adaptive moving averages and other sophisticated smoothing techniques have been developed in an effort to minimize lag without giving up much noise reduction. One such technique is based on standard time series forecasting methods to improve moving averages. To eliminate lag, Mulloy (1994) implements a linear, recursive scheme involving multiple moving averages. When the rate of movement in the market is appropriate to the filter, lag is eliminated; however, the filters tend to "overshoot" (an example of insufficient damping) and deteriorate when market behavior deviates from filter design specifications. Chande (1992) took a nonlinear approach, and developed a moving average that adapts to the market on the basis of volatility. Sometimes lag can be controlled or eliminated by combining several moving averages to create a band-pass filter. Band-pass filters can have effectively zero lag for signals with periodicities near the center of the pass-band; the smoothed signal can be coincident with the original, noisy signal when there is cyclic activity and when the frequency (or periodicity) of the cyclic activity is close to the frequency maximally passed by the filter.

TYPES OF MOVING AVERAGES

All moving averages, from the simple to the complex, smooth time series data by some kind of averaging process. They differ in how they weigh the sample points that are averaged and in how well they adapt to changing conditions. The differences between moving averages arose from efforts to reduce lag and increase responsiveness. The most popular moving averages (equations below) are the *simple moving average*, the *exponential moving average*, and the *front-weighted triangular moving average*. Less popular is Chande's *adaptive moving average* (1992).

$$a_i = \left(\sum_{k=0}^{m} = s_{i-k} \right) / m \qquad\qquad \text{Simple}$$

$$a_i = \left(\sum_{k=0}^{i} c^k s_{i-k} \right) / \left(\sum_{k=0}^{i} c^k \right) \qquad\qquad \text{Exponential}$$

$$a_i = \left[\sum_{k=0}^{2m} (2m + 1 - k)\, s_{i-k} \right] / \left(\sum_{k=0}^{2m} (2m + 1 - k) \right) \quad \text{Front-weighted triangular}$$

In the equations, a_i represents the moving average at the i-th bar, s_i the i-th bar or data point of the original time series, m the period of the moving average, and c (normally set to $2 / (m + 1)$) is a coefficient that determines the effective period for the exponential moving average. The equations show that the moving averages differ in how the data points are weighted. In a simple moving average, all data points receive equal weight or emphasis. Exponential moving averages give more weight to recent points, with the weights decreasing "exponentially" with distance into the past. The front-weighted triangular moving average weighs the more recent points more heavily, but the weights decline in a linear fashion with time; TradeStation calls this a "weighted moving average," a popular misnomer.

Adaptive moving averages were developed to obtain a speedier response. The goal was to have the moving average adapt to current market behavior, much as Dolby noise reduction adapts to the level of sound in an audio signal: Smoothing increases when the market exhibits mostly noise and little movement (more noise attenuation during quiet periods), and smoothing declines (response quickens) during periods of more significant market activity (less noise suppression during loud passages). There are several adaptive moving averages. One that seems to work well was developed by Mark Jurik (www.jurikres.com). Another was "VIDYA" (Variable Index Dynamic Moving Average) developed by Chande.

A recursive algorithm for the exponential moving average is as follows: For each bar, a coefficient (c) that determines the effective length (m) of the moving average is multiplied by the bar now being brought into the average and, to the result, is added $1.0 - c$ multiplied by the existing value of the moving average, yielding an updated value. The coefficient c is set to $2.0 / (1.0 + m)$ where m is the desired length or period. Chande (1992) modified this algorithm by changing the coefficient (c) from a fixed number to a number determined by current market volatility, the market's "loudness," as measured by the standard deviation of the prices over some number of past bars. Because the standard deviation can vary greatly between markets, and the measure of volatility needs to be relative, Chande divided the observed standard deviation on any bar by the average of the standard deviations over all bars on the S&P 500. For each bar, he recomputed the coefficient c in the recursive algorithm as $2.0 / (1.0 + m)$ multiplied by the relative volatility, thus creating a moving average with a length that dynamically responds to changes in market activity.

We implemented an adaptive moving average based on VIDYA that does not require a fixed adjustment (in the form of an average of the standard deviations over all bars) to the standard deviation. Because markets can change dramatically in their average volatility over time, and do so in a way that is irrelevant to the adaptation of the moving average, a fixed normalization did not seem sound. We replaced the standard deviation divided by the normalizing factor (used by Chande) with a ratio of two measures of volatility: one shorter term and one longer term. The relative volatility required for adjusting c, and hence the period of the adaptive moving average, was obtained by dividing the shorter term volatility measure by the longer term volatility measure. The volatility measures were exponential moving averages of the squared differences between successive data points. The shorter moving average of squared deviations was set to a period of p, an adjustable parameter, while the period of the longer moving average was set to p multiplied by four. If the longer term volatility is equal to the most recent volatility (i.e., if their ratio is 1), then the adaptive moving average behaves identically to a standard exponential moving average with period m; however, the effective period of the exponential moving average is monotonically reduced with an increasing ratio of short-term to long-term volatility, and increased with a declining ratio of short-term to long-term volatility.

TYPES OF MOVING AVERAGE ENTRY MODELS

A *moving average entry model* generates entries using simple relationships between a moving average and price, or between one moving average and another. Trend-following and countertrend models exist. The most popular models follow the trend and lag the market. Conversely, countertrend moving average models anticipate reversals and lead, or coincide with, the market. This is not to imply that countertrend systems trade better than trend-following ones. Consistently entering trends, even if late in their course, may be a more reliable way to make money than anticipating reversals that only sometimes occur when expected. Because of the need for a standard exit, and because no serious trader would trade without the protection of money management stops, simple moving average models that are always in the market are not tested. This kind of moving average reversal model will, however, be fairly well-approximated when fast moving averages are used, causing reversal signals to occur before the standard exit closes out the trades.

Trend-following entries may be generated in many ways using moving averages. One simple model is the *moving average crossover*: The trader buys when prices cross above the moving average and sells when they cross below. Instead of waiting for the raw prices to cross a moving average, the trader can wait for a faster moving average to cross a slower one: A buy signal occurs when the faster moving average crosses above the slower moving average, and a sell is signalled when the crossover is in the other direction. Smoothing the raw price series with a fast moving average reduces spurious crossovers and, consequently, minimizes whipsaws.

Moving averages can also be used to generate countertrend entries. Stock prices often react to a moving average line as they would to the forces of support or resistance; this forms the basis of one countertrend entry model. The rules are to buy when prices touch or penetrate the moving average from above, and to sell when penetration is from below. Prices should bounce off the moving average, reversing direction. Countertrend entries can also be achieved by responding in a contrary manner to a standard crossover: A long position is taken in response to prices crossing below a moving average, and a short position taken when prices cross above. Being contrary—doing the opposite of what seems "right"—often works when trading: It can be profitable to sell into demand and buy when prices drop in the face of heavy selling. Since moving averages lag the market, by the time a traditional buy signal is given, the market may be just about to reverse direction, making it time to sell, and vice versa.

Using a moving average in a countertrend model based on support and resistance is not original. Alexander (1993) discussed retracement to moving average support after a crossover as one way to set up an entry. Tilley's (1998) discussion of a two parameter moving average model, which uses the idea of support and resistance to trade mutual funds, is also relevant. Finally, Sweeney (1998) described the use of an end-of-day moving average to define intraday levels of support and resistance.

CHARACTERISTICS OF MOVING AVERAGE ENTRIES

A trend-following moving average entry is like a breakout: Intuitively appealing and certain to get the trader aboard any major trend; it is also a traditional, readily available approach that is easy to understand and implement, even in a spreadsheet. However, as with most trend-following methods, moving averages lag the market, i.e., the trader is late entering into any move. Faster moving averages can reduce lag or delay, but at the expense of more numerous whipsaws.

A countertrend moving average entry gets one into the market when others are getting out, before a new trend begins. This means better fills, better entry prices, and greater potential profits. Lag is not an issue in countertrend systems. The danger, however, is entering too early, before the market slows down and turns around. When trading a countertrend model, a good risk-limiting exit strategy is essential; one cannot wait for the system to generate an entry in the opposite direction. Some countertrend models have strong logical appeal, such as when they employ the concept of support and resistance.

ORDERS USED TO EFFECT ENTRIES

Entries based on moving averages may be effected with stops, limits, or market orders. While a particular entry order may work especially well with a particular model, any entry may be used with any model. Sometimes the entry order can form part of the entry signal or model. A basic crossover system can use a stop order priced at tomorrow's expected moving average value. To avoid intraday whipsaws, only a buy stop or a sell stop (not both) is issued for the next day. If the close is above, a sell stop is posted; if below, a buy stop.

Entry orders have their own advantages and disadvantages. A market order will never miss a signalled entry. A stop order will never miss a significant trend (in a trend-following model), and entry will never occur without confirmation by movement in favor of the trade; the disadvantages are greater slippage and less favorable entry prices. A limit order will get the best price and minimize transaction costs, but important trends may be missed while waiting for a retracement to the limit price. In countertrend models, a limit order may occasionally worsen the entry price: The entry order may be filled at the limit price, rather than at a price determined by the negative slippage that sometimes occurs when the market moves against the trade at the time of entry!

TEST METHODOLOGY

In all tests that follow, the standard portfolio is used. The number of contracts to buy or sell on entry, in any market, at any time, was chosen to approximate the dollar volatility of two S&P 500 contracts at the end of 1998. Exits are the standard ones. All tests are performed using the C-Trader toolkit. The portfolios, exit strategies, and test platform are identical to those used previously, making all results comparable. The tests are divided into trend-following and countertrend ones. They were run using a script containing instructions to set parameters, run optimizations, and generate output for each combination of moving average type, model, and entry order.

The code below is more complex than for breakouts: Instead of a different routine for each combination of moving average, entry rule, and trading order, there is one larger routine in which parameters control the selection of system elements. This technique is required when systems are genetically evolved. Although no genetics are used here, such algorithms are employed in later chapters. This code uses parameters to control model elements, making it easier to handle all the combinations tested in a clean, systematic way.

```
static void Model (float *parms, float *dt, float *opn, float *hi,
float *lo, float *cls, float *vol, float *oi, float *dlrv, int nb,
TRDSIM &ts, float *eqcls) {

    // Implements all moving average models to be tested.
    // File = x10mod01.c
    // parms    - vector [1..MAXPRM] of parameters
    // dt       - vector [1..nb] of dates in YYMMDD form
    // opn          - vector [1..nb] of opening prices
    // hi           - vector [1..nb] of high prices
    // lo       - vector [1..nb] of low prices
    // cls          - vector [1..nb] of closing prices
    // vol          - vector [1..nb] of volumes
    // oi           - vector [1..nb] of open interest numbers
    // dlrv         - vector [1..nb] of average dollar volatilities
    // nb           - number of bars in data series
    // ts           - trading simulator class instance
    // eqcls        - vector [1..nb] of closing equity levels

    // declare local scratch variables
    static int rc, cb, ncontracts, maxhold, fastmalen, slowmalen;
    static int modeltype, ordertype, avgtype, signal;
    static float mmstp, ptlim, stpprice, limprice, tmp;
    static float exitatr[MAXBAR+1];
    static float fastma[MAXBAR+1], slowma[MAXBAR+1];

    // copy parameters to local variables for clearer reference
    fastmalen = parms[1];    // period for faster moving average
    slowmalen = parms[2];    // period for slower moving average
    modeltype = parms[5];    // type of entry model
    avgtype   = parms[6];    // type of moving average
    ordertype = parms[7];    // type of entry order
    maxhold = 10;            // maximum holding period
    ptlim = 4;               // profit target in volatility units
    mmstp = 1;               // stop loss in volatility units
```

```
// skip invalid parameter combinations
if(fastmalen >= slowmalen) {
  set_vector(eqcls, 1, nb, 0.0);
  return;
}

// perform whole-series computations using vector routines
AvgTrueRangeS(exitatr, hi, lo, cls, 50, nb);  // ATR for exit
switch(avgtype) {  // select type of moving average
  case 1:   // simple moving averages
     AverageS(fastma, cls, fastmalen, nb);
     AverageS(slowma, cls, slowmalen, nb);
     break;
  case 2:   // exponential moving averages
     XAverageS(fastma, cls, fastmalen, nb);
     XAverageS(slowma, cls, slowmalen, nb);
     break;
  case 3:   // front-weighted triangular moving averages
     FWTAverageS(fastma, cls, fastmalen, nb);
     FWTAverageS(slowma, cls, slowmalen, nb);
     break;
  case 4:   // VIDYA-style adaptive moving averages
     VIAverageS(fastma, cls, fastmalen, 10, nb);
     VIAverageS(slowma, cls, slowmalen, 10, nb);
     break;
  default: nrerror("Invalid moving average selected");
};

// step through bars (days) to simulate actual trading
for(cb = 1; cb <= nb; cb++) {

  // take no trades before the in-sample period
  // ... same as TradeStation's MaxBarsBack setting
  if(dt[cb] < IS_DATE) { eqcls [cb] = 0.0; continue; }
  // execute any pending orders and store closing equity
  rc = ts.update(opn[cb], hi[cb], lo[cb], cls[cb], cb);
  if(rc != 0) nrerror("Trade buffer overflow");
  eqcls[cb] = ts.currentequity(EQ_CLOSETOTAL);

  // calculate number of contracts to trade
  // ... we want to trade the dollar volatility equivalent
  // ... of 2 new S&P-500 contracts as of 12/31/98
  ncontracts = RoundToInteger(5673.0 / dlrv[cb]);
  if(ncontracts < 1) ncontracts = 1;

  // avoid placing orders on possibly limit-locked days
  if(hi[cb+1] == lo[cb+1]) continue;

  // generate entry signals, stop prices and limit prices
  // using the specified moving average entry model
```

```
#define CrossesAbove(a,b,c)  (a[c]>=b[c]  && a[c-1]<b[c-1])
#define CrossesBelow(a,b,c)  (a[c]<b[c]  && a[c-1]>=b[c-1])
#define TurnsUp(a,c)  (a[c]>=a[c-1]  && a[c-1]<a[c-2])
#define TurnsDn(a,c)  (a[c]<a[c-1]  && a[c-1]>=a[c-2])
signal=0;
switch(modeltype) {
  case 1:   // classic trend-following crossover model
    if(CrossesAbove(fastma, slowma, cb)) signal = 1;
    else if(CrossesBelow(fastma, slowma, cb)) signal = -1;
    limprice = 0.5 * (hi[cb] + lo[cb]);
    stpprice = cls[cb] + 0.5 * signal * exitatr[cb];
    break;
  case 2:   // slope-based trend-following model
    if(TurnsUp(fastma, cb)) signal = 1;
    else if(TurnsDn(fastma, cb)) signal = -1;
    limprice = 0.5 * (hi[cb] + lo[cb]);
    stpprice = cls[cb] + 0.5 * signal * exitatr[cb];
    break;
  case 3:   // counter-trend crossover model
    if(CrossesAbove(fastma, slowma, cb)) signal = -1;
    else if(CrossesBelow(fastma, slowma, cb)) signal = 1;
    limprice = 0.5 * (hi[cb] + lo[cb]);
    stpprice = cls[cb] + 0.5 * signal * exitatr[cb];
    break;
  case 4:   // counter-trend support-resistance model
    if(slowma[cb] > slowma[cb-1]
       && CrossesBelow(fastma, slowma, cb)) signal = 1;
    else if(slowma[cb] < slowma[cb-1]
       && CrossesAbove(fastma, slowma, cb)) signal = -1;
    limprice = 0.5 * (hi[cb] + lo[cb]);
    stpprice = cls[cb] + 0.5 * signal * exitatr[cb];
    break;
  default: nrerror("Invalid model selected");
}
#undef CrossesAbove
#undef CrossesBelow
#undef TurnsUp
#undef TurnsDn

// enter trades using specified order type
if(ts.position() <= 0 && signal == 1) {
  switch(ordertype) {  // select desired order type
    case 1: ts.buyopen('1', ncontracts); break;
    case 2: ts.buylimit('2', limprice, ncontracts); break;
```

```
      case 3: ts.buystop('3', stpprice, ncontracts); break;
      default: nrerror("Invalid buy order selected");
   }
}
else if(ts.position() >= 0 && signal == -1) {
   switch(ordertype) {  // select desired order type
      case 1: ts.sellopen('4', ncontracts); break;
      case 2: ts.selllimit('5', limprice, ncontracts); break;
      case 3: ts.sellstop('6', stpprice, ncontracts); break;
      default: nrerror("Invalid sell order selected");
   }
}


// instruct simulator to employ standard exit strategy
tmp = exitatr[cb];
ts.stdexitcls('X', ptlim*tmp, mmstp*tmp, maxhold);


} // process next bar
}
```

The code contains three segments. The first segment calculates moving averages. A parameter (*avgtype*) selects the kind of average: 1 = simple; 2 = exponential; 3 = front-weighted triangular; and 4 = the modified VIDYA. Even if the model requires only one moving average, two of the same type are computed; this allows the selection of the moving average to be independent of model selection. The average true range is also computed and is required for setting stop-losses and profit targets in the standard exit strategy. Two additional parameters, *fastmalen* and *slowmalen*, specify the period of the faster and the slower moving averages, respectively. The moving averages are saved in the vectors *fastma* and *slowma*.

The next block uses the selected model to generate entry signals, stop prices, and limit prices. First, simple relationships (*CrossesAbove*, *CrossesBelow*, *TurnsUp*, and *TurnsDown*) are defined. Depending on *modeltype*, one of four moving average models then generates the signals: 1 = the classic, trend-following dual moving average crossover; 2 = a slope-based trend-following model; 3 = a countertrend crossover model; and 4 = a countertrend support/resistance model. In the classic, trend-following dual moving average crossover, the trader goes long if a faster moving average of the closing price crosses above a slower moving average, and goes short if the faster moving average crosses below the slower one. As a special case, this model contains the classic crossover that compares prices to a moving average. The special case is achieved when the period of the shorter moving average is set to 1, causing that moving average to decay to the original series, i.e., the closing prices. With a slope-based trend-following model, the trader buys when the moving average was decreasing on previous bars but increases on the current bar (slope turns up), and sells when the opposite occurs. This model requires only the fast moving average. The countertrend model is the opposite of the classic trend-following crossover: The trader buys when the shorter moving average (or the price itself) crosses below the longer moving average, and sells when it crosses above. This model is the contrarian's delight: Doing exactly the opposite of the trend-followers. Last is a crude countertrend support/resistance model in which prices are expected to bounce off the moving average, as if off a line of support or resistance. The rules are almost identical to the countertrend crossover model, except that the slower moving average must be moving in the direction of the entry: If the slower moving average is trending upward, and prices (or the faster moving average) move from above that slower moving average into or below it, the trader buys; conversely, if prices (or the faster moving average) are currently below a downward trending slower moving average, and prices bump into or penetrate that moving average from below, then the trader sells. The additional trend rule prevents an immediate reversal of position after contact or penetration. Without the trend rule, a quick penetration followed by a reversal would trigger two entries: The first would be the desired countertrend entry, occurring when the prices penetrate the moving average, and the second entry (in the opposite direction) would occur as the prices bounce back, again crossing the moving average. The trend check only allows entries to be taken in one direction at a time. A penetration, followed by a bounce in an up-trending market, will take the long entry; a penetration and reversal in a down-trending market will result in a short entry.

In the last block of code, the entry order to be posted is determined by the *ordertype* parameter: 1 = market at open; 2 = limit; 3 = stop. Whether a buy or sell is posted, or no order at all, is determined by whether any signal was generated in the previous block of code; a variable called *signal* carries this information: 1 = buy; − 1 = sell (go short); 0 = do nothing. The limit price (*limprice*) is computed as the sum of today's high and low prices divided by two. Because many of the models have no natural price for setting a stop, a standard stop was used. The standard entry stop price (*stpprice*) is obtained by taking the closing price of the previous bar and adding (if a long position is signalled) or subtracting (if a short is signalled) the 50-bar average true range multiplied by 0.50; the market must move at least one-half of its typical daily range, in the direction of the desired entry, for the entry to occur. This type of stop order adds a breakout test to the moving average system: Once a signal is given, the market must move a certain amount in the direction of the trade to trigger an entry. Because of the large number of tests, statistical significances were not reported unless something notable occurred.

TESTS OF TREND-FOLLOWING MODELS

The group of tests presented here involve moving averages as trend-followers. The models vary in the kinds of moving average, the rules that generate signals, and the orders posted to effect entry. The moving averages tested include the simple, the exponential, the front-weighted triangular, and a modification of VIDYA. Both single and dual moving average crossovers, and models that use slope (rather than crossover) to determine entry, are examined. Entry orders are market-at-open, stop, and limit.

Tests 1 through 12 were of the crossover models. Optimization was performed by stepping the length of the shorter moving average from 1 to 5, in increments of 1, and the longer moving average from 5 to 50, in increments of 5. Only cases in which the longer moving average was strictly longer than the shorter moving average were examined. Brute force optimization was used, controlled by the testing script. The parameters were chosen to maximize the risk-to-reward ratio or, equivalently, minimize the probability (based on a t-test of daily returns) that any profitable performance was due to chance. In Tests 13 through 24 (the slope models), brute-force optimization was performed by stepping the length of the first and, in this case, only moving average from 3 to 40, in increments of 1. As in Tests 1 through 12, the risk-to-reward ratio was maximized. Optimization was only carried out on in-sample data.

Tables 6-1 and 6-2 show, for each of the 24 tests, the specific commodities that the model traded profitably and those that lost, for the in-sample (Table 1) and out-of-sample (Table 6-2) runs. The *SYM* column represents the market being studied; the first row identifies the test. The data provides relatively detailed information about which markets were and were not profitable when traded by each of the models: One dash ($-$) indicates a moderate loss per trade, i.e., $2,000 to $4,000; two dashes (- -) represent a large loss per trade, i.e., $4,000 or more; one plus sign ($+$) means a moderate profit per trade, i.e., $1,000 to $2,000; two pluses ($++$) indicates a large gain per trade, i.e., $2,000 or more; a blank cell means that the loss was between $0 and $1,999 or the profit was between $0 and $1,000 per trade.

Table 6-3 shows, for the entire portfolio, the return-on-account (*ROA%*) and average dollars-per-trade (*$TRD*) broken down by the moving average, model, entry order, and sample. The last two columns on the right, and the last four rows of numbers on the bottom, are averages. The numbers at the bottom have been averaged over all combinations of moving average type and model. The numbers at the right are averaged over order type.

None of the trend-following moving average models was profitable on a portfolio basis. More detailed examination reveals that for the crossover models the limit order resulted in a dramatic benefit on the in-sample data. When compared with an entry at open or on a stop, the limit cut the loss of the average trade almost in half. Out-of-sample, the improvement was not as dramatic, but still significant. The return-on-account showed a similar pattern: The least loss was with the limit order. For slope models, the limit order worked best out-of-sample in terms of dollars per trade. The return-on-account was slightly better with a stop (due to distortions in the *ROA%* numbers when evaluating losing systems), and worse for entry at open. In-sample, the stop order performed best, but only by a trivial amount.

TABLE 6-1

In-Sample Performance Broken Down by Test and Market

SYM	01	02	03	04	05	06	07	08	09	10	11	12	13	14	15	16	17	18	19	20	21	22	23	24
SP		-			-			--	-						--						-			
YX	-		-		-	-		--				-			--	-					--			
US	-		+	-	-		-				-	-	-	-		-			-			-		-
TB	--	--	--	--	-	--	--	--	--	--	--	-	--		--	-	--	--			--	--		--
TY	-			-	+	-	--	--	--	-		-	-		--				-	-		-	-	
BP		++		+				--				-			++					+				
DM					+			--				-			++		-	+						
SF	-	-	++		+		++	++	+	+	++	+			++		+			-		-		-
JY	+	+	++		+	+	++	++	+		-			+	+						+			+
CD		+	--		+	-	+	+	+	-		--		-	-	-	-	-						--
ED	--		--	-		-	-	-	-	-					-	-	-			--			--	-
CL				-	--				-			++						+				-	-	+
HO	-		--		+			-	+		+	--				-								
HU		+				-						-		-	+					-	-			-
GC		-	--				-	--	-		+	--			-		+	--			-			--
SI		-	-	-	-	-	--	--	-			-	--	-	-	-	-	-			-	-		
PL			--			--		++		-		--			+	-		-				--	-	--
PA	-	-	+	-	-	--	-	--	+	--	-					--	-	-	-	-		-	--	-
FC		-		+	++	++	++		+		++		-		-					+				-
LC				+		-															+			+
LH	+			+		+	++	+	++		+	+		-			-	+		-			-	+
PB	+	++		+	++		+	++			++	+			++			+		--	+		+	+
S		+			+	-		--	-												-	-	-	
SM		-		-	--		-	-	--	--	--	-			-	-	-		-	--		-	--	
BO	--	-		-	-		-		-	-		++			+			-						
C	-	-	--	-	--		-	--		--		--	-	-	--	--	-	--		-		--	--	--
O	--	--	--	--	--	--	--	-		--		-	--		-	--	--	--	--	-		-	--	-
W		+			--	-	-			+	--		-	-	-						-	-		-
KW			-	-			+	+		-	-				-	-	-	-		--		-	-	-
MW		+	+				--	--				-		-			--	+		-	+		--	+
KC	--	-	+	-			++		++			-	+							-	+	-		+
CC			-	-			+	-		-			-											
SB	-		+							-		++	-			-	-	-	-	-		-	-	-
JO						--	++		-			-				-		-		-		-	-	-
CT	-		--	-		--	--	-	-			--					-	+	-			--	-	-
LB		++	++		+				+			++			+			-			+	-	-	-

In-sample, the simple moving average provided the best results in average dollars-per-trade. The worst results were for the adaptive moving average. The other two moving averages fell in-between, with the exponential better in the crossover models, and the front-weighted triangular in the slope models. Of the crossover models, the *ROA%* was also the best for the simple moving average. Overall, the crossover models did as well or better than the slope models, possibly because of a faster response to market action in the former. Out-of-sample, the simple moving average was the clear winner for the crossover models, while the front-weighted triangular was the best for the slope models. In terms of the

TABLE 6-2

Out-of-Sample Performance Broken Down by Test and Market

SYM	01	02	03	04	05	06	07	08	09	10	11	12	13	14	15	16	17	18	19	20	21	22	23	24
SP	+	+	--		--	-	+		++	+		--			-			--		-	--		--	--
YX	+	-	--		-	--	++	++	++	+	++	--			--	+		-		-			-	-
US	--	--	--	--	--	-	-	--	+	--	-	-	-		--	-	++	-	-	+	+		+	--
TB	--	--	--	--	--	--	--	--	--	-	+	--	--	--	--	--	--	--	--	--	--	--	--	--
TY	--	--	--	--	--	--	--	--	--	--	--	-	--	--	--		-	-	-			--	-	
BP	-	-	+		--	-	--		--	-	-	+	+							+		+	+	
DM				--					++	+					--		-		-	-	-		-	
SF			++	+		--	-	--	--			-		+		-				+			-	-
JY	++		++	++	+	++	++	++		++	++	++	+		++	+	++	+	+	+	++	+	+	+
CD	--	--		--	--	--		+	-	-	-	--		++	--	-		--	--	-	-	-	-	--
ED	--	--	--	--	--	--	--	--	--	--	--	--	--	--	--	--	--	--	--	+	--	--	--	--
CL		--		--		++	++	++				-			-			-	-	-		-	-	
HO		+	-	++	+	-	+	+	-	++	+	++	+	+	--			++	+	+	++		-	
HU			--	++	+	++	++	++	++						--	+	++	+	+			+		
GC	--	--	-	-		-	--	--	-	--	--		-			-	--		-			-	-	--
SI	+	+	+		++		-		-	-		+			-			-			++	-		
PL		++			-	--	--	--	--	+	++				--			-	--		-	-	-	-
PA	+		--	+	--			++	++	-	++	++	+		++					--	++	-		
FC		+	--	-	--	-	--	--			-	--	-	-	--		--		-	-	-	-	--	-
LC	-	+	--					--			--	--	-		--	-		-	-			-		-
LH	++	++	++	++	++	++	++	++	--	++	++	+			--			++	++		++		-	++
PB		+	++			++	--	++	--		--	+	+					++		++		+	-	++
S	-		-		--	++	--	--	--	--	-	--			+		+	+		-	++		+	
SM			+	++	+		++	-		+	+	+			+		++	+	++	+	++		++	+
BO		-		-	++		--	++		-	-				--					+				+
C	-		--	-	-	-	-		--	-	-	--		+	++			--	-	--	-	-		
O	--	--	-	--		--	--		--	-	--	-			--	-	-	-		--	-			--
W	+	+		+	++	++	+	++	+		+		+	-	++					+				+
KW	+		++	++	++	++	++	+	++					-	++	-	-		-	-	+			
MW		+		-	--		++	-	--	--					--	-	-		-	--	-	-		
KC	++	++	++	++	++	++	++	++	+	+	++	++	++	++	+			+	+			+		
CC		--	--	-		+		+	--	-		-	-		--			-	-		-		--	-
SB		+	++	+	-	+		+			+	-		+	-						--	-		--
JO	--	--	-	-		-	--	-	-	-	+	-		+	-		--	-	-	--	+	-	--	--
CT				--	++		--	++	-	--	+	-	--		-					-	++			
LB		++		+	+	+	-	-			--							--						

ROA%, the exponential moving average appeared the best for the crossover models, with the front-weighted triangular still the best for the slope models.

When looking at individual tests, the particular combination of a front-weighted triangular moving average, the slope model, and entry on stop (Test 21) produced the best out-of-sample performance of all the systems tested. The out-of-sample results for the front-weighted triangular slope models seemed to be better across all order types. There apparently were some strong interactions between the various factors across all tests, e.g., for the crossover model on the in-sample data, entry at the open was consistently close to the worst, entry on stop was somewhere in between, and entry on limit was always best, regardless of the moving average

TABLE 6-3

Performance of Trend-Following Moving Average Entry Models
Broken Down by Order, Moving Average Type, Model, and Sample

Model		In-sample			Out-of-sample			Average In	Average Out
		Open	Limit	Stop	Open	Limit	Stop	In	Out
SMA	ROA%	-9.4	-7.5	-6.5	-23.0	-21.4	-19.7	-7.8	-21.4
Cross	$TRD	-1765	-926	-1045	-1628	-1213	-1337	-1245.3	-1392.7
EMA	ROA%	-9.2	-7.5	-9.1	-20.4	-22.4	-19.9	-8.6	-20.9
Cross	$TRD	-1570	-705	-1534	-1269	-1755	-1223	-1269.7	-1415.7
FWTMA	ROA%	-9.3	-8.2	-9.2	-21.6	-18.0	-23.4	-8.9	-21.0
Cross	$TRD	-1666	-890	-1720	-1984	-1265	-2715	-1425.3	-1988.0
AMA	ROA%	-9.6	-7.1	-8.3	-22.5	-19.0	-23.5	-8.3	-21.7
Cross	$TRD	-1942	-769	-1731	-1798	-1071	-2350	-1480.7	-1739.7
SMA	ROA%	-10.1	-8.7	-9.5	-22.4	-19.2	-23.8	-9.4	-21.8
Slope	$TRD	-1667	-906	-1076	-1083	-615	-2528	-1216.3	-1408.7
EMA	ROA%	-10.1	-9.6	-8.5	-23.1	-20.5	-20.5	-9.4	-21.4
Slope	$TRD	-2137	-1629	-1289	-1714	-1096	-1199	-1685.0	-1336.3
FWTMA	ROA%	-10.0	-9.3	-8.0	-23.4	-19.2	-3.5	-9.1	-15.4
Slope	$TRD	-1842	-1365	-1203	-1647	-1561	-91	-1470.0	-1099.7
AMA	ROA%	-10.1	-9.6	-8.7	-23.4	-22.9	-23.0	-9.5	-23.1
Slope	$TRD	-2353	-1531	-1603	-1872	-1391	-2002	-1829.0	-1755.0
Crossover Models									
Average ROA%		-9.4	-7.6	-8.3	-21.9	-20.2	-21.6	-8.4	-21.2
Average $TRD		-1736	-823	-1508	-1670	-1326	-1906	-1355	-1634
Slope Models									
Average ROA%		-10	-9	-9	-23	-20	-18	-9	-20
Average $TRD		-2000	-1358	-1293	-1579	-1166	-1455	-1550	-1400

used. Out-of-sample, the findings were much more mixed: With the simple moving average, the pattern was similar to that for the in-sample period; however, with the exponential moving average, the limit performed worst, the stop best, and the open not far behind. Out-of-sample, with the front-weighted triangular average, the stop performed by far the worst, with the limit back to the best performer. These results indicate interaction between the moving average, entry order, and time.

The slope model, in-sample, had the entry at open always performing worst; however, although the results were often quite close, the limit and stop orders were twice seen with the limit being favored (simple moving average and adjusted moving average), and twice with the stop being favored (exponential moving average and front-weighted triangular moving average). As before, great variation was seen out-of-sample.

For the simple moving average, the limit order performed best and the stop worst. The more typical pattern was seen for the exponential moving average: The entry at open performed worst, the limit best, and the stop was on the heels of the limit. As already stated, the front-weighted triangular moving average performed very unusually when combined with the stop order. The limit was best for the adaptive moving average, the stop was worst, and the open was slightly better albeit very close to the stop.

As a whole, these models lost on most markets. Only the Japanese Yen and Pork Bellies were profitable both in- and out-of-sample; no other markets were profitable in-sample. Out-of-sample, some profits were observed for Heating Oil, Unleaded Gasoline, Palladium, Live Hogs, Soybean Meal, Wheat, and Coffee. The strong out-of-sample profit for Coffee can probably be explained by the major run-up during the drought around that time. On an individual model-order basis, many highly profitable combinations could be found for Live Hogs, Japanese Yen, Pork Bellies, Coffee, and Lumber. No combinations were profitable in either sample for Oats.

In terms of equity averaged over all averages and models, entry at the open performed, by far, the worst. Entry on limit or stop produced results that were close, with the limit doing somewhat better, especially early in the test period. It should be noted that, with the equity curves of losing systems, a distortion takes place in their reflection of how well a system trades. (In our analyses of these losing systems, we focused, therefore, on the average return-per-trade, rather than on risk-reward ratios, return-on-account, or overall net profits.) The distortion involves the number of trades taken: A losing system that takes fewer trades will appear to be better than a losing system that takes more trades, even if the better appearing system takes trades that lose more on a per-trade basis. The very heavy losses with entry at open may not be a reflection of the bad quality of this order; it may simply be reflecting that more trades were taken with an entry at the open than when a stop or limit order was used.

Figure 6-1 presents the equity curves for all eight model and moving average combinations. The equity curves were averaged across order type. Figure 6-1 provides a useful understanding of how the systems interact with time. Most of the systems had their heaviest losses between late 1988 and early 1995. The best performance occurred before 1988, with the performance in the most recent period being intermediate. In Curve 3, the simple moving average crossover model was the most outstanding: This pattern was greatly exaggerated, making the equity curve appear very distinct; it actually showed a profit in the early period, a heavier relative loss in the middle period, and levelled off (with a potential return to flat or profitable behavior) toward the end of the third period. Finally, it is dramatically evident that the crossover systems (Curves 1 through 4) lost much less heavily than the

FIGURE 6-1

Equity Curves for Each Model and Moving Average Combination

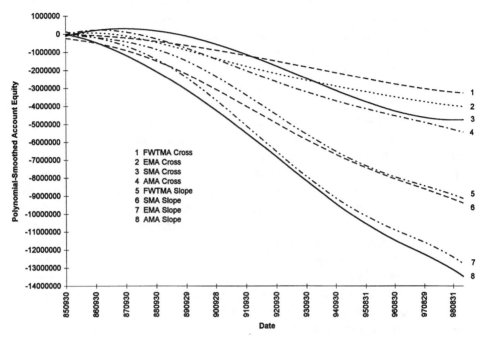

slope-based models (Curves 5 through 8), although this reflects a larger number of trades, not greater losses on a per trade basis.

TESTS OF COUNTER-TREND MODELS

As with trend-following models, countertrend models vary in the moving averages used, the rules that generate signals, and the orders posted to effect entry. The same moving averages used in the trend-following models are studied here. Both single and dual moving average models are examined. Entry orders studied are the market-at-open, stop, and limit.

Tests 25 through 36 evaluate the standard moving average crossover model turned upside-down. As before, entry signals occur when prices cross the average, or when a shorter average crosses a longer one. In traditional trend-following crossover models, the trader buys when the price (or a shorter moving average) crosses above a longer moving average, and sells when it crosses below. In the *contrarian crossover model*, the trader sells when prices cross above, and buys when prices cross below. In these tests, brute force optimization was performed on the in-sample data by stepping the length of the shorter moving average from 1 to 7, in increments of 1; the longer moving average was stepped from 5 to 50, in increments of 5. Only cases where the longer moving average was longer than the shorter moving average were considered. The parameters minimized the probability that any observed profitable performance was due to chance. The model was run on the out-of-sample data using the best parameter set found in-sample.

In tests of the support/resistance model (37 through 48), the trader buys when prices bounce off a moving average from above, and sells when they hit a moving average from below. In this way, the moving average serves as a line of support or resistance where prices tend to reverse. The rules are almost the same as for Tests 25 through 36, except that not every penetration of a moving average results in an entry. If prices are above the moving average and penetrate it, a buy is generated; however, when prices bounce back up through the moving average, the second crossover is not allowed to trigger a sell. If prices are below the moving average and rise into it, a sell is triggered; no buy is triggered when the prices bounce back down. This behavior is achieved by adding one element to the contrarian crossover model: A signal is generated only if it is in the direction of the slope of the slower moving average. Performance was brute force optimized on the in-sample data by stepping the length of the shorter moving average from 1 to 5, in increments of 1, and the longer moving average from 5 to 50, in increments of 5. A moving average length of 1 caused the shorter moving average to become equivalent to the prices; therefore, in the optimization, the model in which prices were compared to the moving average was tested, as was the model in which one moving average was compared to another. Only cases where the longer moving average was strictly longer than the shorter moving average were examined. The parameters were chosen to minimize the probability that any profitable performance was due to chance. The model was then run on the out-of-sample data using the best parameter set found in-sample.

Tables 6-4 and 6-5 show, for Tests 25 through 48, the commodities that the model traded profitably and those that lost, in-sample (Table 6-4) and out-of-sample (Table 6-5). The plus and dash symbols may be interpreted in the same manner as for Tables 6-1 and 6-2.

Table 6-6 provides the results broken down by the moving average, model, order, and sample. The last two columns on the right, and the last four rows of numbers on the bottom, are averages. The numbers at the bottom were averaged over all combinations of moving average type and model. The numbers at the right were averaged over order type.

Overall, the best models in-sample were the simple moving average support/resistance and the front-weighted triangular average support/resistance. The simple average support/resistance with a stop order was unique in that it showed small profits in both samples: an average trade of $227 and a 4.2% return-on-account in-sample, $482 per trade and a 14.8% return-on-account out-of-sample. The front-weighted triangular average with the stop was profitable in-sample, but lost heavily out-of-sample. Both models, especially when combined with a stop, had relatively few trades; consequently, the results are less statistically stable.

TABLE 6-4

In-Sample Performance Broken Down by Test and Market

SYM	25	26	27	28	29	30	31	32	33	34	35	36	37	38	39	40	41	42	43	44	45	46	47	48
SP		+	+	-		-	-	-	-										--		++			
YX	-		+		+				--				-	-	--				-		++			
US			+	-	-	+	--	--		-			-		++					+	+			
TB	--	--	-	--	--	--	--	--	--	--	--	--	--	-	--				--	++				
TY	--	--		-	-	--	--	--		-	-	--	--	-	++				-		--			
BP	-		++	-		+														++	++			
DM	+	+			+			+	--			+	++	++	--				++		++			
SF							-				-	+		-	++				++	-	++			
JY								-		++	+	++	++	++					++					
CD	-		-	-		--		-	--	-		-	--		+				--		-			
ED	--	--	--	--	--	--	--	--	+	--	--	--	--	--					--		--			
CL				+			-	-	+	+	+	++			-				-	++				
HO		+	++		+				++				++	+	++				++		++			
HU	+	++		+	+								--	-					-	++	-			
GC	-	-	-	--	-	--			-	--	--	-		-	--				-		--			
SI	-	-	-			+	++	+	-	-	--	-			+				-		--			
PL	-	-	--				-		-	++	++	-		+	-				+	--	+			
PA				+	+					++	+		+		--				--		--			
FC			-		-		--	--	--		-	--		++	--				++		++			
LC	-		++	-		+	-		+	-	-		++	++	++				++	-	++			
LH	-		-		--	--	--	--	-		-		+		-				-		--			
PB	--	--	++	-		++	-					++	+		++				++	-	-			
S	-		-	-		-			-	-		--	--							--	++			
SM	--	--		--	-	--	-	+	-	-	-	--	-	--	--				--		--			
BO			--	-	-	+						+	++	++							--			
C	-		--	-			-	-	--				--	--	--				--					
O	--	--	-	-			--	--	-	--	--	--	--	--	-				--	+	+			
W			-		-				--	--	-		--	--					--		--			
KW	--	--	-	-			--	--	-			++	-						-	+	++			
MW	-	--	++	--	--	-	-	-		-	--	-	--	-					--		--			
KC			-			-			+	-			++	++					++	++	++			
CC	-	-		-	--		-		++	-		+	+	+	++				++	-	+			
SB	--	--	-	--	--	--	-	-	--	--	--	--	-	--	++				++	++	++			
JO			+	+			-	++			++			++					--	-				
CT		+		+			+					+	++						+	++	++			
LB				-	-								-		+				-		++			

Overall, in-sample, the stop order was best for contrarian crossovers and for support/resistance models, in which the stop led to an average profitable result, and the other two orders led to losses; the market-at-open was the worst order. Out-of-sample, the market-at-open order was still, overall, worst for both the contrarian crossover and the support/resistance models; the limit was best. There were much greater losses out-of-sample than in-sample for both models.

The countertrend models performed less well than the trend-following ones; however, there were outstanding combinations of counter-trend model, average type, and entry order that performed far better than most other combinations tested.

On the basis of the moving average and breakout results, it appears that, with trend-following models, a limit order almost always helps performance; for

TABLE 6-5

Out-of-Sample Performance Broken Down by Test and Market

SYM	25	26	27	28	29	30	31	32	33	34	35	36	37	38	39	40	41	42	43	44	45	46	47	48
SP	-			++	++	++	+		+	++	++	++	++	+	++	++				++	++			
YX		++	+		++	-		-	++	++	++	++	++	++	++				-	-				
US	-	-	-		-	+	++				+	-		++				-		--				
TB	--	--		-	--	--	--		-	--	--	--	--	--					--					
TY	--	--	--	-		--	-	--	--		-	--		-	++				-	++	+			
BP	-	--				++	+	-				-	-	--					--	-	--			
DM	-		++		+			+	+		--		+	+	-					++	++			
SF	+	++	--			--	+	+	-		-	-	-	+	-				++		--			
JY		++		-			--	--			+	+	++	++	++				++	++	++			
CD	-	-	-		++	--			--		+		--		--				--	--	--			
ED	--	--	--	--	--	--	--	--	--	--	--	--	--	-	--				--	++	--			
CL	--	--	--	-	+	--	--	-	-			--	-	--	++				--	++	--			
HO		--	--	--	--	--	-				-		- ·						--		--			
HU	-	--		--	-	-	--	--	--	--			--		++				+	++				
GC	--		--	-	-				--			+		-						--	-			
SI	--	--		--	--	--			++	--	--		++	++					--		++			
PL		+	-			--	++	++	--	-	-	--		-	+				--		++			
PA		++		+	--		+	-				--	++		++						++			
FC	+		-		+				-	-			--	-	++				--	++				
LC	--	--				-	--		++			-	-								--			
LH	-	-		--	--		--	--	--	--	--								--		--			
PB	-	-		-	-	+	++	++	+	-	-	++	--	--						--	-			
S	--	++	--		-				++	++	+	--	+						++	-	--			
SM	+	+	+	--	--	--	--	-	++	--	--		--	--	-				++		+			
BO	-	-	++	+	+		+	+	+		+		-	-	+				-		++			
C	-		-		-		+	+	-	--	--		--	+					-	+	--			
O	-	+		--	--	--	-		--	--	--								++	--	--			
W	--	--	+	--	-		-		-	--		--	--	++					++	++	--			
KW	--	--	++	-	-	--	-	-	-			--	-	++					++	++	+			
MW	-	-	+	+	+	-	--	--	--				-	--					+	++	++			
KC	-	--	++	--	--	-	-	-		-	-		-	--					++	--				
CC	--	--	--	--		--		--	--		--	--		--					--	--				
SB	-	-	-	--	--	--	-		++	--	--	-		+	-					--	+			
JO	+	++	--	+	+	++	+	+	-	-	-	+	++	+	++					--	++			
CT		+	-	-			+	+					--	-					++	--	--			
LB	-	-		-	-	++	--	-	--	-		-		-					++	--	--			

countertrend models, a stop sometimes provides an extra edge. This tendency might result from trend-following models already having a trend detection element: Adding another detection or verification element (such as an entry on a stop) is redundant, offering no significant benefit; however, the addition of a limit order provides a countertrend element and a cheaper entry, thus enhancing performance. With countertrend models, the addition of a trend verification element provides something new to the system and, therefore, improves the results. Sometimes it is so beneficial that it compensates for the less favorable entry prices that normally occur when using stops.

On a market-by-market basis, model-order combinations that were strongly profitable in both samples could be found for T-Bonds, 10-Year Notes, Japanese

TABLE 6-6

Summary of Countertrend Moving Average Entry Models Broken Down by Order, Moving Average Type, Model, and Sample

Model		In-sample				Out-of-sample			Average In	Average Out
		Open	Limit	stop		Open	Limit	Stop	In	Out
SMA-CC	ROA%	-10.2	-9.6	-9.5		-22.7	-20.7	-20.6	-9.8	-21.3
	$TRD	-2220	-1630	-1120		-3221	-1917	-1731	-1657	-2290
EMA-CC	ROA%	-10.1	-10.1	-9.1		-22.8	-22.5	-23.1	-9.8	-22.8
	$TRD	-2350	-1905	-1171		-2471	-2214	-3128	-1809	-2604
FWTMA-CC	ROA%	-9.7	-9.1	-8.5		-20.9	-16.7	-19.9	-9.1	-19.2
	$TRD	-2405	-1869	-1246		-1821	-971	-1343	-1840	-1378
AMA-CC	ROA%	-10.3	-10.3	-9.5		-23.0	-22.8	-20.8	-10.0	-22.2
	$TRD	-1865	-1488	-1033		-2222	-2254	-1604	-1462	-2027
SMA-SR	ROA%	-9.6	-10.2	4.2		-20.4	-16.9	14.8	-5.2	-7.5
	$TRD	-1099	-844	227		-1962	-1512	482	-572	-997
EMA-SR	ROA%	0	0	0		0	0	0	0	0
	$TRD	0	0	0		0	0	0	0	0
FWTMA-SR	ROA%	-8.1	-3.2	8.8		-13.2	-13.8	-22.3	-0.8	-16.4
	$TRD	-841	-261	1015		-1444	-1087	-3566	-29	-2032
AMA-SR	ROA%	0	0	0		0	0	0	0	0
	$TRD	0	0	0		0	0	0	0	0
CC Models										
Average	ROA%	-10.1	-9.8	-9.2		-22.4	-20.7	-21.1	-9.7	-21.4
Average	$TRD	-2210	-1723	-1143		-2434	-1839	-1952	-1691.8	-2074.8
SR Models										
Average	ROA%	-8.8	-6.7	6.5		-16.8	-15.4	-3.7	-3.0	-12.0
Average	$TRD	-970	-553	621		-1703	-1300	-1542	-300.5	-1514.8

Yen, Deutschemark, Swiss Franc, Light Crude, Unleaded Gasoline, Coffee, Orange Juice, and Pork Bellies.

Figure 6-2 depicts equity curves broken down by model and moving average combination; equity was averaged over order type. The best two models were the front-weighted triangular average support/resistance and the simple average support/resistance. The best support/resistance models performed remarkably better than any of the contrarian crossover models. There were three eras of distinct behavior: the beginning of the sample until October 1987, October 1987 until June 1991, and June 1991 through December 1998, the end of the sample. The worst performance was in the last period.

FIGURE 6-2

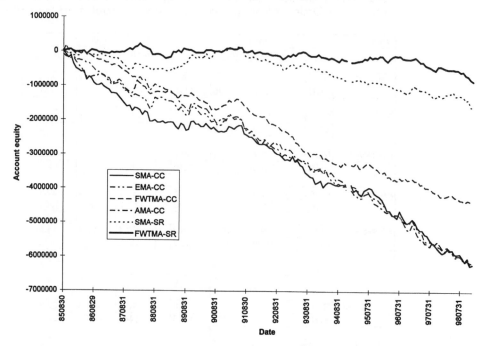

Equity Curves by Model and Moving Average Combination

On the basis of the equity curves in Figure 6-2, as well as others not shown, it is evident that the countertrend models were better in the past, while the trend-following models performed better in recent times. In-sample, the stop order was best for every model-average combination, and, out-of-sample, for three of the six (two combinations had no trades so were not considered); entry at the open was worst in all but two cases. The stop was generally superior to the limit order, in-sample; out-of-sample, the limit was only marginally better than the stop.

CONCLUSION

In general, the trend-following models in Tests 1 through 24 performed better than the countertrend models in Tests 25 through 48, with a number of exceptions discussed above.

The best models apparently are those that combine both countertrend and trend-following elements. For example, attempting to buy on a retracement with a limit, after a moving average crossover or breakout, provides better results than other combinations. In the countertrend moving average models, those that have a trend-following element (e.g., a stop) perform better. Pure countertrend models and pure trend-following models do not fare as well. Moreover, adding a trend-following filter to an already trend-following system does not seem beneficial, but may instead increase entry cost. Traders should try combining one of these countertrend models with something like the ADX trend filter. Although the ADX filter may not have helped breakouts (because, like the stop, it represents another trend-following element added to an already trend-following model), in a countertrend model such an element may provide an edge. As true with breakouts, the limit order performed best, except when the stop was beneficial due to its trend filtering characteristics.

The results suggest certain generalizations. Sometimes a stop can provide enough benefit to overcome the extra transaction costs associated with it, although a limit order generally performs best because of its ability to reduce costs. While such a generalization might help guide a trader's choices, one has to watch for potential interactions within the moving average type-model-order combinations that may cause these generalizations to fail. The variables interact: Although each variable may have its own characteristic effect, when put in combination with other variables, these effects may not maintain their integrity, but may change due to the coupling; this is demonstrated in the tests above. Sometimes variables do maintain their integrity, but not always.

WHAT HAVE WE LEARNED?

- When designing an entry model, try to effectively combine a countertrend element with a trend-following one. This may be done in any number of ways, e.g., buy on a short-term countertrend move when a longer-term trend is in progress; look for a breakout when a countertrend move is in progress; or apply a trend-following filter to a countertrend model.

- If possible, use orders that reduce transaction costs, e.g., a limit order for entry. But do not be rigid: Certain systems might perform better using another kind of order, e.g., if a trend-following element is needed, a stop might be advisable.

- Expect surprises. For the slope-based models, we thought the adaptive moving average, with its faster response, would provide the best performance; in fact, it provided one of the worst.

- Even though traditional indicators, used in standard ways, usually fail (as do such time-honored systems as volatility breakouts), classical concepts like support/resistance may not fail; they may actually be quite useful. In breakouts, models based on the notion of support/resistance held up better than did, e.g., volatility breakouts. Likewise, moving average models using the concept of support/resistance did better than others. The support/resistance implementation was rudimentary, yet, in the best combination, it was one of the best performers; perhaps a more sophisticated version could provide a larger number of more profitable trades. Although support/resistance seems to be an important concept, further research on it will not be easy. There are many variations to consider when defining levels of support and resistance. Determining those levels can be quite challenging, especially when doing so mechanically.

CHAPTER 7

Oscillator-Based Entries

Oscillators have been popular among technical traders for many years. Articles that describe oscillators appear quite frequently in such magazines as *Technical Analysis of Stocks and Commodities* and *Futures*. The subject is also covered in many books on trading.

Most widely used, in both their classic forms and variations, are Appel's (1990) Moving Average Convergence Divergence (MACD) oscillator and MACD-Histogram (MACD-H). Also highly popular are Lane's Stochastic, and Williams's Relative Strength Index (RSI). Many variations on these oscillators have also appeared in the literature. Other oscillators include Lambert's Commodities Channel Index (CCI), the Random Walk Index (which might be considered an oscillator), and Goedde's (1997) Regression Channel Oscillator. In this chapter, the primary focus is on the three most popular oscillators: the MACD, Stochastics, and the RSI.

WHAT IS AN OSCILLATOR?

An *oscillator* is an indicator that is usually computed from prices and that tends to cycle or "oscillate" (hence the name) within a fixed or fairly limited range. Oscillators are characterized by the normalization of range and the elimination of long-term trends or price levels. Oscillators extract information about such transient phenomena as momentum and overextension. *Momentum* is when prices move strongly in a given direction. *Overextension* occurs when prices become excessively high or low ("overbought" or "oversold") and are ready to snap back to more reasonable values.

KINDS OF OSCILLATORS

There are two main forms of oscillators. Linear band-pass filters are one form of oscillator. They may be analyzed for frequency (periodicity) and phase response. The MACD and MACD-H are of this class. Another form of oscillator places some aspect of price behavior into a normalized scale (the RSI, Stochastics, and CCI belong to this class); unlike the first category, these oscillators are not linear filters with clearly defined phase and frequency behavior. Both types of oscillators highlight momentum and cyclical movement, while downplaying trends and eliminating long-term offsets; i.e., they both produce plots that tend to oscillate.

The *Moving Average Convergence Divergence Oscillator*, or *MACD* (and MACD-Histogram), operates as a crude band-pass filter, removing both slow trends and offsets, as well as high-frequency jitter or noise. It does this while passing through cyclic activity or waves that fall near the center of the pass-band. The MACD smooths data, as does a moving average; but it also removes some of the trend, highlighting cycles and sometimes moving in coincidence with the market, i.e., without lag. Ehlers (1989) is a good source of information on this oscillator.

The MACD is computed by subtracting a longer moving average from a shorter moving average. It may be implemented using any kind of averages or low-pass filters (the classic MACD uses exponential moving averages). A number of variations on the MACD use more advanced moving averages, such as the VIDYA (discussed in the chapter on moving averages). Triangular moving averages have also been used to implement the MACD oscillator. Along with the raw MACD, the so-called MACD Histogram (MACD-H) is also used by many traders. This is computed by subtracting from the MACD a moving average of the MACD. In many cases, the moving average of the MACD is referred to as a *signal line*.

The *Stochastic* oscillator is frequently referred to as an *overbought/oversold indicator*. According to Lupo (1994), "The stochastic measures the location of the most recent market action in relation to the highest and lowest prices within the last . . . " *n* bars. In this sense, the Stochastic is a momentum indicator: It answers the question of whether the market is moving to new highs or new lows or is just meandering in the middle.

The Stochastic is actually several related indicators: Fast %K, Slow %K (also known as Fast %D), and Slow %D. *Fast %K* measures, as a percentage, the location of the most recent closing price relative to the highest high and lowest low of the last *n* bars, where *n* is the length or period set for the indicator. *Slow %K*, which is identical to *Fast %D*, applies a 3-bar (or 3-day) moving average to both the numerator and denominator when computing the %K value. *Slow %D* is simply a 3-bar simple moving average of Slow %K; it is occasionally treated as a signal line in the same way that the moving average of the MACD is used as a signal line for the MACD.

There have been many variations on the Stochastic reported over the years; e.g., Blau (1993) discussed a double-smoothing variation. The equations for the classical Lane's Stochastic are described in an article by Meibahr (1992). A version of those equations appears below:

$$A(i) = \text{Highest of } H(i), H(i - 1), \ldots H(i - n + 1)$$
$$B(i) = \text{Lowest of } L(i), L(i - 1), \ldots L(i - n + 1)$$
$$D(i) = [A(i) + A(i - 1) + A(i - 2)] / 3$$
$$E(i) = [B(i) + B(i - 1) + B(i - 2)] / 3$$
$$F(i) = [C(i) + C(i - 1) + C(i - 2)] / 3$$
$$\text{Fast } \%K \text{ for ith bar} = 100 * [C(i) - B(i)] / [A(i) - B(i)]$$
$$\text{Slow } \%K = \text{Fast } \%D = 100 * [F(i) - E(i)] / [D(i) - E(i)]$$
$$\text{Slow } \%D = \text{3-bar simple moving average of Slow } \%K$$

In these equations, i represents the bar index, $H(i)$ the high of the ith bar, $L(i)$ the low of the ith bar, and $C(i)$ the close of the ith bar. All other letters refer to derived data series needed to compute the various Stochastic oscillators. As can be seen from the equations, the Stochastic oscillators highlight the relative position of the close in a range set by recent market highs and lows: High numbers (a maximum of 100) result when the close is near the top of the range of recent price activity and low numbers (a minimum of 0) when the close is near the bottom of the range.

The *Relative Strength Index*, or *RSI*, is another well-known oscillator that assesses relative movement up or down, and scales its output to a fixed range, 0 to 100. The classic RSI makes use of what is essentially an exponential moving average, separately computed for both up movement and down movement, with the result being up movement as a percentage of total movement. One variation is to use simple moving averages when computing the up and down movement components. The equations for the classic RSI appear below:

$$U(i) = \text{Highest of } 0, C(i) - C(i - 1)$$
$$D(i) = \text{Highest of } 0, C(i - 1) - C(i)$$
$$AU(i) = [(n - 1) * AU(i - 1) + U(i)] / n$$
$$AD(i) = [(n - 1) * AD(i - 1) + D(i)] / n$$
$$RSI(i) = 100 * AU(i) / [AU(i) + AD(i)]$$

The indicator's period is represented by n, upward movement by U, downward movement by D, average upward movement by AU, and average downward movement by AD. The bars are indexed by i. Traditionally, a 14-bar RSI ($n = 14$) would be calculated. A good discussion of the RSI can be found in Star (1993).

Finally, there is the *Commodities Channel Index*, or *CCI*, which is discussed in an article by Davies (1993). This oscillator is like a more statistically aware Stochastic: Instead of placing the closing price within bands defined by recent highs and lows, the CCI evaluates the closing price in relation to bands defined by the mean and mean deviation of recent price activity. Although not discussed further in this chapter, the equations for this oscillator are presented below for interested readers:

$$X(i) = H(i) + L(i) + C(i)$$
$$A(i) = \text{Simple n-bar moving average of } X(i)$$
$$D(i) = \text{Average of } |X(i - k) - A(i)| \qquad \text{for } k = 0 \text{ to } n - 1$$
$$CCI(v) = [X(i) - A(i)] / [0.015 * D(i)]$$

In the equations for the Commodities Channel Index, X represents the so-called median price, A the moving average of X, D the mean absolute deviations, n the period for the indicator, and i the bar index.

Figure 7-1 shows a bar chart for the S&P 500. Appearing on the chart are the three most popular oscillators, along with items normally associated with them, e.g., signal lines or slower versions of the oscillator. Also drawn on the subgraph containing the Stochastic are the fixed thresholds of 80 and 20 often used as reference points. For the RSI, similar thresholds of 70 and 30, traditional numbers for that oscillator, are shown. This figure illustrates how these three oscillators appear, how they respond to prices, and what divergence (a concept discussed below) looks like.

GENERATING ENTRIES WITH OSCILLATORS

There are many ways to generate entry signals using oscillators. In this chapter, three are discussed.

One popular means of generating entry signals is to treat the oscillator as an overbought/oversold indicator. A buy is signaled when the oscillator moves below some threshold, into oversold territory, and then crosses back above that threshold. A sell is signaled when the oscillator moves above another threshold, into overbought territory, and then crosses below that threshold. There are traditional thresholds that can used for the various oscillators.

A second way oscillators are sometimes used to generate signals is with a so-called signal line, which is usually a moving average of the oscillator. Signals to take long or short positions are issued when the oscillator crosses above or below (respectively) the signal line. The trader can use these signals on their own in a reversal system or make use of additional, independent exit rules.

Another common approach is to look for price/oscillator divergences, as described by McWhorter (1994). *Divergence* is when prices form a lower low while the oscillator forms a higher low (suggesting a buy), or when prices form a higher high while the oscillator forms a lower high (suggesting a loss of momentum and a possible sell). Divergence is sometimes easy to see subjectively, but almost always difficult to detect accurately using simple rules in a program. Generating signals mechanically for a divergence model requires algorithmic pattern recognition, making the correct implementation of such models rather complex and, therefore, difficult to test. Generating such signals can be done, however;

FIGURE 7-1

Examples of Oscillators and Price-Oscillator Divergence

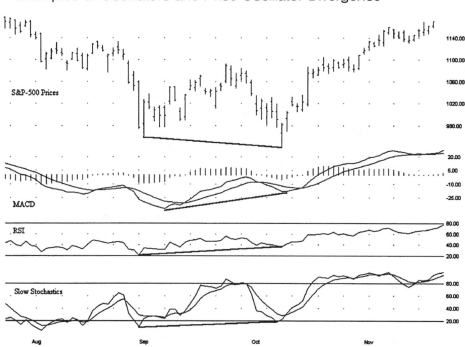

a good example is the "Divergengine" software distributed by Ruggiero Associates. An example of divergence appears in Figure 7-1.

There are a number of issues to consider when using oscillators to generate entries, e.g., smoothing of data and timeliness of entry. The MACD, for example, can sometimes provide the smoothing of a moving average with the timeliness of raw prices. The combination of timeliness and good smoothing may yield entries that are more profitable than those obtained when using moving average entry models. The peaks and valleys in a moving average come significantly after the corresponding peaks and valleys in prices. Consequently, entries generated by looking for these peaks and valleys, or "turning points," are excruciatingly late. Conversely, when cyclic activity in the market has a periodicity that matches the particular MACD used, the peaks and valleys in the output from the MACD come at roughly the same time as the peaks and valleys in the prices; the smoothing of a moving average is achieved without the lag of a moving average. Because the MACD smooths the data, numerous noise-induced trades will be eliminated, as happens with moving averages. Because the MACD can be timely, trades generated may be profitable.

In addition to the MACD, many other oscillators tend to move concurrently with prices or even lead them. For reasons to be discussed later, leading or coincident indicators do not necessarily generate more profitable entries than such lagging indicators as moving averages. Having coincident indicators does not necessarily mean highly profitable signals. The problem is that even though some signals will occur with precise timing, many spurious signals can result, especially in the context of developing trends. When strong trends are present, the anticipated or coincident reversals may simply never take place, leading to entries in the wrong direction. Timeliness may be gained, but reliability may be lost. The question of which trade-off provides a more profitable model—getting in reliably but late, or on time but unreliably—is a matter for empirical study. Such issues are present with any entry method or pattern detection or forecasting model: The greater the delay, the more accurate (but less useful) the detection or indication; the lesser the delay, or the further ahead a forecast must be made, the less accurate (but more useful) the detection or indication. The logic is not unlike that of the Heisenberg Uncertainty Principle.

As an example of how oscillators may be used to generate entries, consider the Stochastic: A simple entry model might buy when this indicator drops below the traditional oversold threshold of 20 and then rises above that threshold. It might sell when the indicator goes beyond the traditional overbought threshold of 80 and then drops back under. The trader must not wait for another signal to close out the current position, as one might do when using a moving average crossover; such a signal might not occur for a long time, so an independent exit is essential. Traders also look for the so-called Stochastic hook, a pattern in which the Stochastic reaches a first low, moves up a little, and then reaches a second low at a higher level than the first. A buy signal is generated as soon as the second low becomes defined. A sell is generated with the exact same pattern flipped over; i.e., a lower high follows a higher high.

As in the case of breakouts and moving averages, oscillator-generated entries can be effected using any of several orders, such as a market at open, limit, or stop. The advantages and disadvantages of these orders have been discussed thoroughly in the previous two chapters.

CHARACTERISTICS OF OSCILLATOR ENTRIES

Oscillator-based entries have the positive characteristic of leading or being coincident with price activity; therefore, they lend themselves to countertrend entries and have the potential to provide a high percentage of winning trades. Oscillators tend to do best in cycling or nontrending (trading range) markets. When they work, oscillators have the appeal of getting the trader in the market close to the bottom or top, before a move has really begun. For trades that work out this way, slippage is low or even negative, good fills are easily obtained, and the trade turns profitable with very little adverse excursion. In such cases it becomes easy to capture a good chunk of the move, even with a suboptimal exit strategy. It is said that the markets trend only about 30% of the time. Our experience suggests that many markets trend even less frequently. With appropriate filtering to prevent taking oscillator-based signals during strong trends, a great entry model could probably be developed. The kind of filtering is exactly the opposite of what was sought when testing breakout systems, where it was necessary to detect the presence, rather than the absence, of trends.

The primary weakness of simple oscillator-based entries is that they perform poorly in sustained trends, often giving many false reversal signals. Some oscillators can easily become stuck at one of their extremes; it is not uncommon to see the Stochastic, for instance, pegged near 100 for a long period of time in the course of a significant market movement. Finally, most oscillator entry models do not capture trends, unlike moving averages or breakouts, which are virtually guaranteed to capture any meaningful trend that comes along. Many traders say that "the trend is your friend," that most money is made going after the "big wave," and that the profits earned on such trends can make up for the frequent smaller losses of trend-following systems. Because oscillator entries go after smaller, countertrend moves, it is essential to have a good exit strategy to minimize the damage that will occur when a trend goes against the trades.

TEST METHODOLOGY

All the tests that follow were performed using oscillator entries to trade a diversified portfolio of commodities. Can oscillator entry models result in profitable trades? How have they fared over time—have they become more or less profitable in recent years? These questions will be addressed below.

The exits are the standard ones, used throughout this book in the study of entry models. Entry rules are discussed along with the model code and under the individual tests. Trades were closed out either when an entry in the opposing direction took place or when the standard exit closed the trade, whichever came first. The test platform is also standard.

Over the years, we have coded into C++ the various oscillators described in articles from *Technical Analysis of Stocks and Commodities* and from other sources. When writing this chapter, we compared the output from our C++ implementations of the classic MACD, Stochastic, and RSI oscillators with (when available) equivalent oscillators in TradeStation. In most cases, there was perfect agreement of the results. However, for one of the Stochastics, the results were extremely different, specifically for Slow %K. Examining the code revealed that TradeStation was computing Slow %K by taking an exponential moving average of Fast %K. Our code, however, computes the 3-bar simple moving averages of both the numerator and the denominator (from which Fast %K would have been computed) to obtain Slow %K. According to the equations in Meibahr's (1992) article, and in other sources we have encountered over the years, our C++ implementation is the correct one. If the reader attempts to replicate some of our work in TradeStation and finds discrepancies, we strongly suggest checking the indicator functions of TradeStation. In addition, when attempting to code a correct implementation for Slow %K in TradeStation's Easy Language, we ran into problems: It appears that TradeStation can give inaccurate results, without any warning, when one user function calls another. When we modified our code so intermediate variables were computed (thus avoiding the need to have nested calls), correct results were obtained. The version of TradeStation used for those tests was 4.02, dating from July 29, 1996.

The following code implements most of the oscillator-based entry models that underlie the tests. The actual computation of the oscillators is handled by calls to external functions.

```c
static void Model (float *parms, float *dt, float *opn, float *hi,
float *lo, float *cls, float *vol, float *oi, float *dlrv, int nb,
TRDSIM &ts, float *eqcls) {

    // Implements the oscillator-based entry models to be tested.
    // File = x11mod01.c
    // parms    - vector [1..MAXPRM] of parameters
    // dt       - vector [1..nb] of dates in YYMMDD form
    // opn      - vector [1..nb] of opening prices
    // hi       - vector [1..nb] of high prices
    // lo       - vector [1..nb] of low prices
    // cls      - vector [1..nb] of closing prices
    // vol      - vector [1..nb] of volumes
    // oi       - vector [1..nb] of open interest numbers
    // dlrv     - vector [1..nb] of average dollar volatilities
    // nb       - number of bars in data series or vectors
    // ts       - trading simulator class instance
    // eqcls    - vector [1..nb] of closing equity levels

    // declare local scratch variables
    static int rc, cb, ncontracts, maxhold, len1, len2, len3;
    static int modeltype, ordertype, osctype, signal, i, j, k;
    static float mmstp, ptlim, stpprice, limprice, tmp;
    static float exitatr[MAXBAR+1];
    static float sigline[MAXBAR+1], oscline[MAXBAR+1];
    static float upperband[MAXBAR+1], lowerband[MAXBAR+1];

    // copy parameters to local variables for clearer reference
    len1      = parms[1];      // shorter or first length parameter
    len2      = parms[2];      // longer or second length parameter
    len3      = parms[3];      // length for divergence test
    modeltype = parms[7];      // type of oscillator entry model
    osctype   = parms[8];      // type of oscillator
    ordertype = parms[9];      // type of entry order
    maxhold   = 10;            // maximum holding period
```

```
        ptlim    = 4;                    // profit target in volatility units
        mmstp    = 1;                    // stop loss in volatility units

    // skip invalid parameter combinations
    if( (osctype==4 && len1>=len2) ) {
        set_vector(eqcls, 1, nb, 0.0);
        return;
}

// perform whole-series computations using fast vector routines
AvgTrueRangeS(exitatr,hi,lo,cls,50,nb);      // ATR for exit
switch(osctype) {    // select oscillator
  case 1:    // classic fast stochastics
    StochOsc(oscline,hi,lo,cls,1,len1,nb);   // Fast %K
    MovAvg(sigline, oscline, 1, 3, nb);      // Fast %D
    set_vector(upperband, 1, nb, 80.0);      // upper threshold
    set_vector(lowerband, 1, nb, 20.0);      // lower threshold
    break;
  case 2:    // classic slow stochastics
    StochOsc(oscline,hi,lo,cls,2,len1,nb);   // Slow %K
    MovAvg(sigline, oscline, 1, 3, nb);      // Slow %D
    set_vector(upperband, 1, nb, 80.0);      // upper threshold
    set_vector(lowerband, 1, nb, 20.0);      // lower threshold
    break;
  case 3:    // classic rsi
    RsiOsc(oscline, cls, 1, len1, nb);       // RSI
    MovAvg(sigline, oscline, 1, 3, nb);      // 3-bar SMA
    set_vector(upperband, 1, nb, 70.0);      // upper threshold
    set_vector(lowerband, 1, nb, 30.0);      // lower threshold
    break;
  case 4:    // classic macd
    MacdOsc(oscline,cls,1,len1,len2,nb);     // classic MACD
    MovAvg(sigline, oscline, 2, 9, nb);      // 9-bar EMA
    for(i=1; i<=nb; i++)
        lowerband[i]=1.5*fabs(oscline[i]);   // thresholds
    MovAvg(upperband,lowerband,1,120,nb);    // as long-term
        for(i=1; i<=nb; i++)                 // mean-deviation
            lowerband[i]= -upperband[i];     // bands
    break;
    default: nrerror("Invalid moving average selected");
};
// step through bars (days) to simulate actual trading
for(cb = 1; cb <= nb; cb++) {

    // take no trades before the in-sample period
    // ... same as TradeStation's MaxBarsBack setting
    if(dt[cb] < IS_DATE) { eqcls[cb] = 0.0; continue; }
```

```
// execute any pending orders and store closing equity
rc = ts.update(opn[cb], hi[cb], lo[cb], cls[cb], cb);
if(rc != 0) nrerror("Trade buffer overflow");
eqcls[cb] = ts.currentequity(EQ_CLOSETOTAL);
// calculate number of contracts to trade
// ... we want to trade the dollar volatility equivalent
// ... of 2 new S&P-500 contracts as of 12/31/98
ncontracts = RoundToInteger(5673.0 / dlrv[cb]);
if(ncontracts < 1) ncontracts = 1;
// avoid placing orders on possibly limit-locked days
if(hi[cb+1] == lo[cb+1]) continue;


// generate entry signals, stop prices and limit prices
// using the specified oscillator-based entry model
#define CrossesAbove(a,b,c)  (a[c]>=b[c] && a[c-1]<b[c-1])
#define CrossesBelow(a,b,c)  (a[c]<b[c] && a[c-1]>=b[c-1])
#define TurnsUp(a,c)  (a[c]>=a[c-1] && a[c-1]<a[c-2])
#define TurnsDn(a,c)  (a[c]<a[c-1] && a[c-1]>=a[c-2])
signal=0;
switch(modeltype) {
  case 1: // overbought-oversold model
    if(CrossesAbove(oscline, lowerband, cb))
       signal = 1;
    else if(CrossesBelow(oscline, upperband, cb))
       signal = -1;
    limprice = 0.5 * (hi[cb] + lo[cb]);
    stpprice = cls[cb] + 0.5 * signal * exitatr[cb];
    break;
  case 2: // signal line model
    if(CrossesAbove(oscline, sigline, cb))
       signal = 1;
  else if(CrossesBelow(oscline, sigline, cb))
    signal = -1;
  limprice = 0.5 * (hi[cb] + lo[cb]);
  stpprice = cls[cb] + 0.5 * signal * exitatr[cb];
  break;
case 3: // divergence model
  i = LowestBar(cls, len3, cb);
  j = LowestBar(oscline, len3, cb);
  if(i < cb && i > cb-6 && j > cb-len3+1 && i-j > 4
     && TurnsUp(oscline, cb)) signal = 1;
  else {
     i = HighestBar(cls, len3, cb);
     j = HighestBar(oscline, len3, cb);
     if(i < cb && i > cb-6 && j > cb-len3+1 && i-j > 4
           && TurnsDn(oscline, cb)) signal = -1;
```

```
      }
      limprice = 0.5 * (hi[cb] + lo[cb]);
      stpprice = cls[cb] + 0.5 * signal * exitatr[cb];
      break;
    default: nrerror("Invalid model selected");
  }
  #undef CrossesAbove
  #undef CrossesBelow
  #undef TurnsUp
  #undef TurnsDn

  // enter trades using specified order type
  if(ts.position() <= 0 && signal == 1) {
    switch(ordertype) { // select desired order type
      case 1: ts.buyopen(`1', ncontracts); break;
      case 2: ts.buylimit(`2', limprice, ncontracts); break;
      case 3: ts.buystop(`3', stpprice, ncontracts); break;
      default: nrerror("Invalid buy order selected");
    }
  }
  else if(ts.position() >= 0 && signal == -1) {
    switch(ordertype) { // select desired order type
      case 1: ts.sellopen(`4', ncontracts); break;
      case 2: ts.selllimit(`5', limprice, ncontracts); break;
      case 3: ts.sellstop(`6', stpprice, ncontracts); break;
      default: nrerror("Invalid sell order selected");
    }
  }

  // instruct simulator to employ standard exit strategy
  tmp = exitatr[cb];
  ts.stdexitcls(`X', ptlim*tmp, mmstp*tmp, maxhold);
  } // process next bar
}
```

The logic of the code is very similar to the code used to test moving averages. First, a number of parameters are copied to local variables to make them easier to understand and refer to in the code that follows. A check is then made for invalid combinations of parameters; e.g., for the MACD (*osctype* = 4), the length of the shorter moving average must be less than the longer moving average; otherwise the test is skipped. In the next large block of code, osctype selects the type of oscillator that will be computed (1 = fast Stochastics, 2 = slow Stochastics, 3 = classic RSI, 4 = classic MACD). The oscillator (*oscline*) is then computed as a data series or vector; any additional curves associated with it, such as a signal line (*sigline*) or slower version of the oscillator, are generated; and upper (*upperband*)

and lower (lowerband) thresholds are either set or computed. For the Stochastics, the standard thresholds of 80 and 20 are used. For the RSI, 70 and 30 are specified (also standard). Although the MACD normally has no thresholds, thresholds placed 1.5 mean deviations above and below zero. Finally, the process of stepping through the data, bar by bar, is begun.

Two main blocks of code are of interest in the loop for stepping through the data. The first block generates a buy or sell signal, as well as limit and stop prices for the specified, oscillator-based entry model. The *modeltype* parameter selects the model to use: 1 = overbought/oversold model, 2 = signal line model, and 3 = divergence model. The oscillator used by the model to generate the buy and sell signals is the one computed earlier, as selected by *osctype*. The final block of code enters trades using the specified order type. The parameter *ordertype* determines the order used: 1 = entry at open, 2 = entry on limit, and 3 = entry on stop. Finally, the simulator is instructed to use the standard exit model to close out any open trades.

The exact logic used for entering the market is discussed in the context of the individual tests below without requiring the reader to refer to or understand the code.

TESTS RESULTS

Tests were performed on three oscillator entry models: Overbought/oversold (Stochastic and RSI used), signal line (Stochastic and MACD used), and divergence (Stochastic, RSI, and MACD used). All individual model-oscillator combinations were examined with entry at the open, on a limit, and on a stop. The results for all three orders are discussed together.

Tables 7-1 and 7-2 contain, for each of the 21 tests, the specific commodities the model traded profitably and those that lost in-sample (Table 7-1) and out-of-sample (Table 7-2). The *SYM* column represents the market being studied; the first row identifies the test number. The tables show which markets were, and were not, profitable when traded by each model: One dash (-) indicates a $2,000 to $4,000 loss per trade; two dashes (- -), a $4,000 or more loss; one plus sign (+) means a $1,000 to $2,000 profit; two pluses (++), a $2,000 or more profit; a blank cell means a $0 to $1,999 loss or a $0 to $1,000 profit.

TESTS OF OVERBOUGHT/OVERSOLD MODELS

The entries were generated when the oscillator crossed below an upper threshold or above a lower one. These are countertrend models: The trader buys when the oscillator shows downward momentum in prices and sells when the oscillator depicts recent positive momentum. In Tests 1 through 6, the Stochastic and the RSI were considered since these indicators have traditional thresholds associated with them and are often used as described above.

TABLE 7-1

In-Sample Performance Broken Down by Test and Market

SYM	01	02	03	04	05	06	07	08	09	10	11	12	13	14	15	16	17	18	19	20	21
SP	-	-		--		--								+	-	+				+	--
YX	-			--	--		-		-	-	-	-		--		+					-
US	--	-	-	--	++	--	-		-		-		--	-	--	-	-			++	--
TB	--	--	--	--	--	--	--	-	--	--	--	--	--			--		--	-	++	++
TY	--		-	--	--	--	-		-	-	-	-	--	-	--		-	-		+	++
BP	-	-		--	--	-										-	+	-	+		++
DM	-			--	--	--								+		--		+	+	++	
SF	-		+	-	--	+						-				+		-	+	++	++
JY	-	-		-	--				-				--	-	--	-	--	-	--	--	--
CD	--	-	--	--	--	--	-		-			-		--	-	-	-			--	-
ED	--	--	--	--	--		--	--	--	--	--	-	--	--	--	--	--	--	--	--	-
CL	--	-	--	--	--	--	-	-			-		-	--	-	++	+	++	++	++	++
HO				--	-	--		-				-		+	++	++	++	++	++	++	++
HU				-	-	+			+			+	+	++		++	+	+			+
GC	-	-	--		++	-	-		-			-		++	-		++	++	++	++	++
SI	-			-	++	--	-	-	-			-		--	--	-	--	++	--		++
PL	-	-	-	++	++				--	-		--	-	--	--		-	-	++	-	++
PA	-	-	-	--	+	--	-		--			+	-	--	-	-	--	-	-	-	++
FC				--	++	--	-	-					--	--	--				+	++	++
LC		+	-	-	--	++		-				--	-	--	--	-		-	++	++	--
LH	-	-	-	--	--	--	-	-	-			++		-	++	-	--	--		-	
PB	-			--		-						++	-	++	-	+	++	++	++	+	++
S	-			--		-						-	++	++	++	++	++	++	+	++	--
SM			--	-	--				-			+	++	+	-	-	+		++	++	
BO		--		--		--	-	-	-				-	--	-	++	++	+	-		++
C	--	--	--	--	--	--	--	-	-	--	-		--	--	--	-	++		--	-	--
O	--	-	--	+	++	++	--	-	--	--	--	-	--	-	--	-		-		--	-
W	--	-	-	--		--	-	-	--	-		--	-	--		--	--	--	--		--
KW	--	--	--	--	-	-	-	-	-		+	-	--	--	--	--	--	--	--		--
MW	--		--	-	-	-	-	-	-				--	--	+	--	--	--	-	--	--
KC	-			--	++	--			+			++	-	--			+	+	++	+	++
CC		-	+	--	--	--	-	-	-	-	-		-	+						++	--
SB	--	--	--	--	--	--	-	-		-	-	++	-	--		+	-	++	++	++	++
JO	--	--	-	--	--	--	-		-			+	--	--	--	--	++	-	--	+	--
CT	-	-	-	--	--	--	-		-	-	--	--		--	+	--	+	--	+	++	+
LB	-		-	-		--	-	-				++	-	--	--	--	-	--	--	++	++

Tests 1 through 3: Stochastic Overbought/Oversold Models. These tests evaluate the model with entry at the open (Test 1), on a limit (Test 2), and on a stop (Test 3). Lane's original Fast %K was used. The length was stepped from 5 to 25 in increments of 1. The best values for this parameter in-sample were 25, 20, and 16 (Tests 1 through 3, respectively). For the Stochastic, the traditional thresholds are 20 (lower) and 80 (upper). As a whole, these models lost heavily in- and out-of-sample (see Table 7-3). As in previous tests, the limit

TABLE 7-2

Out-of-Sample Performance Broken Down by Test and Market

SYM	01	02	03	04	05	06	07	08	09	10	11	12	13	14	15	16	17	18	19	20	21
SP	-	--	-	--	--	--			--		-		--	--		--	--	--	--	--	
YX	--	--	--	-	++	--	-		--		-		--	-	--	--	--	--	--	--	++
US	--	-	--	--	--	--	-		-	-			--	-	--	--	-	--		+	--
TB	--	-	--	--	--	-	--	--	--	--	--	--	--	--	++	--	++	++	--	-	
TY	--	--	--	--	--			-		-	--	--	--	--	--	-	+	--		-	
BP	+	++	++	--	++	--						+	+	++	-	--	--	++	--	-	++
DM		+	-	--	--	--				-			++	++	++	++	++	+	++	++	--
SF	-		-	--	--	--			+		--	++				--	+	--		++	-
JY	--	--		--	--	--							-	++		--			++	++	
CD		--		+		++	-	-	--	+	+		--	--				++		--	++
ED	--	--	--	--	--	--	--	-	--	--	--	--	--	--	++	--	--	--	--	--	
CL	-	-	--	-	--	--	-	-	-		-		--	--	--	--		--	++	++	+
HO			-		++	--				++	+		--	--	--	-	--	-	++		++
HU	-		-	+	--	++				+		+	+	++	+	+			++	+	--
GC	--		-	++	++		-				-	++	--			--	--		--	++	--
SI	-			++	++	--	-				++	--	--	--	--	++	++	++	++	++	
PL	-	--	-	++	++	++	-	-				-	++	+	++		-	++	++	-	
PA	-	+	--	--	--	--	-	-	-	-	-	+	++	++	--		++	--	--		--
FC		+	--	--	++		-			--	--			--	++	-	--	++	--	--	-
LC	-		-	--	--					-	-	--	-	--	-		+	++	++	++	++
LH	-	--	++	-	+	--		-	+	+	+	++	--	--	--	-	-	--	--	--	--
PB		+	-	--	--				+		-	+			--	--	--	--		-	-
S			++	--		--	-	-				+		++	++	+	++	++	++	++	++
SM		-		--	-	--	+	+	+	++	++	+	-	-	--	+	++		++	++	-
BO	--					-				-		-	++	++		+	++	-	--	++	--
C	-	--	-	+	++	+	-	-	-		-		--	-	-	--	--	--		+	++
O	--	--	--	--	++	--	--	-	--	--	--	-	--	--	--	--	--	--	-	-	
W	--	-	-		--		-	-	-				-		--	--		--	--	--	+
KW	--	--	-		--	++	-	-	-				--	--	--	-	--				++
MW	--	--		--	+	-	-	-		-	-	-			--	-	--	--	--	--	--
KC		-		--	--	++		++	++	++	++	--			-	--		++	++	++	
CC	--	-		--		--	--	-	-	++		-								--	-
SB	-		-	+	++	--			--	-		-	--	--	--	--		--		-	--
JO	+	+	+	++	++	++			--	+	+	++	+	++	++		++	--	++	++	+
CT	-	-	--	--	--	--	-						--	--	-	--	-	--	-	+	
LB	+		++	++	++	++				++	++	+				+	+		++		++

order was the best in both samples, having the least loss per trade; the percent of winning trades (37% in-sample, 36% out-of-sample) was also highest with this order. The stop order was intermediate in performance, with the entry at open being the worst. No markets traded well in either sample. Out-of-sample, the British Pound and Orange Juice were profitable across all orders, and Lumber, Soybeans, and Live Hogs made profits with a stop; other small profits were occasionally noted, but had no consistency. This model is among the worst tested.

Tests 4 through 6: RSI Overbought/Oversold Models.   The model was tested with entry at the open (Test 4), on a limit (Test 5), and on a stop (Test 6). The RSI was computed as suggested by its originator, Larry Williams. The length was stepped from 5 to 25 in increments of 1. Across all tests, 25 was the best value for this parameter in-sample. The traditional thresholds were used: 30 (lower) and 70 (upper). The model performed more poorly than the Stochastic overbought/oversold one. The percentage of winning trades was extremely low, ranging from 26% to 37%, depending on sample and test. The average loss per trade reached over $7,000. Net profits were better than for the Stochastic because there were fewer trades; even though the loss per trade was greater, the total loss was smaller. This model did not capture any market inefficiency. The limit order was best, while the stop and open were about equal. Significantly more markets showed positive returns, especially in Test 5 when the limit was used: Profits occurred in-sample for Bonds, COMEX Gold, Silver, Platinum, Feeder Cattle, Oats, and Coffee; out-of-sample, Gold, Silver, Platinum, Feeder Cattle, and Oats still traded profitably. Also profitable out-of-sample were the NYFE, British Pound, Heating Oil, Corn, Sugar, Orange Juice, and Lumber.

Tests of Signal Line Models

These are essentially moving average crossover models, except that an oscillator is substituted for prices when searching for crossovers. In this case, the moving average is called the *signal line*. A short entry is signalled when the oscillator crosses from above to below the signal line; when the oscillator does the reverse, a long entry is generated. Since oscillators show less lag than moving averages and less noise than raw prices, perhaps more timely and reliable signals can be generated. In Tests 7 through 12, the Stochastic and MACD are considered. The Slow %K usually exhibits strong cyclic behavior, appropriate for use with a signal line entry. The MACD is traditionally plotted with the signal line, even if crossovers are not a traditional entry criteria.

Tests 7 through 9: Stochastic Signal Line Models.   The model was tested with entry at the open, on a limit, and on a stop (Tests 7 through 9, respectively). Lane's original Slow %K Stochastic was used because, in preliminary testing, Fast %K produced an incredible excess of trades, resulting from very high noise levels and the indicator pegging near its extremes. The signal line consisted of a 3-bar simple moving average of Slow %K. The length of the Stochastic was stepped from 5 to 25, in increments of 1. The best values for this parameter in-sample were 15, 14, and 11 (Tests 7 through 9). Overall, these models lost heavily on a per trade basis. Due to the large number of trades, the losses were astronomical. The limit order was best, showing the least loss per trade and the highest percent of winning trades across samples. Entry at the open was worst.

This model likes stops, perhaps because they act as trend filters: After countertrend activity is detected (triggering an entry signal), before entry can occur, the market must demonstrate reversal by moving in the direction of the trade. Stops also performed better in countertrend moving average models. Only two markets had positive returns in-sample, but not out-of-sample. Out-of-sample, the stop produced a few small profits; Coffee made more than $2,000 per trade.

Tests 10 through 12: MACD Signal Line Models.   Entry at the open (Test 10), on a limit (Test 11), and on a stop (Test 12) were examined. The classic MACD, employing exponential moving averages, was used. The shorter moving average was stepped from a length of 3 to a length of 15 in increments of 2; the longer moving average was stepped from lengths of 10 through 40 in increments of 5. The moving average serving as the signal line had a fixed traditional period of 9. This was the best performing oscillator model thus far. In-sample, the limit order was best and entry at open was worst. Out-of-sample, the stop was best and the limit order worst. Out-of-sample, the stop produced the highest percentage of wins (40%) seen so far, and the smallest loss per trade. In-sample, only Lumber was substantially profitable with a limit. Live Hogs, Pork Bellies, Coffee, and Sugar were profitable in-sample with a stop. Lumber, Live Hogs, Pork Bellies, and Coffee held up out-of-sample. Many markets unprofitable in-sample, were profitable out-of-sample. The highest number of markets traded profitably with a stop.

TESTS OF DIVERGENCE MODELS

Tests 13 through 21 examine divergences with the Stochastic oscillator, the RSI, and the MACD. Divergence is a concept used by technical traders to describe something easily perceived on a chart but hard to precisely define and detect algorithmically. Figure 7-1 shows examples of divergence. *Divergence* occurs when, e.g., the market forms a lower valley, while the oscillator forms a higher valley of a pair of valleys, indicating a buy condition; selling is the converse. Because wave forms may be irregular, quantifying divergence is tricky. Although our detection algorithm is elementary and imperfect, when examining charts it appears to work well enough to objectively evaluate the usefulness of divergence.

Only buy signals will be discussed; the sells are the exact opposite. The algorithm's logic is as follows: Over a look-back (in the code, *len3*), the lowest bar in the price series and the lowest bar produced by the oscillator are located. Several conditions are then checked. First, the lowest bar of the price series must have occurred at least one bar ago (there has to be a definable valley), but within the past six bars (this valley should be close to the current bar). The lowest bar in the price series has to occur at least four bars after the lowest bar in the look-back period for the oscillator line (the deepest valley produced by the oscillator must occur before the deepest valley produced by the price). Another condition is that the lowest bar produced by the oscillator line is not the first bar in the look-back period (again, there has to be a definable bottom). Finally, the oscillator must have just turned upward (defining the second valley as the signal about to be issued). If all conditions are met, there is ostensibly a divergence and a buy is posted. If a buy has not been posted, a similar set of conditions looks for peaks (instead of valleys); the conditions are adjusted and a sell is posted if the market formed a higher high, while the oscillator formed a lower high. This logic does a reasonable job of detecting divergences seen on charts. Other than the entry orders, the only difference between Tests 13 through 21 is the oscillator being analyzed (in relation to prices) for the presence of divergence.

Tests 13 through 15: Stochastic Divergence Models.   Fast %K was used with the standard entries. Optimization involved stepping the Stochastic length from 5 to 25 in increments of 1 and the divergence look-back from 15 to 25 by 5. The best parameters were length and look-back, respectively, 20 and 15 for open, 24 and 15 for limit, 25 and 15 for stop. This model was among the worst for all orders and in both samples. In-sample, the limit was marginally best; out-of-sample, the stop. In-sample, across all orders, Unleaded Gasoline, Soybeans, and Soybean Meal were profitable; Gold and Pork Bellies were moderately profitable with a limit. Unleaded Gasoline held up out-of-sample across all orders. Soybeans were profitable out-of-sample for the open and stop. More markets were profitable out-of-sample than in-sample, with the stop yielding the most markets with profits. The pattern of more profitable trading out-of-sample than in-sample is *prima facie* evidence that optimization played no role in the outcome; instead, in recent years, some markets have become more tradeable using such models. This may be due to fewer trends and increased choppiness in many markets.

Tests 16 through 18: RSI Divergence Models.   Optimization stepped the RSI period from 5 to 25 in increments of 1, and the divergence look-back from 15 to 25 by 5. Overall, the results were poor. In-sample, the stop was least bad, with the limit close behind. Out-of-sample, the stop was also best, closely followed by the open. Given that the RSI has been one of the indicators traditionally favored by traders using divergence, its poor showing in these tests is noteworthy. Heating Oil was profitable for all orders, Unleaded Gasoline was significantly profitable for the open and stop, Light Crude for the limit and stop. In-sample, Soybeans traded very profitably across orders; Orange Juice, Corn, Soybean Oil, and Pork Bellies traded well with the stop. Out-of-sample, the oils were not consistently profitable, while Soybeans remained profitable across orders; Orange Juice and Soybean Oil still traded profitably with the stop.

Tests 19 through 21: MACD Divergence Models.   The length of the shorter moving average was stepped from 3 to 15 in increments of 2; the length of the longer moving average from 10 to 40 by 5; and the divergence look-back from 15 to 25, also by 5. Only parameter sets where the longer moving average was actually longer than the shorter one were examined.

Finally, models that appear to work, producing positive returns in both samples! With entry at open, trades were profitable across samples. In-sample, the average trade made $1,393; 45% of the trades were winners; and there was only an 8.7% (uncorrected; 99.9% corrected) probability that the results were due to chance; both longs and shorts were profitable. Despite poor statistical significance in-sample, there was profitability out-of-sample: The model pulled $140 per trade (after commissions and slippage), with 38% winning trades; only shorts were profitable.

The limit performed slightly worse in-sample, but much better out-of-sample. Figure 7-2 depicts the equity curve for entry on a limit. In-sample, the average profit per trade was $1,250 with 47% winning trades (the highest so far); longs and shorts were profitable; and the probability was 13.1% (uncorrected; 99.9% corrected) that the results were due to chance. Out-of-sample, the model made $985 per trade; won 44% of the time; was profitable in long and short positions; and was only 27.7% likely due to chance.

In-sample, the stop had the greatest dollars-per-trade return, but the smallest number of trades; only the shorts were profitable. Out-of-sample, the system lost $589 per trade; only short positions were profitable. Regardless of the order used, this model had relatively few trades.

The market-by-market analysis (see Tables 7-1 and 7-2) confirms the potential of these models to make money. The largest number of markets were profitable in-sample. Across samples, all three orders yielded profits for Light Crude and Coffee; many other markets had profitability that held up for two of the orders, but not for the third, e.g., Heating Oil, Live Cattle, Soybeans, Soybean Meal, and Lumber.

SUMMARY ANALYSES

Table 7-3 provides the results broken down by the model, order, and sample. The last two columns on the right, and the last two rows on the bottom, are averages. The numbers at the right are averaged over order type. The numbers at the bottom have been averaged over all models.

The best results across samples were for the MACD divergence model. The limit produced the best combined results in both samples: a 12.5% return (annualized) and $1,250 per trade in-sample, and a 19.5% return (annualized) and $985 per trade out-of-sample. This model is dramatically different from all others.

When considered across all order types and averaged, the overbought/oversold models using the RSI were worst (especially in terms of dollars-per-trade). Also among the worst were the Stochastic divergence, Stochastic overbought/oversold, and RSI divergence models.

When all models were averaged and broken down by order type, the limit order was best and the entry at open worst.

FIGURE 7 - 2

Equity for MACD Divergence Model with Entry on a Limit

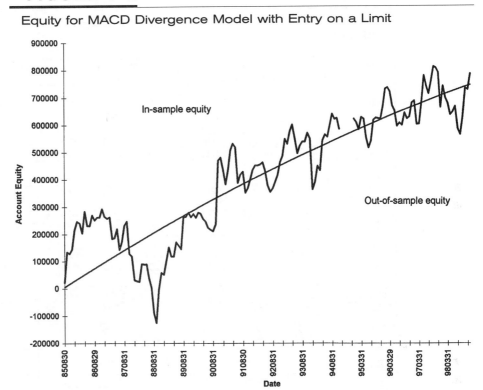

CONCLUSION

With breakouts and moving averages, a limit usually was the best overall performer, perhaps because it minimizes transaction costs; a stop sometimes improved performance, depending on its interaction with the entry model. For some oscillator entries, including the profitable MACD divergence, a limit was again best. Other oscillator models preferred the stop, perhaps due to its trend filtering quality.

There was an interaction between specific oscillators and models. The divergence model, for example, worked well with the MACD, but terribly with the RSI. Such results demonstrate that, when studying a model with an indicator component that may be varied without altering the model's essence, it is important to test all model-indicator combinations as certain ones may perform dramatically better.

WHAT HAVE WE LEARNED?

- In general, for best results, use a limit order. However, test a stop as it sometimes works better.

TABLE 7-3

Performance of Oscillator Models Broken Down by Model, Order, and Sample

Model	In-sample			Out-of-sample			Average	Average
	Open	Limit	Stop	Open	Limit	Stop	In	Out
Stochastic	-10.2	-10.1	-10.1	-23.7	-23.7	-22.5	-10.1	-23.3
ob/os	-3672	-2228	-2586	-3130	-2504	-2650	-2828.7	-2761.3
RSI	-10.1	-9.9	-9.9	-21.1	-18.3	-21.1	-10.0	-20.2
ob / os	-7073	-4093	-6878	-3537	-1978	-3824	-6014.7	-3113.0
Stochastic	-10.3	-10.3	-10.2	-23.5	-23.3	-23.5	-10.3	-23.5
signal line	-2656	-1813	-2026	-2324	-1330	-1968	-2165.0	-1874.0
MACD	-10.2	-9.6	-7.8	-22.2	-20.6	-18.7	-9.2	-20.5
signal line	-1808	-1210	-1476	-1259	-1434	-533	-1498.0	-1075.3
Stochastic	-10.1	-10.1	-9.8	-21.7	-21.2	-19.9	-10.0	-20.9
divergence	-3245	-2443	-3008	-3259	-3182	-2179	-2898.7	-2873.3
RSI	-9.8	-8.9	-7.1	-21.7	-18.8	-20.1	-8.6	-20.2
divergence	-2278	-1529	-1309	-3065	-3400	-2935	-1705.3	-3133.3
MACD	26.3	12.5	27.2	2.2	19.5	-5.3	22.0	5.5
divergence	1393	1250	2062	140	985	-589	1568.3	178.7
Average								
ROA%	-4.9	-6.6	-4.0	-18.8	-15.2	-18.7	-5.2	-17.6
$TRD	-2762.7	-1723.7	-2174.4	-2347.7	-1834.7	-2096.9	-2220.3	-2093.1

- When testing a model that can be used with multiple indicators, try several to see whether any yield distinct improvements.
- Attempt to algorithmically implement concepts normally employed in a highly variable and subjective manner. Sometimes this can be exceptionally difficult, requiring fuzzy logic or neural network technology, along with other specialized methods.

CHAPTER 8

Seasonality

Imagine that tomorrow is June 7, 1997. You need to decide whether or not to trade. If you do trade, you will enter at the open and exit at the close. You also need to decide how to enter the market: Should you go long or short? As part of the decision process, you examine the behavior of the market on all June 7s that occurred within a look-back window of some number of years (e.g., 10). You tabulate the number of June 7s on which trading occurred, the average open-to-close change in price, and the percentage of time the market rallied or collapsed. Perhaps, in the past 10 years, there were eight instances when the market was open and June 7 was a trading day; of those instances, perhaps the market closed higher than it opened six times (75%) and the average change in price was 2.50 (a reasonable figure for the S&P 500). On the basis of this information, you place a trading order to enter long tomorrow at the open and to exit at the close. Tomorrow evening you repeat the procedure for June 8, the evening after that for June 9, and so on. This is one form of seasonal trading. Will you make a profit trading this way? Will your trading at least be better than chance? These are the questions that arise when discussing seasonal trading and that this chapter attempts to answer.

WHAT IS SEASONALITY?

The term *seasonality* is used in many different ways by traders. Some construe seasonality as events that are strictly related the four seasons, e.g., the increased demand for heating oil in the winter or gasoline in the summer. Others have a more liberal interpretation that includes weather patterns and election cycles.

Over the years, a number of articles in academic journals have demonstrated that stocks show larger returns around the first of each month. There has been some discussion of the so-called January Effect, in which stocks tend to rise in January. Hannula (1991) used seasonal cycles in his own trading, providing as an example a chart for EXABYTE stock with strong seasonal patterns marked. He also discussed another phenomenon, sometimes observed with seasonal patterns, in which the highs and lows occasionally invert, a pattern that we also have witnessed and that may be worth exploring. Other factors that influence various markets have definite dates of occurrence and so should induce seasonal effects; e.g., the dates for filing taxes occur at the same time every year. The legendary trader, Gann, apparently made heavy use of recurrent yearly behavior in his trading. Bernstein's (1995) home-study course on seasonality suggests trading off significant tops and bottoms, and when there has been consistent movement in a tradable over a number of years; this approach, as well as Hannula's, may tend to involve trades lasting several weeks to several months.

In 1990, we first published the *Calendar Effects Chart*, a set of tables and a chart that show date-specific behavior in the S&P 500 cash index. The chart illustrates a general up-trend from January through September, and then an up and down decline until October 24. The market then, on average, bottoms, after which time it steeply rises until the end of the year. On a more detailed level, rapid gains seem to occur throughout most of January, the first half of April, and the first half of June. A peak can be seen on October 8, and a very steep decline that leads to a bottom on October 24. When the tables and chart for this publication were generated, extreme movements were clipped at ±2 percent to prevent them from having undue influence on the results. Consequently, the steep decline in October, and the other patterns mentioned, cannot be attributed to events in specific years, for instance, the crash in 1987. For some dates, there were incredibly consistent patterns; e.g., if an entry occurred on the close of April 14 and the trade was exited one day later, over 90% of the time a small profit would have been made. Entry on May 6, with exit one day later, resulted in a profit 100% of the time, as did entry on July 13. The market declined 90% of the time from October 18 to 19, and 89% of the time from October 16 to 17. Although the crash may have involved a much greater than normal amount of movement, the presence of a decline at the time when the crash occurred was not at all unexpected. In an attempt to capture high-probability, short-term movements, the *Calendar Effects Chart* could have been used to enter trades that last one or two days. For example, such a methodology would have caused a trader to go short at the close on October 16 and exit on October 19, thus capturing the crash. The data contained in this publication could also have been used to help maintain positions during periods of steep ascent or decline.

There have been other studies indicating the presence of strong seasonal effects in the market that can be exploited for profitable trading. An investigation we conducted (Katz and McCormick, April 1997) found that short-term seasonal behavior could be used to trade the S&P 500: The system used fairly fast moving average crossovers that were computed on seasonally anticipated prices. Because the antici-pated prices could be computed at least one year ahead, lag in the moving average crossover was easily compensated for with a displacement that enabled the system to take trades at crossovers occurring several days after the fact. The trades taken by the system typically lasted between 7 and 8 days, a fairly short-term seasonal trad-ing model. The system was profitable: It pulled an astonishing $329,900 from the S&P 500 between January 3, 1986, and November 8, 1996. The test did not include transaction costs, but even with $15 round-turn commissions and $75 per trade slip-page, a profit of $298,310 (about a 10% reduction) resulted. The return on account was 732%, not annualized; assuming fixed contract trading, this amounted to over 70% per year, annualized, on a constant one-contract, no-reinvestment basis. There were 351 trades taken, of which 60% were winners. Both the longs and shorts were profitable. The average trade pulled $939 from the market—not bad for a simple, seasonality-based trading model. Findings like these suggest there are strong sea-sonal patterns in the markets producing inefficiencies that can be exploited by traders, and that are worthy of investigation.

For our current purposes, *seasonality* is defined as cyclic or recurrent phe-nomena that are consistently linked to the calendar. The term is being used in a broad sense to mean market behavior related to the time of the year or to particular dates, including anniversaries of critical events (e.g., the October 16, 1987, crash). In short, seasonality is being construed as calendar-related cyclic phenomena. It should be made clear, however, that while all seasonality is cyclic, not all cycles are seasonal.

GENERATING SEASONAL ENTRIES

There are many ways to time entries using seasonal rhythms. Two basic approaches will be examined: momentum and crossover. To calculate momentum, a series of price changes is computed and *centered smoothing* (a smoothing that induces no delays or phase shifts, in this case, a centered triangular moving average) is applied. Each price change (or difference) in the series of price changes is then normalized: It is divided by the 50-day average true range. For every bar, the date is determined. Instances of the same date are then found in the past (or perhaps future). For each such instance, the momentum is examined. The average of the momentums becomes the value placed in the seasonal momentum series for the current bar. The *seasonal momentum series* measures the expected rate of change (or momentum) in prices at a given time. It is based on the historical movement of prices on the specified date in different years. The number in the seasonal momentum series for the current bar is determined only by events about 1 year or more ago. This is why it is possible to use the centered moving average and other techniques that look ahead in time, rela-tive to the bar being considered. Entries are taken as follows: When the seasonal momentum crosses above some positive threshold, a buy is posted. When the momentum crosses below some negative threshold, a sell is posted. Buying or sell-ing can happen on any of the standard three orders: at open, on limit, or on stop. Entries may also be generated by computing the price differences, normalizing them, applying an integration or summing procedure to the series (to obtain a kind of pseudo-price series, based on previous instances of each date), and then applying a moving average crossover model to the series. Because the value at any bar in the series is determined only by bars that are about 1 year old or older, the delay in the crossovers can be compensated for by simply looking ahead a small number of bars.

Both of the methods described above are somewhat *adaptive* in nature; i.e., they do not require specific information about which dates a buy or sell order should be placed. The adaptive quality of the aforementioned methods is impor-tant since different markets respond to seasonal influences in different ways, a fact that logic, as well as our earlier research, supports.

In the current study, several rules for handling confirmations and inversions are also tested to determine whether better results can be obtained over the basic models. *Confirmation* means additional data is available that supports the signals produced by the model. For example, suppose a model generated a buy signal for a given bar. If everything is behaving as it should, the market should be form-ing a bottom around the time of the buy. If, however, the market is forming a top, the buy signal might be suspect, in that the market may not be adhering to its typ-ical seasonal timing. When such apparently contradictory circumstances exist, it would be helpful to have additional criteria to use in deciding whether to act upon the signal, in determining if it is correct. The *crossover-with-confirmation model* implements the crossover model with an additional rule that must be satisfied before the signal to buy or sell can be acted upon: If a buy signal is issued, the Slow %K on the signal bar must be less than 25%, meaning the market is at or near the bottom of its recent range. If a sell signal is issued, Slow %K must be greater than 75%, indicating that the market is at or near the top of its range, as would be expected if following its characteristic seasonal behavior. The *confirmation-and-inversion model* adds yet another element: If a buy signal is issued by the basic model, and the market is near the top of its range (Slow %K greater than 75%), then it is assumed that an inversion has occurred and, instead of issuing a buy sig-nal, a sell signal is posted. If a sell signal is generated, but the market is near the bottom of its range (Slow %K less than 25%), a buy signal is issued.

CHARACTERISTICS OF SEASONAL ENTRIES

Consider trading a simple moving average crossover system. Such a system is usually good at capturing trends, but it lags the market and experiences frequent whipsaws. If slower moving averages are used, the whipsaws can be avoided, but the lag is made worse. Now add seasonality to the equation. The trend-fol-lowing moving average system is applied, not to a series of prices, but to a series that captures the seasonal ebb and flow of the market. Then compute the seasonal series so it represents that ebb and flow, as it will be several days from now—just far enough ahead to cancel out the annoying lag! The result: A system without lag (despite the use of slow, smooth, moving averages) that follows seasonal trends. The ability to remove lag in this way stems from one of the characteristics of seasonality: Seasonal patterns can be estimated far in advance. In other words, seasonality-based models are *predictive*, as opposed to merely responsive.

Since seasonality-based models are predictive, and allow turning points to be identified before their occurrence, seasonal-based trading lends itself to countertrend trading styles. Moreover, because predictions can be made far in advance, very high quality smoothing can be applied. Therefore, the kind of whipsaw trading encountered in responsive models is reduced or eliminated. Another nice characteristic of seasonality is the ability to know days, weeks, months, or even years in advance when trades will occur—certainly a convenience.

Seasonality also has a downside. The degree to which any given market may be predicted using a seasonal model may be poor. Although there may be few whipsaws, the typical trade may not be very profitable or likely to win. If inversions do occur, but the trading model being used was not designed to take them into account, sharp losses could be experienced because the trader could end up going short at an exact bottom, or long at an exact top.

The extent to which seasonal models are predictive and useful and the possibility that inversion phenomena do exist and need to be considered are questions for empirical study.

ORDERS USED TO EFFECT SEASONAL ENTRIES

Entries based on seasonality may be effected in at least three ways: with stops, limits, or market orders. While a particular entry option may work especially well with a particular model, any entry may be used with any model.

Entry orders themselves have their own advantages and disadvantages. The advantage of a *market order* is that no signaled entry will be missed. *Stop orders* ensure that no significant trends (in a trend-following model) will elude the trader, and that entry will not occur without confirmation by movement in favor of the trade (possibly beneficial in some countertrend models). The disadvantages are greater slippage and less favorable entry prices. A *limit order* gets the trader the best price and minimizes transaction costs. However, important trends may be missed while waiting indefinitely for a retracement to the limit price. In countertrend models, a limit order may occasionally worsen the entry price. The entry order may be filled at the limit price, rather than at a price determined by the negative slippage that sometimes occurs when the market is moving against the trade at the time of entry!

TEST METHODOLOGY

The data sample used throughout the tests of seasonal entry methods extends from August 1, 1985, to December 31, 1994 (the in-sample period), and from January 1, 1995, through February 1, 1999 (the out-of-sample period). For seasonality studies, an in-sample period of only 10 years means there is a shortage of data on which to develop the model. When generating seasonal entries was discussed, mention was made about calculating seasonal momentum (or average price behavior) based on equivalent dates in previous years. Because of the data shortage, when considering the in-sample data, calculations will be based not only on past years, but also on future years. This is accomplished using the "jackknife."

Target dates are run throughout the series, bar after bar. If only past years are included, for the early data points, there are very few past years or none at all. Since it takes at least 6 years of past data to get a reasonable seasonal average, there would be no seasonality calculations for most of the in-sample period, which itself is only 10 years. Consequently, there is very little data on which to optimize essential parameters or determine how seasonal models perform on the in-sample data. The *jackknife*, a well-known statistical technique (also known as the "leave-one-out method"), helps solve the data shortage problem

Suppose a seasonality estimate for June 1, 1987, is being calculated. If only past data from the in-sample period is used, the estimate would be based on data from 1986 and 1985. If, however, the jackknife is applied, not only would data from the past be available, but so would data from the "future," i.e., the other years of the in-sample period (1988 through 1994). If the year (1987) that serves as the target bar for the calculations is removed from the in-sample period, the seasonality estimate for that bar would now be based on 9 years of data, a reasonably adequate sample. The jackknife procedure is justified because the data being examined to make the prediction is fairly independent of the data actually being predicted by the seasonality estimate. Since the data used in generating the prediction is at least 1 year away from the target date, it is not contaminated with current market behavior. The process provides an effectively larger sample than could otherwise be obtained, and does so without seriously compromising the available number of degrees of freedom.

For bars in the out-of-sample period, all past years are used to generate the seasonality estimates. For example, to calculate the seasonality for January 14, 1999, the *all-past-years technique* is used: Data from 1998 all the way back to 1985 are included in the analysis. In this way, no calculation for the out-of-sample period is ever based on any future or current data.

All the tests that follow are performed using seasonal entries to trade a diversified portfolio of commodities. The exits are the standard ones, used throughout this book to study entry models. Trades are closed out either when an entry in the opposing direction occurs or when the standard exit closes the trade, whichever comes first. The test platform is also standard. Here is the code for the seasonal trading tests:

```
void SeasonalAvg (float *a, float *v, float *dt, int mode,
int m, int n) {

   // Calculates a seasonal (date-specific) average for each bar
   // based on bars from previous and (in some cases) subsequent
   // years with the same dates. Operates on whole data series.
   // a       - out: series [1..n] of seasonal averages
   // v       - in:  original data series [1..n]
   // dt      - in:  series [1..n] of corresponding dates
   // mode    - in:  method of analysis:
   //                   1 = Jacknife IS, all past years OOS
   //                   2 = Fixed lookback in years
   // m       - in:  date (mode = 1) or lookback (mode = 2)
   // n       - in:  number of bars in all series

   static int i, j, cnt;
   static unsigned long k;
   static float sum, sdate;

   if(mode == 1) {                          // jacknife mode
      for(i = 1; i <= n; i++) {             // for each target bar
         sum = 0.0; cnt = 0;
         for(j = 1; j < 100; j++) {    // walk backwards
            sdate = ((int)dt[i] - 10000 * j); // source date
            if (sdate < dt[3]) break;  // run to beginning
            k = max(0, (int)(i-260.893*j));   // approx index
            hunt(dt, n, sdate, &k);    // find exact index
            if(sdate > dt[k]) k++;
            if(sdate != dt[k]) continue;
            cnt++; sum += v[k];            // accumulate average
         }
         for(j = 1; j < 100; j++) {    // walk forwards
            sdate = ((int)dt[i] + 10000 * j);  // source date
            if(sdate > m) break;           // avoid oos data
            k = min(n, (int)(i+260.893*j)); // approx index
            hunt(dt, n, sdate, &k);    // find exact index
            if(sdate > dt[k]) k++;
            if(sdate != dt[k]) continue;
            cnt++; sum += v[k];            // accumulate average
         }
         a[i] = sum / (cnt + 1.0E-20); // finish average
      }                                    // next target bar
   }
   else if(mode == 2) {                    // fixed lookback mode
      for(i = 1; i <= n; i++) {            // for each target bar
         sum = 0.0; cnt = 0;
```

```
                for(j = 1; j < 100; j++) {     // walk backwards
                if(cnt >= m) break;            // enough years run
                sdate = ((int)dt[i] - 10000 * j);   // source date
                if (sdate < dt[3]) break;      // run to beginning
                k = max(0, (int)(i-260.893*j));     // approx index
                hunt(dt, n, sdate, &k);        // find exact index
                if(sdate > dt[k]) k++;
                if(sdate != dt[k]) continue;
                cnt++; sum += v[k];            // accumulate average
            }
            for(j = 1; j < 100; j++) {         // walk forwards
               if(cnt >= m) break;             // enough years run
               sdate = ((int)dt[i] + 10000 * j);   // source date
               k = min(n, (int)(i+260.893*j));     // approx index
               hunt(dt, n, sdate, &k);         // find exact index
               if(sdate > dt[k]) k++;
                if(sdate != dt[k]) continue;
               cnt++; sum += v[k];             // accumulate average
             }
             a[i] = sum / cnt;                 // finish average
         }                                     // next target bar
     }
}


static void Model (float *parms, float *dt, float *opn, float *hi,
float *lo, float *cls, float *vol, float *oi, float *dlrv, int nb,
TRDSIM &ts, float *eqcls) {
    // Implements a variety of seasonality-based trading models.
    // File = x12mod01.c
    // parms   - vector [1..MAXPRM] of parameters
    // dt      - vector [1..nb] of dates in YYMMDD form
    // opn     - vector [1..nb] of opening prices
    // hi      - vector [1..nb] of high prices
    // lo      - vector [1..nb] of low prices
    // cls     - vector [1..nb] of closing prices
    // vol     - vector [1..nb] of volumes
    // oi      - vector [1..nb] of open interest numbers
    // dlrv    - vector [1..nb] of average dollar volatilities
    // nb      - number of bars in data series or vectors
    // ts      - trading simulator class instance
    // eqcls   - vector [1..nb] of closing equity levels

    // declare local scratch variables
    static int rc, cb, ncontracts, maxhold, ordertype, signal;
    static int avglen, disp, k, modeltype, matype;
    static float mmstp, ptlim, stpprice, limprice, tmp, thresh;
```

```
static float exitatr[MAXBAR+1];
static float savg[MAXBAR+1], pchg[MAXBAR+1], stoch[MAXBAR+1];
static float ma1[MAXBAR+1], ma2[MAXBAR+1];

// copy parameters to local variables for clearer reference
avglen     = parms[1];   // length of moving averages
disp       = parms[2];   // displacement factor
thresh     = parms[3];   // threshold for momentum models
matype     = parms[7];   // average type:
               // 1=simple moving average
               // 2=exponential
               // 3=front-weighted triangular
               // 4=triangular
               // 5=centered simple
               // 6=centered exponential
               // 7=centered triangular
modeltype = parms[8];   // model type:
               //   1=momentum
               //   2=crossover
               //   3=crossover with confirmation
               //   4=crossover with confirmation and inversion
ordertype = parms[9];   // entry: 1=open, 2=limit, 3=stop
maxhold = 10;           // maximum holding period
ptlim = 4;              // profit target in volatility units
mmstp = 1;              // stop loss in volatility units
// perform whole-series computations using vector methods
AvgTrueRangeS(exitatr,hi,lo,cls,50,nb);    // ATR for exit
pchg[1] = 0.0;
for(cb = 2; cb <= nb; cb++) {
   tmp = cls[cb] - cls[cb-1];              // price change
   tmp = tmp / exitatr[cb];                // normalization
   pchg[cb] = clip(tmp, -2.0, 2.0);        // clipping
}
switch(modeltype) {
  case 1:                   // series for momentum model
    SeasonalAvg(savg,pchg,dt,1,OOS_DATE,nb);  // seasonals
    MovAvg(savg,savg,matype,avglen,nb);       // smoothing avg
    for(cb = 1; cb <= nb; cb++)
        ma2[cb] = fabs(savg[cb]);
    MovAvg(ma1, ma2, 1, 100, nb);             // avg deviation
    break;
  case 2: case 3: case 4: // series for crossover models
    SeasonalAvg(savg,pchg,dt,1,OOS_DATE,nb);  // seasonals
    for(cb = 2; cb <= nb; cb++)
        savg[cb] += savg[cb-1];               // integration
    MovAvg(ma1,savg,matype,avglen,nb);        // smoothing avg
```

```
      MovAvg(ma2,ma1,matype,avglen,nb);          // crossover avg
      if(modeltype == 3 || modeltype == 4)       // stochastic osc
          StochOsc(stoch,hi,lo,cls,1,9,nb);      //   9-bar Fast %K
      break;
    default: nrerror("TRAPSMOD: invalid modeltype");
}
// step through bars (days) to simulate actual trading
for(cb = 1; cb <= nb; cb++) {

    // take no trades before the in-sample period
    // ... same as TradeStation's MaxBarsBack setting
    if(dt[cb] < IS_DATE) { eqcls[cb] = 0.0; continue; }

    // execute any pending orders and save closing equity
    rc = ts.update(opn[cb], hi[cb], lo[cb], cls[cb], cb);
    if(rc != 0) nrerror("Trade buffer overflow");
    eqcls[cb] = ts.currentequity(EQ_CLOSETOTAL);

    // take no trades in last 30 bars of data sample
    // to leave room in arrays for seasonal look-aheads
    if(cb > nb-30) continue;

    // calculate number of contracts to trade
    // ... we want to trade the dollar volatility equivalent
    // ... of 2 new S&P-500 contracts as of 12/31/98
    ncontracts = RoundToInteger(5673.0 / dlrv[cb]);
    if(ncontracts < 1) ncontracts = 1;

    // avoid placing orders on possibly limit-locked days
    if(hi[cb+1] == lo[cb+1]) continue;

    // generate entry signals, stop prices and limit prices
    // for all seasonality-based entry models
    signal = 0;
    switch(modeltype) {
      case 1:   // basic thresholded momentum entry model
        k = cb + disp;
        tmp = thresh * ma1[k];
        if(savg[k] > tmp && savg[k-1] <= tmp)
            signal = 1;
        else if(savg[k] < -tmp && savg[k-1] >= -tmp)
            signal = -1;
        break;
      case 2: // basic crossover entry model
        k = cb + disp;
        if(CrossesAbove(ma1, ma2, k)) signal = 1;
        else if(CrossesBelow(ma1, ma2, k)) signal = -1;
        break;
```

```
      case 3: // crossover with confirmation
        k = cb + disp;
        if(CrossesAbove(ma1, ma2, k)) {
           if(stoch[cb] < 25.0) signal = 1;
        }
        else if(CrossesBelow(ma1, ma2, k)) {
           if(stoch[cb] > 75.0) signal = -1;
        }
        break;
      case 4: // crossover with confirmation and inversion
        k = cb + disp;
        if(CrossesAbove(ma1, ma2, k)) {
           if(stoch[cb] < 25.0) signal = 1;
           else if(stoch[cb] > 75.0) signal = -1;
        }
        else if(CrossesBelow(ma1, ma2, k)) {
           if(stoch[cb] > 75.0) signal = -1;
           else if(stoch[cb] < 25.0) signal = 1;
        }
        break;
      default: nrerror("TRAPSMOD: invalid modeltype");
    }
    limprice = 0.5 * (hi[cb] + lo[cb]);
    stpprice = cls[cb] + 0.5 * signal * exitatr[cb];

    // enter trades using specified order type
    if(ts.position() <= 0 && signal == 1) {
      switch(ordertype) { // select desired order type
        case 1: ts.buyopen('1', ncontracts); break;
        case 2: ts.buylimit('2', limprice, ncontracts); break;
        case 3: ts.buystop('3', stpprice, ncontracts); break;
        default: nrerror("Invalid buy order selected");
      }
    }
    else if(ts.position() >= 0 && signal == -1) {
      switch(ordertype) { // select desired order type
        case 1: ts.sellopen('4', ncontracts); break;
        case 2: ts.selllimit('5', limprice, ncontracts); break;
        case 3: ts.sellstop('6', stpprice, ncontracts); break;
        default: nrerror("Invalid sell order selected");
      }
    }
    // instruct simulator to employ standard exit strategy
    tmp = exitatr[cb];
    ts.stdexitcls('X', ptlim*tmp, mmstp*tmp, maxhold);

  } // process next bar
}
```

After declaring local variables and arrays, the first major block of code copies various parameters to local variables for more convenient and understandable reference. The parameters are described in comments in this block of code.

The next block of code performs all computations that are carried out on complete time series. The 50-bar average true range is calculated and saved in a vector (*exitatr*); it will be used later for the placement of money management stops and profit targets in the standard exit strategy. The average true range in this vector (or data series) is also used to normalize the price changes in the code that immediately follows.

After calculating the average true range, normalized and clipped price changes are calculated. Each bar in the series *pchg* reflects the change in price from the close of the previous bar to the close of the current bar. The price changes are normalized by dividing them by the average true range. They are then clipped to limit the influence of sharp spikes or statistical outliers. Normalization is performed because markets change in their volatility over time, sometimes very dramatically. For example, the current S&P 500 has a price almost five or more times its price 15 years ago, with a corresponding increase in the size of the average daily move. If the price changes were not normalized and represented in terms of recent volatility, any seasonal estimate conducted over a number of years would be biased. The years with greater volatility would contribute more to the estimate than the years with lesser volatility. In the case of the S&P 500, the most recent years would almost totally dominate the picture. Using normalized price changes, each year contributes about equally. Clipping to remove outliers is performed so the occasional, abnormal price change does not skew the estimates. Clipping is performed at -2 and $+2$ average true range units.

The *modeltype* selection then determines which calculations occur next. A *modeltype* of 1 selects the basic momentum model. The seasonals are computed from the clipped and normalized price changes, the jackknife is used on the in-sample period, and the all-past-years technique is used for the out-of-sample period. These calculations are accomplished with a call to the function called *SeasonalAvg*. The series of seasonal estimates is then smoothed using a moving average of the type, specified by the parameter *matype*, and of a length set by *avglen*, another parameter. A series of average absolute deviations of the seasonal momentums is then computed. This series is nothing more than a 100-bar simple moving average of the absolute values of seasonal momentum, which is used in later computations of threshold values. The *modeltypes* of 2, 3, and 4 all represent variations of the crossover model. The seasonals are computed, and then the seasonal estimates of price change for every bar are integrated (a running sum is calculated), creating a new series that behaves almost like a price series. The synthesized, price-like series represents the movement in prices based on typical behavior in previous and perhaps future years. Two moving averages are then computed: *ma1* (a moving average of the integrated seasonal time series of *matype*, having a length of *avglen*) and *ma2* (used as a signal line for detecting crossovers, calculated by taking a moving average of *ma1*; the kind of average taken is again specified by *matype* and the length by *avglen*). If the *modeltype* is 3 or 4, additional calculations are performed for models in which confirmation and/or inversions are detected; in the current study, a 9-bar Fast %K is calculated and saved in the vector *stoch*.

The next block of code consists of a loop that steps sequentially through all bars in the data series. This loop is the same one that has been seen in every previous chapter on entry strategies. The first few lines of code deal with such issues as updating the simulator, calculating the number of contracts to trade, and avoiding limit-locked days. The next few lines generate entry signals for all the seasonality-based entry models. Depending on the value of the modeltype parameter, either of four different approaches is used to generate entry signals.

A *modeltype* of 1 represents the basic momentum threshold entry model. A threshold is calculated by multiplying a threshold-determining parameter (*thresh*) by the average absolute deviation of the seasonal momentum over the past 100 bars. A long signal is issued if the seasonal momentum (*savg*), on the current bar plus a displacement parameter (*disp*), crosses above the threshold. If the seasonal momentum, at the current bar plus the displacement, crosses below the negative of the threshold, a sell signal is generated. In other words, if sufficiently strong seasonal momentum is predicted for a given date, plus or minus some number of days or bars (*disp*), then a trade is taken in the direction of the expected movement.

For *modeltype* 2, which represents the basic crossover entry model, the moving averages of the integrated seasonals, at the current bar plus a displacement factor, are calculated. If the first moving average crosses above the second, a buy is generated. If it crosses below, a sell is generated. The displacement factor allows the model to look for such crossings some number of days down the line (ahead in time). In this manner, the displacement can neutralize the lag involved in the moving averages. Because the seasonal averages are based on data that is usually a year old, it is perfectly acceptable to look ahead several days.

A *modeltype* of 3 represents the same crossover model, but with the addition of confirmation. Confirmation is achieved by checking the Stochastic oscillator of the actual price series to determine whether it is consistent with what one would be expected if the market were acting in a seasonal fashion.

If *modeltype* is 4, the crossover model, with the addition of confirmation and inversion, is selected. When there is a *modeltype* of 4, a buy signal is issued if the first moving average crosses above the second, and the seasonal pattern is confirmed by a Stochastic of less than 25. The model assumes that an inversion has occurred and issues a sell signal if the Stochastic is over 75. If the first moving average crosses below the second moving average, and the normal seasonal pattern is confirmed by a Stochastic that is over 75, a sell signal is issued. Inversion is assumed and a buy signal issued if the Stochastic is less than 25.

Finally, the limit price (*limprice*) is set at the midpoint of the current bar. The stop price (*stpprice*), for entry on a stop, is set at the close of the current bar plus (if entering long) or minus (if entering short) one-half of the 50-bar average true range. The remaining code blocks are identical to those in previous chapters: They involve actually posting trades using the specified order (*ordertype*) and instructing the simulator to employ the standard exit strategy.

TEST RESULTS

Tests are performed on two seasonality-based entry models: the crossover model (both with and without confirmation and inversions) and the momentum model. Each model is examined using the usual three entry orders: enter at open, on limit, and on stop.

Tables 8-1 and 8-2 provide information on the specific commodities that the model traded profitably, and those that lost, for the in-sample (Table 8-1) and out-of-sample (Table 8-2) runs. The *SYM* column represents the market being studied. The rightmost column (*COUNT*) contains the number of profitable tests for a given market. The numbers in the first row represent test identifiers. The last row (*COUNT*) contains the number of markets on which a given model was profitable. The data in these tables provide relatively detailed information about which markets are and are not profitable when traded by each of the models: One dash (-) indicates a moderate loss per trade, i.e., $2,000 to $4,000; two dashes (--) represent a large loss per trade, i.e., $4,000 or more; one plus sign (+) means a moderate profit per trade, i.e., $1,000 to $2,000; two pluses (++) indicate a large gain per trade, i.e., $2,000 or more; and a blank cell means that the loss was between $0 and $1,999 or the profit was between $0 and $1,000 per trade. (For information about the various markets and their symbols, see Table II-1 in the "Introduction" to Part II.)

Tests of the Basic Crossover Model

A simple moving average (*ma1*) of a specified length (*avglen*) was computed for the integrated, price-like seasonality series. A second moving average (*ma2*) was taken of the first moving average. A buy signal was generated when *ma1* crossed above *ma2*. A sell signal was generated when *ma1* crossed below *ma2*. (This is the same moving-average crossover model discussed in the chapter on moving averages, except here it is computed on a predicted, seasonal series, rather than on prices.) The entries were effected by either a market at open (Test 1), a limit (Test 2), or a stop order (Test 3).

Optimization for these tests involved stepping the length of the moving averages (*avglen*) from 5 to 20 in increments of 5 and the displacement (*disp*) from 0 to 20 in increments of 1. For entry at the open, the best performance (in terms of in-sample risk-to-reward ratio) was achieved with a moving average length of 20 and a displacement of 5. Entry on a limit was best with a length of 20 and a dis-

TABLE 8-1

In-Sample Performance Broken Down by Test and Market

SYM	01	02	03	04	05	06	07	08	09	10	11	12	COUNT
SP			+				+	-	++	-		++	4
YX			++	--	-	-			++		--	++	3
US	--	--			++	++		++				++	4
TB	--	--	--	--	-	--	--	-	++	--	--	++	2
TY	--	-	--	--	++	++	-	--	--	-	--	++	3
BP	--	+	--				--		-			-	1
DM	--	--	--	-		++	--	--	-	++	++	--	3
SF	-	-	+	--	--	--	-	--	--	-	++		2
JY	--	++		+	+	++	--	--		-	--		4
CD	-		-	-	-		-	++	+	-		--	2
ED	--	--	-	--	--		--	--	++	--		-	1
CL	+	+	+	++	++	++		+	++	--	--		8
HO		+	-	++	-	++	++	++	-	++			6
HU	++	++	++	+		++	+	++	+		--		8
GC	-		--	--		--	--		--		+	--	1
SI	+	+	++	-			+	--	++	--	-	+	6
PL	+	-	-	-	--	--	++		++	-	++	++	5
PA	++	++		-	--	--				++		-	3
FC	+		++	++	++	++	-		-	+	-		6
LC		+	+	+		--	++	+	--	++			5
LH	++	+	++	++	+	++	-	+	-			--	7
PB	-	--	--	++	++	+	++	--	++		+	+	7
S		+	++	-	-	--		+	+		-	++	5
SM	+	+	-	--	--	--	++	++		-	-	-	4
BO		--	+			--	--			+			2
C	--		-	+		-	--	-	--	--	--	--	1
O	--		+	+		+		+	-	-		--	3
W	-	--	-			--	--	--			--	-	0
KW	-	--			-	++	-		--	--		--	1
MW		+		--	-	--	--			--	--		1
KC	+	++	++	+	+	++	++	+	++		++	+	11
CC	+		-				++	++	++	-		++	5
SB	-	+	+				+	+		++	++	+	7
JO	+		+	+		++		+	-	--	--	--	5
CT		+	++	+	++	++	++		--	--	-	--	6
LB	+	++		-			+	+	++		--		5
COUNT	12	15	15	13	9	15	13	15	14	7	7	12	

placement of 8. Entry on a stop required a length of 20 and a displacement of 6. The model seemed to prefer longer moving averages (more smoothing), and somewhat earlier signals were required by the limit order when compared with the stop or market-at-open orders.

In-sample, none of the results were profitable when both long and short positions were traded. However, the losses were much smaller on a per-trade basis than those observed in many of the other tests presented in earlier chapters. The stop order performed best. The market-at-open order performed worst. The limit order came in not too far behind the stop. For both the stop and limit orders, trading was

TABLE 8-2

Out-of-Sample Performance Broken Down by Test and Market

SYM	01	02	03	04	05	06	07	08	09	10	11	12	COUNT
SP	+		++	-	++	--	--		--	--		--	3
YX	-	-	--	--	++	--	++	--	++	--		++	4
US			--	++	++	++	--		--	+		--	4
TB	--	-	-	-	--	--	--		-	-		--	0
TY	+		--	++	++	++	--	--	++	-	--	++	6
BP	+	++	++	--	--	--	++	--	++		--	++	6
DM			--	--	--	-	--	+		-	+	+	3
SF	--	--	-	--	-	--	--	--	+	++	-	++	3
JY		-	--	++	++	++	-	--	-	++	+	--	5
CD		-	--	++	-	++			--	--		--	2
ED	--	--	-	--	--	--	--	--	--	--	--	--	0
CL				+	+	++	--	--	++	--	-	--	4
HO	--	++	--	++		++	--		++	--	--	--	4
HU	++	++	++	++		++	++		++	--	--		7
GC	+	++	++		-	--	+	--	--		--	--	4
SI	-		+	-	--	--	+		++	++	++	++	6
PL	+	++	++	++	++	++		-	++		-	++	8
PA	+	++	++	++	++	++	--	--		--	--	-	6
FC			-	-	-	-	+	-	+	-		++	3
LC				++	++		++	--	--	-	++	--	4
LH		++	++	++	++	++	+	+	--	--	--		7
PB			++	-	++		+		--		--	--	3
S	-	+	--	+	-	++	--	-	--	-	++	+	5
SM	++	-	++	++		++	++				--	+	6
BO	++		-	++	+	--			--	--			3
C		-	--	-	--	--	--	--	--	--	--	--	0
O	-	--	-	--	--	--	--	--	++	--	--	++	2
W		+		--	--	--			--	-	-	--	1
KW		++	++	--	+	--	++	++		--	--	--	5
MW		++		-	+	--	-	--	-	--	-	-	2
KC	++		++	++	++	++	-		++	++	++	--	8
CC	-	--	--	--	--	--	--	-	+	++		-	2
SB			++	--	--	--	--	-	++	--	--	++	3
JO		+			-	--	--	--	+		++	-	3
CT	++		++		--	+	++	-	+	++	-	++	7
LB			++	++	++	++	++	++	++	-		++	7
COUNT	11	12	14	16	16	15	13	4	17	7	7	14	

actually profitable for long positions. In all cases, 20-bar moving averages provided the best results, but the displacement varied depending on the order. A look-ahead of 5 bars was optimal for entry at the open, 8 bars for entry on a limit, and 6 bars for entry on a stop. This makes sense, in that one would want to post a limit order earlier than a market-on-open order so as to give the limit some time to be filled. Out-of-sample, the results showed the same ordering of overall performance as measured by the average profit per trade (*$TRD*), with the stop order actually producing a positive return of $576 per trade, representing an 8.3% annual return on account; this system, although not great, was actually profitable on recent data. For the stop entry, both in- and out-of-sample trading was profitable when only the long trades were considered, but the short side lost in both samples. This is a pattern that has been observed a number of times in the various tests. The percentage of wins for all orders and samples was between 40 and 43%.

It is interesting that, even for the losing variations, the losses here were much smaller than what seems typical for many of the models so far tested.

With entry at the open, equity declined until November 1988. It retraced approximately 50% of the way until July 1989, making a small U-shaped formation, with the second of a double-top around November 1990. Equity then declined rather steeply until November 1992 and, in a more choppy fashion, throughout the remainder of the in-sample period and the first third of the out-of-sample period. The decline ended in April 1996 when equity gradually climbed throughout the remainder of the out-of-sample period.

With entry on a limit, equity was fairly flat until January 1987, rose very rapidly to a peak in May 1987, and then declined until November 1992. From then through July 1994, equity rose steeply. Afterward, choppy performance was observed with no significant trend.

The stop order produced strong equity growth until June 1988. Equity then declined in a choppy fashion through most of the in-sample period and about the first quarter of the out-of-sample period. It reached bottom in December 1995 and then rose sharply through the end of the out-of-sample period in February 1999.

Across all three entry orders, the best-performing market was Unleaded Gasoline, in which strong, consistent profits were observed in both samples. Palladium was also a strong market for this model: Both the entry at open and entry on limit produced profits in- and out-of-sample, with the entry on limit having strong profits in both samples, and the entry on stop producing strong profits out-of-sample and neutral results in-sample. Live Hogs was another good market to trade seasonally: Every order type yielded profits in-sample, while two of the three order types yielded profits out-of-sample; both the limit and stop orders were profitable in both samples. Yet another good market to trade with this model is Coffee: All three orders produced in-sample profits, while the market at open and stop orders produced strong profits out-of-sample. Finally, Cotton did not do too badly: The stop order yielded strong profits in both samples, and no order resulted in strong losses in either sample. Finding good performance for Unleaded Gasoline is totally in accord with expectations. What is moderately surprising is that Heating Oil, for which there is a strong seasonal demand characteristic, was only profitable in both samples when using the limit order. Coffee also traditionally has strong seasonal patterns caused by, e.g., recurrent frosts that damage crops, create shortages, and drive up prices. Surprisingly, the wheats did not produce many profits in-sample. The only exception was a small profit for Minnesota Wheat with a limit order. More profits in the wheat group were seen out-of-sample, where the limit order led to profitable trading in all three wheat markets and the stop order in Kansas Wheat.

A number of other markets showed profitable, but less consistent, trading across sample and order type. Again, it is impressive to see the great number of markets that trade well across both samples, especially when compared with many of the other models that have been tested in the preceding chapters.

It is also interesting that there is a discrepancy between the performance of the seasonality model in the current tests and in our earlier tests of the S&P 500 (Katz and McCormick, April 1997). The differences are probably due to such factors as tuning. In the earlier tests, the moving averages were specifically tuned to the S&P 500; in the current tests, they were tuned to the entire portfolio. Moreover, compared with other markets, the seasonal behavior of the S&P 500 appears to involve fairly rapid movements and, therefore, requires a much shorter moving average to achieve optimal results. Finally, the earlier tests did not use separate exits and so a seasonal trend lasting several weeks could be captured. In the current test, only the first 10 days could be captured, after which time the standard exit closes out the trade. It is likely that the performance observed, not just on the S&P 500, but on all the markets in the portfolio, would be better if the standard exit were replaced with an exit capable of holding onto a sustained trend.

Tests of the Basic Momentum Model

For the momentum model, the unintegrated seasonal price change series was smoothed with a centered simple moving average of a specified length (*avglen*). The centered average introduces no lag because it examines as many future data points, relative to the current bar, as it does past data points. The use of a centered moving average is legitimate, because the seasonality estimate at the current bar is based on data that is at least 1 year away. For this series of smoothed seasonal price changes, a series of average absolute deviations was computed: To produce the desired result, the absolute value for each bar in the smoothed seasonal series was computed and a 100-bar simple moving average was taken. A buy signal was issued if the seasonal momentum, at the current bar plus some displacement (*disp*), was greater than some multiple (*thresh*) of the average absolute deviation of the seasonal momentum. A sell signal was issued if the seasonal momentum, at the same displaced bar, was less than minus the same multiple of the average absolute deviation. Entries were executed at the open (Test 4), on a limit (Test 5), or on a stop (Test 6).

Optimization was carried out for the length of the moving averages, the displacement, and the threshold. The length was stepped from 5 to 15 in increments of 5; the displacement from 1 to 10 in steps of 1; and the threshold from 1.5 to 2.5 in increments of 0.5. The best in-sample performance was observed with a length of 15 and a threshold of 2.5, regardless of entry order. For the market at open and for the stop a displacement of 2 was required. The limit worked best with a displacement of 1. In agreement with expectations, these displacements are much smaller than those that were optimal for the crossover model where there was a need to compensate for the lag associated with the moving averages.

Overall, the results were much poorer than for the seasonal crossover model. In-sample, profitability was only observed with the stop order. No profitability was observed out-of-sample, regardless of the order. The losses on a per-trade basis were quite heavy. Interestingly, the long side performed less well overall than the short side. This reverses the usual pattern of better-performing long trades than short ones.

With both entry at open and on limit, equity declined in a choppy fashion from the beginning of the in-sample period through the end of the out-of-sample period. The decline was less steep with the limit order than with entry at open. With the stop order, equity was choppy, but basically flat, until May 1990, when it began a very steep ascent, reaching a peak in September 1990. Equity then showed steady erosion through the remaining half of the in-sample and most of the out-of-sample periods. The curve flattened out, but remained choppy, after April 1997.

The model traded the T-Bonds, 10-Year Notes, Japanese Yen, Light Crude, Heating Oil, Unleaded Gasoline, Live Hogs, and Coffee fairly well both in- and out-of-sample. For example, T-Bonds and 10-Year Notes were very profitable in both samples when using either the limit or stop orders. Japanese Yen performed best with the stop, showing heavy profits in both samples, but was profitable with the other orders as well. The same was true for Light Crude. Heating Oil showed heavy profits with the entry at open and on stop in both samples, but not with entry on limit. This was also true for Unleaded Gasoline. Live Hogs performed best, showing heavy profits in both samples, with entry at open or on stop. This market was profitable with all three orders in both samples. Coffee was also profitable with all three orders on both samples, with the strongest and most consistent profits being with the stop. For the most part, this model showed losses on the wheats.

In-sample, 15 markets were profitable to one degree or another using a stop, 13 using a market order at the open, and 9 using a limit. Out-of-sample, the numbers were 15, 16, and 16, respectively, for the stop, open, and limit.

Even though the momentum model performed more poorly on the entire portfolio, it performed better on a larger number of individual markets than did the crossover model. The momentum model, if traded on markets with appropriate seasonal behavior, can produce good results.

Tests of the Crossover Model with Confirmation

This model is identical to the basic crossover model discussed earlier, except that entries were only taken if seasonal market behavior was confirmed by an appropriate reading of the Fast %K Stochastic. Specifically, if the seasonal crossover suggested a buy, the buy was only acted upon if the Fast %K was below 25%; i.e., the market has to be declining or near a bottom (as would be expected on the basis of the seasonal buy) before a buy can occur. Likewise, a seasonal sell was not taken unless the market was near a top, as shown by a Fast %K greater than 75%. As always, the standard exits were used. Entries were executed at the open (Test 7), on a limit (Test 8), or on a stop (Test 9).

Optimization for these tests involved stepping the length of the moving averages (*avglen*) from 5 to 20 in increments of 5 (*P1*) and the displacement (*disp*) from 0 to 20 in increments of 1 (*P2*). For entry at the open, a moving average length of 15 and a displacement of 7 were best. Entry on a limit was best with a length of 15 and a displacement of 6. Entry on a stop required a length of 20 and a displacement of 9.

On a per-trade basis, the use of confirmation by the Fast %K worsened the results for both sampling periods when entry was at the open or on a limit; with both of these orders, trades lost heavily in both samples. When the confirmed seasonal was implemented using a stop order for entry, relatively profitable performance in both samples was seen. In-sample, the average trade pulled $846 from the market, while the average trade pulled $1,677 out of the market in the verification sample. In-sample, 41% of the trades were profitable and the annual return was 5.8%. The statistical significance is not great, but at least it is better than chance; both long and short positions were profitable. Out-of-sample, 44% of the trades were winners, the return on account was 19.6%, and there was a better than 77% chance that the model was detecting a real market inefficiency; both longs and shorts were profitable. Compared with other systems, the number of trades taken was somewhat low. There were only 292 trades in-sample and 121 out-of-sample. All in all, we again have a profitable model. Seasonality seems to have validity as a principle for entering trades.

The equity curve for entry at open showed a gradual decline until May 1989. It was then fairly flat until August 1993, when equity began to decline through the remainder of the in-sample period and most of the out-of-sample period. The limit order was somewhat similar, but the declines in equity were less steep. For the stop order, the picture was vastly different. Equity declined at a rapid pace until May 1987. Then it began to rise at an accelerating rate, reaching a peak in June 1995, the early part of the out-of-sample period. Thereafter, equity was close to flat. The greatest gains in equity for the stop order occurred between June 1990 and May 1991, between May 1993 and September 1993, and between January 1995 and June 1995. The last surge in equity was during the out-of-sample period.

Compared with the previous two models, there were fewer markets with consistent profitability across all or most of the order types. Lumber was the only market that showed profitability across all three order types both in- and out-of-sample. Unleaded Gasoline yielded profits across all three order types in-sample, and was highly profitable out-of-sample with entry at open or on stop. Coffee and Cocoa were profitable for all order types in-sample, but profitable only for the stop order out-of-sample. For the stop order, the NYFE, Silver, Palladium,

Light Crude, Lumber, and Coffee were highly profitable in both samples. Again, there was no profitability for the wheats. There was enough consistency for this model to be tradable using a stop order and focusing on appropriate markets.

Tests of the Crossover Model with Confirmation and Inversions

This model is the same as the crossover model with confirmation. However, additional trades were taken where inversions may have occurred; i.e., if a seasonal buy was signaled by a crossover, but the market was going up or near a top (as indicated by the Fast %K being greater than 75%), a sell signal was posted. The assumption with this model is that the usual seasonal cycle may have inverted or flipped over, where a top is formed instead of a bottom. Likewise, if the crossover signaled a sell, but the Fast %K indicated that the market was down by being less than 25%, a buy was posted. These signals were issued in addition to those described in the crossover with confirmation model. Entries were executed at the open (Test 10), on a limit (Test 11), or on a stop (Test 12).

Optimization for these tests involved stepping the length of the moving averages (*avglen*) from 5 to 20 in increments of 5 (*P1*) and the displacement (*disp*) from 0 to 20 in increments of 1 (*P2*). For entry at the open, a moving-average length of 15 and a displacement of 2 were best. Entry on a limit was best with a length of 20 and a displacement of 4. Entry on a stop again required a length of 20 and a displacement of 9.

For entry at the open, the equity curve showed a smooth, severe decline from one end of the sampling period to the other. There was a steeply declining equity curve for the limit order, although the overall decline was roughly half that of the one for entry at open. For entry on stop, the curve declined until May 1987. It then became very choppy but essentially flat until August 1993. From August 1993 until June 1995, the curve steeply accelerated, but turned around and sharply declined throughout the rest of the out-of-sample period. Adding the inversion element was destructive to the crossover model. The seasonal patterns studied apparently do not evidence frequent inversions, at least not insofar as is detectable by the approach used.

Adding the inversion signals to the model dramatically worsened performance on a per-trade basis across all entry orders. Losses were seen for every combination of sample and order type, except for a very small profit with a stop in the out-of-sample period. There were no markets that showed consistently good trading across multiple order types in both samples, although there were isolated instances of strong profits for a particular order type in certain markets. The NYFE again traded very profitably with a stop order, as did 10-Year Notes, in both samples. Platinum and Silver also traded well in- and out-of-sample with a stop order. Soybeans traded very profitably with a stop order in-sample, but only somewhat profitably out-of-sample. There were consistent losses, or no profits at all, across all orders and samples for the wheats.

Summary Analyses

Results from the different tests were combined into one table and two charts for overall analysis. Table 8-3 provides performance numbers broken down by sample, entry order, and model. For each model, there are two rows of numbers: The first row contains the figures for annualized return-on-account, and the second row contains the average dollar profit or loss per trade. The two rightmost columns contain averages across all order types for the in-sample and out-of-sample performance. The last two rows contain the average across all models for each type of order.

Of the three types of orders, it is evident that the stop performed best. The limit and entry at open performed about equally well, but much worse than the stop. In fact, for the stop, the average across all four models actually showed a positive return and small profits on a per-trade basis both in-sample and out-of-sample.

When examining models averaged across all order types, the in-sample performance was best using the crossover-with-confirmation model and worst for the crossover-with-confirmation and inversion model. Out-of-sample, the basic crossover model showed the best performance, while the crossover with confirmation and inversion had the worst.

As can be seen, in-sample the best performance was observed when the stop order was used with the crossover-with-confirmation model. This is also the combination of order and model that performed best out-of-sample.

TABLE 8-3

Performance of Seasonal Entry Models Broken Down by Model, Order, and Sample

Model	In-sample			Out-of-sample			Average	Average
	Open	Limit	Stop	Open	Limit	Stop	In	Out
Seasonal	-9.7	-4.1	-1.3	-5.8	-1.7	8.3	-5.0	0.3
crossover	-1127.0	-424.0	-179.0	-300.0	-56.0	576.0	-576.7	73.3
Seasonal	-9.4	-7.4	3.3	-13.6	-13.7	-16.4	-4.5	-14.6
momentum	-1069.0	-757.0	275.0	-952.0	-785.0	-1750.0	-517.0	-1162.3
Crossover with	-9.6	-7.2	5.8	-13.8	-21.1	19.6	-3.7	-5.1
confirmation	-1195.0	-832.0	846.0	-1512.0	-3408.0	1677.0	-393.7	-1081.0
Crossover with	-9.6	-8.9	-2.2	-20.4	-22.6	0.9	-6.9	-14.1
conf. + inver.	-1669.0	-1696.0	-229.0	-2545.0	-2642.0	95.0	-1198.0	-1697.3
Average	-9.6	-6.9	1.4	-13.4	-14.8	3.1	-5.0	-8.4
	-1265.0	-927.3	178.3	-1327.3	-1722.8	149.5	-671.3	-966.8

In earlier chapters, other types of entry models were tested and the limit order was usually found to perform best. In the case of seasonality, the stop order had a dramatic, beneficial impact on performance, despite the additional transaction costs. Previously it appeared that countertrend principles may perform better when combined with some trend-following or confirming element, such as an entry on a stop. It seems that, with seasonality, the kind of confirmation achieved by using something like a stop is important, perhaps even more so than the kind achieved using the Fast %K. In other words, if, based on seasonal patterns, the market is expected to rise, confirmation that it is indeed rising should be obtained before a trade is entered.

Overall, it seems that there is something important about seasonality: It has a real influence on the markets, as evidenced by the seasonality-based system with the stop performing better, or at least on par, with the best of the entry models. This was one of the few profitable entry models tested. Seasonal phenomena seem to have fairly strong effects on the markets, making such models definitely worth further exploration.

It would be interesting to test a restriction of the seasonality model to markets on which it performed best or to markets that, for fundamental reasons, would be expected to have strong seasonal behavior. From an examination of the market-by-market analysis (discussed earlier in the context of individual tests), there is quite a bit of *prima facie* evidence that certain markets are highly amenable to seasonal trading. When breakout models were restricted to the currencies, dramatic benefits resulted. Perhaps restricting seasonal models to appropriate markets would be equally beneficial.

When looking over all the tests and counting the number of instances in which there were significant, positive returns, an impression can be obtained of the markets that lend themselves to various forms of seasonal trading. Across all tests, Coffee had one of the highest number of positive returns in-sample and no losses—true also for its out-of-sample performance. Coffee, therefore, appears to be a good market to trade with a seasonal model, which makes sense since Coffee is subject to weather damage during frost seasons, causing shortages and thus major increases in price. For Coffee, 11 out of the 12 tests in-sample and 8 out of 12 tests out-of-sample were profitable. Unleaded Gasoline was another commodity that had a large number of positive returns across all tests in both samples: in-sample 8 and out-of-sample 11. Light Crude had 8 in-sample but only 4 out-of-sample positive returns. Live Hogs was another market showing a large number of positive returns in both samples.

Figure 8-1 illustrates equity growth broken down by type of order and averaged across all models. As can be seen, the stop order performed best, while entry at open performed worst, and the limit order was in between the two.

Figure 8-2 shows equity growth broken down by model, with averaging done over orders. The crossover-with-confirmation model had the overall best performance, especially in the later half of the testing periods. The basic crossover model

FIGURE 8-1

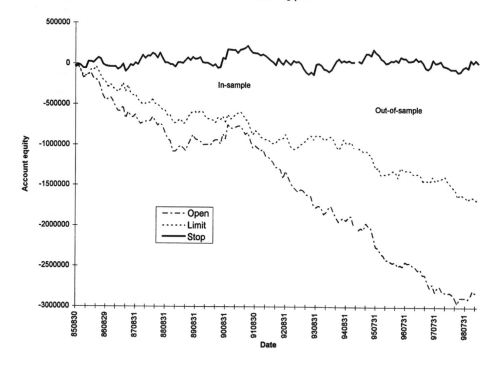

Equity Growth as a Function of Order Type

started out the best, but after 1990, performance deteriorated. However, the equity trend seemed to reverse to the upside after 1995 in the out-of-sample period, a time when the other models tended to have declining equity when considered across all order types.

CONCLUSION

These explorations into seasonality have demonstrated that there are significant seasonal effects to be found in the markets. Decisions about how to trade can be made based on an examination of the behavior of the market at nearby dates for a number of years in the past. The information contained on the same date (or a date before or a date after) for a number of years in the past is useful in making a determination about what the market will do in the near future. Although the seasonal effect is not sufficient to be really tradable on the whole portfolio, it is sufficient to overcome transaction costs leading to some profits. For specific markets, however, even the simple models tested might be worth trading. In other words, seasonal phenomena appear to be real and able to provide useful information. There are times of the year when a market rises and times of the year when a market falls,

FIGURE 8-2

Equity Growth as a Function of Model

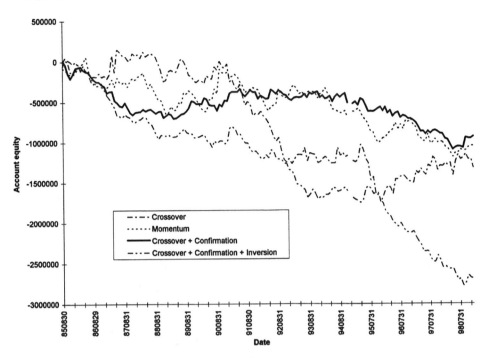

and models like those tested in the chapter can capture such seasonal ebbs and flows in a potentially profitable manner.

Seasonality, as defined herein, has been demonstrated to be worthy of serious consideration. If the kinds of simple entry models illustrated above are elaborated by adding confirmations and by using an exit better than the standard one, some impressive trading results are likely to result.

WHAT HAVE WE LEARNED?

- Recurrent seasonal patterns appear to have real predictive validity and are definitely worthy of further study.
- The usefulness of seasonal patterns for trading varies from market to market, with certain markets being particularly amenable to seasonal trading. Trading a basket of seasonally reactive markets could be a highly lucrative endeavor.
- To obtain the best results, raw seasonal information should be combined with some form of confirmation or trend detection. Making use of additional information can improve the performance of an unadorned seasonal model.

CHAPTER 9

Lunar and Solar Rhythms

In the previous chapter, seasonal rhythms were defined as recurrent phenomena connected to the calendar. Seasonality involves the orbital position and tilt of the earth in relation to the sun. Every year, on approximately the same date, the earth reaches a similar phase in its movement around the sun. Other solar bodies generate similar rhythms, most notably the moon, with its recurrent phases, and "sunspot" phenomena. In this chapter, market cycles determined by external forces will again be analyzed, but this time the relationship between market behavior and planetary and solar rhythms will be examined.

LEGITIMACY OR LUNACY?

Discussion of planetary influences conjures up images of what some regard as astrological nonsense. However, it seems arrogant to dismiss, *a priori*, the possible influence of lunar, solar, and other such forces, simply because of the pervasive *belief* that astrology (which Webster defines as "the pseudo-science which claims to foretell the future by studying the supposed influence of the relative positions of the moon, sun, and stars on human affairs") is ludicrous. Such beliefs are often based on the absence of knowledge. But what is already *known* about so-called astrology, especially in the form of planetary and solar effects on earthly events?

Scientists have demonstrated some correlation between personality and planetary positions. In one study (Mayo, White, and Eysenck, 1978), published in the *Journal of Social Psychology*, researchers tested the claim that introversion and extroversion are determined by the zodiac sign a person is born under. A personality test was given to 2,324 individuals to determine whether they were introverts or extroverts. The hypothesis was that individuals born under the signs Aries, Gemini,

Leo, Libra, Sagittarius, and Aquarius were likely to be extroverts, while those under Taurus, Cancer, Virgo, Scorpio, Capricorn, and Pisces, tend to be introverts. The results of the study were significantly consistent with the hypothesis, as well as with other related studies (Gauquelin, Gauquelin, and Eysenck, 1979).

It is also known that the moon's gravitational force influences the aquatic, terrestrial, and atmospheric tides of the earth. The moon has been shown to affect when coral spawn, when oysters open, when certain crimes are likely to be more prevalent, and when "lunatics" (derived from the Latin word "luna," which translates as "moon") become more agitated. Moreover, women give birth and/or ovulate more frequently during the full moon.

When faced with the facts, the possibility of the moon influencing market behavior is not so outlandish. Even Larry Williams (1979) found that the prices of Silver, Wheat, Corn, and Soybean Oil rally when the moon is full and drop when the moon is new!

Every amateur radio operator knows, "sunspots" exert a major influence on long distance radio transmission. Sunspots appear as dark spots on the surface of the sun. One theory is that they are produced by peculiarities in the gravitational influences of neighboring planets on the Sun's tidal rhythms. Another theory explains sunspots as due to shifts in the sun's magnetic poles. During high sunspot activity, "skip" occurs: Short wavelength radio transmissions, which normally carry only as far as line-of-sight, bounce off the ionosphere and may span distances of up to several thousand miles. Many have experienced this phenomenon when watching television: A signal from a distant station will appear superimposed on a local one. Conversely, during low solar activity, long distance communication is much less likely at short wavelengths; anyone trying to achieve "DX" (long distance communications), will need longer wavelengths.

Sunspot activity and solar flares are also correlated with terrestrial magnetic storms that can disrupt sensitive electronics equipment and even knock out power grids. Magnetic storms induced by solar eruptions in March 1989 shut down the Hydro-Quebec power system, blacking out parts of Montreal and Quebec for up to nine hours (Space Science Institute, 1996).

Changes in solar activity are even suspected of causing major fluctuations in the earth's climate, as when the "Little Ice Age" occurred in the 1600s, after 100 years of attenuated solar activity (Center for Solar and Space Research, 1997).

More relevant to traders: Edward R. Dewey, who established the Foundation for the Study of Cycles in 1940, believed that there was a relationship between sunspots and industrial production. Perhaps such a relationship is mediated by climatological effects on agriculture, making it worthwhile to examine the correlation between solar activity and agricultural commodity prices.

Our interest in sunspots peaked upon noticing that, during 1987, there were only three days when the sunspot number (an index of solar activity) was greater than 100. Two of those days were October 15 and 16! The probability of the correspondence between Black Monday and heightened solar activity is less than one in 100.

In the section below on "Lunar Cycles and Trading," the impact of the lunar phase on prices is examined. The impact of solar activity is examined in "Sunspots and Market Activity."

LUNAR CYCLES AND TRADING

In a previous study (Katz and McCormick, June 1997), we found that lunar cycles could be used to profitably trade the NYFE. From 1990 to 1997, a simple lunar system produced a net profit of $75,550. There were 170 trades, 60% profitable. The average one contract trade made $444.41; the return-on-account was 365% (not annualized). The long side performed better (520%) than the short (-37%). The signals often marked turning points to the very day. Silver also responded well, with signals picking off exact tops and bottoms; both longs and shorts were profitable with a 190% return over the same period as for the NYFE. Even Wheat traded profitably long and short with a 242% return. Given only one parameter (a displacement in days since the full or new moon), and many trades, the results are impressive and probably robust.

Our results were encouraging enough to justify further study of entries based on these phenomena. The study will involve the phases of the moon, i.e., full moon, first quarter, last quarter, new moon, and all phases in between. Can the lunar phase predict whether the market is bottoming or topping? Do bottoms (or tops) form at the time of the full moon, or perhaps five days before the full moon, or at the new moon? Since the lunar cycle may affect different markets differently, the adaptive approach taken with seasonality is again used.

GENERATING LUNAR ENTRIES

There are many ways to time entries based on the lunar rhythm. Two approaches are employed in the tests: momentum and crossover. To calculate momentum, a series of price changes is computed and then a *centered smoothing* (one that induces no delays or phase shifts) is applied. For normalization, each price change in the smoothed series is divided by the 50-day average true range. For each bar, we ask: "What phase is the moon in currently?" As many past instances as possible are found in which the moon was in the identical phase and the momentum of prices on the corresponding bars is examined. The average of the momentums becomes the value placed in the *lunar momentum series*, which reflects the expected rate-of-change (momentum) in prices at a given time based on historical price movement at the phase of the moon existing on the current bar. Each number in the lunar momentum series is determined only by events about 27 or more days ago; this is why centered smoothing, and other techniques that look ahead in time relative to any specified bar, are permissible. Entries are taken when momentum crosses above a positive threshold (a buy signal is issued), or when momentum crosses below a negative threshold (a sell is posted). Buying or selling can take place at the open, on a limit, or on a stop. The momentum calculations and generation of entries closely follow those for seasonality, but, instead of looking to previous instances of the same date in earlier years, previous instances of the moon having a phase identical to that on the target bar are examined.

Entries can also be generated by computing the price differences, normalizing them, and integrating the series to obtain a pseudo-price series based on previous instances of the correct lunar phase. A moving average crossover model is then applied to that series. Because the value at any bar in the series is determined only by bars roughly 27 or more days ago, the delay in the crossovers can be compensated for by looking ahead a small number of bars.

Both methods are *adaptive* in that no specific information is required about the phase of the moon on which to place a buy or sell order. The adaptive quality is important because different markets respond to the moon differently, as seen in our earlier study. Both methods differ from the previous research, where buys or sells occurred a fixed number of days before or after a full or a new moon.

Several rules for handling confirmations and inversions are also tested to determine whether better results can be obtained over the basic models. An example of *confirmation* is the following: If a buy signal occurs on a given bar and everything behaves as expected, the market should bottom around the time of the buy; if instead it tops, the buy signal might be suspect, i.e., the market may not be adhering to its typical seasonal or lunar timing. The *crossover with confirmation model* implements the crossover model with an additional rule that must be satisfied before a buy or sell can be issued. If a buy signal occurs, the Slow %K on the signal bar must be less than 25%, meaning the market is near the bottom of its recent historical range. Likewise, if the model generates a sell signal, a check is made to see whether Slow %K is greater than 75%, indicating that the market is near the top of its range, as would be expected if it is responding to lunar influence. The *confirmation and inversion model* adds another element: If a buy is signalled, and the market is near the top of its range (Slow %K greater than 75%), then an inversion is assumed and, instead of issuing a buy, a sell order is posted. If a sell is signalled, but the market is near the bottom of its recent range, a buy order is issued.

The characteristics of lunar entries are similar to seasonal entries: Both are predictive, rather than responsive, and thus lend themselves to countertrend trading. And, as with any predictive entry, they may be out of tune with market behavior. As with seasonal entries, cycle or rhythm inversions may occur.

LUNAR TEST METHODOLOGY

All tests were performed using lunar entries to trade a diversified portfolio. Can lunar entry models result in profitable trades? How have such models fared over time? Have they become more or less profitable in recent years? The tests will address these questions.

The exits are the standard ones. Entry rules are discussed when presenting individual tests. Trades are closed out when either an entry in the opposing direction takes place, or when the standard exit closes the trade, whichever comes first. The following code implements the lunar-based entry models that underlie all tests.

```
int LunarEventDates (int n) {

    // Calculates the date of a phase of the moon, starting with
    // events in Jan, 1900.
    // n        - in:  event or phase instance number
    //                 0,4,8,...  New moons
    //                 1,5,9,...  First quarter moons
    //                 2,6,10,..  Full moons
    //                 3,7,11,..  Second quarter moons
    // return  - out: Julian date of event occurrence

    static long ndate;
    static float timzon = -5.0 / 24.0;   // eastern standard time
    static float frac;

    flmoon(n >> 2, n & 3, &ndate, &frac);
    frac = 24.0 * (frac + timzon);
    if(frac < 0.0) {                      // correct the times
        ndate—;
        frac += 24.0;
    }
    if(frac > 12.0) {
        ndate++;
        frac -= 12.0;
    }
    else frac += 12.0;
    return ndate;                         // julian date of event
}


int LunarEquivDate (int date, int n) {

    // Calculates the date of the n-th previous (n < 0) or
    // future (n > 0) instance of a moon phase equivalent to
```

```
    // that which exists on the current date.
    // date   - in:  current date in YYYMMDD format
    // n      - in:  lunar cycles back (-) or forward (+)
    // return - out: date of previous or future cycle as YYYMMDD

    static long nstar, ndate1, ndate2, curdate, ntarg, nans;
    static int mm, dd, yyyy;

    curdate = julday((date/100)%100, date%100, 1900+date/10000);
    while(curdate >= ndate2) {
        ndate1 = LunarEventDates(++nstar);
        ndate2 = LunarEventDates(nstar + 1);
    }
    while(curdate < ndate1) {
        ndate1 = LunarEventDates(—nstar);
        ndate2 = LunarEventDates(nstar + 1);
    }
    if(curdate < ndate1 || curdate >= ndate2
      || abs(ndate2 - ndate1 - 7) > 2)
        nrerror("LunarEquivDate: calculation error");
    nans = LunarEventDates(nstar + 4 * n);
    nans += (curdate - ndate1);
    caldat(nans, &mm, &dd, &yyyy);
    return 10000*(yyyy-1900) + 100*mm + dd;
}


void LunarAvg (float *a, float *v, float *dt, int mode, int m, int n) {

    // Calculates a lunar (phase-date-specific) average for each
    // bar based on bars from previous and (in some cases)
    // subsequent equivalent lunar phase dates.
    // Operates on whole data series.
    // a      - out: series [1..n] of lunar averages
    // v      - in:  original price data series [1..n]
    // dt     - in:  series [1..n] of corresponding dates
    // mode   - in:  method of analysis:
    //                    1 = Jacknife IS, all past cycles OOS
    //                    2 = Fixed lookback in moon cycles
    // m      - in:  date (for mode = 1) or lookback (for mode = 2)
    // n      - in:  number of bars in all series

    static int i, j, cnt;
    static unsigned long k;
    static float sum, sdate, tiny=1.0E-20;
```

```
if(mode == 1) {                         // jacknife mode
    for(i = 1; i <= n; i++) {           // for each target bar
        sum = 0.0;  cnt = 0;
        for(j = 2; j < 1000; j++) {     // walk backwards
            sdate = LunarEquivDate (dt[i], -j); // source date
            if(sdate < dt[3]) break;    // run to beginning
            hunt(dt, n, sdate, &k);     // find index
            if(sdate > dt[k]) k++;
            cnt++;  sum += v[k];        // accumulate average
        }
        for(j = 2; j < 1000; j++) {     // walk forwards
            sdate = LunarEquivDate (dt[i], j);  // source date
            if(sdate > m) break;        // avoid oos data
            hunt(dt, n, sdate, &k);     // find index
            if(sdate > dt[k]) k++;
            cnt++;  sum += v[k];        // accumulate average
        }
        a[i] = sum / (cnt + tiny);      // finish average
    }                                   // next target bar
}
else if(mode == 2) {                    // fixed lookback mode
    for(i = 1; i <= n; i++) {           // for each target bar
        sum = 0.0;  cnt = 0;
        for(j = 2; j < 1000; j++) {     // walk backwards
            if(cnt >= m) break;         // enough cases run
            sdate = LunarEquivDate(dt[i], -j);  // source date
            if (sdate < dt[3]) break;   // run to beginning
            hunt(dt, n, sdate, &k);     // find index
            if(sdate > dt[k]) k++;
            cnt++;  sum += v[k];        // accumulate average
        }
        for(j = 2; j < 1000; j++) {     // walk forwards
            if(cnt >= m) break;         // enough cases run
            sdate = LunarEquivDate(dt[i], j)    // source date
            hunt(dt, n, sdate, &k);     // find index
            if(sdate > dt[k]) k++;
            cnt++;  sum += v[k];        // accumulate average
        }
        a[i] = sum / (cnt + tiny)       // finish average
    }                                   // next target bar
}
}
```

```c
static void Model (float *parms, float *dt, float *opn, float *hi,
float *lo, float *cls, float *vol, float *oi, float *dlrv, int nb,
TRDSIM &ts, float *eqcls) {

    // Implements a variety of lunar-cycle trading models.
    // File = x13mod01.c
    // parms    - vector [1..MAXPRM] of parameters
    // dt       - vector [1..nb] of dates in YYMMDD form
    // opn      - vector [1..nb] of opening prices
    // hi       - vector [1..nb] of high prices
    // lo       - vector [1..nb] of low prices
    // cls      - vector [1..nb] of closing prices
    // vol      - vector [1..nb] of volumes
    // oi       - vector [1..nb] of open interest numbers
    // dlrv     - vector [1..nb] of average dollar volatilities
    // nb       - number of bars in data series or vectors
    // ts       - trading simulator class instance
    // eqcls    - vector [1..nb] of closing equity levels

    // declare local scratch variables
    static int rc, cb, ncontracts, maxhold, ordertype, signal;
    static int avglen, disp, k, modeltype, matype, mktindx;
    static float mmstp, ptlim, stpprice, limprice, tmp, thresh;
    static float exitatr[MAXBAR+1], savg[MAXBAR+1];
    static float ma1[MAXBAR+1], ma2[MAXBAR+1], stoch[MAXBAR+1];
    static float *exitatrtab[MAXMKT+1], *savgtab[MAXMKT+1];

    // copy parameters to local variables for clearer reference
    avglen    = parms[1];  // length of moving averages
    disp      = parms[2];  // displacement factor
    thresh    = parms[3];  // threshold for momentum models
    matype    = parms[7];  // average type:
                // 1=simple moving average
                // 2=exponential
                // 3=front-weighted triangular
                // 4=triangular
                // 5=centered simple
                // 6=centered exponential
                // 7=centered triangular
    modeltype = parms[8];  // model type:
                // 1=momentum
                // 2=crossover
                // 3=crossover with confirm
                // 4=crossover with confirm and inversions
    ordertype = parms[9];  // entry: 1=open, 2=limit, 3=stop
    maxhold   = 10;         // maximum holding period
```

```
ptlim    = 4;              // profit target in volatility units
mmstp    = 1;              // stop loss in volatility units

// Perform whole-series computations that are unaffected by
// any parameters.  These may be performed once for each
// market, and saved in tables for repeated use, thereby
// dramatically reducing execution time.
mktindx = ts.model();                          // market index
if(exitatrtab[mktindx] == NULL) {              // allocated ?
    exitatrtab[mktindx] = vector(1, nb);       // exitatr table
    savgtab[mktindx] = vector(1, nb);          // savg table
    AvgTrueRangeS(exitatrtab[mktindx],
        hi,  lo,  cls,  50,  nb);              // 50-bar atr
    float *pchg = vector(1, nb);               // scratch vector
    pchg[1] = 0.0;
    for(cb = 2; cb <= nb; cb++) {
        tmp = cls[cb] - cls[cb-1];             // price change
        tmp /= exitatrtab[mktindx][cb];        // normalization
        pchg[cb] = clip(tmp, -2.0, 2.0);       // clipping
    }
    LunarAvg(savgtab[mktindx],
        pchg, dt, 2, 60, nb);                  // lunar seasonal
    free_vector(pchg, 1, nb);
    printf("Mkt: %d\n", mktindx);              // show progress
}

// perform other whole-series computations
memcpy(exitatr, exitatrtab[mktindx], sizeof(float)*nb);
memcpy(savg, savgtab[mktindx], sizeof(float)*nb);
switch(modeltype) {
  case 1:                     // series for momentum model
    MovAvg(savg,savg,matype,avglen,nb);        // smoothing avg
    for(cb = 1; cb <= nb; cb++)
        ma2[cb] = fabs(savg[cb]);
    MovAvg(ma1, ma2, 1, 100, nb);              // avg deviation
    break;
  case 2: case 3: case 4:  // series for crossover models
    for(cb = 2; cb <= nb; cb++)
        savg[cb] += savg[cb-1];                // integration
    MovAvg(ma1,savg,matype,avglen,nb);         // smoothing avg
    MovAvg(ma2,ma1,matype,avglen,nb);          // crossover avg
    if(modeltype == 3 || modeltype == 4)       // stochastic osc
        StochOsc(stoch,hi,lo,cls,1,9,nb);      //   9-bar Fast %K
    break;
  default: nrerror("TRAPSMOD: invalid modeltype");
}
```

```
// step through bars (days) to simulate actual trading
for(cb = 1; cb <= nb; cb++) {

    // take no trades before the in-sample period
    // ... same as TradeStation's MaxBarsBack setting
    if(dt[cb] < IS_DATE) { eqcls[cb] = 0.0;  continue; }

    // execute any pending orders and save closing equity
    rc = ts.update(opn[cb], hi[cb], lo[cb], cls[cb], cb);
    if(rc != 0) nrerror("Trade buffer overflow");
    eqcls[cb] = ts.currentequity(EQ_CLOSETOTAL);

    // take no trades in last 30 bars of data sample
    // to leave room in arrays for seasonal look-aheads
    if(cb > nb-30) continue;

    // calculate number of contracts to trade
    // ... we want to trade the dollar volatility equivalent
    // ... of 2 new S&P-500 contracts as of 12/31/98
    ncontracts = RoundToInteger(5673.0 / dlrv[cb]);
    if(ncontracts < 1) ncontracts = 1;

    // avoid placing orders on possibly limit-locked days
    if(hi[cb+1] == lo[cb+1]) continue;

    // generate entry signals, stop prices and limit prices
    // for all models
    signal = 0;
    switch(modeltype) {
      case 1:  // basic thresholded momentum entry model
        k = cb + disp;
        tmp = thresh * ma1[k];
        if(savg[k] > tmp && savg[k-1] <= tmp)
            signal = 1;
        else if(savg[k] < -tmp && savg[k-1] >= -tmp)
            signal = -1;
        break;
      case 2:  // basic crossover entry model
        k = cb + disp;
        if(CrossesAbove(ma1, ma2, k)) signal = 1;
        else if(CrossesBelow(ma1, ma2, k)) signal = -1;
        break;
      case 3:  // crossover with confirmation
        k = cb + disp;
        if(CrossesAbove(ma1, ma2, k)) {
```

```
                                  if(stoch[cb] < 25.0) signal = 1;
                          }
                          else if(CrossesBelow(ma1, ma2, k)) {
                              if(stoch[cb] > 75.0) signal = -1;
                          }
                          break;
                      case 4:  // crossover with confirmation and inversion
                          k = cb + disp;
                          if(CrossesAbove(ma1, ma2, k)) {
                              if(stoch[cb] < 25.0) signal = 1;
                              else if(stoch[cb] > 75.0) signal = -1;
                          }
                          else if(CrossesBelow(ma1, ma2, k)) {
                              if(stoch[cb] > 75.0) signal = -1;
                              else if(stoch[cb] < 25.0) signal = 1;
                          }
                          break;
                  }
                  limprice = 0.5 * (hi[cb] + lo[cb]);
                  stpprice = cls[cb] + 0.5 * signal * exitatr[cb];

                  // enter trades using specified order type
                  if(ts.position() <= 0 && signal == 1) {
                    switch(ordertype) { // select desired order type
                        case 1: ts.buyopen('1', ncontracts); break;
                        case 2: ts.buylimit('2', limprice, ncontracts); break;
                        case 3: ts.buystop('3', stpprice, ncontracts); break;
                        default: nrerror("Invalid buy order selected");
                    }
                  }
                  else if(ts.position() >= 0 && signal == -1) {
                      switch(ordertype) {   // select desired order type
                          case 1: ts.sellopen('4', ncontracts); break;
                          case 2: ts.selllimit('5', limprice, ncontracts); break;
                          case 3: ts.sellstop('6', stpprice, ncontracts); break;
                          default: nrerror("Invalid sell order selected");
                      }
                  }

                  // instruct simulator to employ standard exit strategy
                  tmp = exitatr[cb];
                  ts.stdexitcls('X', ptlim*tmp, mmstp*tmp, maxhold);

              } // process next bar
      }
```

Several functions required to calculate lunar rhythms for any market in an adaptive manner precede the code implementing the trading model. The implementation function, *Model*, follows the standard conventions: After declarations, parameters are copied into local variables for easier reference. Comments indicate what the parameters control. The next block computes the 50-bar average true range (*exitatrtab*), used in the exits and for normalization, as well as the lunar seasonal series (*savgtab*), the predicted price changes for each bar. These series are computed only once for each market and tabled; this may be done as no relevant parameters change from test to test as *Model* is repeatedly called. A second block calculates the model-specific time series needed to generate entry signals. If *modeltype* is 1, the simple momentum model is used; 2 = the crossover model; 3 = crossover with confirmation; and 4 = crossover with confirmation and inversion. Among the series that may be computed are: smoothed lunar momentum, integrated lunar momentum (price-like series), moving averages for the crossover model, and Slow %K for models involving confirmation and inversion. Depending on *modeltype*, several other parameters may become important. One parameter, *avglen*, controls the length of all moving averages: For the momentum model, it controls the length of the centered triangular moving average; and for the crossover models, it controls the length of the two moving averages those models require. Another parameter, *disp*, sets the displacement: This is the look-ahead used, e.g., to compensate for the lag of the moving averages. The parameter *thresh* is the threshold used in the momentum model for both short and long trades (short trades use the negative of *thresh*). Variable *matype* controls the type of certain moving averages: 1 = simple, 2 = exponential, 6 = centered exponential, 7 = centered triangular; other moving averages are available, but are not used in the analyses. After all series are calculated, a loop is entered that steps, day by day, through the market to simulate trading. This loop contains code to update the simulator, determine the number of contracts, avoid trading on limit-locked days, etc. The next block, appearing within the bar-stepping loop, generates entry signals. The rules are determined by *modeltype*. Finally, a block handles posting the appropriate trading order, as selected by the *ordertype*: 1 = entry at open, 2 = on limit, 3 = on stop.

LUNAR TEST RESULTS

Tests were run on four entry models: crossover, momentum, crossover with confirmation, and crossover with confirmation and inversions. Each model was studied with entry at open, on limit, and on stop. Table 9-1 summarizes the results of all tests, broken down by sample, entry order, and model. For each model, there is a row of numbers containing the annualized portfolio return, and a row with the average portfolio dollar profit or loss per trade. Averages across all order types for in-sample and out-of-sample performance are in the two rightmost columns. The last two rows contain the average across all models for each type of order.

Tables 9-2 and 9-3 present information for each of the 12 tests on the specific commodities that the model traded profitably and those that lost, for the in-sample (Table 9-2) and out-of-sample (Table 9-3) runs. The first column, *SYM*, is the market being studied. The last column (*COUNT*) is the number of profitable tests for a given market. The numbers in the first row are Test identifiers. The last row (*COUNT*) contains the number of markets profitable for a given model. Tables 9-2 and 9-3 provide information about which markets are and are not profitable when traded by each model: One dash (-) indicates a loss per trade of $2,000 to $4,000; two dashes (- -) represent a loss of $4,000 or more; one plus sign (+) means a profit per trade of $1,000 to $2,000; two pluses (++) indicate gains of $2,000 or more; a blank cell means a loss between $0 and $1,999 or a profit between $0 and $1,000 per trade.

Tests of the Basic Crossover Model

A moving average (*ma1*) was computed for the integrated, price-like lunar series. A second moving average (*ma2*) was taken of the first moving average. A buy signal was generated when *ma1* crossed above *ma2*. A sell signal was generated when *ma1* crossed below *ma2*. This is the same moving average crossover model discussed in the chapter on moving averages, except here it is computed on a lunar series, rather than on prices. The entries were effected by either a market at open (Test 1), a limit (Test 2), or a stop order (Test 3).

Optimization involved stepping the length of the moving averages (*avglen*) from 5 to 15 in increments of 5, and the displacement (*disp*) from 0 to 15 in incre-

TABLE 9-1

Performance of Lunar Models Broken Down by Model, Order, and Sample

Model	In-sample			Out-of-sample			Average	Average
	Open	Limit	Stop	Open	Limit	Stop	In	Out
Lunar	-9.3	-6.0	-5.6	-14.3	-10.2	-10.4	-7.0	-11.6
crossover	-1287	-406	-686	-894	-643	-702	-793	-746
Lunar	-10.1	-9.9	-8.1	-14.8	-19.7	-8.3	-9.4	-14.2
momentum	-2410	-1560	-1288	-1316	-1942	-372	-1753	-1210
Crossover with	-8.1	-6.6	1.8	-20.5	-21.3	-18.6	-4.3	-20.1
confirm	-1251	-655	234	-3465	-3896	-2449	-557	-3270
Crossover with	-9.4	-10.0	-7.8	-20.6	-20.9	-20.1	-9.1	-20.5
conf. & inv.	-1546	-1078	-998	-2937	-3203	-2995	-1207	-3045
Average	-9.3	-8.1	-4.9	-17.6	-18.0	-14.4	-7.4	-16.6
	-1624	-925	-685	-2153	-2421	-1630	-1078	-2068

TABLE 9-2

In-Sample Performance Broken Down by Test and Market

SYM	01	02	03	04	05	06	07	08	09	10	11	12	COUNT
SP				+	+	+		--	--	--		--	3
YX	-	-		+	+	+	--	+	--	+	+	++	7
US	+	++	-				--	--		--		--	2
TB	+			--	--		--	--	++	--	--	--	2
TY	+	+		--			-		++	--	+	-	4
BP	--	--	--	+		+	+	+		--	--	++	5
DM	+	++	+	++	+	+			++	-	++		8
SF		+		+	++	++	+		++	+	+	+	9
JY	++	++		--		+	+	+	+	++		++	8
CD	+	++	-			--	++		++	++		--	5
ED	--	--		--		--	--	--	++		--	--	1
CL	+	+	++	+								+	5
HO			++		+		++	+	++	++	-		6
HU			++				+	+				++	4
GC				--	-	-	+			+	+	-	3
SI		+		-	--	--	--	--	+			+	3
PL		+	--	--	-	-	-				--	+	2
PA	-	+	++	-	-	-	-		--	--	--	--	2
FC	-		--				--	--		--	++	+	2
LC	-		-	-	-				-		+	--	1
LH	--	--					--	-	++	--	--	--	1
PB	+	++					-	--	++	--	++	--	4
S		+	-		+	-	++	++	+			+	6
SM		+	+	-			++	++	+	+	+	--	7
BO				--		-	-		++	-		+	2
C	--	-	-	--	--				--		--	--	0
O	--	--	--	--	--	--	--	--	--			-	0
W				--	-	-	--	--	--			--	0
KW	-	-		--	-		+	++	--	-	--	--	2
MW	--	--	--	--			--				-		0
KC	-	-	++	+	+	-	--	--	--	--		--	3
CC				+		+			++			+	4
SB		+	--	--	--	--	-		-	-	+	++	3
JO	--	--	--		+	+	-		--	++	--	+	4
CT		+	--	-	-	+	++	++	-	++	+		6
LB	-	--	--		-		-	-	++	--	--	++	2
COUNT	08	15	07	08	08	09	11	09	16	09	11	15	

TABLE 9-3

Out-of-Sample Performance Broken Down by Test and Market

SYM	01	02	03	04	05	06	07	08	09	10	11	12	COUNT
SP													0
YX													0
US	++	++	++	++	+	--	--	--		++	--	++	7
TB	--	-	+	-	-	--		-	--		-	++	2
TY	-	+	++	++	-	--	--	--		--		--	3
BP	++	++	--		++	-	++	++		+	++	--	7
DM		++	++	++			--	--	--	--	--	--	3
SF	++	++	-		++	++	++	++	++	++	--	--	8
JY		++	--	-		++	--	--	--	--			2
CD	--	--	--		--		--	--	++	--	--		1
ED	--	--	--	--	--	--	--	--	+	--	--	++	2
CL			-	-	-	+	--	--		--	--	+	2
HO	+		+		-	-			-	-	--	++	3
HU		--	--	-			--	--	++		--	-	1
GC	--	--	++	++	++		++	-	--		--		4
SI	--	-	--	-	--	-	--	--		--		--	0
PL	+	+	++						++		++	--	5
PA	++	+	--	--	--	-			-	--		++	3
FC			++	++				--	--	-		--	2
LC	+	+		--	--		+	++	++	++	-	++	7
LH	+	-	--			++	--	--	-	--	--	--	2
PB	++	+		--	--	-	++	++	++	+		--	6
S		-	--	--	-				-		-		0
SM	+	--	--	--		++	--	--	--	--	--		2
BO	-	-	+	+	--	-		--	-		-		2
C	--	--	--			++	--	--	++	--	--	--	2
O	-	-		--		--	-	--	--	-		--	0
W	+	++	+		-	--	--	-	--	--	-	--	3
KW	++	++	++			++	++	++	--	++	++	+	9
MW	--	--		++	-	++	--			--	--	--	2
KC	-				++	++	--	--	--	++	--	--	3
CC	++	++	--	++	++		--	--	--	--	--		4
SB	++	+	++	--	--	-	-		--	+	--	-	4
JO	++	++	++		--	-	++	++	++	++	++	--	8
CT		++		--	--		--	--	+	-	++	++	4
LB	++	++	+	++	++	++	--	++	--	--	++	+	9
COUNT	16	17	14	9	7	10	7	7	10	9	6	10	

ments of 1. For entry at the open, the best performance (in terms of in-sample risk-to-reward ratio) was achieved with a moving average length of 15 and a displacement of 8; entry on a limit was best with a length of 15 and a displacement of 6; entry on a stop required a length of 15 and a displacement of 12.

No tests showed profits in either sample. In-sample, best performance (least average loss per trade) was with entry on limit; entry on stop produced poorer results; entry at open was the worst. With the limit order, 43% of the 1,759 trades were profitable. Out-of-sample, the limit order produced the smallest average loss per trade and the stop yielded the largest loss. Overall, the system did not do well on the entire portfolio. The relative performance of shorts and longs was inconsistent across orders and samples. In-sample, longs lost substantially more than shorts, the opposite of what was frequently seen in tests of other models.

Equity steadily declined from the beginning to the end of the data series for entry at open. For entry on limit, equity was choppy but up, peaking in September 1989. It then declined until July 1992, rose slightly until February 1994, and declined steadily until July 1998, when it suddenly began increasing. With a stop, equity showed a choppy decline from one end of the data series to the other.

In-sample, the number of markets with positive returns using a limit, a market-at-open, and a stop were 15, 8, and 7, respectively. Out-of-sample, the limit produced the best results (17), followed by the market-at-open (16), and the stop (14). More market-order combinations produced profits out-of-sample than in-sample; it seems that many markets are becoming more affected by lunar rhythms in recent years. In-sample, only the Deutschemark and Light Crude were profitable across all three entry orders. Out-of-sample, the Deutschemark was highly profitable with limit and stop orders; Light Crude slightly lost with the stop. T-Bonds strongly profitable in both samples with the limit. Pork Bellies was profitable in both samples with entry at open and on limit. Considering only the limit order, profit in both samples was observed for the Deutschemark, Swiss Franc, Japanese Yen, Platinum, Palladium, Sugar, and Cotton.

Tests of the Basic Momentum Model

A centered moving average smoothed the unintegrated lunar price change series. No lag was induced because the centered average examines as many future (relative to the current bar), as it does past, data points. This smoothing is legitimate because, in the calculations, the lunar estimate at the current bar involves data at least two lunar cycles (about two months) away. For the smoothed lunar price changes, a series of average absolute deviations was computed and a 100-bar simple moving average was taken to produce the desired result. A buy was issued when lunar momentum, at the current bar plus some displacement (*disp*), was greater than some multiple (*thresh*) of the average absolute deviation of the lunar momentum. A sell was issued when lunar momentum, at the same displaced bar, was less than minus the same multiple of the average absolute deviation. Entries were executed at the open (Test 4), on a limit (Test 5), or on a stop (Test 6).

Optimization was for the length of the moving averages (stepped from 5 to 15 in increments of 5), the displacement (1 to 10 in steps of 1), and the threshold (1.5 to 2.5 in steps of 0.5). Best results were achieved with the length, displacement, and threshold parameters set to 10, 10, 2 for the market-at-open and 15, 9, 1.5 for the limit and stop.

Overall, results were worse than for the crossover model. Heavy losses occurred in both samples across all order types. The same poor performance was observed when seasonal effects were analyzed with the momentum model. Longs again performed better than shorts.

With entry at open, portfolio equity declined smoothly and severely, with the rate of loss gradually decreasing over time. With a limit order, equity steadily decreased. With a stop, equity dropped sharply from the beginning of the sample until August 1988, then declined gradually.

In-sample, the S&P 500, NYFE, Deutschemark, and Swiss Franc were somewhat profitable across all orders. Out-of-sample, the S&P 500 and NYFE neither profited nor lost, but the Deutschemark did well with entry at open, and the Swiss Franc with entry on limit and on stop. As with the crossover model, there were many more profitable market-order combinations.

Tests of the Crossover Model with Confirmation

This is identical to the basic crossover model except that entries were only taken when an appropriate reading of the Fast %K Stochastic confirmed lunar market behavior. Specifically, if the lunar crossover suggested a buy, it was only acted upon if Fast %K was below 25%; before a buy occurred, the market had to be down or near a bottom, as expected on the basis of the lunar rhythm. Likewise, a lunar sell was not taken unless the market was near a possible top, i.e., Fast %K greater than 75%. Entries were at the open, on a limit, or a stop (Tests 4 to 6, respectively).

The length of the moving averages (*avglen*) was optimized from 3 to 15 in increments of 3, and displacement (*disp*) from 0 to 15 in increments of 1. Best performance was achieved for entry at the open, and on a limit, with a moving average length of 15 and a displacement of 12; the best stop entry occurred with a length of 12 and a displacement of 5.

In-sample, the results were somewhat better than the basic crossover model: When combined with the stop, the crossover with confirmation yielded about $234 per trade. Out-of-sample, however, the average loss was more than for either of the previous two models, regardless of order. The stop showed the smallest loss per trade and was best. This is another system not profitable on a whole portfolio basis. The equity curves showed nothing but losses across all three orders.

In-sample, the Japanese Yen, Heating Oil, Soybeans, and Soybean Meal were profitable with all three orders; out-of-sample, only losses or, at best, unprofitable trading occurred in these markets. Kansas Wheat showed consistent behavior across samples: Results were profitable with entry at open and on limit, and unprofitable with entry on stop. Across samples, the British Pound and Swiss Franc were profitable, as was the Canadian Dollar, Eurodollar, and Pork Bellies with entry on a stop. Since the number of trades was fairly small for many markets and the whole portfolio, results are probably not trustworthy.

Tests of the Crossover Model with Confirmation and Inversions

This is the same as the crossover model with confirmation, but additional trades were taken at possible inversions. If a lunar buy was signalled by a crossover, but the market was high (Fast %K being greater than 75%), a sell (not a buy) was posted; the assumption is the usual lunar cycle may have inverted, forming a top instead of a bottom. Likewise, if the crossover signalled a sell, but the market was down, a buy was issued. These signals were posted in addition to those described in the crossover with confirmation model. Entries occurred at the open (Test 10), on a limit (Test 11), or a stop (Test 12).

The length of the moving averages (*avglen*) was stepped from 3 to 15 in increments of 3, and the displacement (*disp*) from 0 to 15 in increments of 1. For entry at the open, the best moving average length was 15 and displacement, 12; entry on a limit was best with a length of 15 and a displacement of 8; entry on a stop required a length of 12 and displacement of 15.

This model lost heavily across samples and orders. As with seasonality, inversions did not benefit performance. The equity curve paints a dismal picture.

In-sample, the NYFE was profitable across all three orders, but the S&P 500 lost for two of the orders and was flat for the other. The Swiss Franc was also profitable in-sample across all three orders; out-of-sample, it was very profitable for entry at open, but lost for the other two orders. There was a great deal of inconsistency in results between the samples.

SUMMARY ANALYSES

When considered over all models, the stop performed best in both samples. The worst performers were, in-sample, the open and, out-of-sample, the limit. In-sample, when considered over all order types, crossover with confirmation was the best. Out-of-sample, the basic lunar crossover model performed best and crossover with confirmation worst.

There were many strong interactions between sample, model, and order. Some of the results stem from the small number of trades. The best of the seasonal model-order combinations yielded better and more consistent performance than the best of the lunar ones.

CONCLUSION

When entire portfolios are considered, entry models based on lunar rhythms do not do as well as those based on seasonal rhythms. The poor showing of the lunar effect contradicts our earlier study (Katz and McCormick, June 1997). The differences may stem from two possible factors: entry models and exits. In the current tests, the models were optimized on an entire portfolio, which may not be appropriate for the lunar rhythm (the earlier model entered the market a specified number of days after full or new moon). The methods used in this chapter were altered from the previous study because of the need to optimize using common parameters across all markets. Doing this with the earlier approach would require that trades be entered *n*-days after the full or new moon, regardless of the market being traded; since lunar rhythms are distinct for each market (as demonstrated in our previous study), this approach was inappropriate. The earlier model was, therefore, redesigned to be self-adaptive, i.e., as it proceeds through lunar cycles, the appropriate timing for trading is decided by analysis of previous lunar cycles.

Another possible reason for the conflicting results may be the interaction between the exits and entries. The lunar model, and perhaps the seasonal model, has the property of pinpointing tradeable tops and bottoms, but only a percentage of the time. Such systems work best with very tight stops that quickly cut losses when predictions go wrong, but that allow profits to accumulate when correct.

In general, the lunar models performed poorly, but there were individual markets with consistent, positive performance—encouraging, given the model was not optimized to them. Results suggest that some great systems are hiding here if entries were tailored to them, e.g., in our earlier study, the lunar model traded Silver well; in the current study, Silver was not strongly responsive. Although the lunar models lost money on the portfolio, they lost very much less on a per-trade basis than did, for instance, most moving average and oscillator entry models.

SOLAR ACTIVITY AND TRADING

An earlier study (Katz and McCormick, September 1997) examined the effects of sunspots on the S&P 500 and Wheat. In-sample, a simple sunspot model pulled $64,000 from the S&P 500 between 1984 and 1992. There were 67 trades, 31% profitable. The average winning trade was $5,304.76, much larger than the average loser (-$1,030.43). The average trade was $955.22 with a return of 561% (not annualized). The long side was profitable, but the short side was substantially more so, highlighting the tendency of unusual solar activity to coincide with market crashes. The better performance of short trades is especially significant, since this market was in a secular uptrend during most of the testing period. Profitability continued out-of-sample, from 1993 through 1996, with a 265% return, 23 trades (30% profitable), and with an average trade yielding $891.30. The results for Wheat were also good across samples. In-sample, 57% of 84 trades were profitable with a $203.27 average trade and 859% return (not annualized). Out-of-sample, there were 29 trades, 55% profitable, a $260.78 average trade, and 406% return.

Our initial research suggested further study would be worthwhile. The tests below examine the effects of solar activity on the standard portfolio. Daily sunspot numbers from 1985 through 1999, from the Royal Observatory of Belgium, were used to generate entries.

GENERATING SOLAR ENTRIES

There are many ways to generate entries based on solar activity. The method used below is a simple variation of a breakout model, applied to sunspot counts, not prices. The rules are: If the current sunspot number is higher than the current upper threshold, and the sunspot counts for a certain number (*lb2*) of previous bars were lower than their corresponding thresholds, then either a buy or sell signal (depending on previous market behavior in response to upside breakouts in the sunspot numbers) is issued. If the current sunspot number is lower than the current lower threshold, and the sunspot counts for the same number of previous bars were all higher than their corresponding thresholds, then either a sell or a buy signal (again, depending on previous market behavior) is issued. The signals are not responded to immediately, but only after a specified number of days (*disp*). The breakout thresholds are determined as follows: The upper threshold, used for a given bar, is the highest sunspot number found in a certain larger number of previous bars (*lb1*), while the lower threshold is set at the lowest of the sunspot numbers in those previous bars. "Previous market behavior" refers to whether the market was near the bottom or top of its near-future range when a particular kind of breakout occurred. If a given direction of solar breakout is historically associated with the market being near the bottom of its near-future range, a buy signal is generated; on the other hand, if the market is characteristically near the top of its near-future range, a sell signal is generated.

Like lunar phenomena and seasonality, entries based on solar activity share the assumption that market behavior is influenced by external factors and that the independent, influential variable has predictive value, i.e., market behavior is anticipated rather than responded to. As with any predictive system, the forecasts may be more or less correct. Trades resulting from incorrect predictions can be incredibly bad, even if many trades resulting from correct predictions are perfect, as is often the case with predictive systems. Being anticipatory, the models lend themselves to countertrend entries, which means better fills, less slippage, and better risk control, assuming appropriate stops are used (not done here because of the need to maintain the standard exit).

The code for these tests is similar to that for lunar analysis and so is not presented here. It is available on the companion software CD (see offer at back of book).

SOLAR TEST RESULTS

Tests were performed on the solar entry model using entry at open (Test 1), on a limit (Test 2), and on a stop (Test 3). The breakout look-back (*lb1*) was stepped from 25 to 40 in increments of 5; the repeat prevention look-back (*lb2*) from 10 to 15 by 5; and the displacement (*disp*) from 0 to 2 by 1. For entry at the open, the best in-sample performance was with a breakout look-back of 35, a repeat prevention look-back of 15, and a displacement of 2. For the limit, a breakout look-back of 40, a repeat prevention look-back of 15, and a displacement of 0 were optimal. For the stop, the best values were: for the breakout look-back, 35; for the repeat prevention look-back, 15; and for the displacement, 2.

Table 9-4 shows both the in- and out-of-sample performance for specific commodities. The columns and rows contain the same kinds of data as in Tables 9-2 and 9-3 above.

The solar model performed about as well as the lunar ones and, in sample, did best with a stop order. In-sample, entry at the open was worst (-$1631 per trade); a limit was slightly better (-$1519), substantially so when only long trades were considered. The stop order was the best, losing only $52 per trade; were it not for transaction costs, this order would have been very profitable in-sample.

The model required the theoretically expected displacement. The best displacement for the limit was zero, understandable since the goal is to respond quickly, before the market turns, when a limit can enter on the noise. With the stop, a displacement of 2 was best: Movement needs to begin to trigger the stop and cause entry. The average loss per trade worsened, from -$52 to -$2,000, when displacement deviated just one or two bars from its optimal value. This implies a relationship between the timing of the market and solar events otherwise small changes in the displacement should have little or no effect.

With the stop order, the highest percentage of wins (in-sample) was obtained and the long side was actually profitable. Out-of-sample, the stop was again best, but the average loss per trade was a substantial $1,329.

Equity was examined only for the stop, since the other orders performed so poorly. Equity rose very rapidly until June 1988, then, until October 1990, it was choppy and fairly flat. Between October 1990 and June 1994, equity declined sharply, then was choppy and slightly down.

Interestingly, some of our previous findings (Katz and McCormick, September 1997) were confirmed. With the stop, which generally performed best on the whole portfolio, the S&P 500 was very profitable in both samples. The average trade returned $4,991 in-sample; the return was 20.4% annualized; and,

TABLE 9-4

Performance Broken Down by Sample, Test, and Market

SYM	In-sample 01	02	03	Count		Out-of-sample 01	02	03	Count
SP			++	1		-	--	++	1
YX			++	1		--	--		0
US	--	-	-	0		-	--	--	0
TB	--	--		0		--	--	--	0
TY	--		--	0		--	--	--	0
BP		+	++	2		--	--	--	0
DM		-		0		-	-	-	0
SF				0			-	-	0
JY	+			1				-	0
CD		-	+	1		++		--	1
ED	--	--	++	1		--	--	--	0
CL			++	1		-	--	-	0
HO	+		+	2			--	-	0
HU	-	-		0		--		--	0
GC		-	-	0		--	-	--	0
SI	-	--	--	0			--	+	1
PL	+		-	1		++	--	+	2
PA	+	++	--	2			--	-	0
FC	--	-	--	0		-	+	++	2
LC	-		-	0			++		1
LH	+			1		--	--	-	0
PB	+		+	2		--			0
S			+	1			--	+	1
SM	+		+	2		--	--	--	0
BO	-	--		0		-	--	--	0
C	--	-		0		-	--	--	0
O	--	-	++	1		-	+	-	1
W		-		0		+	+	+	3
KW		+		1		+	+	++	3
MW		-	++	1			+	++	2
KC			++	1		++	++		2
CC	-	-	-	0		-	-		0
SB	-		-	0		--	-	+	1
JO		+		1		-	--	++	1
CT			+	1				++	1
LB	--	--		0		+	+	+	3
Count	7	4	14			6	8	12	

the t-test indicated a greater than 80% probability that the effect was real and would hold up. Both long and short trades were profitable. In-sample there were 37 trades (40% winners). Out-of-sample, longs and shorts both continued to be profitable; it was surprising that the shorts were profitable because the market was in a steep up-trend during most of that period. Out-of-sample, the return was 39.5% annualized, with an 80% probability of being real; there were 11 trades (45% winners), and the average trade returned $5,640. These are excellent results.

The observation that sharp down-turns can occur after solar flares has been supported. With the stop order, Minnesota Wheat, Soybeans, and Cotton were also profitable in both samples. Minnesota Wheat pulled 13.5% annually in-sample, again with a better than 80% chance of the results being real, and 30.5% out-of-sample, with almost an 85% probability of the effect not being due to chance. Interestingly, Light Crude and Heating Oil were highly profitable in-sample, but lost moderately out-of-sample. There were a few profits in other markets, but no consistency between in- and out-of-sample performance with the stop.

CONCLUSION

Like seasonality and lunar phase, solar activity appears to have a real influence on some markets, especially the S&P 500 and Minnesota Wheat. As with lunar cycles, this influence is not sufficiently strong or reliable to be a primary element in a portfolio trading system; however, as a component in a system incorporating other factors, or as a system used to trade specific markets, solar activity is worth attention. We personally do not believe solar influences directly determine the market. We do suspect that they act as triggers for events that are predisposed to occur, or as synchronizers of already-present market rhythms with similar period-icities. For example, if a market is highly over-valued and unstable, as was the S&P 500 in October 1987, a large solar flare might be sufficient to trigger an already-imminent crash.

WHAT HAVE WE LEARNED?

- Lunar and solar phenomena may have real impact on commodities mar-kets. In the case of solar phenomena, such impact on the S&P 500 has been confirmed. With lunar phenomena, there is more inconsistency in the results, but influence is clearly detectable.
- The phenomena are probably worth including in a more elaborate trading model, e.g., as inputs to a neural network.
- Models that capture such influences almost certainly need to be tuned to specific markets in a more effective way than has been done here. Such market specificity might be the reason for the better results observed when tests were conducted on individual markets.

- As with other countertrend models that pinpoint turning points (including seasonality), it is probably necessary to use an exit that includes a fairly tight stop. If a turning point is correctly identified, the stop is never hit and the trade quickly turns profitable. On the other hand, when a prediction error occurs, as frequently happens, the stop quickly kills the trade, cutting losses short. The use of tight stops may be another factor that accounts for better performance in our earlier studies (Katz and McCormick, June and September 1997) than in the current tests.

- Given the highly probable influence of solar and lunar rhythms on certain markets, it might be worth exploring some other planetary rhythms, including the kinds of planetary configurations and cycles that are the focus of astrologers.

- Entry orders interact with models. Limit orders, for example, do not always perform best. It seems a stop order sometimes improves performance. The reason may be that a stop order introduces verification of the beginning of a trend before entry can occur, something that may be important when using a prediction-based counter-trend strategy.

CHAPTER 10

Cycle-Based Entries

A *cycle* is a rhythmic oscillation that has an identifiable frequency (e.g., 0.1 cycle per day) or, equivalently, periodicity (e.g., 10 days per cycle). In the previous two chapters, phenomena that are cyclic in nature were discussed. Those cycles were exogenous in origin and of a known, if not fixed, periodicity. Seasonality, one such form of cyclic phenomena, is induced by the periodicity and recurrence of the seasons and, therefore, is tied into an external driving force. However, while all seasonality is cyclic, not all cycles are seasonal.

In this chapter, cycles that can be detected in price data alone, and that do not necessarily have any external driving source, are considered. Some of these cycles may be due to as yet unidentified influences. Others may result only from resonances in the markets. Whatever their source, these are the kinds of cycles that almost every trader has seen when examining charts. In the old days, a trader would take a comb-like instrument, place it on a chart, and look for bottoms and tops occurring with regular intervals between them. The older techniques have now been made part of modern, computerized charting programs, making it easy to visually analyze cycles. When it comes to the mechanical detection and analysis of cycles, *maximum entropy spectral analysis* (MESA) has become the preeminent technique.

CYCLE DETECTION USING MESA

Currently, there are at least three major software products for traders that employ the maximum entropy method for the analysis of market cycles: Cycle Trader (Bressert), MESA (Ehlers, 800-633-6372), and TradeCycles (Scientific Consultant Services, 516-696-3333, and Ruggiero Associates, 800-211-9785). This kind of analysis has been found useful by many market technicians. For example, Ruggiero (October 1996) contends that adaptive breakout systems that make use of the maximum entropy method (MEM) of cycle analysis perform better than those that do not.

Maximum entropy is an elegant and efficient way to determine cyclic activity in a time series. Its particular strength is its ability to detect sharp spectral features with small amounts of data, a desirable characteristic when it comes to analyzing market cycles. The technique has been extensively studied, and implementations using maximum entropy have become polished relative to appropriate preprocessing and postprocessing of the data, as required when using that algorithm.

A number of problems, however, exist with the maximum entropy method, as well as with many other mathematical methods for determining cycles. MEM, for example, is somewhat finicky. It can be extremely sensitive to small changes in the data or in such parameters as the number of poles and the look-back period. In addition, the price data must not only be de-trended or differenced, but also be passed through a low-pass filter for smoothing before the data can be handed to the maximum entropy algorithm; the algorithm does not work very well on noisy, raw data. The problem with passing the data through a filter, prior to the maximum entropy cycle extraction, is that lag and phase shifts are induced. Consequently, extrapolations of the cycles detected can be incorrect in terms of phase and timing unless additional analyses are employed.

DETECTING CYCLES USING FILTER BANKS

For a long time, we have been seeking a method other than maximum entropy to detect and extract useful information about cycles. Besides avoiding some of the problems associated with maximum entropy, the use of a novel approach was also a goal: When dealing with the markets, techniques that are novel sometimes work better simply because they are different from methods used by other traders. One such approach to detecting cycles uses banks of specially designed band-pass filters. This is a method encountered in electronics engineering, where filter banks are often used for spectral analysis. The use of a filter bank approach allows the bandwidth, and other filter characteristics, to be tailored, along with the overlap between successive filters in the bank. This technique helps yield an effective, adaptive response to the markets.

A study we conducted using filter banks to explore market cycles produced profitable results (Katz and McCormick, May 1997). Between January 3, 1990, and November 1, 1996, a filter bank trading model, designed to buy and sell on cycle tops and bottoms, pulled $114,950 out of the S&P 500. There were 204 trades, of which 50% were profitable. The return-on-account was 651% (not annualized). Both the long and short sides had roughly equal profitability and a similar percentage of winning trades. Various parameters of the model had been optimized, but almost all parameter values tested yielded profitable results. The parameters determined on the S&P 500 were used in a test of the model on the T-Bonds without any changes in the parameters, this market also traded profitably, returning a 254% profit. Given the relative crudeness of the filters used, these results were very encouraging.

In that study, the goal was simply to design a zero-lag filtering system. The filters were analogous to resonators or tuned circuits that allow signals of certain frequencies (those in the pass-band) to pass through unimpeded, while stopping signals of other frequencies (those in the stop-band). To understand the concept of using *filters*, think of the stream of prices from the market as analogous to the electrical voltage fluctuations streaming down the cable from an aerial on their way to a radio receiver. The stream of activity contains noise (background noise or "hiss" and static), as well as strong signals (modulated cycles) produced by local radio stations. When the receiver is tuned across the band, a filter's resonant or center frequency is adjusted. In many spots on the band, no signals are heard, only static or noise. This means that there are no strong signals, of the frequency to which the receiver is tuned, to excite the resonator. Other regions on the band have weak signals present, and when still other frequencies are tuned in, strong, clear broadcasts are heard; i.e., the filter's center (or resonant frequency) corresponds to the cyclic electrical activity generated by a strong station. What is heard at any spot on the dial depends on whether the circuits in the radio are resonating with anything, i.e., any signals coming in through the aerial that have the same frequency as that to which the radio is tuned. If there are no signals at that frequency, then the circuits are only randomly stimulated by noise. If the radio is tuned to a certain frequency and a strong signal comes in, the circuits resonate with a coherent excitation. In this way, the radio serves as a *resonating filter* that may be tuned to different frequencies by moving the dial across the band. When the filter receives a signal that is approximately the same frequency as its resonant or center frequency, it responds by producing sound (after demodulation). Traders try to look for strong signals in the market, as others might look for strong signals using a radio receiver, dialing through the different frequencies until a currently broadcasting station—strong market cycle—comes in clearly.

To further explore the idea of *resonance*, consider a tuning fork, one with a resonant frequency of 440 hertz (i.e., 440 cycles per second), that is in the same room as an audio signal generator connected to a loud speaker. As the audio generator's frequency is slowly increased from 401 hertz to 402 to 403, etc., the resonant frequency of the tuning fork is gradually approached. The nearer the audio generator's frequency gets to that of the tuning fork, the more the tuning fork picks up the vibration from the speaker and begins to emit its tone, that is, to resonate with the audio generator's output. When the exact center point of the fork's tuning (440 hertz) is reached, the fork oscillates in exact unison with the speaker's cone; i.e., the correlation between the tuning fork and the speaker cone is perfect. As the frequency of the sound emitted from the speaker goes above (or below) that of the tuning fork, the tuning fork still resonates, but it is slightly out of synch with the speaker (*phase shift* occurs) and the resonance is weaker. As driving frequencies go further away from the resonant frequency of the tuning fork, less and less signal is picked up and responded to by the fork. If a large number of tuning forks (resonators or filters) are each tuned to a slightly different frequency, then there is the potential to pick up a multitude of frequencies or signals, or, in the case of the markets, cycles. A particular filter will resonate very strongly to the cycle it is tuned to, while the other filters will not respond because they are not tuned to the frequency of that cycle.

Cycles in the market may be construed in the same manner as described above—as if they were audio tones that vary over time, sometimes stronger, sometimes weaker. Detecting market cycles may be attempted using a bank of filters that overlap, but that are separate enough to enable one to be found that strongly resonates with the cyclic activity dominant in the market at any given time. Some of the filters will resonate with the current cyclic movement of the market, while others will not because they are not tuned to the frequency/periodicity of current market activity. When a filter passes a signal that is approximately the same frequency as the one to which it is tuned, the filter will behave like the tuning fork, i.e., have zero lag (no phase shift); its output will be in synchrony with the cycle in the market. In addition, the filter output will be fairly close to a perfect sine wave and, therefore, easy to use in making trading decisions. The filter bank used in our earlier study contained Butterworth band-pass filters, the code of which was rather complex, but was fully disclosed in the Easy Language of TradeStation.

Butterworth Filters

Butterworth filters are not difficult to understand. A *low-pass Butterworth filter* is like a moving average: It both attenuates higher-frequency (shorter-periodicity) signals (or noise) and passes lower-frequency (higher-periodicity) signals unimpeded; in other words, it smooths data. While an exponential moving average has a stop-band cutoff of 6 decibels (db) per *octave* (halving of the output for every halving of the signal's period below the cutoff period), a 4-pole Butterworth filter (the kind used in our May 1997 study) has a stop-band attenuation of 18 decibels per octave (output drops by a factor of 8 for every halving of a signal's period below the cut-off period). The sharper attenuation of unwanted higher-frequency (lower-periodicity) activity with the Butterworth filter comes at a price: greater lag and distorting phase shifts.

A *high-pass Butterworth filter* is like a moving-average difference oscillator (e.g., $X - MA(X)$, where X is the input signal): Both attenuate lower-frequency signals (e.g., trend), while passing higher-frequency signals unimpeded. The attenuation in the stop-band is sharper for the 4-pole Butterworth filter (18 db per octave) than for the moving-average oscillator (6 db per octave). Both the moving-average oscillator and the Butterworth high-pass filter produce lead (rather than lag) at the expense of increased noise (short-period activity) and distorting phase shifts.

If both high-pass and low-pass filters are combined by connecting the output of the first to the input of the second, a *band-pass filter* is obtained: Frequencies that are higher or lower than the desired frequency are blocked. A signal with a frequency (or periodicity) that falls in the center of the filter's "pass-band" is passed with little or no attenuation, and without lag. The phase shifts of the high-pass (lead) and low-pass (lag) component filters cancel out; this is comparable to the behavior of the tuning fork, as well as to the MACD, which is actually a rudimentary band-pass filter built using moving averages. Also, like moving averages, the stop-band attenuation of the MACD is not very sharp. The stop-band attenuation of the Butterworth band-pass filter, on the other hand is very sharp. Because only a small range of frequencies pass through such a filter, its output is very smooth, close to a sine wave. Moreover, because the lag and lead cancel at the center frequency, there is no lag. Smooth output and no lag? That sounds like the perfect oscillator! But there is a catch: Only the filter with a center frequency that matches the current cyclic activity in the market can be used.

The output from an appropriately tuned filter should be in synchronization with the cyclic activity in the market at a given time. Such output will be very smooth, leading to solid trading decisions with few or no whipsaws, and should be usable in the generation of trading signals. In fact, if a filter is chosen that is tuned to a slightly higher frequency than the filter with the most resonance, there will be a slight lead in the filter output, which will make it slightly predictive.

One problem with band-pass filters constructed using Butterworth high- and low-pass components is the dramatically large phase shifts that occur as the periodicity of the signal moves away from the center of the pass-band. Such phase shifts can completely throw off any attempt at trade timing based on the output of the filter.

Wavelet-Based Filters

Butterworth filters are not necessarily the optimal filters to use when applying a filter bank methodology to the study of market cycles. The drawbacks to using Butterworth filters include the fact that they do not necessarily have the response speed desired when trading markets and making quick, timely decisions. Problems with measuring the instantaneous amplitude of a particular cycle are another consideration. And as noted earlier, the phase response of Butterworth filters is less than ideal. Wavelets, on the other hand, provide an elegant alternative.

The theory of filter banks has recently become much more sophisticated with the introduction of *wavelet theory*. On a practical level, wavelet theory enables the construction of fairly elegant digital filters that have a number of desirable properties. The filters used in the tests below are loosely based upon the *Morelet* wavelet. The Morelet wavelet behaves very much like a localized Fourier transform. It captures information about cyclic activity at a specific time, with as rapid a decrease as possible in the influence (on the result) of data points that have increasing distance from the time being examined. Unlike Butterworth filters, Morelet wavelets are maximally localized in time for a given level of selectivity or sharpness. This is a very desirable feature when only the most current information should influence estimates of potentially tradable cycles. The filters constructed for the tests below also have the benefit of a much better phase response, highly important when attempting to obtain accurate market timing in the context of varying cycles. The advanced filters under discussion can easily be used in banks, employing a methodology similar to the one used in our May 1997 study.

The kind of wavelet-based filters used in the tests below are designed to behave like *quadrature mirror filters*; i.e., there are two outputs for each filter: an in-phase output and an in-quadrature output. The *in-phase output* coincides precisely with any signal in the market with a frequency that lies at the center of the pass-band of the filter. The *in-quadrature output* is precisely 90 degrees out-of-phase, having zero crossings when the in-phase output is at a peak or trough, and having peaks and troughs when the in-phase output is crossing zero. In a mathematical sense, the outputs can be said to be orthogonal. Using these filters, the instantaneous amplitude of the cyclic activity (at the frequency the filter is tuned to) can be computed by simply taking the square of the in-phase output, adding it to the square of the in-quadrature output, and taking the square root of the sum. There is no need to look back for peaks and valleys in the filtered output, and to measure their amplitude, to determine the strength of a cycle. There is also no need to use any other unusual technique, such as obtaining a correlation between the filter output and prices over approximately the length of one cycle of bars, as we did in 1997. Instead, if a strong cycle is detected by one of the filters in the bank, the pair of filter outputs can generate a trading signal at any desired point in the phase of the detected cycle.

Figure 10-1 shows a single filter responding to a cycle of fixed amplitude (*original signal*), with a frequency that is being swept from low to high (left to right on graph). The center of the filter was set to a period of 12. The second line down from the top (*in-phase filter output*) illustrates the in-phase output from the filter as it responds to the input signal. It is evident that as the periodicity of the original signal approaches the center of the filter's pass-band, the amplitude of the in-phase output climbs, reaching a maximum at the center of the pass-band. As the periodicity of the original signal becomes longer than the center of the pass-band, the amplitude of the in-phase output declines. Near the center of the pass-band, the in-phase output from the filter is almost perfectly aligned with the original input signal. Except for the alignment, the *in-quadrature filter output* (third line) shows the same kind of amplitude variation in response to the changing periodicity of the driving signal. Near the center of the filter pass-band, the in-quadrature output is almost exactly 90 degrees out-of-phase with the in-phase output. Finally, the

FIGURE 10-1

Signal Processing Behavior of the Quadrature Mirror Wavelet Filter Pair

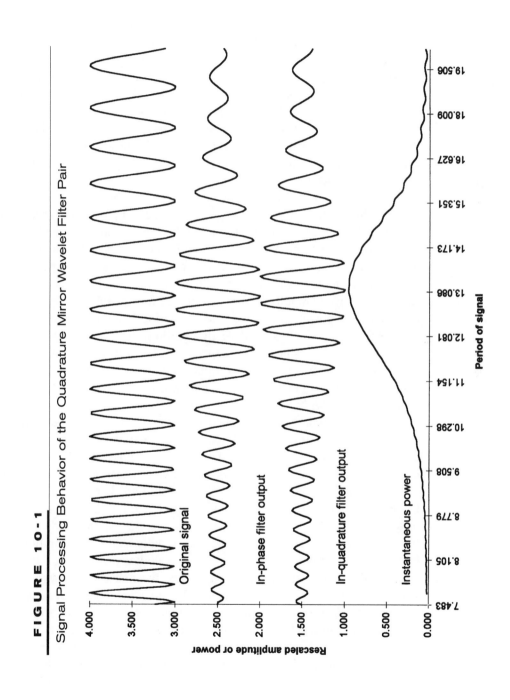

fourth line depicts *instantaneous power*, as estimated from the filter outputs. This represents the strength or amplitude of cyclic activity in the signal near the center of the filter pass-band. The curve for instantaneous power is exceedingly smooth, reaches a peak when the signal has a periodicity matching the tuning of the filter, and declines thereafter. In the chart, the center of the pass-band appears to occur at a period of 13, rather than 12, the period to which the filter was set. The reason for the slight distortion is that the periodicity of the original signal was being rapidly swept from low to high. Since the filter needs to look back several cycles, the spectral estimate is distorted. Nevertheless, it seems apparent that trades based on the filtered output would be highly profitable. The scaling of the *y*-axis is irrelevant; it was done in the manner presented to make the signals appear clearly, at separate locations, on the chart.

Figure 10-2 depicts the frequency (or periodicity) and phase response of the filter. In this case, the filter is set to have a center, or pass-band, periodicity of 20. The relative power curve shows the strength of the output from the filter as the signal frequency is varied, but held constant in power. The filter passes the signal to a maximum extent when it has a frequency at the center of the pass-band, and as the frequency moves away from the center frequency of the filter, the output of the filter smoothly and rapidly declines. There are no side lobes in the response curve, and the output power drops to zero as the periodicity goes down or up. The filter has absolutely no response to a steady trend or a fixed offset—a highly desirable property for traders, since there is then no need to fuss with de-trending, or any other preprocessing of the input signal, before applying the filter. The phase response also shows many desirable characteristics. For the most part, the phase response is well within ±90 degrees within the pass-band of the filter. At the center of the pass-band, there is no phase shift; i.e., the in-phase filter output is exactly in synchronization with the input series—a trader timing his trades would achieve perfect entries. As with the power, the phase response is smooth and extremely well behaved. Any engineer or physicist seeing this chart should appreciate the quality of these filters. When a similar chart was generated for the Butterworth band-pass filters (used in our 1997 study), the results were much less pleasing, especially with regard to the filter's phase response and offset characteristics. Severe phase shifts developed very rapidly as the periodicity of the signal moved even slightly away from the center periodicity of the filter. In real-life circumstances, with imprecisely timed cycles, the phase response of those filters would likely play total havoc with any effort to achieve good trade timing.

Figure 10-3 shows the impulse response for both outputs from the wavelet filter pair: the in-quadrature output and the in-phase output. These curves look almost as though they were exponentially decaying sines or cosines. The decay, however, is not quite exponential, and there are slight, though imperceptible, adjustments in the relative amplitudes of the peaks to eliminate sensitivity to offset or trend.

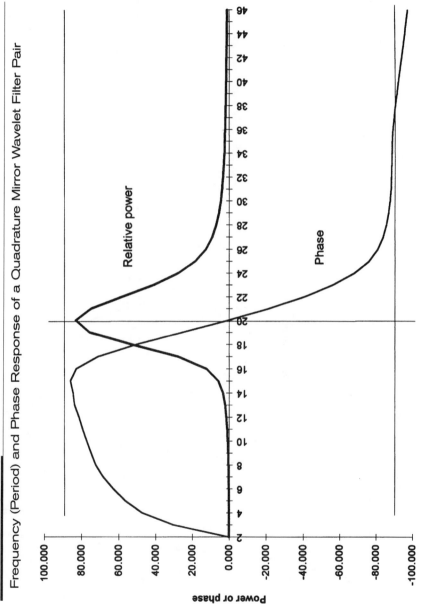

FIGURE 10-2

Frequency (Period) and Phase Response of a Quadrature Mirror Wavelet Filter Pair

Period = 1 / frequency   Center period of filter set to 20 bars

211

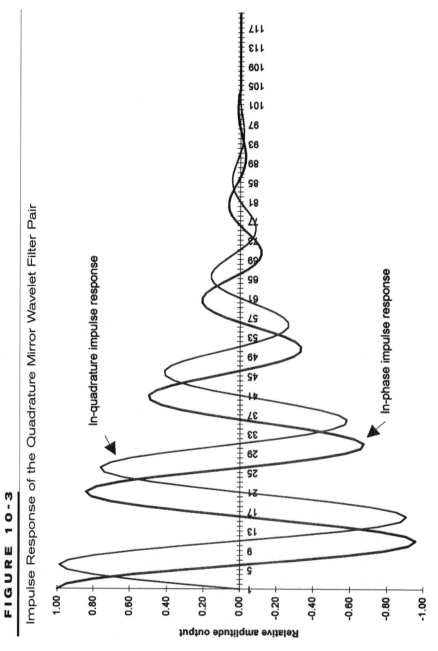

FIGURE 10-3

Impulse Response of the Quadrature Mirror Wavelet Filter Pair

In addition to the data provided in the charts, a number of other tests were conducted using "plasmodes." A *plasmode* is a set of data constructed to have the characteristics that are assumed to exist in the real data. The intention is to test the ability of some algorithm or analytic technique to properly extract, detect, or analyze those characteristics. A good cycle-based trading system should be able to do a good job trading a synthetic data series containing lots of noise and occasional embedded cycles. If it cannot, there could be no expectation of it trading well in any real market. The kind of filters used in the tests below perform very well in tests involving plasmodes.

GENERATING CYCLE ENTRIES USING FILTER BANKS

One way to generate cycle entries is to set up a series of filters, each for a different frequency or periodicity (e.g., going down a certain percentage per filter throughout some range or spectrum that will be analyzed). If one of these filters shows strong resonance, while the others show little or no activity, there is presumably a strong cycle in the market. An entry is generated by looking at the pair of filter outputs and buying at the next bar, if the cycle phase is such that a cyclic bottom will occur on that bar, or selling at the next bar, if a cycle top is evident or would be expected on that bar. Since the strongest-responding filter should produce no undesirable lag or phase error, such cyclic entries should provide exceedingly timely signals if the market is evidencing cyclic behavior. Attempting to buy cycle bottoms and sell cycle tops is one of the traditional ways in which cycle information has been used to trade the markets. Cycle information derived from filter banks, or by other means, can also enhance other kinds of systems or adapt indicators to current market conditions. An example of how information regarding the signal-to-noise ratio and periodicity of the dominant cycle (if there is any) may be used within another system, or to adapt an indicator to current market conditions, can be found in Ruggiero (1997).

CHARACTERISTICS OF CYCLE-BASED ENTRIES

A cycle-based entry of the kind studied below (which attempts to buy bottoms and sell tops) has several strong characteristics: a high percentage of winning trades, low levels of slippage, and the ability to capture as much of each move as possible. This is the kind of trading that is a trader's dream. The assumption being made is that there are well-behaved cycles in the market that can be detected and, more importantly, extrapolated by this kind of technology. It has been said that the markets evidence cyclic activity up to 70% of the time. Even if clear cycles that lead to successful trades only occur some smaller percentage of the time, because of the nature of the model, the losses can be kept small on the failed trades by the use of tight stops. The main disadvantage of a cycle-based entry is that the market may

have become efficient relative to such trading methodologies, thanks to the proliferation of fairly powerful cycle analysis techniques, e.g., maximum entropy. The
trading away of well-behaved cycles may hamper all cycle detection approaches.
Since cycle entries of the kind just discussed are countertrend in nature, if the
cycles show no follow-through, but the trends do, the trader can get wiped out
unless good money management practices (tight stops) are employed. Whether or
not a sophisticated cycle analysis works, at least as implemented here, is the question to be answered by the tests that follow.

TEST METHODOLOGY

In all tests of cycle-based entry models, the standard portfolio of 36 commodities
is used. The number of contracts in any market at any time to buy or sell on entry
was chosen to approximate the dollar volatility of two S&P 500 contracts at the
end of 1998. Exits are the standard ones in which a money management stop closes out any trade that moves more than one volatility unit into the red, a profit target limit closes out trades that push more that four volatility units into the profit
zone, and a market-at-close order ends any trade that has not yet been closed out
by the stop-loss or profit target after 10 days has elapsed. Entry rules are specified
in the discussion of the model code and the individual tests. All tests are performed
using the standard C-Trader toolkit. Here is the code implementing the wavelet filter entry model along with the standard exit strategy:

```
static void Model (float *parms, float *dt, float *opn, float *hi,
float *lo, float *cls, float *vol, float *oi, float *dlrv, int nb,
TRDSIM &ts, float *eqcls) {

    // Implements filter-bank cycle trading models.
    // File = x14mod01.c
    // parms    - vector [1..MAXPRM] of parameters
    // dt       - vector [1..nb] of dates in YYMMDD form
    // opn      - vector [1..nb] of opening prices
    // hi       - vector [1..nb] of high prices
    // lo       - vector [1..nb] of low prices
    // cls      - vector [1..nb] of closing prices
    // vol      - vector [1..nb] of volumes
    // oi       - vector [1..nb] of open interest numbers
    // dlrv     - vector [1..nb] of average dollar volatilities
    // nb       - number of bars in data series or vectors
    // ts       - trading simulator class instance
    // eqcls    - vector [1..nb] of closing equity levels

    // declare local scratch variables
    static int rc, cb, ncontracts, maxhold, ordertype, signal;
```

```
static int disp, k, modeltype, fcount, goodcycle, domperndx;
static float mmstp, ptlim, stpprice, limprice, tmp;
static float width, oldwidth, lper, sper, per, ratio;
static float exitatr[MAXBAR+1], **inphase, **inquad, **power;
static float peakpower, phase, peaknoise, domperiod;
static float buyphase, sellphase, phaseb, oldphase, oldphaseb;
static WAVFILT filter[20];

// copy parameters to local variables for clearer reference
width     = parms[1];    // filter bandwidth (0.05 .. 0.20)
disp      = parms[2];    // time displacement in degrees
modeltype = parms[8];    // model: 1=trade cycle turns
ordertype = parms[9];    // entry: 1=open, 2=limit, 3=stop
maxhold   = 10;          // maximum holding period
ptlim     = 4;           // profit target in volatility units
mmstp     = 1;           // stop loss in volatility units

// make the closing prices a period-sweeped sine wave for debugging
// this is a testing plasmode: the model should trade a
// pure cycle well.
// #define USESINEWAVE
#ifdef USESINEWAVE
per = 3.0;
ratio = exp (log (30.0 / 3.0) / (nb - 1));
sper=0.0;
for (cb = 1; cb <= nb; cb++) {
   sper += 2.0 * PI * (1.0 / per);
   cls[cb] = sin(sper);
   per *= ratio;
}
#endif

// initialize bank of equally-spaced wavelet filters
// re-initialize if the width parameter has changed
if(width != oldwidth) {
   lper = 30.0;           // longest period filter
   sper = 3.0;            // shortest period filter
   fcount = 20;           // number of filters in bank
   ratio = exp (log (lper / sper) / (fcount - 1));
   per = sper;
   for(k = 1; k <= fcount; k++) {
       filter[k-1].build_kernel(per, width);
       per *= ratio;
   }
   oldwidth = width;
}
```

```
// calculate filter outputs and adjusted power spectrum
// if matrices (tables) not yet allocated, allocate them
if(inphase == NULL) inphase = matrix(1,fcount,1,MAXBAR);
if(inquad == NULL) inquad = matrix(1,fcount,1,MAXBAR);
if(power == NULL) power = matrix(1,fcount,1,MAXBAR);
for(k = 1; k <= fcount; k++) {
    filter[k-1].apply (cls, inphase[k], inquad[k], nb);
    for(cb = 1; cb <= nb; cb++)
        power[k][cb] = (inphase[k][cb] * inphase[k][cb] +
            inquad[k][cb] * inquad[k][cb])
                / filter[k-1].period();
}


// writes a sample bar-by-bar spectral analysis to a file
// again, this is used for debugging
// #define WRITESAMPLE
#ifdef WRITESAMPLE
FILE *fil = fopen("test.dat", "wt");
for(cb = nb-1200; cb < nb; cb++) {
    domperndx = 0;
    peakpower = -1.0;
    for(k = 1; k <= fcount; k++) {
        if(power[k][cb] > peakpower) {
            peakpower = power[k][cb];
            domperndx = k;
        }
    }
    phase = (180.0 / PI) * atan2(inquad[domperndx][cb],
                                inphase[domperndx][cb]);

    for(k = 1; k <= fcount; k++) {
        if(power[k][cb] > 0.90 * peakpower)
            fprintf(fil, " **");
        else if(power[k][cb] > 0.75 * peakpower)
            fprintf(fil, " ++");
        else if(power[k][cb] > 0.5 * peakpower)
            fprintf(fil, " + ");
        else
            fprintf(fil, "   ");
    }
    fprintf(fil, "%4d %7d %7d %7d %8.1f\n",
        (int)filter[domperndx-1].period(),
        (int)(inphase[domperndx][cb]),
        (int)(inquad[domperndx][cb]),
        (int)phase, cls[cb]);
}
fclose(fil);
```

```
exit(0);
#endif

// used to debug signals
// #define SIGNALDEBUG
#ifdef SIGNALDEBUG
   FILE *fil = fopen("testsig.dat", "wt");
#endif

// perform other whole-series calculations
AvgTrueRangeS(exitatr,hi,lo,cls,50,nb);          // ATR for exit
switch(modeltype) {
  case 1:
     // Do nothing! Placeholder for future code.
     break;
  default: nrerror("Invalid model type");
}

// step through bars (days) to simulate actual trading
for(cb = 1; cb <= nb; cb++) {

   // take no trades before the in-sample period
   // ... same as TradeStation's MaxBarsBack setting
   if(dt[cb] < IS_DATE) { eqcls[cb] = 0.0; continue; }

   // execute any pending orders and save closing equity
   rc = ts.update(opn[cb], hi[cb], lo[cb], cls[cb], cb);
   if(rc != 0) nrerror("Trade buffer overflow");
   eqcls[cb] = ts.currentequity(EQ_CLOSETOTAL);

   // take no trades in last 30 bars of data sample
   // to leave room in arrays for seasonal look-aheads
   if(cb > nb-30) continue;

   // calculate number of contracts to trade
   // ... we want to trade the dollar volatility equivalent
   // ... of 2 new S&P-500 contracts as of 12/31/98
   ncontracts = RoundToInteger(5673.0 / dlrv[cb]);
   if(ncontracts < 1) ncontracts = 1;

   // avoid placing orders on possibly limit-locked days
   if(hi[cb+1] == lo[cb+1]) continue;

   // generate entry signals, stop prices and limit prices
   signal = 0;
   switch(modeltype) {
```

```
    case 1:
      // check for a good, pure cycle to trade
      domperndx = 0;
      peakpower = -1.0;
      for(k = 1; k <= fcount; k++) {
          if(power[k][cb] > peakpower) {
              peakpower = power[k][cb];
              domperndx = k;
          }
      }
      goodcycle = FALSE;
      if(domperndx > 3 && domperndx < fcount-1) {
          peaknoise = 0.0;
          for(k = 1; k <= fcount; k++) {
              if(abs(k - domperndx) > 2) {
                  if(power[k][cb] > peaknoise)
                      peaknoise = power[k][cb];
              }
          }
          if(peakpower > 1.5 * peaknoise) goodcycle = TRUE;
      }
      // generate the trading signals
      if(goodcycle) {
          domperiod = filter[domperndx-1].period();
          phase = (180.0 / PI) *
                      atan2(inquad[domperndx][cb],
                          inphase[domperndx][cb]);
          oldphase = (180.0 / PI) *
                      atan2(inquad[domperndx][cb-1],
                          inphase[domperndx][cb-1]);
          phaseb = (phase<0.0) ? (360.0+phase) : phase;
          oldphaseb = (oldphase<0.0)
              ? (360.0+oldphase) : oldphase;
          sellphase = 0.0 - (disp + 180.0 / domperiod);
          buyphase = 180.0 + sellphase;
          if(phaseb > buyphase && oldphaseb <= buyphase)
              signal = 1;                       // buy signal
          if(phase > sellphase && oldphase <= sellphase)
              signal = -1;                      // sell signal
      }
      break;
}
limprice = 0.5 * (hi[cb] + lo[cb]);
stpprice = cls[cb] + 0.5 * signal * exitatr[cb];

// print out debugging data
```

```
        #ifdef SIGNALDEBUG
            fprintf(fil, "%8d %8.1f %8d %8d %8d %8d\n",
                cb, cls[cb], signal,
                (int)filter[domperndx-1].period(),
                (int)peakpower, (int)peaknoise );
        #endif

        // enter trades using specified order type
        if(ts.position() <= 0 && signal == 1) {
          switch(ordertype) { // select desired order type
            case 1: ts.buyopen('1', ncontracts); break;
            case 2: ts.buylimit('2', limprice, ncontracts); break;
            case 3: ts.buystop('3', stpprice, ncontracts); break;
            default: nrerror("Invalid buy order selected");
          }
        }
        else if(ts.position() >= 0 && signal == -1) {
          switch(ordertype) { // select desired order type
            case 1: ts.sellopen('4', ncontracts); break;
            case 2: ts.selllimit('5', limprice, ncontracts); break;
            case 3: ts.sellstop('6', stpprice, ncontracts); break;
            default: nrerror("Invalid sell order selected");
          }
        }

        // instruct simulator to employ standard exit strategy
        tmp = exitatr[cb];
        ts.stdexitcls('X', ptlim*tmp, mmstp*tmp, maxhold);

    } // process next bar

    // close up when in debug mode
    #ifdef SIGNALDEBUG
       fclose(fil);
       exit(0);
    #endif
}
```

The code above implements the model being tested. The first significant block of code specifically relevant to a cyclic trading model initializes the individual filters that make up the filter bank. This code is set up to run only on the first pass, or when a parameter specifically affecting the computations involved in initializing the filter bank (e.g., the *width* parameter) has changed; if no relevant parameter has changed, there is no point in reinitializing the filters every time the *Model* function is called.

The next block of code applies each of the filters in the bank to the input signal. In this block, two arrays are allocated to hold the filter bank outputs. The first array contains the in-phase outputs (*inphase*), and the second contains the in-quadrature outputs (*inquad*). The inputs to the filters are the raw closing prices. Because the filters are mathematically optimal, and designed to eliminate offsets and trends, there is no need to preprocess the closing prices before applying them, as might be necessary when using less sophisticated analysis techniques. Each row in the arrays represents the output of a single filter with a specified center frequency or periodicity. Each column represents a bar. The frequencies (or periodicities) at which the filters are centered are all spaced evenly on a logarithmic scale; i.e., the ratio between the center frequency of a given filter and the next has a fixed value. The selectivity or bandwidth (*width*) is the only adjustable parameter in the computation of the filter banks, the correct value of which may be sought by optimization.

The usual bar-stepping loop is then entered and the actual trading signals generated. First, a good, pure cycle to trade is identified, which involves determining the power at the periodicity that has the strongest resonance with current market activity (*peakpower*). The cycle periodicity at which the peak power occurs is also assessed. If the periodicity is not at one of the end points of the range of periodicities being examined (in this case the range is 3 bars to 30 bars), one of the conditions for a potentially good cycle is met. A check is then made to see what the maximum power (*peaknoise*) is at periodicities at least 2 filters away from the periodicity at which peak power occurs If *peakpower* is more than 1.5 times the *peaknoise* (a signal-to-noise ratio of 1.5 or greater), the second condition for a good cycle is met. The phase angle of that cycle is then determined (easy to do given the pair of filter outputs), making adjustments for the slice that occurs at 180 degrees in the plane of polar coordinates. The code then checks whether the phase is such that a cycle bottom or a cycle top is present. A small displacement term (*disp*) is incorporated in the phase assessments. It acts like the displacements in previous models, except that here it is in terms of phase angle, rather than bars. There is a direct translation between phase angle and number of bars; specifically, the period of the cycle is multiplied by the phase angle (in degrees), and the sum is then divided by 360, which is the number of bars represented by the phase angle. If the displaced phase is such that a bottom can be expected a certain number of degrees before or after the present bar, a buy is posted. If the phase angle is such that a top can be expected, a sell signal is issued. The limit and stop prices are then calculated, as usual. Finally, the necessary trading orders are posted.

Many other blocks of code present in the above listing have not been discussed. These were used for debugging and testing. Comments embedded in the code should make their purpose fairly clear.

TEST RESULTS

Only one model was tested. Tests were performed for entry at the open (Test 1), entry on a limit (Test 2), and entry on a stop (Test 3). The rules were simple: Buy predicted cycle bottoms and sell predicted cycle tops. Exits took place when a cycle signal reversed an existing position or when the standard strategy closed out the trade, whichever came first. This simple trading model was first evaluated on a noisy sine wave that was swept from a period of about 4 bars to a period of about 20 bars to verify behavior of the model implementation. On this data, buy and sell signals appeared with clockwork precision at cycle tops and bottoms. The timing of the signals indicates that when real cycles are present, the model is able to detect and trade them with precision.

Table 10-1 contains the best in-sample parameters, as well as the performance of the portfolio on both the in-sample and verification sample data. In the table, *SAMP* = whether the test was on the optimization sample (*IN* or *OUT*); *ROA%* = the annualized return-on-account; *ARRR* = the annualized risk-to-reward ratio; *PROB* = the associated probability or statistical significance; *TRDS* = the number of trades taken across all commodities in the portfolio; *WIN%* = the percentage of winning trades; *$TRD* = the average profit/loss per trade; BARS = the average number of days a trade was held; *NETL* = the total net profit on long trades, in thousands of dollars; and *NETS* = the total net profit on short trades, in thousands of dollars. Two parameters were optimized. The first (*P1*) represents the bandwidth for each filter in the filter bank. The second parameter (*P2*) represents the phase displacement in degrees. In all cases, the parameters were optimized on the in-sample data by stepping the bandwidth from 0.05 to 0.2 in increments of 0.05, and by stepping the phase angle displacement from -20 degrees to $+20$ degrees in increments of 10 degrees. Only the best solutions are shown.

It is interesting that, overall, the cycle model performed rather poorly. This model was not as bad, on a dollars-per-trade basis, as many of the other systems tested, but it was nowhere near as good as the best. In-sample, the loss per trade was $1,329 with entry at open, $1,037 with entry on limit, and $1,245 with entry on stop. The limit order had the highest percentage of wins and the smallest average loss per

TABLE 10-1

Portfolio Performance with Best In-Sample Parameters on Both In-Sample and Out-of-Sample Data

SAMP	P1	P2	P3	ROA%	RRR	PROB	TRDS	WIN%	$TRD	BARS	NETL	NETS
Test 01	Basic cycle model, entry at open											
IN	0.2	20	0	-10.2	-0.66	0.980	1312	40	-1329	6	255	-2000
OUT	0.2	20	0	-23.2	-1.70	1.000	547	34	-3741	6	-693	-1352
Test 02	Basic cycle model, entry on limit											
IN	0.2	20	0	-9.5	-0.46	0.926	1103	41	-1037	7	621	-1764
OUT	0.2	20	0	-22.8	-1.47	0.999	475	34	-3551	7	-652	-1034
Test 03	Basic cycle model, entry on stop											
IN	0.1	20	0	-8.3	-0.53	0.951	957	40	-1245	7	-195	-996
OUT	0.1	20	0	-15.0	-0.35	0.762	403	41	-944	7	-220	-160

trade. The long side was slightly profitable with entry at open, was somewhat more profitable with entry on limit, and lost with entry on stop. The behavior out-of-sample, with entry at open and on limit, was a lot worse than the behavior of the model in-sample. The loss per trade grew to $3,741 for entry at open and to $3,551 for entry on limit. The percentage of winning trades also declined, to 34%. The performance of the cycle model on the verification sample was among the worst observed of the various models tested. The deterioration cannot be attributed to optimization: Several other parameter sets were examined, and regardless of which was chosen, the cycle model still performed much worse out-of-sample. With entry on stop, the out-of-sample performance did not deteriorate. In this case, the loss ($944) was not too different from the in-sample loss. Although the stop order appears to have prevented the deterioration of the model that was seen with the other orders, in more recent times the system is a loser.

The decline of system performance in recent years was unusually severe, as observed from the results of the other models tested. One possible reason may be the recent proliferation of sophisticated cycle trading tools. Another explanation might be that major trading firms are conducting research using sophisticated techniques, including wavelets of the kind studied here. These factors may have contributed to making the markets relatively efficient to basic cycle trading.

Table 10-2 shows the in-sample and out-of-sample behavior of the cycle model broken down by market and entry order (test). The *SYM* column represents the market being studied. The center and rightmost columns (*COUNT*) contain the number of profitable tests for a given market. The numbers in the first row represent test identifiers: 01, 02, and 03 represent entry at open, on limit, and on stop, respectively. The last row (*COUNT*) contains the number of markets on which a given model was profitable. The data in this table provides relatively detailed information about which markets are and are not profitable when traded by each of the models: One dash (-) indicates a moderate loss per trade, i.e., $2,000 to $4,000; two dashes (--) represent a large loss per trade, i.e., $4,000 or more; one plus sign (+) means a moderate profit per trade, i.e., $1,000 to $2,000; two pluses (++) indicate a large gain per trade, i.e., $2,000 or more; and a blank cell means that the loss was between $0 and $1,999 or the profit was between $0 and $1,000 per trade. (For information about the various markets and their symbols, see Table II-1 in the "Introduction" to Part II.)

Only the 10-Year Notes and Cotton showed strong profits across all three entry orders in-sample. Out-of-sample, performance on these markets was miserable. The S&P 500, a market that, in our experience, has many clear and tradable cycles, demonstrated strong profitability on the in-sample data when entry was at open or on limit. This market was strongly profitable out-of-sample with entry on limit and on stop, but somewhat less profitable with entry at open. Interestingly, the NYFE, although evidencing strong in-sample profits with entry at open and on limit, had losses out-of-sample across all three orders. There are a few other prof-

TABLE 10-2

Performance Data Broken Down by Market and Test

SYM	In-sample					Out-of-sample			
	01	02	03	Count		01	02	03	Count
SP	++	++	--	2		+	++	++	3
YX	++	++	--	2		--	-	-	0
US	++	++	-	2		-		++	1
TB	--	--	++	1		--	--	--	0
TY	++	++	++	3		--	--		0
BP	+	+	+	3			+	--	1
DM		-	+	1		--	--	--	0
SF			+	1		--	--	++	1
JY	--	--		0		--	--	++	1
CD	--	--		0		--	--		0
ED	+	++	-	2		--	--	--	0
CL		+	++	2		--	--		0
HO		--		0				--	0
HU	+	-	--	1				-	0
GC	+	++	-	2		--	--		0
SI		--		0		--	++		1
PL		-		0		+	--	++	2
PA	--	-	+	1			-	+	1
FC				0		-	--	--	0
LC			--	0		--	--		0
LH	++	--	-	1			+	-	1
PB	+			1		--	--	-	0
S				0		--	--	--	0
SM			-	0		++	++	--	2
BO		+	-	1			-	+	1
C	--	--		0		--	--	++	1
O	+		--	1		++	++	--	2
W	--	--	-	0		--	--	++	1
KW	--	--	--	0		--	--		0
MW	--	-	--	0		--	-		0
KC	--	-		0		++	++	++	3
CC	--	--		0			-	-	0
SB	-		++	1		--	--	--	0
JO	--	--	-	0		++	++	--	2
CT	++	++	++	3		+	--	--	1
LB	--	-	--	0		--	--	--	0
Count	12	10	9			7	8	10	

itable in-sample market-order combinations, as well as out-of-sample market-order combinations. However, very little correspondence between the two was observed. Perhaps markets that have not had cycles in the past (in-sample) have cycles in the present (out-of-sample), and vice versa. At least the S&P 500 behaved as expected on the basis of prior research and may be one of the few markets consistently amenable to cycle trading in this crude form.

Figure 10-4 depicts the equity for the portfolio with entry at open. Equity declined slowly and then became rather flat until about August 1992, at which time it began a steady and rapid decline.

CONCLUSION

In our May 1997 study, the filter bank method appeared to have potential as the basis for an effective trading strategy. At times it worked incredibly well, and was almost completely insensitive to large variations in its parameters, whereas at other times it performed poorly. The results may simply have been due to the fact that the implementation was "quick and dirty." Back then, the focus was on the S&P 500, a market that continued to trade well in the present study.

The results of the current study are disappointing, all the more given the theoretical elegance of the filters. It may be that other approaches to the analysis of cycles, e.g., the use of maximum entropy, might have provided better performance; then again, maybe not. Other traders have also experienced similar disappointments using a variety of techniques when trading cycles in a simple, buy-the-bottom/sell-the-top manner. It may be that cycles are too obvious and detectable by any of a number of methods, and may be traded away very quickly whenever they develop in the market. This especially seems the case in recent years with the proliferation of cycle analysis software. The suggestion is not that cycles should be abandoned as a concept, but that a more sophisticated use of detected cycles must be made. Perhaps better results would ensue if cycles were combined with other kinds of entry criteria, e.g., taking trades only if a cycle top corresponds to an expected seasonal turning-point top.

Further studies are needed to determine whether the cycle model does indeed have the characteristic of giving precise entries when it works, but failing miserably when it does not work. Looking over a chart of the S&P 500 suggests this is the case. There are frequently strings of four or five trades in a row, with entries that occur precisely at market tops and bottoms, as if predicted with perfect hindsight. At other times, entries occur exactly where they should not. With a system that behaves this way, our experience indicates that, combined with a proper exit, sometimes great profits can be achieved. More specifically, losses have to be cut very quickly when the model fails, but trades should not be prematurely terminated when the model is correct in its predictions. Because of the precision of the model when the predictions are correct, an extremely tight stop could perhaps

FIGURE 10-4

Portfolio Equity Growth for Countertrend Cycle Trading

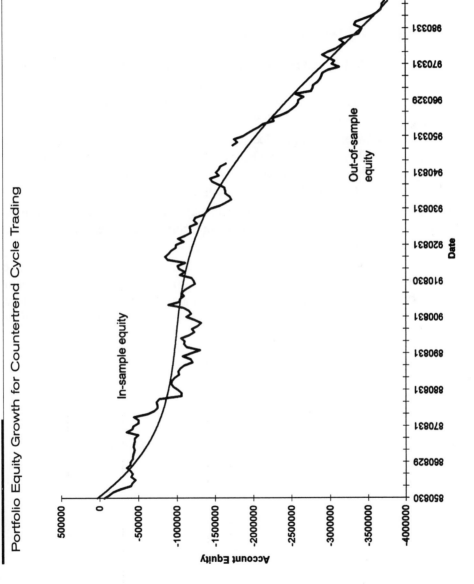

accomplish the goal. When an exact cycle top or bottom is caught, the market begins to move immediately in the favored direction, with hardly any adverse excursion, and the stop is never hit. When the model fails, the stop is hit very quickly, resulting in only a small loss. Given the fairly loose stop of the standard exit, the benefits of sophisticated cycle trading may not have been realized.

WHAT HAVE WE LEARNED?

- Models that are theoretically sound, elegant, and appealing do not necessarily work well when trading real markets.
- Exception to Rule 1: The S&P 500 may respond to such methods; it did so both in our earlier study and in the current one.
- When the model does work, it does so remarkably well. As stated earlier, when examining its behavior on the S&P 500 and several other markets, one can quickly and easily find strings of signals that pick off tops and bottoms with the precision of hindsight.
- The previous point suggests that exits specifically designed for a system that yields high precision when correct, but fails badly when incorrect, may be required.
- The markets appear to have become more efficient relative to cycle models, as they have to breakout models. Obvious market behavior (such as clear, tradable cycles) are traded away before most traders can capitalize on them. The lesson: Anything too theoretically appealing or obvious will tend not to work.

CHAPTER 11

Neural Networks

Neural network technology, a form of artificial intelligence (or AI), arose from endeavors to emulate the kind of information processing and decision making that occurs in living organisms. The goal was to model the behavior of neural tissue in living systems by using a computer to implement structures composed of simulated neurons and neural interconnections (synapses). Research on neural networks began in the 1940s on a theoretical level. When computer technology became sophisticated enough to accommodate such research, the study of neural networks and their applications began in earnest. It was not, however, until the mid-to-late 1980s that neural network technology became of interest to the financial community. By 1989, a few vendors of neural network development tools were available, and there was one commercial S&P 500 forecasting system based on this technology (Scientific Consultant Services' NexTurn). In the early 1990s, interest peaked, more development tools appeared, but the fervor then waned for reasons discussed later.

While it is not within the scope of this book to present a full tutorial on neural network technology, below is a brief discussion to provide basic understanding. Those interested in exploring this subject in greater depth should read our contributions to the books *Virtual Trading* (Lederman and Klein, 1995) and *Computerized Trading* (Jurik, 1999), in which we also present detailed information on system development using neural networks, as well as our articles in *Technical Analysis of Stocks and Commodities* (Katz, April 1992; Katz and McCormick, November 1996, November 1997). *Neural Networks in Finance and Investing* (Trippi and Turban, 1993) should also be of interest.

WHAT ARE NEURAL NETWORKS?

Neural networks (or "nets") are basically building blocks that learn and are useful for pattern recognition, classification, and prediction. They hold special appeal to traders because nets are capable of coping both with probability estimates in uncertain situations and with "fuzzy" patterns, i.e., those recognizable by eye but difficult to define in software using precise rules; and they have the potential to recognize almost any pattern that exists. Nets can also integrate large amounts of information without becoming stifled by detail and can be made to adapt to changing markets and market conditions.

A variety of neural networks are available, differing in terms of their "architecture," i.e., the ways in which the simulated neurons are interconnected, the details of how these neurons behave (signal processing behavior or "transfer functions"), and the process through which learning takes place. There are a number of popular kinds of neural networks that are of some use to traders: the Kohonen and the Learning Vector Quantization (LVQ) networks, various adaptive resonance networks, and recurrent networks. In this chapter, the most popular and, in many respects, the most useful kind of network is discussed: the "feed-forward" network.

As mentioned above, nets differ in the ways they learn. The system developer plays the role of the neural network's teacher, providing the net with examples to learn from. Some nets employ "supervised learning" and others "unsupervised learning." *Supervised learning* occurs when the network is taught to produce a correct solution by being shown instances of correct solutions. This is a form of *paired-associate learning*: The network is presented with pairs of inputs and a desired output; for every set of inputs, it is the task of the net to learn to produce the desired output. *Unsupervised learning*, on the other hand, involves nets that take the sets of inputs they are given and organize them as they see fit, according to patterns they find therein. Regardless of the form of learning employed, the main difficulty in developing successful neural network models is in finding and "massaging" historical data into training examples or "facts" that highlight relevant patterns so that the nets can learn efficiently and not be put astray or confused; "preprocessing" the data is an art in itself.

The actual process of learning usually involves some mechanism for updating the neural connection weights in response to the training examples. With feed-forward architectures, back-propagation, a form of steepest-descent optimization, is often used. Genetic algorithms are also effective. These are very computationally intensive and time-consuming, but generally produce better final results.

Feed-Forward Neural Networks

A *feed-forward network* consists of layers of neurons. The *input layer*, the first layer, receives data or *inputs* from the outside world. The inputs consist of *independent variables* (e.g., market or indicator variables upon which the system is to be based) from which some inference is to be drawn or a prediction is to be made. The input layer is massively connected to the next layer, which is often called the *hidden layer* because it has no connections to the outside world. The outputs of the hidden layer are fed to the next layer, which may be another hidden layer (if it is, the process repeats), or it may be the *output layer*. Each neuron in the output layer produces an *output* composed of the predictions, classifications, or decisions made by the network. Networks are usually identified by the number of neurons in each layer: For example, a 10-3-1 network is one that has 10 neurons in its first or input layer, 3 neurons in its middle layer, and 1 neuron in its output layer. Networks vary in size, from only a few neurons to thousands, from only three layers to dozens; the size depends on the complexity of the problem. Almost always, a three- or four-layer network suffices.

Feed-forward networks (the kind being used in this chapter) implement a particular form of *nonlinear* multiple regression. The net takes a number of input variables and uses them to predict a target, exactly as in regression. In a standard *linear* multiple regression, if the goal is to predict cholesterol (the dependent variable or target) on the basis of dietary fat intake and exercise (the independent variables or inputs), the data would be modeled as follows: predicted cholesterol $= a + b *$ fat intake $+ c *$ exercise; where a, b, and c represent parameters that would be determined by a statistical procedure. In a least-squares sense, a line, plane, or hyperplane (depending on the number of independent variables) is being fitted to the points in a data space. In the example above, a plane is being fit: The x-axis represents fat intake, the y-axis is exercise, and the height of the plane at each xy coordinate pair represents predicted cholesterol.

When using neural network technology, the two-dimensional plane or n-dimensional hyperplane of linear multiple regression is replaced by a smooth n-dimensional curved surface characterized by peaks and valleys, ridges and troughs. As an example, let us say there is a given number of input variables and a goal of finding a nonlinear mapping that will provide an output from the network that best fits the target. In the neural network, the goal is achieved via the "neurons," the nonlinear elements that are connected to one another. The weights of the connections are adjusted to fit the surface to the data. The learning algorithm adjusts the weights to get a particular curved surface that best fits the data points. As in a standard multiple regression model, in which the coefficients of the regression are needed to define the slope of the plane or hyperplane, a neural model requires that parameters, in the form of connection weights, be determined so that the particular surface generated (in this case a curved surface with hills and dales) will best fit the data.

NEURAL NETWORKS IN TRADING

Neural networks had their heyday in the late 1980 and early 1990s. Then the honeymoon ended. What happened? Basically, disillusionment set in among traders who believed that this new technology could, with little or no effort on the trader's part, magically provide the needed edge. System developers would "train" their nets on raw or mildly preprocessed data, hoping the neural networks themselves would discover something useful. This approach was naïve; nothing is ever so simple, especially when trading the markets. Not only was this "neural newbie" approach an ineffective way to use neural networks, but so many people were attempting to use nets that whatever edge was originally gained was nullified by the response of the markets, which was to become more efficient with regard to the technology. The technology itself was blamed and discarded with little consideration to the thought that it was being inappropriately applied. A more sophisticated, reasoned approach was needed if success was going to be achieved.

Most attempts to develop neural network forecasting models, whether in a simplistic manner or more elaborately, have focused on individual markets. A serious problem with the use of individual markets, however, is the limited number of data points available on which to train the net. This situation leads to grand opportunities for curve-fitting (the bad kind)—something that can contribute greatly to the likelihood of failure with a neural network, especially with less than ideal data preprocessing and targets. In this chapter, however, neural networks will be trained on a whole portfolio of tradables, resulting in the availability of many tens of thousands of data points (facts), and a reduction in curve-fitting for small to moderate-sized networks. Perhaps, in this context, a fairly straightforward attempt to have a neural network predict current or near-future market behavior might be successful. In essence, such a network could be considered a universal market forecaster, in that, trained across an entire portfolio of tradables, it might be able to predict on all markets, in a non-market-specific fashion.

FORECASTING WITH NEURAL NETWORKS

Neural networks will be developed to predict (1) where the market is in terms of its near-future range and (2) whether tomorrow's open represents a turning point. Consider, first, the goal of predicting where the market is relative to its near-future range. An attempt will be made to build a network to predict a time-reversed Stochastic, specifically the time-reversed Slow %K. This is the usual Stochastic, except that it is computed with time running backward. The time-reversed Slow %K reflects where the current close lies with respect to the price range over the next several bars. If something could predict this, it would be useful to the trader: Knowing that today's close, and probably tomorrow's open, lies near the bottom of the range of the next several days' prices would suggest a good buy point; and knowing that today's close, or tomorrow's open, lies near the top of the range would be useful in deciding to sell. Consider, second, the goal of predicting whether tomorrow's open is a top, a bottom, or neither. Two neural networks will be trained. One will predict whether tomorrow's open represents a bottom turning point, i.e., has a price that is lower than the prices on earlier and later bars. The other will predict whether tomorrow's open represents a top turning point, i.e., has a price that is higher than the prices on earlier or later bars. Being able to predict whether a bottom or a top will occur at tomorrow's open is also useful for the trader trying to decide when to enter the market and whether to go long or short. The goal in this study is to achieve such predictions in any market to which the model is applied.

GENERATING ENTRIES WITH NEURAL PREDICTIONS

Three nets will be trained, yielding three entry models. Two models will be constructed for turning points. One model will be designed to detect bottoms, the other model to detect tops. For the bottom detection model, if the neural net indicates that the probability that tomorrow's open will be a bottom is greater than some threshold, then a buy order will be posted. For the top detection model, if the neural net indicates that the probability that tomorrow's open will be a top is greater than some other threshold, then a sell order will be posted. Neither model will post an order under any other cicumstances. These rules amount to nothing more than a simple strategy of selling predicted tops and buying predicted bottoms. If, with better than chance accuracy, the locations of bottoms and tops can be detected in time to trade them, trading should be profitable. The detection system does not have to be perfect, just sufficiently better than chance so as to overcome transaction costs.

For the model that predicts the time-reversed Slow %K, a similar strategy will be used. If the prediction indicates that the time-reversed Slow %K is likely to be less than some lower threshold, a buy will be posted; the market is near the bottom of its near-future range and so a profit should quickly develop. Likewise, if the predicted reverse Slow %K is high, above an upper threshold, a sell will be posted.

These entries share the characteristics of other entries based on predictive, rather than responsive, analysis. The entries lend themselves to countertrend trading and, if the predictions are accurate, can dramatically limit transaction costs in the form of slippage, and provide good fills since the trader will be buying when others are selling and vice versa. A good predictive model is the trader's Holy Grail, providing the ability to sell near tops and buy near bottoms. As with other predictive-based entries, if the predictions are not sufficiently accurate, the benefits will be outweighed by the costs of bad trades when the predictions go wrong, as they often do.

TIME-REVERSED SLOW %K MODEL

The first step in developing a neural forecasting model is to prepare a *training fact set*, which is the sample of data consisting of examples from which the net learns; i.e., it is the data used to train the network and to estimate certain statistics. In this case, the fact set is generated using the in-sample data from all commodities in the portfolio. The number of facts in the fact set is, therefore, large—88,092 data points. A fact set is only generated for training, not for testing, for reasons that will be explained later.

To generate the facts that make up the fact set for this model, the initial step of computing the time-reversed Slow %K, which is to serve as the target, must be taken. Each fact is then created and written to a file by stepping through the in-sample bars for each commodity in the portfolio. For each current bar (the one currently being stepped through), the process of creating a fact begins with computing each input variable in the fact. This is done by calculating a difference between a pair of prices, and then dividing that difference by the square-root of the number of bars that separate the two prices. The square-root correction is used because, in a random market, the standard deviation of a price difference between a pair of bars is roughly proportional to the square-root of the number of bars separating the two prices. The correction will force each price difference to contribute about equally to the fact. In this experiment, each fact contains 18 price changes that are computed using the square-root correction. These 18 prices change scores will serve as the 18 inputs to the neural network after some additional processing.

The pairs of prices (used when computing the changes) are sampled with increasing distance between them; i.e., the further back in time, the greater the distance between the pairs. For the first few bars prior to the current bar, the spacing between the prices differenced is only 1 bar; i.e., the price of the bar prior to the current bar is be subtracted from the price of the current bar; the price 2 bars before the current bar is subtracted from the price 1 bar ago, etc. After several such price change scores, the sampling is increased to every 2 bars, then every 4, then every 8, etc. The exact spacings are in a table inside the code. The rationale behind this procedure is to obtain more detailed information on very recent price behavior. The further back the prices are in time, the more likely only longer-term movements will be significant. Therefore, less resolution should be required. Sampling the bars in this way ought to provide sufficient resolution to detect cycles and other phenomena that range from a period of 1 or 2 bars through 50 bars or more. This approach is in accord with a suggestion made by Mark Jurik (jurikres.com).

After assembling the 18 input variables consisting of the square-root–corrected price differences for a fact, a normalization procedure is applied. The intention is to preserve wave shape while discarding amplitude information. By treating the 18 input variables as a vector, the normalization consists of scaling the vector to unit length. The calculations involve squaring each vector element or price difference, summing the squares, taking the square-root, and then dividing each element by the resultant number. These are the input variables for the neural network. In actual fact, the neural network software will further scale these inputs to an appropriate range for the input neurons.

The target (dependent variable in regression terms) for each fact is simply the time-reversed Slow %K for the current bar. The input variables and target for each fact are written in simple ASCII format to a file that can be analyzed with a good neural network development package.

The resultant fact set is used to train a net to predict the time-reversed Slow %K, i.e., to predict the relative position of today's close, and, it is hoped, tomorrow's open, with respect to the range of prices over the next 10 bars (a 10-bar time-reversed Slow %K).

The next step in developing the neural forecaster is to actually train some neural networks using the just-computed fact set. A series of neural networks, varying in size, are trained. The method used to select the most appropriately sized and trained network is not the usual one of examining behavior on a test set consisting of out-of-sample data. Instead, the correlation coefficients, which reflect the predictive capabilities of each of the networks, are corrected for shrinkage based on the sample size and the number of parameters or connection weights being estimated in the corresponding network. The equation employed to correct for shrinkage is the same one used to correct the multiple correlations derived from a multivariate regression (see the chapters on optimization and statistics). Shrinkage is greater for larger networks, and reflects curve-fitting of the undesirable kind. For a larger network to be selected over a smaller network, i.e., to overcome its greater shrinkage, the correlation it produces must be sufficiently greater than that produced by the smaller network. This technique enables networks to be selected without the usual reference to out-of-sample data. All networks are fully trained; i.e., no attempt is being made to compensate for loss of degrees of freedom by undertraining.

The best networks, selected on the basis of the shrinkage-corrected correlations, are then tested using the actual entry model, together with the standard exit, on both in- and out-of-sample data and across all markets. Because shrinkage results from curve-fitting, excessively curve-fit networks should have very poor shrinkage-corrected correlations. The large number of facts in the fact set (88,092) should help reduce the extent of undesirable curve-fitting for moderately sized networks.

Code for the Reverse Slow %K Model

```
static void PrepareNeuralInputs (float *var, float *cls, int cb) {

    // Simple preprocessing of raw closing price data
    // into inputs for the neural network.
    // var      - out: vector [1..18] of variables for neural inputs
    // cls      - in: vector [1..] of closing prices
    // cb       - in: current bar index

    static pbars[] = { 0, 0,1,2,3,4,5,6,8,10,12,16,20,24,32,34,
        40,48,64,96 };
```

```
static float pfac[19], amp;
static int notfirstpass, k;
// initialize price difference adjustment factor table
if(notfirstpass == FALSE) {
    for(k = 1; k <= 18; k++)
        pfac[k] = 1.0 / sqrt(pbars[k+1] - pbars[k]);
    notfirstpass = TRUE;
}


// calculate adjusted price differences and squared amplitude
amp = 0.0;
for(k = 1; k <= 18; k++) {
    var[k] = pfac[k] *
        (cls[cb - pbars[k]] - cls[cb - pbars[k+1]]);
    amp += var[k] * var[k];
}


// normalize the price difference vector to unit amplitude
amp = 1.0 / sqrt(amp);
for(k = 1; k <= 18; k++)
    var[k] = amp * var[k];
}

static void Model (float *parms, float *dt, float *opn, float *hi,
float *lo, float *cls, float *vol, float *oi, float *dlrv, int nb,
TRDSIM &ts, float *eqcls) {

// Implements a simple neural network trading model. This
// model trades off predictions of the time-reversed Slow %K.
// File = x15mod01.c
// parms   - vector [1..MAXPRM] of parameters
// dt      - vector [1..nb] of dates in YYMMDD form
// opn     - vector [1..nb] of opening prices
// hi      - vector [1..nb] of high prices
// lo      - vector [1..nb] of low prices
// cls     - vector [1..nb] of closing prices
// vol     - vector [1..nb] of volumes
// oi      - vector [1..nb] of open interest numbers
// dlrv    - vector [1..nb] of average dollar volatilities
// nb      - number of bars in data series or vectors
// ts      - trading simulator class instance
// eqcls   - vector [1..nb] of closing equity levels

// declare local scratch variables
static int rc, cb, ncontracts, maxhold, ordertype;
static int mode, signal, factcount, k, netnum;
```

```
static FILE *fil;
static NEURALNET *nnet; static char netname[20];
static float thresh, netout, var[19];
static float mmstp, ptlim, stpprice, limprice, tmp;
static float exitatr[MAXBAR+1], revstoch[MAXBAR+1];

// copy parameters to local variables for clearer reference
thresh = parms[1];        // threshold for neural output
netnum = parms[2];        // neural-network number
mode = parms[6];          // train (mode=1) or test (mode=2)
ordertype = parms[9];     // type of entry order
maxhold = 10;             // maximum holding period
ptlim = 4;                // profit target in volatility units
mmstp = 1;                // stop loss in volatility units

// perform whole-series computations using vector routines
AvgTrueRangeS(exitatr,hi,lo,cls,50,nb);        // ATR for exit
RevStochOsc(revstoch,hi,lo,cls,2,10,nb);       // reverse Slow %K

// prepare a fact set for training a neural network
if(mode == 1) {              // fact preparation mode (p6=1)

  // open output file and write N-TRAIN fact file
  // header before processing the first market
  if(strcmp(ts.symbol(), "SP") == 0) {
     fil = fopen("y15fac01.dat", "wt");
     fprintf(fil, "%d\n%d\n", (int)18, (int)1);
     factcount = 0;
  }

  // write actual in-sample facts to the fact file
  // this is done for every market in the portfolio
  for(cb = 1; cb <= nb; cb++) {
     if(dt[cb] < IS_DATE) continue;     // lookback
     if(dt[cb+10] > OOS_DATE) break;    // ignore OOS data
     fprintf(fil, "%6d", ++factcount);  // fact num
     PrepareNeuralInputs(var, cls, cb);
     for(k = 1; k <= 18; k++)
         fprintf(fil, "%7.3f", var[k]);        // inputs
     fprintf(fil,"%7.3f\n",revstoch[cb]);      // target
     if((cb % 1000) == 1)
         printf("CB = %d\n", cb);              // progress info
  }

  // close output file and quit after processing the last market
  if(strcmp(ts.symbol(), "LB") == 0) {
```

```
        fclose(fil);
        exit(0);
    }
}


// simulate trading with a trained neural network
if(mode == 2) {   // trading simulation mode (p6=2)

    // load the trained net before processing the first market
    if(strcmp(ts.symbol(), "SP") == 0) {
        sprintf(netname, "/nets/nn%d.net", netnum);
        nnet = nt1load(netname);
        if(nnet == NULL) nrerror(nt1errm(nt1errc()));
    }

    // step through bars (days) to simulate actual trading
    for(cb = 1; cb <= nb; cb++) {

     // take no trades before the in-sample period
     // ... same as TradeStation's MaxBarsBack setting
     if(dt[cb] < IS_DATE) { eqcls[cb] = 0.0; continue; }

     // execute any pending orders and store closing equity
     rc = ts.update(opn[cb], hi[cb], lo[cb], cls[cb], cb);
     if(rc != 0) nrerror("Trade buffer overflow");
     eqcls[cb] = ts.currentequity(EQ_CLOSETOTAL);

     // calculate number of contracts to trade
     // ... we want to trade the dollar volatility equivalent
     // ... of 2 new S&P-500 contracts as of 12/31/98
     ncontracts = RoundToInteger(5673.0 / dlrv[cb]);
     if(ncontracts < 1) ncontracts = 1;

     // avoid placing orders on possibly limit-locked days
     if(hi[cb+1] == lo[cb+1]) continue;

     // generate entry signals, stop prices and limit prices
     // using the trained neural network
     signal=0;
     PrepareNeuralInputs(var, cls, cb);
     nt1set_inputv(nnet, &var[1]);       // feed net the inputs
     nt1fire (nnet);                      // run the net
     netout = nt1get_output(nnet, 0);    // get the output
     if(netout > thresh) signal = -1;    // sell signal
     if(netout < (100 - thresh))
         signal = 1; // buy signal
```

```
            limprice = 0.5 * (hi[cb] + lo[cb]);
            stpprice = cls[cb] + 0.5 * signal * exitatr[cb];

            // enter trades using specified order type
            if(ts.position() <= 0 && signal == 1) {
              switch(ordertype) { // select desired order type
                case 1: ts.buyopen('1', ncontracts); break;
                case 2: ts.buylimit('2', limprice, ncontracts); break;
                case 3: ts.buystop('3', stpprice, ncontracts); break;
                default: nrerror("Invalid buy order selected");
              }
            }
            else if(ts.position() >= 0 && signal == -1) {
              switch(ordertype) { // select desired order type
                case 1: ts.sellopen('4', ncontracts); break;
                case 2: ts.selllimit('5', limprice, ncontracts); break;
                case 3: ts.sellstop('6', stpprice, ncontracts); break;
                default: nrerror("Invalid sell order selected");
              }
            }

            // instruct simulator to employ standard exit strategy
            tmp = exitatr[cb];
            ts.stdexitcls(`X', ptlim*tmp, mmstp*tmp, maxhold);

        } // process next bar

        // unload the trained net after processing last market
        if(strcmp(ts.symbol(), "LB") == 0) nt1disp(nnet);
      }
    }
```

The code is comprised of two functions: the usual function that implements the trading model (*Model*), and a procedure to prepare the neural network inputs (*PrepareNeuralInputs*). The procedure that prepares the inputs requires the index of the current bar (*cb*) and a series of closing prices (*cls*) on which to operate.

The *PrepareNeuralInputs* function, given the index to the current bar and a series of closing prices, calculates all inputs for a given fact that are required for the neural network. In the list, *pbars*, the numbers after the first zero (which is ignored), are the lookbacks, relative to the current bar, which are used to calculate the price differences discussed earlier. The first block of code, after the declarations, initializes a price adjustment factor table. The table is initialized on the first pass through the function and contains the square-roots of the number of bars between each pair of prices from which a difference is computed. The next block of code calculates the adjusted price differences, as well as the sum of the squares of these differences, i.e., the squared amplitude or length of the resultant vector. The final block of code in this function normalizes the vector of price differences to unit length.

The general code that implements the model follows our standard practice. After a block of declarations, a number of parameters are copied to local variables for convenient reference. The 50-bar average true range, which is used for the standard exit, and the time-reversed 10-bar Slow %K, used as a target, are then computed.

One of the parameters (*mode*) sets the mode in which the code will run. A *mode* of 1 runs the code to prepare a fact file: The file is opened, the header (consisting of the number of inputs, 18, and the number of targets, 1) is written, and the fact count is initialized to zero. This process only occurs for the first market in the portfolio. The file remains open during all further processing until it is closed after the last tradable in the portfolio has been processed. After the header, facts are written to the file. All data before the in-sample date and after the out-of-sample date are ignored. Only the in-sample data are used. Each fact written to the file consists of a fact number, the 18 input variables (obtained using *PrepareNeuralInputs*), and the target (which is the time-reversed Slow %K). Progress information is displayed for the user as the fact file is prepared.

If *mode* is set to 2, a neural network that has been trained using the fact file discussed above is used to generate entries into trades. The first block of code opens and loads the desired neural network before beginning to process the first commodity. Then the standard loop begins. It steps through bars to simulate actual trading. After executing the usual code to update the simulator, calculate the number of contracts to trade, avoid limit-locked days, etc., the block of code is reached that generates the entry signals, stop prices, and limit prices. The *PrepareNeuralInputs* function is called to generate the inputs corresponding to the current bar, these inputs are fed to the net, the network is told to run itself, the output from the net is retrieved, and the entry signal is generated.

The rules used to generate the entry signal are as follows. If the output from the network is greater than a threshold (*thresh*), a sell signal is issued; the net is predicting a high value for the time-reversed Slow %K, meaning that the current closing price might be near the high of its near-future range. If the output from the network (the prediction of the time-reversed Slow %K) is below 100 minus *thresh*, a buy signal is issued. As an example, if *thresh* were set to 80, any predicted time-reversed Slow %K greater than 80 would result in the posting of a sell signal, and any predicted time-reversed Slow %K less than 20 would result in the issuing of a buy signal.

Finally, there are the two blocks of code used to issue the actual entry orders and to implement the standardized exits. These blocks of code are identical to those that have appeared and been discussed in previous chapters.

Test Methodology for the Reverse Slow %K Model

The model is executed with the *mode* parameter set to 1 to generate a fact set. The fact set is loaded into N-TRAIN, a neural network development kit (Scientific

Consultant Services, 516-696-3333), appropriately scaled for neural processing, and shuffled, as required when developing a neural network. A series of networks are then trained, beginning with a small network and working up to a fairly large network. Most of the networks are simple, 3-layer nets. Two 4-layer networks are also trained. All nets are trained to maximum convergence and then "polished" to remove any small biases or offsets. The process of polishing is achieved by reducing the learning rate to a very small number and then continuing to train the net for about 50 runs.

Table 11-1 contains information regarding all networks that were trained for this model, along with the associated correlations and other statistics. In the table, *Net Name* = the file name to which the net was saved; *Net Size* = the number of layers and the number of neurons in each layer; *Connections* = the number of connections in the net optimized by the training process (similar to the number of regression coefficients in a multiple regression in terms of their impact on curve-fitting and shrinkage); and *Correlation* = the multiple correlation of the network output with the target (this is not a squared multiple correlation but an actual correlation). Corrected for Shrinkage covers two columns: The left one represents the correlation corrected for shrinkage under the assumption of an effective sample size of 40,000 data points or facts in the training set. The right column represents the correlation corrected for shrinkage under the assumption of 13,000 data points or facts in the training set. The last line of the table contains the number of facts or data points (*Actual N*) and the number of data points assumed for each of the shrinkage corrections (*Assumed*).

The number of data points specified to the shrinkage adjustment equation is smaller than the actual number of facts or data points in the training set. The reason

TABLE 11-1

Training Statistics for Neural Nets to Predict Time-Reversed Slow %K

Net Name	Net Size	Connections	Correlation	Corrected for Shrinkage	
NN1.NET	18-4-1	76	0.093	0.082	0.054
NN2.NET	18-6-1	114	0.118	0.105	0.072
NN3.NET	18-8-1	152	0.122	0.106	0.058
NN4.NET	18-10-1	190	0.124	0.104	0.029
NN5.NET	18-12-1	228	0.144	0.123	0.058
NN6.NET	18-16-1	304	0.156	0.130	0.031
NN7.NET	18-20-1	380	0.172	0.143	0.022
NN8.NET	18-14-4-1	312	0.169	0.145	0.070
NN9.NET	18-20-6-1	486	0.201	0.169	0.055
Actual N	88092		Assumed	40000	13000

is the presence of redundancy between facts. Specifically, a fact derived from one bar is likely to be fairly similar to a fact derived from an immediately adjacent bar. Because of the similarity, the "effective" number of data points, in terms of contributing statistically independent information, will be smaller than the actual number of data points. The two corrected correlation columns represent adjustments assuming two differently reduced numbers of facts. The process of correcting correlations is analogous to that of correcting probabilities for multiple tests in optimization: As a parameter is stepped through a number of values, results are likely to be similar for nearby parameter values, meaning the effective number of tests is somewhat less than the actual number of tests.

Training Results for Time-Reversed Slow %K Model

As evident from Table 11-1, the raw correlations rose monotonically with the size of the network in terms of numbers of connections. When adjusted for shrinkage, by assuming an effective sample size of 13,000, the picture changed dramatically: The nets that stood out were the small 3-layer net with 6 middle layer neurons, and the smaller of the two 4-layer networks. With the more moderate shrinkage correction, the two large 4-layer networks had the highest estimated predictive ability, as indicated by the multiple correlation of their outputs with the target.

On the basis of the more conservative statistics (those assuming a smaller effective sample size and, hence, more shrinkage due to curve-fitting) in Table 11-1, two neural nets were selected for use in the entry model: the 18-6-1 network (*nn2.net*) and the 18-14-4-1 network (*nn8.net*). These were considered the best bets for nets that might hold up out-of-sample. For the test of the entry model using these nets, the model implementation was run with *mode* set to 2. As usual, all order types (at open, on limit, on stop) were tested.

TURNING-POINT MODELS

For these models, two additional fact sets are needed. Except for their targets, these fact sets are identical to the one constructed for the time-reversed Slow %K. The target for the first fact set is a 1, indicating a bottom turning point, if tomorrow's open is lower than the 3 preceding bars and 10 succeeding bars. If not, this target is set to 0. The target for the second fact set is a 1, indicating a top, if tomorrow's open has a price higher than the preceding 3 and succeeding 10 opens. Otherwise this target is set to 0. Assuming there are consistent patterns in the market, the networks should be able to learn them and, therefore, predict whether tomorrow's open is going to be a top, a bottom, or neither.

Unlike the fact set for the time-reversed Slow %K model, the facts in the sets for these models are generated only if tomorrow's open could possibly be a turning point. If, for example, tomorrow's open is higher than today's open, then tomorrow's open cannot be considered a turning point, as defined earlier, no matter what happens thereafter. Why ask the network to make a prediction when there is no uncertainty or need? Only in cases where there is an uncertainty about whether tomorrow's open is going to be a turning point is it worth asking the network to make a forecast. Therefore, facts are only generated for such cases.

The processing of the inputs, the use of statistics, and all other aspects of the test methodology for the turning-point models are identical to that for the time-reversed Slow %K model. Essentially, both models are identical, and so is the methodology; only the subjects of the predictions, and, consequently, the targets on which the nets are trained, differ. Lastly, since the predictions are different, the rules for generating entries based on the predictions are different between models.

The outputs of the trained networks represent the probabilities, ranging from 0 to 1, of whether a bottom, a top, or neither is present. The two sets of rules for the two models for generating entries are as follows: For the first model, if the bottom predictor output is greater than a threshold, buy. For the second model, if the top predictor output is greater than a threshold, sell. For both models, the threshold represents a level of confidence that the nets must have that there will be a bottom or a top before an entry order is placed.

```
// write actual in-sample facts to the fact file
for(cb = 1; cb <= nb; cb++) {
    if(dt[cb] < IS_DATE) continue;          // lookback
    if(dt[cb+10] > OOS_DATE) break;          // ignore OOS data
    if(opn[cb+1] >= Lowest(opn, 3, cb))
        continue;                            // skip these facts
    fprintf(fil, "%6d", ++factcount);        // fact number
    PrepareNeuralInputs(var, cls, cb);
    for(k = 1; k <= 18; k++)
        fprintf(fil, "%7.3f", var[k]);        // standard inputs
    if(opn[cb+1] < Lowest(opn, 9, cb+10))
        netout = 1.0; else netout = 0.0; // calculate target
    fprintf(fil, "%6.1f\n", netout); // target
    if((cb % 500) == 1)
        printf("CB = %d\n", cb);        // progress info
}


// generate entry signals, stop prices and limit prices
signal=0;
if(opn[cb+1] < Lowest(opn, 3, cb)) { // run only these
    PrepareNeuralInputs(var, cls, cb);   // preprocess data
    nt1set_inputv(nnet, &var[1]);        // feed net inputs
    nt1fire(nnet);                       // run the net
    netout = nt1get_output(nnet, 0);     // get output
    netout *= 100.0;                     // scale to percent
```

```
        if(netout > thresh) signal = 1;        // issue buy signal
    }
    limprice = 0.5 * (hi[cb] + lo[cb]);
    stpprice = cls[cb] + 0.5 * signal * exitatr[cb];
```

Since the code for the bottom predictor model is almost identical to that of the time-reversed Slow %K model, only the two blocks that contain changed code are presented above. In the first block of code, the time-reversed Slow %K is not used. Instead, a series of ones or zeros is calculated that indicates the presence (1) or absence (0) of bottoms (bottom target). When writing the facts, instead of writing the time-reversed Slow %K, the bottom target is written. In the second block of code, the rules for comparing the neural output with an appropriate threshold, and generating the actual entry buy signals, are implemented. In both blocks, code is included to prevent the writing of facts, or use of predictions, when tomorrow's open could not possibly be a bottom. Similar code fragments for the top predictor model appear below.

```
// write actual in-sample facts to the fact file
for(cb = 1; cb <= nb; cb++) {
    if(dt[cb] < IS_DATE) continue;            // lookback
    if(dt[cb+10] > OOS_DATE) break;           // ignore OOS data
    if(opn[cb+1] <= Highest(opn, 3, cb))
        continue;                             // skip these facts
    fprintf(fil, "%6d", ++factcount);         // fact number
    PrepareNeuralInputs(var, cls, cb);
    for(k = 1; k <= 18; k++)
        fprintf(fil, "%7.3f", var[k]);        // inputs
    if(opn[cb+1] > Highest(opn, 9, cb+10))
        netout = 1.0; else netout = 0.0;      // calculate target
    fprintf(fil, "%6.1f\n", netout);          // write target
    if((cb % 500) == 1)
        printf("CB = %d\n", cb);              // progress info
}


// generate entry signals, stop prices and limit prices
signal=0;
if(opn[cb+1] > Highest(opn, 3, cb)) {         // run only these
    PrepareNeuralInputs(var, cls, cb);        // preprocess data
    nt1set_inputv(nnet, &var[1]);             // feed net inputs
    nt1fire(nnet);                            // run the net
    netout = nt1get_output(nnet, 0);          // get output
    netout *= 100.0;                          // scale to percent
    if(netout > thresh) signal = -1;          // sell signal
}
limprice = 0.5 * (hi[cb] + lo[cb]);
stpprice = cls[cb] + 0.5 * signal * exitatr[cb];
```

Test Methodology for the Turning-Point Model

The test methodology for this model is identical to that used for the time-reversed Slow %K model. The fact set is generated, loaded into N-TRAIN, scaled, and shuffled. A series of nets (from 3- to 4-layer ones) are trained to maximum convergence and then polished. Statistics such as shrinkage-corrected correlations are calculated.

Training Results for the Turning-Point Model

Bottom Forecaster.   The structure of Table 11-2 is identical to that of Table 11-1. As with the net trained to predict the time-reversed Slow %K, there was a monotonic relationship between the number of connections in the network and the multiple correlation of the network's output with the target; i.e., larger nets evinced higher correlations. The net was trained on a total of 23,900 facts, which is a smaller fact set than that for the time-reversed Slow %K. The difference in number of facts resulted because the only facts used were those that contained some uncertainty about whether tomorrow's open could be a turning point. Since the facts for the bottom forecaster came from more widely spaced points in the time series, it was assumed that there would be less redundancy among them. When corrected for shrinkage, effective sample sizes of 23,919 (equal to the actual number of facts) and 8,000 (a reduced effective fact count) were assumed. In terms of the more severely adjusted correlations, the best net in this model appeared to be the largest 4-layer network; the smaller 4-layer network was also very good. Other than these two nets, only the 3-layer network with 10 middle-layer neurons was a possible choice. For tests of trading performance, the large 4-layer network (*nn9.net*) and the much smaller 3-layer network (*nn4.net*) were selected.

TABLE 11-2

Training Statistics for Neural Nets to Predict Bottom Turning Points

Net Name	Net Size	Connections	Correlation	Corrected for Shrinkage	
NN1.NET	18-4-1	76	0.109	0.094	0.050
NN2.NET	18-6-1	114	0.121	0.100	0.025
NN3.NET	18-8-1	152	0.146	0.122	0.049
NN4.NET	18-10-1	190	0.166	0.141	0.064
NN5.NET	18-12-1	228	0.167	0.137	-0.019
NN6.NET	18-16-1	304	0.185	0.148	-0.060
NN7.NET	18-20-1	380	0.225	0.188	0.057
NN8.NET	18-14-4-1	312	0.219	0.188	0.096
NN9.NET	18-20-6-1	486	0.294	0.260	0.166
Actual N	23900		Assumed	23900	8000

TABLE 11-3

Training Statistics for Neural Nets to Predict Top Turning Points

Net Name	Net Size	Connections	Correlation	Corrected for	Shrinkage
NN1.NET	18-4-1	76	0.103	0.088	0.035
NN2.NET	18-6-1	114	0.117	0.097	-0.022
NN3.NET	18-8-1	152	0.138	0.116	0.017
NN4.NET	18-10-1	190	0.158	0.133	0.037
NN5.NET	18-12-1	228	0.166	0.138	-0.029
NN6.NET	18-16-1	304	0.197	0.166	0.033
NN7.NET	18-20-1	380	0.218	0.183	0.015
NN8.NET	18-14-4-1	312	0.229	0.202	0.119
NN9.NET	18-20-6-1	486	0.274	0.240	0.124
Actual N	25919		Assumed	25919	8000

Top Forecaster.   Table 11-3 contains the statistics for the nets in this model; they were trained on 25,919 facts. Again, the correlations were directly related in size to the number of connections in the net, with a larger number of connections leading to a better model fit. When mildly corrected for shrinkage, only the smaller 4-layer network deviated from this relationship by having a higher correlation than would be expected. When adjusted under the assumption of large amounts of curve-fitting and shrinkage, only the two 4-layer networks stood out, with the largest one (*nn9.net*) performing best. The only other high correlation obtained was for the 18-10-1 net (*nn4.net*). To maximize the difference between the nets used in the trading tests, the largest 4-layer net, which was the best shrinkage-corrected performer, and the fairly small (18-10-1) net were chosen.

TRADING RESULTS FOR ALL MODELS

Table 11-4 provides data regarding whole portfolio performance with the best in-sample parameters for each test in the optimization and verification samples. The information is presented for each combination of order type, network, and model. In the table, *SAMP* = whether the test was on the training or verification sample (*IN* or *OUT*); *ROA%* = the annualized return-on-account; *ARRR* = the annualized risk-to-reward ratio; *PROB* = the associated probability or statistical significance; *TRDS* = the number of trades taken across all commodities in the portfolio; *WIN%* = the percentage of winning trades; $*TRD* = the average profit/loss per trade; *BARS* = the average number of days a trade was held; *NETL* = the total net profit on long trades, in thousands of dollars; *NETS* = the total net profit on short trades, in thousands of dollars. Columns *P1*, *P2*, and *P3* represent parameter val-

TABLE 11-4

Portfolio Performance with Best In-Sample Parameters for Each Test in the Optimization and Verification Samples

SAMP	P1	P2	P3	ROA%	ARRR	PROB	TRDS	WIN%	$TRD	BARS	NETL	NETS
Test 01 Reverse Slow %K, 18-6-1 net, entry at open												
IN	60	2	0	192.9	1.90	0.000	653	52	6917	7	3204	1312
OUT	60	2	0	-2.9	-0.09	0.576	279	38	-233	7	477	-542
Test 02 Reverse Slow %K, 18-6-1 net, entry on limit												
IN	60	2	0	181.9	2.06	0.000	577	53	7879	7	3337	1209
OUT	60	2	0	-2.9	-0.13	0.604	259	38	-331	7	285	-371
Test 03 Reverse Slow %K, 18-6-1 net, entry on stop												
IN	60	2	0	134.6	1.57	0.000	379	52	8496	7	2249	970
OUT	59	2	0	2.7	0.05	0.458	182	39	362	7	364	-298
Test 04 Reverse Slow %K, 18-14-4-1 net, entry at open												
IN	60	8	0	534.7	3.78	0.000	2200	56	7080	7	10662	4914
OUT	60	8	0	-17.7	-0.69	0.922	984	40	-1214	7	-404	-790
Test 05 Reverse Slow %K, 18-14-4-1 net, entry on limit												
IN	60	8	0	547.4	4.01	0.000	1909	59	8203	8	10408	5251
OUT	60	8	0	-17.4	-0.50	0.848	860	40	-961	7	-216	-610
Test 06 Reverse Slow %K, 18-14-4-1 net, entry on stop												
IN	59	8	0	328.9	2.78	0.000	1548	53	6304	8	6067	3690
OUT	59	8	0	-16.2	-0.50	0.848	621	41	-1154	7	-587	-128
Test 07 Long Turning Point, 18-10-1 net, entry at open												
IN	32	4	0	311.1	2.80	0.000	718	61	9316	8	6689	0
OUT	32	4	0	-16.8	-0.83	0.955	307	35	-2327	7	-714	0
Test 08 Long Turning Point, 18-10-1 net, entry on limit												
IN	32	4	0	308.4	2.79	0.000	698	61	9373	8	6542	0
OUT	32	4	0	-16.1	-0.77	0.943	300	36	-2197	7	-659	0
Test 09 Long Turning Point, 18-10-1 net, entry on stop												
IN	32	4	0	236.8	2.09	0.000	294	68	10630	9	3125	0
OUT	32	4	0	-11.1	-0.56	0.876	91	32	-2868	7	-261	0
Test 10 Long Turning Point, 18-20-6-1 net, entry at open												
IN	54	9	0	768.0	4.80	0.000	699	83	18588	9	12993	0
OUT	54	9	0	-13.4	-0.64	0.906	291	38	-2001	7	-582	0
Test 11 Long Turning Point, 18-20-6-1 net, entry on limit												
IN	54	9	0	742.0	4.70	0.000	676	83	18569	9	12552	0
OUT	54	9	0	-12.7	-0.60	0.889	284	38	-1886	7	-535	0
Test 12 Long Turning Point, 18-20-6-1 net, entry on stop												
IN	50	9	0	468.8	2.94	0.000	339	77	15392	9	5217	0

TABLE 11-4

Portfolio Performance with Best In-Sample Parameters for Each Test in the Optimization and Verification Samples (Continued)

OUT	50	9	0	-1.8	-0.09	0.577	93	39	-518	7	-48	0
Test 13 Short Turning Point, 18-10-1 net, entry at open												
IN	34	4	0	206.8	1.86	0.000	377	62	8448	8	0	3185
OUT	34	4	0	12.1	0.17	0.361	152	49	580	7	0	88
Test 14 Short Turning Point, 18-10-1 net, entry on limit												
IN	34	4	0	209.0	1.90	0.000	370	62	8701	8	0	3219
OUT	34	4	0	8.0	0.13	0.399	147	48	405	7	0	59
Test 15 Short Turning Point, 18-10-1 net, entry on stop												
IN	36	4	0	175.4	1.44	0.000	125	68	12553	8	0	1569
OUT	36	4	0	-6.2	-0.19	0.654	50	48	-1138	7	0	-56
Test 16 Short Turning Point, 18-20-6-1 net, entry at open												
IN	48	9	0	601.9	2.81	0.000	256	78	18550	8	0	4748
OUT	48	9	0	-19.4	-1.08	0.987	91	27	-5314	7	0	-483
Test 17 Short Turning Point, 18-20-6-1 net, entry on limit												
IN	48	9	0	603.8	2.83	0.000	252	78	18905	8	0	4764
OUT	48	9	0	-19.7	-1.05	0.984	90	27	-5163	7	0	-464
Test 18 Short Turning Point, 18-20-6-1 net, entry on stop												
IN	30	9	0	387.3	2.48	0.000	1268	55	6320	8	0	8014
OUT	30	9	0	-22.5	-0.98	0.977	541	39	-2076	7	0	-1123

ues: $P1$ = the threshold, $P2$ = the number of the neural network within the group of networks trained for the model (these numbers correspond to the numbers used in the file names for the networks shown in Tables 11-1 through 11-3), $P3$ = not used. In all cases, the threshold parameters (column $P1$) shown are those that resulted in the best in-sample performance. Identical parameters are used for verification on the out-of-sample data.

The threshold for the time-reversed Slow %K model was optimized for each order type by stepping it from 50 to 90 in increments of 1. For the top and bottom predictor models, the thresholds were stepped from 20 to 80 in increments of 2. In each case, optimization was carried out only using the in-sample data. The best parameters were then used to test the model on both the in-sample and out-of-sample data sets. This follows the usual practice established in this book.

Trading Results for the Reverse Slow %K Model

The two networks that were selected as most likely to hold up out-of-sample, based on their shrinkage-adjusted multiple correlations with the target, were analyzed for trading performance. The first network was the smaller of the two, having 3 layers (18-6-1 network). The second network had 4 layers (18-14-4-1 network).

Results Using the 18-6-1 Network.   In-sample, as expected, the trading results were superb. The average trade yielded a profit of greater than $6,000 across all order types, and the system provided an exceptional annual return, ranging from 192.9% (entry at open, Test 1) to 134.6% (entry on stop, Test 3). Results this good were obtained because a complex model containing 114 free parameters was fitted to the data. Is there anything here beyond curve-fitting? Indeed there is. With the stop order, out-of-sample performance was actually slightly profitable—nothing very tradable, but at least not in negative territory: The average trade pulled $362 from the market. Even though losses resulted out-of-sample for the other two order types, the losses were rather small when compared with those obtained from many of the tests in other chapters: With entry at open, the system lost only $233 per trade. With entry on limit (Test 2), it lost $331. Again, as has sometimes happened in other tests of countertrend models, a stop order, rather than a limit order, performed best. The system was profitable out-of-sample across all orders when only the long trades were considered. It lost across all orders on the short side.

In-sample performance was fabulous in almost every market in the portfolio, with few exceptions. This was true across all order types. The weakest performance was observed for Eurodollars, probably a result of the large number of contracts (hence high transaction costs) that must be traded in this market. Weak performance was also noted for Silver, Soybean Oil, T-Bonds, T-Bills, Canadian Dollar, British Pound, Gold, and Cocoa. There must be something about these markets that makes them difficult to trade, because, in-sample, most markets perform well. Many of these markets also performed poorly with other models.

Out-of-sample, good trading was obtained across all three orders for the T-Bonds (which did not trade well in-sample), the Deutschemark, the Swiss Franc, the Japanese Yen, Unleaded Gasoline, Gold (another market that did not trade well in-sample), Palladium, and Coffee. Many other markets were profitable for two of the three order types. The number of markets that could be traded profitably out-of-sample using neural networks is a bit surprising. When the stop order (overall, the best-performing order) was considered, even the S&P 500 and NYFE yielded substantial profits, as did Feeder Cattle, Live Cattle, Soybeans, Soybean Meal, and Oats.

Figure 11-1 illustrates the equity growth for the time-reversed Slow %K predictor model with entry on a stop. The equity curve was steadily up in-sample, and continued its upward movement throughout about half of the out-of-sample period, after which there was a mild decline.

Results of the 18-14-4-1 Network.   This network provided trading performance that showed more improvement in-sample than out-of-sample. In-sample, returns

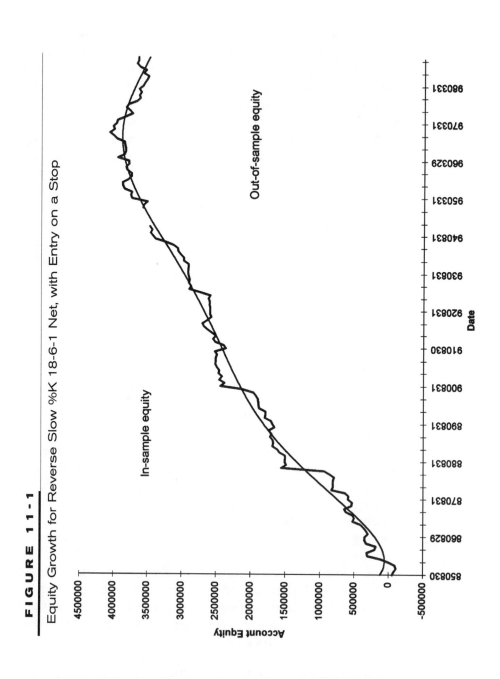

FIGURE 11-1

Equity Growth for Reverse Slow %K 18-6-1 Net, with Entry on a Stop

ranged from a low of 328.9% annualized (stop order, Test 6) to 534.7% (entry at open, Test 4). In all cases, there was greater than $6,000 profit per trade. As usual, the longs were more profitable than the shorts. Out-of-sample, every order type produced losses. However, as noted in the previous set of tests, the losses were smaller than typical of losing systems observed in many of the other chapters; i.e., the losses were about $1,000 per trade, rather than $2,000. This network also took many more trades than the previous one. The limit order performed best (Test 5). The long side evidenced smaller losses than the short side, except in the case of the stop order, where the short side had relatively small losses. The better in-sample performance and worsened out-of-sample performance are clear evidence of curve-fitting. The larger network, with its 320 parameters, was able to capitalize on the idiosyncrasies of the training data, thereby increasing its performance in-sample and decreasing it out-of-sample.

In-sample, virtually every market was profitable across every order. There were only three exceptions: Silver, the Canadian Dollar, and Cocoa. These markets seem hard to trade using any system. Out-of-sample, several markets were profitable across all three order types: the Deutschemark, the Canadian Dollar, Light Crude, Heating Oil, Palladium, Feeder Cattle, Live Cattle, and Lumber. A few other markets traded well with at least one of the order types.

The equity curve showed perfectly increasing equity until the out-of-sample period, at which point it mildly declined. This is typical of a curve resulting from overoptimization. Given a sample size of 88,092 facts, this network may have been too large.

Trading Results for the Bottom Turning-Point Model

The two networks that were selected, on the basis of their corrected multiple correlations with the target, as most likely to hold up out-of-sample are analyzed for trading performance below. The first network was the smaller of the two, having 3 layers (18-10-1 network). The second network was a network with 4 layers (18-20-6-1 network).

Results of the 18-10-1 Network.   In-sample, this network performed exceptionally well—nothing unusual, given the degree of curve-fitting involved. Out-of-sample, there was a return to the scenario of a heavily losing system. For all three order types (at open, on limit, and on stop, or Tests 7, 8, and 9, respectively), the average loss per trade was in the $2,000 range, typical of many of the losing models tested in previous chapters. The heavy per-trade losses occurred although this model was only trading long positions, which have characteristically performed better than shorts.

In-sample, only four markets did not perform well: the British Pound, Silver, Live Cattle, and Corn. Silver was a market that also gave all the previously tested networks problems. Out-of-sample, the network was profitable across all three order types for the S&P 500, the Japanese Yen, Light Crude, Unleaded Gasoline, Palladium, Soybeans, and Bean Oil. A number of other markets were also profitable with one or two of the orders.

The equity curve showed strong steady gains in-sample and losses out-of-sample.

Results of the 18-20-6-1 Network.   These results were derived from Tests 10–12 (at open, on limit, and on stop, respectively). In-sample performance for this network soared to unimaginable levels. With entry at open, the return was 768% annualized, with 83% of the 699 trades taken being profitable. The average trade produced $18,588 profit. Surprisingly, despite the larger size of this network (therefore, the greater opportunity for curve-fitting), the out-of-sample performance, on a dollars-per-trade basis, was better than the smaller network, especially in the case of the stop entry, where the loss per trade was down to $518.

All markets were profitable across all orders in-sample, without exception. Out-of-sample, the S&P 500, the British Pound, Platinum, Palladium, Soybean Meal, Wheat, Kansas Wheat, Minnesota Wheat, and Lumber were profitable across all three order types.

Trading Results for the Top Turning-Point Model

The two networks that were selected as most likely to hold up out-of-sample, based on their corrected multiple correlations with the target, are analyzed for trading performance below. The first network was the smaller of the two, having 3 layers (18-10-1 network). The second network had 4 layers (18-20-6-1 network).

Results of the 18-10-1 Network.   As usual, the in-sample performance was excellent. Out-of-sample performance was profitable for two of the orders: entry at open (Test 13) and on limit (Test 14). There were moderate losses for the stop order (Test 15). This is slightly surprising, given that the short side is usually less profitable than the long side.

The market-by-market breakdown reveals that only the Canadian Dollar, Feeder Cattle, Bean Oil, Wheat, and Cocoa were not profitable across all three order types, in-sample. Out-of-sample, strong profits were observed across all three orders for the Deutschemark, the Japanese Yen, Light Crude, Heating Oil, Feeder Cattle, Live Cattle, and Corn. The Japanese Yen, Light Crude, and, to some extent, Corn shared profitability with the corresponding bottom (long) turning-point model; in other words, these markets held up out-of-sample for both the bottom network and the top (short) network.

The equity curve (Figure 11-2) for entry at open depicts rapidly rising equity until August 1993, and then more slowly rising equity throughout the remainder of the in-sample period and through about two-thirds of the out-of-sample period. Equity then declined slightly.

FIGURE 11-2

Equity Growth for Short Turning Points, 18-10-1 Net, with Entry at Open

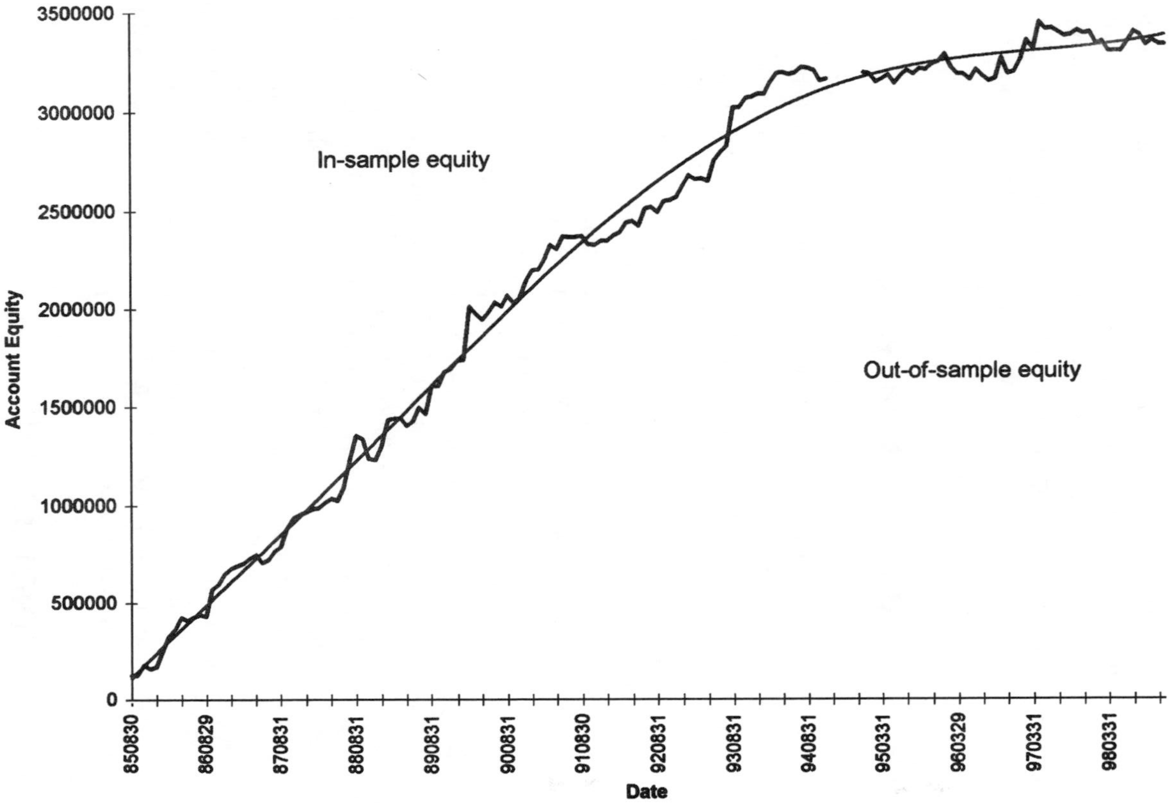

Results of the 18-20-6-1 Network.   As expected, this network, the larger of the two, produced greater and more consistent in-sample profits due to a higher amount of curve-fitting. Out-of-sample, this network performed terribly across all order types (at open, on limit, and on stop, or Tests 16, 17, and 18, respectively). The least bad results were obtained with the stop order.

In-sample, only Silver, Wheat, Sugar, and Orange Juice did not trade profitably across all orders. Out-of-sample, only Cocoa showed profitability for all three orders. Surprisingly, all the metals showed strong out-of-sample profitability for the entry at open and on limit, as did Feeder Cattle, Cocoa, and Cotton.

Portfolio equity showed incredibly smooth and steep gains in-sample, with losses out-of-sample for all order types.

SUMMARY ANALYSES

Table 11-5 provides in-sample and Table 11-6 contains out-of-sample performance statistics for all of the neural network models broken down by test and market. The *SYM* column represents the market being studied. The rightmost column (*COUNT*) contains the number of profitable tests for a given market. The numbers in the first row represent test identifiers. The last row (*COUNT*) contains the number of markets on which a given model was profitable. The data in this table provides relatively detailed information about which markets are and are not profitable when traded by each of the models: One dash (-) indicates a moderate loss per trade, i.e., $2,000 to $4,000; two dashes (--) represent a large loss per trade, i.e., $4,000 or more; one plus sign (+) means a moderate profit per trade, i.e., $1,000 to $2,000; two pluses (++) indicate a large gain per trade, i.e., $2,000 or more; and a blank cell means that the loss was between $0 and $1,999 or the profit was between $0 and $1,000 per trade. (For information about the various markets and their symbols, see Table II-1 in the "Introduction" to Part II.)

In-sample, every order and every model yielded exceptionally strong positive returns (see Table 11-7). When averaged over all models, the entry at open and on limit performed best, while the entry on stop was the worst; however, the differences are all very small. In-sample, the best dollars-per-trade performance was observed with the large turning-point networks for the long (bottom) and short (top) sides. Out-of-sample, the stop order provided the best overall results. The time-reversed Slow %K and the short (top) turning-point models performed best when averaged across all order types.

CONCLUSION

When a neural newbie model was tested on an individual market (Katz and McCormick, November 1996), the conclusion was that such an approach does not work at all. The out-of-sample behavior in some of the current tests was much bet-

TABLE 11-5

In-Sample Results Broken Down by Test and Market

SYM	01	02	03	04	05	06	07	08	09	10	11	12	13	14	15	16	17	18	Count
SP	++	++	++	++	++	++	++	++	++	++	++	++	++	++	++	++	++	++	18
YX	++	++	++	++	++	++	++	++	++	++	++	++	++	++	++	++	++	++	18
US			+	++	++	+	++	++	++	++	++	++	+	+	++	++	++	++	16
TB		+	-	+	++	+	++	++	++	++	++	++	++	++	++	++	++	-	15
TY	++	++	++	++	++	++	++	++	++	++	++	++	++	++	++	++	++	++	18
BP		+	++	++	++	-	-	--		++	++	++	++	++	++	++	++	++	13
DM	++	++	++	++	++	++	++	++	++	++	++	++	++	++	++	++	++	++	18
SF	++	++	++	++	++	++	++	++	++	++	++	++	++	++	++	++	++	++	18
JY	++	++	++	++	++	++	++	++	--	++	++	++	++	++	++	++	++	+	17
CD		+		+	++		++	++	+	++	++	++	--	--	++	++	++	++	13
ED	--		--	++	++	++	++	++	++	++	++	++	+	+	++	++	++	++	15
CL	++	++	++	++	++	++	++	++	++	++	++	++	++	++	++	++	++	++	18
HO	++	++	++	++	++	++	++	++	++	++	++	++	++	++	++	++	++	++	18
HU	++	++	++	++	++	++	++	++	++	++	++	++	++	++	++	++	++	++	18
GC	-	+		++	++	++	++	++	++	++	++	++	++	++	++	++	++	++	16
SI	--		--				-	-	--	++	++	++	++	++	++			++	7
PL	+	++	--	++	++	++	++	++	++	++	++	++	++	++	++	++	++	+	17
PA	++	++	++	++	++	+	++	++	++	++	++	++	++	++	++	++	++	++	18
FC	++	++	++	++	++	++	++	++	++	++	++	++			++	++	++	++	16
LC	+	++	+	++	++	++			++	++	++	++	++	++	++	++	++	++	16
LH	++	++	++	++	++	+	++	++	++	++	++	++	++	++	--	++	++	++	17
PB	++	++	++	++	++	++	++	++	++	++	++	++	++	++	++	++	++	++	18
S	++	++	++	++	++	++	++	++	++	++	++	++	++	++	+	++	++	+	18
SM	++	++	++	++	++	++	++	++	++	++	++	++	++	++	++	++	++	++	18
BO			--	++	++	++	+		++	++	++	++	++	++	-	++	++	++	13
C	+	++	++	++	++	++			++	++	++	++	++	++	++	++	++	++	16
O	++	++	++	+	+	++	+	+	++	++	++	++	++	++	++	++	++	++	18
W	-	++	+	++	++	++	++	++	++	++	++	++			++			++	13
KW	++	++	++	++	++	++	++	++	++	++	++	++	++	++	++	++	++	++	18
MW	++	++	++	++	++	++	+	++	+	++	++	++	++	++	++	+	++	++	18
KC	++	++	++	++	++	++	++	++	++	++	++	++	++	++	++	++	++	++	18
CC			++		+		+	+	++	++	++	++	++	++	--	++	++	++	13
SB	++	+	++	++	++	++	++	++	++	++	++	++	++	++	++	--	--	-	15
JO	++	++	++	++	++	++	++	++	++	++	++	++	++	++	++	++	++		17
CT	++	++	++	++	++	++	++	++	+	++	++	++	++	++	++	++	++	++	18
LB	++	++	++	++	++	++	++	++	++	++	++	++	++	++	++	++	++	+	18
Count	26	30	29	34	35	33	32	31	33	36	36	36	33	33	33	33	33	33	

ter than expected, based on our earlier explorations of simple neural network models. In the current tests, the more encouraging results were almost certainly due to the large number of data points in the training set, which resulted from training the model across an entire portfolio, rather than on a single tradable. In general, the larger the optimization (or training) sample, the greater the likelihood of continued performance in the verification sample. Sample size could be increased by

TABLE 11-6

Out-of-Sample Results Broken Down by Test and Market

SYM	01	02	03	04	05	06	07	08	09	10	11	12	13	14	15	16	17	18	Count
SP	-	-	++	+			++	++	++	++	++	+	--	--		--	--		8
YX	--	--	++	+		+	+	+			--	-				--	--		5
US	++	++	+	--	--	--				-	-	-	--	--					3
TB	--	--	--	--	--	--	++	++		--	--	--	--	--		--	--	--	2
TY	++	++					-	-		--	--	-	--	--	--	--	--	--	2
BP	+	-		+		++	++	++		++	++	++	-	-				++	9
DM	++	++	++	++	++	++	--	--	--	--	--	--	++	++	++	--	--	--	9
SF	++	++	++		+		--	--	--	--	--	--	++	++				-	6
JY	++	+	++			++	++	++	++	-	-	--	++	++	++			++	11
CD	--	--	--	+	+	+	--	--	++	--	--	-	--	--	--				4
ED		-	+	--	--	--		-	--	--	--	--	++	++		--	--	--	3
CL		+	--	++	++	+	++	++	++	+	+		++	++	++	--	--		12
HO	-	--	--	++	++	++	--	--		--	--	-	++	++	++	--	--	+	7
HU	++	+	++		+	--	++	++	++	--	--	--	+	+	--	--	--	--	9
GC	+	+	++	-	--	++	--	--		--	--	--	++	++		++	++	--	8
SI				-	-	+	--	--	++	--	--		++	+	++	++	++	-	7
PL	++	++	--			--	--	--	--	++	++	++	--	--	++	++	++	-	8
PA	++	++	++	++	+	+	++	++	++	++	++	++	--	--	--	++	++		14
FC	-	-	++	++	++	+	-			--	--	--	++	++	++	++	++	-	10
LC	--	++	++	++	+	++	+	+	--	--	--		++	+	++	--	--	++	11
LH	-	-	--	--	--		-		++	-		-	--	--		--	--	--	1
PB	-	-	--		-	-	+	+	--	-	-	++	--		--	--	--		3
S			++			++	++	++	+	--	--		--	--	--	--	--		5
SM			++	-		--			--	++	++	++	+	+	--	--	--	--	6
BO	--	--	--	--	--	--	+	+	++	--	--	--	--	--	-		+	+	5
C	++	++				--	++	++		--	--	--	++	++	++	--	--	+	8
O	--	--	++	--	--	--	--	--	--			--	--	--	--	+	+	-	3
W	--	--	--			-	--	--		++	++	++	--	--	--	--	--	-	3
KW		--	+		--	+	--	--	++	++	++	++	--	--	--	--	--	+	7
MW	--		-	-	-	++	--	--	--	++	++	++	--	--	+	--	--	--	5
KC	++	++	+	-	-	++	-			-	-		--	--	--	--	--	+	5
CC	+	++	-			--	--	--	--	--	--	--	++	++	--	++	++	++	7
SB	--	--	--	--	--		-	-		--	--	-	++	++		--	--	--	2
JO	--	--	--	--		--	--	--	--	++	++	--			--				2
CT	-		--			--	-	-		--	--	--	--	--	--	++	++		2
LB	--	--	--	++	++	++	-	-	--	++	++	++	++	++		--	--	+	9
Count	13	14	17	11	10	17	13	13	11	11	11	11	16	16	10	08	09	10	

going back further in history, which would be relatively easy to accomplish since many commodities contracts go back well beyond the start of our in-sample period (1985). It could also be increased by enlarging the portfolio with additional markets, perhaps a better way to bolster the training sample.

A maxim of optimization is that the likelihood of performance holding up increases with reduction in the number of model parameters. Given the somewhat positive results obtained in some of the tests, it might be worthwhile to experiment

TABLE 11-7

Performance of Neural Network Models Broken Down by Model, Order, and Sample

Model		In-sample			Out-of-sample			Average In	Average Out
		Open	Limit	Stop	Open	Limit	Stop	In	Out
Reverse Slow %K	ROA%	192.9	181.9	153.9	-2.9	-2.9	2.7	176.2	-1.0
18-6-1	$TRD	6917	7879	6764	-233	-331	362	7187	-67
Reverse Slow %K	ROA%	534.7	547.4	328.9	-17.7	-17.4	-16.2	470.3	-17.1
18-14-4-1	$TRD	7080	8203	6304	-1214	-961	-1154	7196	-1110
Turning Point Long	ROA%	311.1	308.4	236.8	-16.8	-16.1	-11.1	285.4	-14.6
18-10-1	$TRD	9316	9373	10630	-2327	-2197	-2868	9773	-2464
Turning Point Long	ROA%	768.0	742.0	468.8	-13.4	-12.7	-1.8	659.6	-9.3
18-20-6-1	$TRD	18588	18569	15392	-2001	-1886	-518	17516	-1468
Turning Point Short	ROA%	206.8	209.0	175.4	12.1	8.0	-6.2	197.1	4.6
18-10-1	$TRD	8448	8701	12553	580	405	-1138	9901	-51
Turning Point Short	ROA%	601.9	603.8	387.3	-19.4	-19.7	-22.5	531.0	-20.5
18-20-6-1	$TRD	18550	18905	6320	-5314	-5163	-2076	14592	-4184
Average	ROA%	435.9	432.1	291.8	-9.7	-10.1	-9.2	386.6	-9.7
	$TRD	11483	11938	9661	-1752	-1689	-1232	11027	-1557

with more sophisticated models. Specifically, better input preprocessing, in the sense of something that could reduce the total number of inputs without much loss of essential predictive information, would probably lead to a very good trading system. With a smaller number of inputs, there would be fewer parameters (connection weights) in the network to estimate. Consequently, curve-fitting, an apparently significant issue judging by the results and shrinkage levels, would be less of a problem.

WHAT HAVE WE LEARNED?

- Under certain conditions, even neural newbie models can work. The critical issue with neural networks is the problem of achieving an adequate ratio of sample size to free parameters for the purpose of minimizing harmful (as opposed to beneficial) curve-fitting.
- Curve-fitting is a problem with neural networks. Any methods by which the total number of parameters to be estimated can be reduced, without too much loss of predictive information, are worth exploring; e.g., more sophisticated information-compressing input preprocessing would probably improve out-of-sample performance and reduce the effects of pernicious curve-fitting.

- For similar reasons, large samples are critical to the training of successful neural network trading models. This is why training on whole portfolios provides better results than training on individual tradables, despite the loss of market specificity. One suggestion is to increase the number of markets in the portfolio and, thereby, achieve a larger in-sample training set. Carrying this to an extreme, perhaps a neural network should be trained on hundreds of commodities, stocks, and various other trading instruments, in an effort to develop a "universal market forecaster." If there are any universal "technical" price patterns that exist in all markets and that have predictive validity, such an effort might actually be worthwhile.

- Some markets trade poorly, even in-sample. Other markets tend to hold up out-of-sample. This has been found with other models in earlier chapters: Some markets are more amenable to trading using certain techniques than are other markets. Selecting a subset of markets to trade, based on continued out-of-sample performance, might be an approach to take when developing and trading neural network systems.

CHAPTER TWELVE

Genetic Algorithms

Extrapolating from models of biology and economics, mathematician/psychologist, John Holland, developed a genetic optimization algorithm and introduced it to the world in his book, *Adaptation in Natural and Artificial Systems* (1975). Genetic algorithms (or GAs) only became popular in computer science about 15 years later (Yuret and de la Maza, 1994). The trading community first took notice around 1993, when a few articles (Burke, 1993; Katz and McCormick, 1994; Oliver, 1994) and software products appeared. Since then, a few vendors have added a genetic training option to their neural network development shells and a few have "industrial strength" genetic optimization toolkits.

In the trading community, GAs never really had the kind of heyday experienced by neural networks. The popularity of this technology probably never grew due to its nature. Genetic algorithms are a bit difficult for the average person to understand and more than a bit difficult to use properly. Regardless of their image, from our experience, GAs can be extremely beneficial for system developers.

As with neural networks, while a brief discussion is included to provide basic understanding, it is not within the scope of this book to present a full tutorial on genetic algorithms. Readers interested in studying this subject further should read Davis (1991), as well as our contributions to the book *Virtual Trading* (Katz and McCormick, 1995a, 1995b) and our articles (Katz and McCormick, July/August 1994, December 1996, January 1997, February 1997).

WHAT ARE GENETIC ALGORITHMS?

A genetic algorithm solves a problem using a process similar to biological evolution. It works by the recombination and mutation of gene sequences. Recombination and mutation are *genetic operators*; i.e., they manipulate genes. A *gene* is a string of codes (the genotype) that is decoded to yield a functional organism with specific characteristics (the phenotype). A *chromosome* is a string of genes. In the case of genetic optimization, as carried out on such problems as those being addressed here, the string of codes usually takes the form of a series of numbers.

During the simulated evolutionary process, a GA engages in mating and selecting the members of the population (the chromosomes). *Mating* involves crossover and mutation. In *crossover*, the elements that comprise the genes of different chromosomes (members of the population or solutions) are combined to form new chromosomes. *Mutation* involves the introduction of random alterations to these elements. This provides additional variation in the sets of chromosomes being generated. As with the process of biological *selection* (where less-fit members of the population leave fewer progenies), the less-fit solutions are weeded out so the more-fit solutions can proliferate, yielding another *generation* that may contain some better solutions than the previous one. The process of recombination, random mutation, and selection has been shown to be an extremely powerful problem-solving mechanism.

EVOLVING RULE-BASED ENTRY MODELS

What would happen if a GA were allowed to search, not merely for the best parameters (the more common way a GA is applied by traders), but also for the best rules? In this chapter, the consequences of using a GA to evolve a complete entry model, by discovering both the rules *and* the optimal parameters for those rules, will be explored. Although somewhat complex, this methodology proved to be effective in our first investigation (Katz and McCormick, February 1997).

How can a GA be used to discover great trading rules? The garden variety GA just juggles numbers. It is necessary to find a way to map sets of numbers in a one-to-one fashion to sets of rules. There are many ways this can be accomplished. A simple and effective method involves the construction of a set of rule templates. A *rule template* is a partial specification for a rule, one that contains blanks that need to be filled in. For example, if some of the rules in previous chapters were regarded as rule templates, the blanks to be filled in would be the values for the look-backs, thresholds, and other parameters. Using rule templates, as defined in this manner, a one-to-one mapping of sets of numbers to fully specified rules can easily be achieved. The first number (properly scaled) of any set is used as an index into a table of rule templates. The remaining numbers of the set are then used to fill in the blanks, with the result being a fully specified rule. The code below contains a C++ function (*Rules*) that implements this mapping strategy; it will be discussed later. Although C++ was used in the current study, this method can also be implemented in TradeStation using the TS-EVOLVE software from Scientific Consultant Services (516-696-3333).

The term *genetic search* applies to the use of a genetic algorithm to search through an incredibly large set of potential solutions to find those that are best, i.e., that have the greatest fitness. In the current application, the intention is to use the evolutionary process to discover sets of numbers (genotypes) that translate to rule-based entry models (phenotypes) with the greatest degree of *fitness* (defined in terms of desirable trading behavior). In short, we are going to attempt to engage in the selective breeding of rule-based entry methods! Instead of beginning with a particular principle on which to base a model (e.g., seasonality, breakouts, etc.), the starting point is an assortment of ideas that might contribute to the development of a profitable entry. Instead of testing these ideas one by one or in combinations to determine what works, something very unusual will be done: The genetic process of evolution will be allowed to breed the best possible entry model from the raw ideas.

The GA will search an extremely broad space of possibilities to find the best rule-based entry model that can be achieved given the constraints imposed by the rule templates, the data, and the limitation of restricting the models to a specified number of rules (to prevent curve-fitting). To accomplish this, it is necessary to find the best sets of numbers (those that map to the best sets of rule-based entry models) from an exceedingly large universe of possibilities. The kind of massive search for solutions would be almost impossible—certainly impractical, in any realistic sense—to accomplish without the use of genetic algorithms. There are alternatives to GAs, e.g., brute force searching may be used, but we do not have thousands of years to wait for the results. Another alternative might be through the process of *rule induction*, i.e., where an attempt is made to infer rules from a set of observations; however, this approach would not necessarily allow a complex function, such as that of the risk-to-reward ratio of a trading model, to be maximized. Genetic algorithms provide an efficient way to accomplish very large searches, especially when there are no simple problem-solving heuristics or techniques that may otherwise be used.

EVOLVING AN ENTRY MODEL

In this exercise, a population of three-rule entry models are evolved using OptEvolve, a C++ genetic optimizer (Scientific Consultant Services, 516-696-3333). Each gene corresponds to a block of four numbers and to a rule, via the one-to-one mapping of sets of numbers to sets of rules. Each chromosome contains three genes. A chromosome, as generated by the GA, therefore consists of 12 numbers: The first four numbers correspond to the first gene (or rule), the next four correspond to the second gene (or rule), and the last four correspond to the third gene (or rule). The GA itself has to be informed of the gene size so it does not break up intrinsic genes when performing crossover. Crossover should only occur at the *boundaries* of genes, i.e., four number blocks. In the current example, this will be achieved by setting the "chunk size," a property of the genetic optimizer component, to four.

As mentioned, each gene is composed of four numbers. The first number is nothing more than an index into a table of possible rule templates. For example, if that number is 1, a price-comparison template in which the difference between two closing prices is compared with a threshold (see code) is selected. The remaining three numbers in the gene then control the two lookback periods for the prices being compared and the threshold. If the first number of the four-number block is 2, a price-to-moving-average comparison template would be selected. In that case, two of the remaining three numbers would control the period of the moving average and the direction of the comparison (whether the price should be above or below the moving average). In general, if the first number in the block of four numbers that represents a gene is n, then the nth-rule template is used, and any required parameters are determined by reference to the remaining three numbers in the four-number block. This decoding scheme makes it easy to maintain an expandable database of rule templates. Each of the three blocks of four numbers is mapped to a corresponding rule. For any 12-number chromosome, a 3-rule entry model is produced.

The Rule Templates

The first rule template (*case 1* in function *Rules*) defines a comparison between two prices and a threshold: The rule takes on a value of *TRUE* if the closing price lb1 bars ago is greater than some threshold factor (*thr*) plus the closing price *lb2* bars ago. Otherwise, the rule takes on the value of *FALSE*. The unknowns (*lb1*, *lb2*, and *thr*) are left as the blanks to be filled in during instantiation. This template has been included because the kind of rule it represents was useful in previous investigations.

The second rule template (*case 2*) involves simple moving averages, which are often used to determine trend. Usually the market is thought to be trending up if the price is above its moving average and trending down if the price is below its moving average. There are only two unknowns in this template: The first (*per*) controls the number of bars in the moving average, and the second (*v4*) controls the direction of comparison (above or below).

The third rule template (*case 3*) is identical to the second (*case 2*), except that an exponential moving average is used rather than a simple moving average.

Much discussion has occurred regarding the importance of open interest. Larry Williams (1979) mentioned that a decline in total open interest, during a period when the market has been moving sideways, indicates potential for a strong rally. A shrinking of open interest may be interpreted as a decline in available contracts, producing a condition where demand may outweigh supply. The fourth rule template (*case 4*) simply computes the percentage decline in open interest from *lb1* bars ago to 1 bar ago (open interest is generally not available for the current bar) and compares it with a threshold (*thr*). If the percentage decline is greater than the threshold, the rule takes on the value *TRUE*. Otherwise it evaluates to *FALSE*. The threshold and the lookback (*lb1*) are the unknowns to be filled in at the time of instantiation.

The fifth rule template (*case 5*) is similar to the fourth template, but a rise, rather than fall, in total open interest is being sought. If the increase, as a percentage, is greater than a threshold, then the rule evaluates to *TRUE*. Otherwise it evaluates to *FALSE*. As previously, the lookback and the threshold are unknowns that must be supplied to instantiate the rule.

The sixth rule template (*case 6*) can be called a "new high" condition: The template asks whether an *lb1*-bar new high has occurred within the last *lb2* bars. A particular instance of the rule might read: "If a new 50-day high has occurred within the last 10 days, then *TRUE*, else *FALSE*." This rule attempts to capture a simple breakout condition, allowing for breakouts that may have occurred several bars ago (perhaps followed by a pull-back to the previous resistance-turned-support that another rule has detected as a good entry point). There are two blanks to be filled in to instantiate this template: *lb1* and *lb2*.

The seventh rule template (*case 7*) is identical to the sixth rule template, except that new lows, rather than new highs, are being detected.

The eighth rule template (*case 8*) examines the average directional movement index with respect to two thresholds (*thr1* and *thr2*). This is a measure of trendiness, as discussed in the chapter on breakouts. If the average directional movement (ADX) is above a lower threshold and below an upper threshold, the rule evaluates to *TRUE*. Otherwise, the rule evaluates to *FALSE*.

The ninth rule template (*case 9*) performs a threshold comparison on the Stochastic oscillator that is similar to that performed in Rule 8.

The tenth rule template (*case 10*) evaluates the direction of the slope of the MACD oscillator. The lengths (*lb1* and *lb2*) of the two moving averages that compose the MACD, and the direction of the slope (*v4*) required for the rule to evaluate to *TRUE*, are specified as parameters.

TEST METHODOLOGY

Below are the steps involved in evolving an entry model based on the rule templates being used in this study:

1. Retrieve a 12-element chromosome from the genetic optimizer component. This represents a potential solution, one that initially will be random and probably not very good.
2. Instantiate the rule templates to obtain three fully defined rules (one for each gene), and compute their *TRUE/FALSE* values for all bars in the data series, based upon the decoding of the genes/chromosome.

3. Proceed bar by bar through the data. If, on a given bar, all three instantiated rules evaluate to *TRUE*, and if there is no current long (or short) position, then post an order to the simulator component to buy (or sell) at tomorrow's open.

4. If a position is being held, use the standard exit strategy to handle the exit.

5. Evaluate the trading performance of the potential solution. For this exercise, the basic "goodness" of a solution is defined as the annualized risk-to-reward ratio, a figure that is actually a rescaled t-statistic.

6. Tell the genetic optimizer how fit (in the above sense) the potential solution (the chromosome it provided) was. This allows the genetic optimizer component to update the population of chromosomes it maintains.

7. If the solution meets certain criteria, generate performance summaries and other information, and save this data to a file for later perusal.

8. Repeat the above steps again and again until a sufficient number of "generations" have passed.

As the above steps are repeated, the solutions, i.e., the "guesses" (actually, "offspring"), provided by the genetic optimizer, will get better and better, on average. Because of the way the genetic process works, large numbers of distinct, yet effective, solutions will emerge during the evolutionary process. Most of the solutions will have been recorded in a file generated in the course of repeatedly performing the first seven computational steps. In the "Code" section of this chapter, a discussion can be found of some of the C++ code that actually implements the above steps, including the instantiation and computation of the rules.

Because of the nature of the rules, asymmetries are likely. Consequently, long entry models are evolved and tested separately from short entry models. Model performance is evaluated on the entire portfolio. The goal is to find a set of rules that, when applied in the same way to every tradable, produce the best overall portfolio performance. The procedure being used here differs from the one in our earlier investigation (Katz and McCormick, February 1997) where sets of rules, specific to each of several markets, were evolved, an approach that was much more subject to the effects of curve-fitting. As observed with several other models that were originally tested on individual tradables, some performance may be lost when requiring a common model across all markets without market-specific optimization or tuning. In the tests that follow, the standard C++ software platform, as well as the standard entry orders and exit strategy, are used.

```
static int EventPresent (int *es, int m, int cb) {
    // Used by the Rules function to simplify coding
    int i;
    for(i=cb-m+1; i<=cb; i++)
```

```
        if(es[i]) return TRUE;
    return FALSE;
}


static void Rules (float *opn, float *hi, float *lo, float *cls,
float *vol, float *oi, float *atr, int nb, int v1, float v2,
float v3, float v4, int *ans) {

    // Procedure implements the rule templates that are used in
    // the genetic process of evolving a rule-based entry model.
    // opn, hi, lo, cls   - standard price data series [1..nb]
    // vol, oi            - volume and open interest [1..nb]
    // nb                 - number of bars
    // v1, v2, v3, v4     - rule selector and parameters
    // ans                - output data series [1..nb]

    // local macro functions
    #define LinearScale(x,a,b)  ((x)*((b)-(a))/1000.0+(a))
    #define BiasedPosScale(x,a)  (0.000001*(x)*(x)*(a))
    #define Compare(a,b,dir)  (((dir)>=0)?((a)>(b)):((a)<(b)))

    // local variables
    static int lb1, lb2, per, cb, maxlb=100;
    static float thr, fac, thr2, thr1, tmp, tiny=1.0E-20;
    static int IsNewHigh[MAXBAR+1], IsNewLow[MAXBAR+1];
    static float Ser1[MAXBAR+1];

    // rule template implementations
    switch(v1) {                              // select rule

      case 1: // price momentum to threshold comparison
        lb1 = (int)BiasedPosScale(v2, 50.0);
        lb2 = (int)BiasedPosScale(v3, 50.0);
        fac = LinearScale(v4, -2.5, 2.5) * sqrt(abs(lb1 - lb2));
        for(cb=maxlb; cb<=nb; cb++) {
            thr = fac * atr[cb];
            ans[cb] = cls[cb-lb1] - cls[cb-lb2] > thr ;
        }
        break;

      case 2: // price to simple moving average comparison
        per = 2 + (int)BiasedPosScale(v2, 48.0);
        AverageS(Ser1, cls, per, nb);
        for(cb=maxlb; cb<=nb; cb++)
            ans[cb] = Compare(cls[cb], Ser1[cb], v4-500.0);
        break;
```

```
case 3: // price to exponential moving average comparison
 per = 2 + (int)BiasedPosScale(v2, 48.0);
 XAverageS(Ser1, cls, per, nb);
 for(cb=maxlb; cb<=nb; cb++)
      ans[cb] = Compare(cls[cb], Ser1[cb], v4-500.0);
 break;

case 4: // open interest decline threshold comparison
 lb1 = 2 + (int)BiasedPosScale(v2, 48.0);
 thr = LinearScale(v3, 0.01, 0.50);
 for(cb=maxlb; cb<=nb; cb++) {
    tmp = (oi[cb-lb1] - oi[cb-1]) / (oi[cb-lb1] + tiny);
    ans[cb] = tmp > thr ;
 }
 break;

case 5: // open interest incline threshold comparison
 lb1 = 2 + (int)BiasedPosScale(v2, 48.0);
 thr = LinearScale(v3, 0.01, 0.99);
 for(cb=maxlb; cb<=nb; cb++) {
    tmp = (oi[cb-1] - oi[cb-lb1]) / (oi[cb-lb1] + tiny);
    ans[cb] = tmp > thr ;
 }
 break;

case 6: // recent new highs
 lb1 = 2 + (int)BiasedPosScale(v2, 48.0);
 lb2 = 1 + (int)BiasedPosScale(v3, 8.0);
 for(cb=lb1+3; cb<=nb; cb++)
      IsNewHigh[cb] = hi[cb] > Highest(hi, lb1, cb-1) ;
 for(cb=maxlb; cb<=nb; cb++)
      ans[cb] = EventPresent(IsNewHigh, lb2, cb);
 break;

case 7: // recent new lows
 lb1 = 2 + (int)BiasedPosScale(v2, 48.0);
 lb2 = 1 + (int)BiasedPosScale(v3, 8.0);
 for(cb=lb1+3; cb<=nb; cb++)
    IsNewLow[cb] = lo[cb] < Lowest(lo, lb1, cb-1) ;
 for(cb=maxlb; cb<=nb; cb++)
    ans[cb] = EventPresent(IsNewLow, lb2, cb);
 break;

case 8: // average directional movement test
 thr1 = LinearScale(v2, 5.0, 50.0);
 thr2 = thr1 + LinearScale(v3, 5.0, 20.0);
 AvgDirMov(hi, lo, cls, nb, 14, Ser1);
```

```
          for(cb=maxlb; cb<=nb; cb++)
              ans[cb] = (Ser1[cb] > thr1 && Ser1[cb] < thr2)
                  && Compare(Ser1[cb], Ser1[cb-1], v4-500.0);
          break;

       case 9: // stochastic Slow %K test
        thr = LinearScale(v2, 5.0, 95.0);
        fac = LinearScale(v3, 1.0, 20.0);
        thr1 = thr - fac;
        thr2 = thr + fac;
        StochOsc(Ser1, hi, lo, cls, 2, 10, nb);
        for(cb=maxlb; cb<=nb; cb++)
            ans[cb] = (Ser1[cb] > thr1 && Ser1[cb] < thr2)
                && Compare(Ser1[cb], Ser1[cb-1], v4-500.0);
        break;

       case 10: // macd slope direction
        lb1 = 2 + (int)BiasedPosScale(v2, 18.0);
        lb2 = lb1 + 1 + (int)BiasedPosScale(v3, 48.0);
        MacdOsc(Ser1, cls, 1, lb1, lb2, nb);
        for(cb=maxlb; cb<=nb; cb++)
            ans[cb] = Compare(Ser1[cb], Ser1[cb-2], v4-500.0);
        break;

       default:
        nrerror("Undefined rule template selected");
         break;
       }

    // first maxlb elements of result must be FALSE
    memset(&ans[1], 0, sizeof(*ans) * maxlb);

    #undef BiasedPosScale
    #undef LinearScale

}

static void Model (float *parms, float *dt, float *opn, float *hi,
float *lo, float *cls, float *vol, float *oi, float *dlrv, int nb,
TRDSIM &ts, float *eqcls) {

    // Implements a genetically-evolved rule-based entry model.
    // File = x16mod01.c
    // parms    - vector [1..MAXPRM] of parameters
    // dt       - vector [1..nb] of dates in YYMMDD form
    // opn      - vector [1..nb] of opening prices
```

```
// hi      - vector [1..nb] of high prices
// lo      - vector [1..nb] of low prices
// cls     - vector [1..nb] of closing prices
// vol     - vector [1..nb] of volumes
// oi      - vector [1..nb] of open interest numbers
// dlrv    - vector [1..nb] of average dollar volatilities
// nb      - number of bars in data series or vectors
// ts      - trading simulator class instance
// eqcls   - vector [1..nb] of closing equity levels

// declare local scratch variables
static int rc, cb, ncontracts, maxhold, ordertype, signal;
static int disp, k, modeltype;
static float mmstp, ptlim, stpprice, limprice, tmp;
static float exitatr[MAXBAR+1];
static int rule1[MAXBAR+1], rule2[MAXBAR+1], rule3[MAXBAR+1];

// copy parameters to local variables for clearer reference
modeltype = parms[14];   // model: 1=long, 2=short
ordertype = parms[15];   // entry: 1=open, 2=limit, 3=stop
maxhold   = 10;          // maximum holding period
ptlim     = 4;           // profit target in volatility units
mmstp     = 1;           // stop loss in volatility units

// perform whole-series calculations
AvgTrueRangeS(exitatr,hi,lo,cls,50,nb);       // ATR for exit
switch(modeltype) {
  case 1: case 2:        // for both long and short models
    // evaluate the three distinct rules for all bars
      Rules (opn, hi, lo, cls, vol, oi, exitatr, nb,
        parms[1], parms[2], parms[3], parms[4], rule1);
      Rules (opn, hi, lo, cls, vol, oi, exitatr, nb,
        parms[5], parms[6], parms[7], parms[8], rule2);
      Rules (opn, hi, lo, cls, vol, oi, exitatr, nb,
        parms[9], parms[10], parms[11], parms[12], rule3);
      break;
  default: nrerror("Invalid model type");
}

// step through bars (days) to simulate actual trading
for(cb = 1; cb <= nb; cb++) {

  // take no trades before the in-sample period
  // ... same as TradeStation's MaxBarsBack setting
  if(dt[cb] < IS_DATE) { eqcls[cb] = 0.0; continue; }
```

```
// execute any pending orders and save closing equity
rc = ts.update(opn[cb], hi[cb], lo[cb], cls[cb], cb);
if(rc != 0) nrerror("Trade buffer overflow");
eqcls[cb] = ts.currentequity(EQ_CLOSETOTAL);

// calculate number of contracts to trade
// ... we want to trade the dollar volatility equivalent
// ... of 2 new S&P-500 contracts as of 12/31/98
ncontracts = RoundToInteger(5673.0 / dlrv[cb]);
if(ncontracts < 1) ncontracts = 1;

// avoid placing orders on possibly limit-locked days
if(hi[cb+1] == lo[cb+1]) continue;

// generate entry signals, stop prices and limit prices
signal = 0;
switch(modeltype) {
  case 1: // trade long side
    if(rule1[cb] && rule2[cb] && rule3[cb]) signal = 1;
    break;
  case 2: // trade short side
    if(rule1[cb] && rule2[cb] && rule3[cb]) signal = -1;
    break;
}
limprice = 0.5 * (hi[cb] + lo[cb]);
stpprice = cls[cb] + 0.5 * signal * exitatr[cb];

// enter trades using specified order type
if(ts.position() <= 0 && signal == 1) {
  switch(ordertype) { // select desired order type
    case 1: ts.buyopen('1', ncontracts); break;
    case 2: ts.buylimit('2', limprice, ncontracts); break;
    case 3: ts.buystop('3', stpprice, ncontracts); break;
    default: nrerror("Invalid buy order selected");
  }
}
else if(ts.position() >= 0 && signal == -1) {
  switch(ordertype) { // select desired order type
    case 1: ts.sellopen('4', ncontracts); break;
    case 2: ts.selllimit('5', limprice, ncontracts); break;
    case 3: ts.sellstop('6', stpprice, ncontracts); break;
    default: nrerror("Invalid sell order selected");
  }
}
```

```
        // instruct simulator to employ standard exit strategy
        tmp = exitatr[cb];
        ts.stdexitcls('X', ptlim*tmp, mmstp*tmp, maxhold);

    } // process next bar
}
```

The C++ code implements the rule templates and system trading strategy. The function *Rules* implements the rule templates. Arguments *v1*, *v2*, *v3*, and *v4* (which correspond to the four numbers that comprise any one of the three genes) provide all the information required to instantiate a rule template. Argument *v1* is used to select, via a "switch statement," the required rule template from the 10 that are available; arguments *v2*, *v3*, and *v4*, are used to fill in the blanks (required parameters, desired directions of comparison, etc.) to yield a fully defined rule. The rule is then immediately evaluated for all bars, and the evaluations (1 for *TRUE*, 0 for *FALSE*) are placed in *ans*, a floating-point vector used to return the results to the caller.

The macro, *BiasedPosScale(x,a)*, is used to map numbers ranging from 0 to 1,000 to a range of 0 to *a*, with more numbers mapping to smaller values than larger ones. The macro is used to compute such things as lookbacks and moving-average periods from *v2*, *v3*, or *v4*, the values of which are ultimately derived from the genetic algorithm and scaled to range from 0 to 1,000. The macro is non-linear (*Biased*) so that a finer-grained exploration occurs for smaller periods or lookbacks than for larger ones. For example, suppose there is a moving average, with a period that ranges from 2 to 100 bars. The intention is to search as much between periods 2, 3, and 4 as between 30, 50, and 90; i.e., the scale should be spread for small numbers. This is desired because, in terms of trading results, the change from a 2-bar moving average to a 5-bar moving average is likely to be much greater than the change from a 50-bar to a 60-bar moving average.

The macro, *LinearScale(x,a,b)*, performs a linear mapping of the range 0 . . . 1,000 to the range a . . . b. The macro is usually used when calculating thresholds or deviations. In the rule template code, all parameters are scaled inside *Rules*, rather than inside the GA as is the usual practice. The GA has been instructed to produce numbers between 0 and 1,000, except for chromosome elements 1, 5, and 9, which are the first numbers in each gene, and which serve as rule template selectors. The reason for local scaling is that templates for different kinds of rules require parameter and control values having different ranges to be properly instantiated.

The process of evolving trading systems involves asking the genetic optimizer to provide a "guess" as to a chromosome. The genetic optimizer then randomly picks two members of the population and mates them (as specified by the crossover, mutation rate, and chunk-size properties). The resultant offspring is then returned as a potential solution. When the GA component is told the fitness of the solution it has just provided, it compares that fitness with that of the least-fit member of the population it maintains. If the fitness of the offspring is greater than the fitness of the least-fit member, the GA replaces the least-fit member with the offspring solution. This process is repeated generation after generation, and is handled by the shell code (not shown), which, in turn, makes repeated calls to function *Model* to simulate the trading and evaluate the system's fitness.

The code for function *Model* is almost identical to that used in earlier chapters. Prior to the bar indexing loop in which trading orders are generated, the function *Rules* is invoked three times (once for each gene), with the results being placed in time series *rule1*, *rule2*, and *rule3*. A 50-bar average true range is also calculated, as it is necessary for the standard exit and for rule evaluation. Inside the loop, the rule evaluations are checked for the current bar (*rule1[cb]*, *rule2[cb]*, *rule3[cb]*), and if all evaluations are *TRUE*, a buy (or a sell, if the short side is being examined) is generated. Entries are programmed in the standard manner for each of the three orders tested. Only the in-sample data is used to in the evolutionary process.

The output produced by the shell program permits the selection of desirable solutions that may be traded on their own or as a group. The solutions may be easily translated into understandable rules to see if they make sense and to use as elements in other systems.

TEST RESULTS

Six tests were performed. The evolutionary process was used to evolve optimal entry rules for the long and short sides with each of the three entry orders: at open, on stop, and on limit. In all cases, a maximum of 2,500 generations of genetic processing was specified. The task of computing all the solutions and saving them to files took only a few hours on a fast Pentium, which demonstrates the practicality of this technique. For each test, the genetic process produced a tabular file (GFiles 1 through 6) consisting of lines corresponding to each of the generations; i.e., each line represents a specific solution. Most of the early solutions were close to random and not very good, but the quality of the solutions improved as generations progressed; this is normal for a GA. Each line contains information regarding the performance of the particular solution that corresponds to the line, as well as to the complete chromosome, i.e., the set of parameters that represents the gene, which, in turn, corresponds to the solution expressed in the line.

The best solutions for the long entry at open and for the short entry at open were selected. These solutions were used to generate the six tests conducted below. More specifically, the solution that provided the best long entry at open was tested and its performance was evaluated in the usual way on both samples. The same solution was also tested and evaluated with entry on stop and on limit. The same procedure was followed for the short side: The best evolved solution for a short entry at open was determined. It was then tested on both samples with each of the other two order types. The optimal solution for each order type was not selected separately from our genetic runs because doing so would not allow comparability across orders. For example, the optimal entry at open might involve a breakout, while the optimal entry for a stop might involve countertrend momentum—totally different models. By assuming that the entry-at-open model (in which all trades generated by the model are taken) represents a good, overall model, the normal course of evaluating that model with the other orders was followed. Since the model is kept constant, this approach permits meaningful comparisons to be made across orders.

Solutions Evolved for Long Entries

Table 12-1 furnishes some of the performance data for the top 20 solutions for long entries at the open (GFile 1). Each line represents a different trading model. The parameters are not shown, but the line or generation number (*LINE*), the probability or statistical significance (*PROB*, the decimal point is omitted but implied in the formatting of these numbers), the average dollars-per-trade (*$TRD*), the total number of trades taken (*TRDS*), the profit factor (*PFAC*), the annualized return-on-account (*%ROA*), and the net profit or loss (*NET*) in raw numbers are provided.

TABLE 12-1

The Top 20 Solutions Evolved for Long Entries at the Open

LINE	PROB	$TRD	TRDS	PFAC	ROA%	NET
2306	000067	17264	43	3.60	82.2	742352
1889	000092	7467	254	1.81	53.8	1896618
2239	000257	11571	105	3.27	100.0	1214955
2381	000413	19031	25	5.82	100.0	475775
2382	000471	13550	70	4.09	100.0	948500
2054	000499	8618	177	1.91	80.8	1525386
1564	000591	3201	854	1.38	57.4	2733654
1912	000747	4901	437	1.53	52.1	2141737
1473	000758	11415	70	2.92	53.0	799050
1770	000879	5941	364	1.57	41.5	2162524
2226	000899	8887	110	2.08	88.2	977570
698	000951	6602	231	1.76	78.6	1525062
1075	000971	7617	126	2.11	58.4	959742
1904	001100	15591	25	5.10	95.0	389775
2360	001146	23673	15	10.44	86.9	355095
1619	001206	25045	14	17.05	100.0	350630
2132	001400	6133	245	1.69	77.5	1502585
1403	001402	6026	311	1.62	48.5	1874086
1185	001415	23463	15	9.63	80.1	351945
2159	001415	23463	15	9.63	80.1	351945

The performance of most of these models is nothing short of impressive. The better models are statistically significant beyond the 0.00007 level, which means these solutions have a very high probability of being real and holding up in the future. Many of the returns were greater than 50% annualized. In some cases, they reached much higher levels. While the limit order had many of the best solutions, all orders had many good, if not great, solutions. As in our earlier study, the GA succeeded admirably in finding many tradable models.

Solutions Evolved for Short Entries

Table 12-2 provides a small proportion of GFfile 4, the file for evolved models generated for short entries at the open. As in Test 1, the top 20 solutions, in terms of statistical significance or risk-to-reward ratio, are presented. Again, it can be seen that there were many good solutions. However, they were not as good as those for the longs. The solutions were not as statistically significant as for the longs, and the return-on-account numbers were somewhat smaller. A somewhat more distressing difference is that, in most cases, the number of trades was very small; the models appear to have been picking rare events. All else aside, the evolutionary process was able to find numerous, profitable rule sets for the short entries.

TABLE 12-2

The Top 20 Solutions Generated for Short Entries at the Open

LINE	PROB	$TRD	TRDS	PFAC	ROA%	NET
1671	003264	11929	36	2.99	54.9	429444
1474	004558	10742	34	2.88	57.2	365228
1413	008045	11744	22	2.87	50.8	258368
155	010383	27167	11	4.71	49.7	298837
1521	010383	27167	11	4.71	49.7	298837
1248	012249	9622	48	2.30	53.0	461856
1512	012789	8757	36	2.50	20.5	315252
1586	014758	10331	50	2.47	62.5	516550
1522	014895	7985	32	2.25	40.9	255520
1825	015355	11519	22	2.87	44.8	253418
1532	018217	4603	104	1.68	33.3	478712
1711	019089	20137	11	4.54	42.9	221507
1747	019483	7103	34	2.09	34.9	241502
1893	019955	13450	13	3.17	44.0	174850
1508	020676	10615	28	2.44	27.6	297220
1754	021607	12664	14	2.74	39.4	177296
1847	022971	8242	35	2.53	43.6	288470
537	023029	12111	14	2.51	33.1	169554
1325	023029	12111	14	2.51	33.1	169554
1324	023643	14738	10	3.62	22.0	147380

Test Results for the Standard Portfolio

The best solution shown in Table 12-1 (long trades) and the best solution from Table 12-2 (short trades) were run with all three entry orders. Tests 1 through 3 represent the best evolved model for long entry at the open tested with entry at open, on limit, and on stop (respectively). Tests 4 through 6 represent the best evolved model for short entry over all three orders. Table 12-3 contains the performance data for the best evolved entry-at-open models, both long and short, on the optimization and verification samples using each of the three entry orders. In the table, *SAMP* = whether the test was on the optimization sample (*IN* or *OUT*); *ROA%* = the annualized return-on-account; *ARRR* = the annualized risk-to-reward ratio; *PROB* = the associated probability or statistical significance; *TRDS* = the number of trades taken across all commodities in the portfolio; *WIN%* = the percentage of winning trades; *$TRD* = average profit/loss per trade; *BARS* = the

TABLE   1 2 - 3

Performance of the Best Evolved Entry-at-Open Model on the Optimization and Verification Samples with Each of the Three Entry Orders

SAMP	ROA%	ARRR	PROB	TRDS	WIN%	$TRD	BARS	NETL	NETS
Test 01 Long entry at open model, entry at open									
IN	82.2	1.22	0.000	43	62	17264	7	742	0
OUT	63.0	0.66	0.089	17	47	10231	6	173	0
Test 02 Long entry-at-open model, entry on limit									
IN	65.8	0.99	0.001	36	61	14846	8	534	0
OUT	87.7	0.86	0.038	14	50	14920	6	208	0
Test 03 Long entry-at-open model, entry on stop									
IN	42.2	0.88	0.003	22	72	16247	8	357	0
OUT	11.7	0.20	0.344	8	50	4246	6	33	0
Test 04 Short entry-at-open model, entry at open									
IN	54.9	0.87	0.003	36	69	11929	8	0	429
OUT	-10.0	-0.21	0.669	17	35	-2711	6	0	-46
Test 05 Short entry-at-open model, entry on limit									
IN	16.5	0.51	0.056	34	64	7424	8	0	252
OUT	-10.8	-0.24	0.686	14	42	-3351	6	0	-46
Test 06 Short entry-at-open model, entry on stop									
IN	23.1	0.60	0.031	24	54	7493	6	0	179
OUT	-13.0	-0.25	0.696	13	30	-3704	5	0	-48

average number of days a trade was held; *NETL* = the total net profit on long trades, in thousands of dollars; and *NETS* = the total net profit on short trades, in thousands of dollars.

Tests 1 through 3: Long-Entry-At-Open Model Tested with Entry at Open, on Limit, and on Stop. As can be seen in Table 12-3, the entry model produced by the evolutionary process was profitable across all three order types, both in-sample (as would be expected given the optimization power of GAs) and out-of-sample. In-sample, no return was less than 42% (annualized) for any order. The dollars-per-trade figures were all greater than $14,000, and not one system had less than 60% wins! Out-of-sample, there was more variation. With entry at open and on limit, performance continued to be stellar, with the average trade above $10,000 and the return on account above 60%. With a stop order, performance was not quite as good: The return on account was only 11%, and the average trade yielded $4,246. The only distressing aspect of the results is the small number of trades taken. For example, in-sample, with entry at open, there were only 43 trades taken over a 10-year span on a portfolio of 36 commodities. Out-of-sample, there were only 17 trades over a 5-year period; the trading frequency was roughly constant at approximately 4 trades per year.

The rules were apparently detecting unusual (but tradable) market events; the model engaged in what might be termed "rare event trading," which is not necessarily a bad thing. An assortment of systems, each trading different rare events, could yield excellent profits. When working with a system such as this, trading a portfolio of systems, as well as a portfolio of commodities, would be suggested. In the current situation, however, few trades would place the statistical reliability of the findings in question. The entire problem can be dealt with by using a somewhat more complex way of handling larger combinations of rules.

Tests 4 through 6: Short-Entry-at-Open Model Tested on Entry at Open, on Limit, and on Stop. In all cases, the performance of the best evolved short entry at open model, when tested over the three order types, was poorer on the in-sample data than the long model. Out-of-sample, the results deteriorated significantly and losses occurred. Unlike the long model, this one did not hold up. It should be noted, however, that if both the long and short models had been traded together on out-of-sample data, the profits from the long side would have vastly outweighed the losses from the short side; i.e., the complete system would have been profitable. The pattern of longs trading better than shorts is a theme that has been recurrent throughout the tests in this book. Perhaps the pattern is caused by the presence of a few markets in the standard portfolio that have been in extreme bullish mode for a long time. The way commodities markets respond to excess supply, as contrasted to the way they respond to shortages, may also help explain the tendency.

Market-by-Market Test Results

Table 12-4 contains the market-by-market results for the best evolved entry-at-open models, both long and short, tested on the optimization and verification samples using each of the three entry orders. Given the small number of trades taken, many of the empty cells in this table simply reflect the absence of trades. The *SYM* column represents the market being studied. The center and rightmost columns (*COUNT*) contain the number of profitable tests for a given market. The numbers in the first row represent test identifiers: *01, 02,* and *03* represent tests with entry at open, on limit, and on stop, respectively, for the long side; *04, 05,* and *06* represent corresponding tests for the short side. The last row (*COUNT*) contains the number of markets on which a given model was profitable. The data in this table provides relatively detailed information about which markets are and are not profitable when traded by each of the models: One dash (-) indicates a moderate loss per trade, i.e., $2,000 to $4,000; two dashes (--) represent a large loss per trade, i.e., $4,000 or more; one plus sign (+) means a moderate profit per trade, i.e., $1,000 to $2,000; two pluses (++) indicate a large gain per trade, i.e., $2,000 or more; and a blank cell means that the loss was between $0 and $1,999 or the profit was between $0 and $1,000 per trade. (For information about the various markets and their symbols, see Table II-1 in the "Introduction" to Part II.)

Tests 1 through 3: Long-Entry-at-Open Model Tested on Entry at Open, on Limit, and on Stop.   Table 12-4 indicates that, in-sample, the model was strongly profitable for the NYFE (but not the S&P 500), the British Pound, the Deutschemark, the Japanese Yen, Palladium, most of the Wheats, Kansas Wheat, Cocoa, and Lumber, and Light Crude (if entry at open is omitted). Out-of-sample, the NYFE had no trades, the British Pound and the Deutschemark continued to be strongly profitable across all three order types, and many of the other markets in which strong in-sample profitability was observed had no trades. Out-of-sample, some markets that had not traded in-sample traded profitably (especially Unleaded Gasoline, Silver, and Coffee), which indicates that the model continued to perform well, not merely in a different time period, but on a different set of markets.

Tests 4 through 6: Short-Entry-at-Open Model Tested on Entry at Open, on Limit, and on Stop.   In-sample, the T-Bills, the Deutschemark, the Swiss Franc, the Canadian Dollar, Pork Bellies, Oats, Kansas Wheat, Orange Juice, and Lumber all showed strong profits. The British Pound and Deutschemark held up out-of-sample. The Swiss Franc was profitable out-of-sample, but only with the limit order. It lost when entry was at open or on stop. The other markets either did not trade out-of-sample or had losses. Out-of-sample, the NYFE traded strongly profitably across all three order types, but did not trade profitably in-sample.

Figure 12-1 depicts portfolio equity growth for long trades taken with entry at open. As is evident, there was a steady, stair-like growth in equity, the stair-like

TABLE 12-4

Breakdown of Performance By Market and Test

SYM	IN-SAMPLE RESULTS							OUT-OF-SAMPLE RESULTS						
	01	02	03	04	05	06	COUNT	01	02	03	04	05	06	COUNT
SP							0				--	--	--	0
YX	++	++	++	--	--	--	3				++	++	++	3
US							0							0
TB	-	-		++	++		2	-	++	--	--		--	1
TY	--	--					0							0
BP	++	++	++	+	--	++	5	++	++	++	++		++	5
DM	++	++		++	++	++	5	++	++		++	++	++	5
SF	--	--	--	++	++	++	3				--	++	--	1
JY	++	++	++		++	--	4				--	--	--	0
CD	+	-	+	++	++	+	5	--	--	--	--	--	--	0
ED							0							0
CL	-	++	++				2							0
HO	--	--	--				0							0
HU					-	++	1	++		++				2
GC	--	-					0							0
SI							0	++	++					2
PL	++	++	++				3							0
PA							0							0
FC							0							0
LC							0							0
LH							0							0
PB				++		++	2							0
S							0							0
SM							0							0
BO							0							0
C							0							0
O				++	++	++	3							0
W	++		++				2							0
KW	++	++		++	+	++	5							0
MW	++			--	--	--	1							0
KC							0	++	++	-				2
CC	++	++	++				3							0
SB							0							0
JO				++	++	++	3							0
CT			--				0							0
LB	++	++	++	++	++	++	6				--	--		0
COUNT	11	9	9	10	9	10		5	5	2	3	3	3	

FIGURE 12-1

Portfolio Equity Growth for Long Model with Entry at the Open

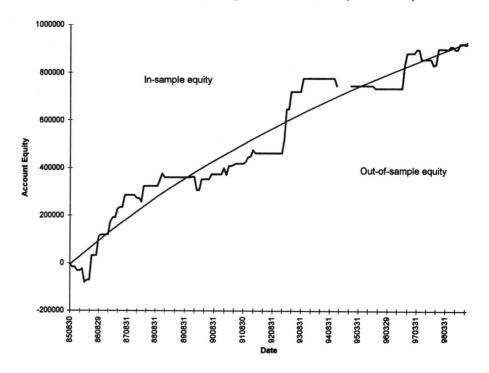

quality resulting from the small number of trades taken. The occasional, strongly profitable trade caused a sudden step up in equity. The least-squares line fitted to the equity curve reveals consistent growth in both samples, but slightly greater in the early years.

The equity growth for the long model with entry on limit, which helps to control transaction costs, is shown in Figure 12-2. Again, the stair-like growth in equity is apparent. However, the equity growth was more even; i.e., there was no slowing down of growth in recent years—in fact, the fitted line is almost straight. Out-of-sample performance was almost identical to in-sample performance.

Figure 12-3 shows portfolio equity growth for the best evolved short-entry-at-open model, evaluated with entry actually at the open. Again, the stair-like appearance is present. However, except for a strong spurt of growth between August 1989 and June 1993, the curve is essentially flat. Overall, the equity was seen rising, except for the flat regions.

FIGURE 12-2

Portfolio Equity Growth for Long Model with Entry on a Limit

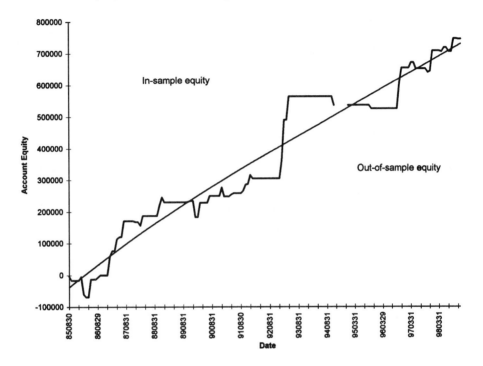

The Rules for the Solutions Tested

Rules for Long Entry.   The chromosome that represented the best solution for long entries at the open contained three genes. Each gene was composed of four numbers and corresponded to a specific rule.

   The numbers for Gene 1 were 4, 850, 65, and 653, which specified an open-interest decline rule (*case 4*), a look-back of 34, and a threshold of 0.042, respectively. The last number (653) was not used or translated because the rule did not require three blanks to be filled in, only two. If this information is taken and translated into plain language, the rule says that the open interest must decline at least 4.2% over the past 34 bars for the rule to evaluate as *TRUE*. In other words, the open interest 34 bars ago (relative to the current bar) minus the open interest 1 bar ago, divided by the open interest 34 bars ago, was greater than 0.042.

   The numbers for Gene 2 were 1, 256, 530, and 709. The first number (1) specified a simple price comparison rule (*case 1*). When the additional numbers were translated to the correct lookbacks and thresholds, it is apparent that this rule fires (evaluates as *TRUE*) when the close 3 days ago is greater than the close 14 days ago plus 3.46 times the average true range.

FIGURE 12-3

Portfolio Equity Growth for Short Model with Entry at the Open

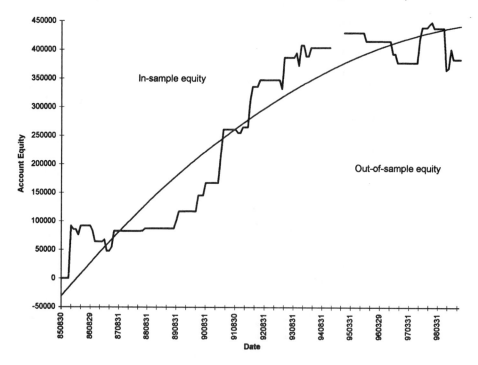

The numbers for Gene 3 were 5, 940, 47, and 610. Rule template 5 (*case 5*), which is the open-interest incline rule, was specified by the first number. Fully instantiating this rule reveals that the rule evaluates as *TRUE* if the market's open interest has risen at least 5.6% in the past 44 days.

If the conditions for all three rules, specified by Genes 1 through 3, were met on a given bar, a buy signal was generated.

It is interesting that two rules involved open interest, a variable not usually considered in many popular approaches to trading. It is also noteworthy that the two open-interest rules, when put together, seem almost contradictory: The current open interest had to be greater than the open interest 44 bars ago, but less than the open interest 34 bars ago. The model appears to be somewhat trend-following in that a recent closing price had to be greater than an older closing price before an entry was taken. However, time was left for a small pull-back; i.e., the increase in price only had to be observed 3 bars ago, not in the current bar. The set of rules is not one that would be easy to discover in a normal manner, without the aid of a genetic algorithm.

Rules for Short Entry.   A similar analysis can be done for the shorts as for the longs. The numbers corresponding to the chromosome that represented the best solution for short entries at the open were 5, 890, 391, and 532 (Gene 1); 5, 705, 760, and 956 (Gene 2); and 10, 163, 999, and 196 (Gene 3). When the string of three genes was translated, it was revealed that two rules deal with open interest and one with the MACD oscillator. The first open-interest rule states that the open interest 1 bar ago must be at least 38% greater than the open interest 38 bars ago. The second open-interest rule states that the open interest 1 bar ago must be at least 75% greater than the open interest 25 bars ago. The third rule states that the slope of the MACD—with a shorter moving average length of 2 and a longer moving average length of 50—must be down, suggesting a current downward trend. If the conditions for all three rules, specified by the three genes, were met on a given bar, a sell signal was generated. Again, these rules would not have been easily discovered when developing a trading model in a more traditional manner.

CONCLUSION

As was the case in our earlier study, the use of a GA to select and instantiate rule templates continued to work well as a means of developing a trading system, or, at least, an entry model. Results were still impressive, despite such problems as inadequate numbers of trades in many of the solutions generated. The approach is certainly one that can serve as the basis for further development efforts. In this exercise, only a small base of rule templates, involving such fairly simple elements as price comparisons, moving averages, and indicators, were used. Undoubtedly, much better results could be obtained by using a more sophisticated and complete set of rule templates as grist for the genetic mill.

WHAT HAVE WE LEARNED?

- Long positions tend to perform better than short positions for the markets in our standard portfolio and with the models that were tested. Therefore, it is probably more worthwhile to place development efforts on a system that emphasizes the long rather than short side.

- Genetic algorithms appear to be an effective means of discovering small inefficiencies that are buried in a mountain of efficient market behaviors.

- When used correctly, and in such a manner as discussed above, overoptimization (curve-fitting) does not seem to be a serious problem, despite the optimization power of genetic algorithms. Restrictions on the number and complexity of the rules in any solution seems to be the key element in controlling the curve-fitting demon.

- Evolution, as used herein, has the great benefit of producing explicit rules that can be translated into plain language and understood. Unlike neural network systems, the trading rules produced by GAs are not hidden in an inscrutable black box.

- Using genetics in the manner described above has the benefit of producing a large number of distinct, yet profitable, solutions. It would be easy evolve and then put together a portfolio of systems.

PART THREE

THE STUDY OF EXITS
Introduction

In Part II, the focus was on the timing of trade entries. The extent to which various methodologies are useful in the process of deciding when, where, and how to enter a trade was examined. Tests were conducted on everything from cycles to sunspot activity, from simple rule-based approaches to advanced genetic algorithms and neural networks. In order that a reasonably fair comparison of entry methods could be made, the exit strategy was intentionally kept simple and constant across all tests. A fixed money management stop, a profit target limit, and an exit at market after a given number of bars, or days, in the trade were used. In Part III, attention will be shifted to the problem of how to get out of a trade once in, i.e., to exit strategies, an issue that has often been neglected in the trading literature.

THE IMPORTANCE OF THE EXIT

In many ways, a good exit is more critical and difficult to achieve than a good entry. The big difference is that while waiting for a good opportunity to enter a trade, there is no market risk. If one opportunity to enter is missed, another will always come along—and a good, active trading model should provide many such opportunities. When a trade is entered, however, exposure to market risk occurs simultaneously. Failing to exit at an appropriate moment can cost dearly and even lead to the dreaded margin call! We actually know someone who made a quick, small fortune trading, only to lose it all (and then some) because the exit strategy failed to include a good money management stop! To get out of a trade that has gone bad, it is not a good idea to simply wait for the next entry opportunity to come along. Similarly, erring on the side of safety and exiting at the drop of a hat can also drain a trading account, albeit less dramatically through slow attrition. The problem with frequent and hasty exits is that many small losses will occur due to the sacrifice of many potentially profitable trades, and trades that are profitable will be cut short before reaching their full profit potential. A good exit strategy must, above all, strictly control losses, but it must not sacrifice too many potentially profitable trades in the process; i.e., it should allow profitable trades to fully mature.

How important is the exit strategy? If risk can be tightly controlled by quickly bailing from losing trades, and done in such a way that most winning trades are not killed or cut short, it is possible to turn a losing system into a profitable one! It has been said that if losses are cut short, profits will come. A solid exit strategy can make a profitable system even more lucrative, while reducing equity volatility and drawdown. Most importantly, during those inevitable bad periods, a good exit strategy that incorporates solid money management and capital preservation techniques can increase the probability that the trader will still be around for the next potentially profitable trade.

GOALS OF A GOOD EXIT STRATEGY

There are two goals that a good exit strategy attempts to achieve. The first and most important goal is to strictly control losses. The exit strategy must dictate how and when to get out of a trade that has gone wrong so that a significant erosion of trading capital can be prevented. This goal is often referred to as *money management* and is frequently implemented using stop-loss orders (money management stops). The second goal of a good exit strategy is to ride a profitable trade to full maturity. The exit strategy should determine not only when to get out with a loss, but also when and where to get out with a profit. It is generally not desirable to exit a trade prematurely, taking only a small profit out of the market. If a trade is going favorably, it should be ridden as long as possible and for as much profit as reasonably possible. This is especially important if the system does not allow multiple reentries into persistent trends. "The trend is your friend," and if a strong trend to can be ridden to maturity, the substantial profits that will result can more than compensate for many small losses. The profit-taking exit is often implemented with trailing stops, profit targets, and time- or volatility-triggered market orders. A complete exit strategy makes coordinated use of a variety of exit types to achieve the goals of effective money management and profit taking.

KINDS OF EXITS EMPLOYED IN AN EXIT STRATEGY

There are a wide variety of exit types to choose from when developing an exit strategy. In the standard exit strategy, only three kinds of exits were used in a simple, constant manner. A *fixed money management exit* was implemented using a stop order: If the market moved against the trade more than a specified amount, the position would be stopped out with a limited loss. A *profit target exit* was implemented using a limit order: As soon as the market moved a specified amount in favor of the trade, the limit would be hit and an exit would occur with a known profit. The *time-based exit* was such that, regardless of whether the trade was profitable, if it lasted more than a specified number of bars or days, it was closed out with an at-the-market order.

There are a number of other exit types not used in the standard exit strategy: trailing exits, critical threshold exits, volatility exits, and signal exits. A *trailing exit*, usually implemented with a stop order and, therefore, often called a *trailing stop*, may be employed when the market is moving in favor of the trade. This stop is moved up, or down, along with the market to lock in some of the paper profits in the event that the market changes direction. If the market turns against the trade, the trailing stop is hit and the trade is closed out with a proportion of the profit intact. A *critical threshold exit* terminates the trade when the market approaches or crosses a theoretical barrier (e.g., a trendline, a support or resistance level, a Fibonacci retracement, or a Gann line), beyond which a change in the interpretation of current market action is required. Critical threshold exits may be implemented using stop or limit orders depending on whether the trade is long or short and whether current prices are above or below the barrier level. If market volatility or risk suddenly increases (e.g., as in the case of a "blow-off" top), it may be wise to close out a position on a *volatility exit*. Finally, a *signal exit* is simply based on an expected reversal of market direction: If a long position is closed out because a system now gives a signal to go short, or because an indicator suggests a turning point is imminent, a signal exit has been taken. Many exits based on pattern recognition are signal exits.

Money Management Exits

Every exit strategy must include a *money management exit*. A money management exit is generally implemented using a stop order. Therefore, it is often referred to as a *money management stop*. Such a stop closes out a trade at a specified amount of adverse excursion (movement against the trade), or at a specified price below (if long) or above (if short) the price at which the trade was entered. A money management stop generally stays in place for the duration of the trade. Its purpose is to control the maximum risk considered tolerable. Of course, the potential risk may be greater than what was expected. The market could go limit up (or down) or have a large overnight gap. Trading without a money management stop is like flying in a rickety old plane without a parachute.

The issue is not whether a money management stop should be used. Rather, it is determining the optimal placement of the stop. There are many ways to decide where to place money management stops. The simplest placement occurs by assessing the maximum amount of money that can be risked on a given trade. For example, if a trade on the S&P 500 is entered and the trader is not be willing to risk more than $1,500, a money management stop that uses a $1,500 stop-loss order would be specified. If the market moves against the trade more than $1,500 (three S&P points), the stop gets hit and the position is closed out. Another way to set the money management stop is on the basis of volatility. In volatile markets and periods, it may be a good idea to give trades more room to breathe, i.e., to avoid having the stop so close to the market that potentially profitable trades get stopped out with losses.

A good way to set a money management stop is on the basis of a price barrier, such as a trendline or support/resistance level. In such cases, the stop also serves as a critical threshold exit. For example, if there are a number of trend and support lines around 936.00 on the S&P 500, and a long position at 937.00 has just been entered, it might be worth considering the placement of a stop a little below 936.00, e.g., at 935.50. Setting a protective stop at 935 is logical since a break through support suggests that the trend has changed and that it is no longer smart to be long the S&P 500. In this example, only $750 is at risk, substantially less than the $1,500 risked when using the money management stop that was based on a dollar amount. A *tighter* stop can often be set using a barrier or critical price model than would be the case using a simple dollar-amount model.

As hinted above, setting a money management stop involves a compromise. It is good to have a very tight stop, since losing trades then involve only tiny, relatively painless losses. However, as the stop is *tightened* (i.e., moved closer to the entry or current price), the likelihood of it getting triggered increases, even if the market eventually moves in favor of the trade. For example, if a $50 stop loss is set, almost all trades on the S&P 500, regardless of entry method, will be stopped out with small losses. As a stop gets tighter, the percentage of winning trades will decrease. The stop eventually ends up sacrificing most of what would have been profitable trades. On the other hand, if the stop is too loose, although the winning trades are retained, the adverse excursion on those winners, and the losses on the losing trades, will quickly become intolerable. The secret is to find a stop that effectively controls losses without sacrificing too many of the trades that provide profits.

Trailing Exits

A *trailing exit* is usually implemented with a so-called trailing stop. The purpose behind this kind of exit is to lock in some of the profits, or to provide protection with a stop that is tighter than the original money management stop, once the market begins to move in the trade's favor. If a long position in the S&P 500 is taken and a paper profit ensues, would it not be desirable to preserve some of that profit in case the market reverses? This is when a trailing stop comes in useful. If a $1,500 money management stop is in place and the market moves more than $1,500 against the trade, the position is closed with a $1,500 loss. However, if the market moves $1,000 in the trade's favor, it might be wise to move the old money management stop closer to the market's current price, perhaps to $500 above the current market price. Now, if the market reverses and the stop gets hit, the trade will be closed out with a $500 profit, rather than a $1,500 loss! As the market moves further in favor of the trade, the trailing stop can be moved up (or down, if in a short position), which is why it is called a *trailing* stop, i.e., it is racheted up (or down), trailing the market—locking in more of the increasing paper profit.

Once it is in place, a good trailing stop can serve both as an adaptive money management exit and as a profit-taking exit, all in one! As an overall exit strategy, it is not bad by any means. Trailing stops and money management stops work hand in hand. Good traders often use both, starting with a money management stop, and then moving that stop along with the market once profits develop, converting it to a trailing stop. Do not be concerned about driving the broker crazy by frequently moving stops around to make them trail the market. If trading is frequent enough to keep commissions coming in, the broker should not care very much about a few adjustments to stop orders. In fact, a smart broker will be pleased, realizing that his or her client is much more likely to survive as an active, commission-producing trader, if money management and trailing stop exits are used effectively.

How is the placement of a trailing stop determined? Many of the same principles discussed with regard to money management exits and stops also apply to trailing exits and stops. The stop can be set to trail, by a fixed dollar amount, the highest (or lowest, if short) market price achieved during the trade. The stop can be based on a volatility-scaled deviation. A moving threshold or barrier, such as a trend or Gann line, can be used if there is one present in a region close enough to the current market action. Fixed barriers, like support/resistance levels, can also be used: The stop would be jumped from barrier to barrier as the market moves in the trade's favor, always keeping the stop comfortably trailing the market action.

Profit Target Exits

A *profit target exit* is usually implemented with a limit order placed to close out a position when the market has moved a specified amount in favor of the trade. A limit order that implements a profit target exit can either be fixed, like a money management stop, or be moved around as a trade progresses, as with a trailing stop. A fixed profit target can be based on either volatility or a simple dollar amount. For example, if a profit target of $500 is set on a long trade on the S&P 500, a sell-at-limit order has been placed: If the market moves $500 in the trade's favor, the position is immediately closed. In this way, a quick profit may be had.

There are advantages and disadvantages to using a profit target exit. One advantage is that, with profit target exits, a high percentage of winning trades can be achieved while slippage is eliminated, or even made to work in the trader's favor. The main drawback of a profit target exit is that it can cause the trader to prematurely exit from large, sustained moves, with only small profits, especially if the entry methods do not provide for multiple reentries into ongoing trends. All things being equal, the closer the profit target is to the entry price, the greater the chances are of it getting hit and, consequently, the higher the percentage of winning trades. However, the closer the profit target, the smaller the per-trade profit. For instance, if a $50 profit target is set on a trade in the S&P 500 and the money management stop is kept far out (e.g., at $5,000), more than 95% of the trades will be winners! Under such circumstances, however, the wins will yield small profits that will certainly be wiped out, along with a chunk of principal, by the rare $5,000 loss, as well as by the commissions. On the other hand, if the profit target is very wide, it will only occasionally be triggered, but when it does get hit, the profits will be substantial. As with exits that employ stops, there is a compromise to be made: The profit target must be placed close enough so that there can be benefit from an increased percentage of winning trades and a reduction in slippage, but it should not be so close that the per-trade profit becomes unreasonably small. An exit strategy does not necessarily need to include a profit target exit. Some of the other strategies, like a trailing stop, can also serve to terminate trades profitably. They have the added benefit that if a significant trend develops, it can be ridden to maturity for a very substantial return on investment. Under the same conditions, but using a profit target exit, the trade would probably be closed out a long time before the trend matures and, consequently, without capturing the bulk of the profit inherent in the move.

Personally, we prefer systems that have a high percentage of winning trades. Profit targets can increase the percentage of wins. If a model that is able to reenter active trends is used, profit target exits may be effective. The advantages and disadvantages really depend on the nature of the system being trading, as well as on personal factors.

One kind of profit target we have experimented with, designed to close out dead, languishing trades that fail to trigger other types of exits, might be called a *shrinking target*. A profit target that is very far away from the market is set. Initially, it is unlikely to be triggered, but it is constantly moved closer and closer to where the market is at any point in the trade. As the trade matures, despite the fact that it is not going anywhere, it may be possible to exit with a small profit when the profit target comes into a region where the market has enough volatility to hit it, resulting in an exit at a good price and without slippage.

Time-Based Exits

Time-based exits involve getting out of the market on a market order after having held a trade for a fixed period of time. The assumption is that if the market has not, in the specified period of time, moved sufficiently to trigger a profit target or some other kind of exit, then the trade is probably dead and just tying up margin. Since the reason for having entered the trade in the first place may no longer be relevant, the trade should be closed out and the next opportunity pursued.

Volatility Exits

A *volatility exit* depends on recognizing that the level of risk is increasing due to rapidly rising market volatility, actual or potential. Under such circumstances, it is prudent to close out positions and, in so doing, limit exposure. For instance, when volatility suddenly expands on high volume after a sustained trend, a "blow-off" top might be developing. Why not sell off long positions into the buying frenzy? Not only may a sudden retracement be avoided, but the fills are likely to be very good, with slippage working with, rather than against, the trader! Another volatility exit point could be a date that suggests a high degree of risk, e.g., anniversaries of major market crashes: If long positions are exited and the market trends up instead, it is still possible to jump back in. However, if a deep downturn does occur, the long position can be reentered at a much better price!

What else constitutes a point of increased risk? If an indicator suggests that a trend is about to reverse, it may be wise to exit and avoid the potential reversal. If a breakout system causes a long entry into the S&P 500 to occur several days before the full moon, but lunar studies have shown that the market often drops when the moon is full and the trade is still being held, then it might be a good idea to close the position, thus avoiding potential volatility. Also remember, positions need not be exited all at once. Just a proportion of a multicontract position can be closed out, a strategy that is likely to help smooth out a trader's equity curve.

Barrier Exits

A *barrier exit* is taken when the market touches or penetrates some barrier, such as a point of support or resistance, a trendline, or a Fibonacci retracement level. Barrier exits are the best exits: They represent theoretical barriers beyond which interpretation of market action must be revised, and they often allow very close stops to be set, thereby dramatically reducing losses on trades that go wrong. The trick is to find a good barrier in approximately the right place. For example, a money management stop can serve as a barrier exit when it is placed at a strong support or resistance level, if such a level exists close enough to the entry price to keep potential loss within an acceptable level. The trailing exit also can be a barrier exit if it is based on a trendline.

Signal Exits

Signal exits occur when a system gives a signal (or indication) that is contrary to a currently held position and the position is closed for that reason. The system generating the signal need not be the same one that produced the signal that initiated the trade. In fact, the system does not have to be as reliable as the one used for trade entry! Entries should be conservative. Only the best opportunities should be selected, even if that means missing many potential entry points. Exits, on the other hand, can be liberal. It is important to avoid missing any reversal, even at the expense of a higher rate of false alarms. A missed entry is just one missed opportunity out of many. A missed exit, however, could easily lead to a downsized account! Exits based on pattern recognition, moving average crossovers, and divergences are signal exits.

CONSIDERATIONS WHEN EXITING THE MARKET

There are a number of issues to take into account when attempting to exit the market. Some orders, such as stops, may result in poor executions and substantial transaction costs due to such factors as "gunning" and slippage. Other orders, such as limits, may simply not be filled at all. There are also trade-offs to consider; e.g., tight stops might keep losses small but, at the same time, kill potentially winning trades and increase the number of losses. Loose stops allow winning trades to develop, but they do so at the cost of less frequent, but potentially catastrophic, losses. In short, there are aspects to exiting that involve how the orders are placed and how the markets respond to them.

Gunning

Sometimes putting stops in the market as they really are may not be prudent, especially when tight stops are being used. Floor traders may try to *gun* the stops to pick up a few ticks for themselves. In other words, the floor traders may intentionally try to force the market to hit the stops, causing them to be executed. When stops are taken out this way, the trader who placed them usually ends up losing. How can this be avoided? Place a *catastrophe stop* with the broker, just in case trading action cannot be taken quickly enough due to busy phones or difficult market conditions. The catastrophe stop is placed far enough away from the market that it is beyond the reach of gunning and similar "mischief." No one would like to see this stop hit, but at least it will keep the trader from getting killed should something go badly wrong. The real stop should reside only with the trader, i.e., in the system on the computer: When this stop gets hit, the computer displays a message and beeps, at which time the broker can be immediately phoned and the trade exited. Handled this way, tight stops can be used safely and without the risk of being gunned.

Trade-Offs with Protective Stops

Usually, as stops are moved in tighter, risk control gets better, but many winning trades could be sacrificed, resulting in the decline of profit. Everyone would love to use $100 stops in the S&P 500 because the losses on losing trades would be fairly small. However, most systems would lose 95% of the time! Certain systems allow stops to be tight, just because of the way the market moves relative to the entry point. Such systems yield a reasonable percentage of winning trades. When developing systems, it is good to build in a tight stop tolerance property. Such systems are often based on support and resistance or other barrier-related models. Many systems do not have a tight stop characteristic and so require wider stops. Nevertheless, there is always a trade-off between having tight stops to control risk, but not so tight that many winning trades are sacrificed. Loose stops will not sacrifice winning trades, but the bad trades may run away and be devastating. A compromise must be found that, in part, depends on the nature of the trading system and the market being traded.

Slippage

Slippage is the amount the market moves from the instant the trading order is placed or, in the case of a stop, triggered, to the instant that order gets executed. Such movement translates into dollars. When considered in terms of stops, if the market is moving against the trade, the speed at which it is moving affects the amount that will be lost due to slippage. If the market is moving quickly and a stop gets hit, a greater loss due to slippage is going to be experienced than if the market was moving more slowly. If there was a stop loss on the S&P 500 of $500 and the market really started moving rapidly against the trade, $200 or $300 of slippage could easily occur, resulting in a $700 or $800 loss, instead of the $500 loss that was anticipated. If the market is moving more slowly, then the slippage might only be $25 or $50, resulting in a $525 or $550 loss. Slippage exists in all trades that involve market or stop orders, although it may, in some circumstances, work for rather than against the trader. Limit orders (e.g., "sell at $x or better") are not subject to slippage, but such orders cannot close out a position in an emergency.

Contrarian Trading

If possible, exit long trades when most traders are buying, and exit short trades when they are selling. Such behavior will make it easier to quickly close out a trade, and to do so at an excellent price, with slippage working for rather than against the trader. Profit targets usually exit into liquidity in the sense just discussed. Certain volatility exits also achieve an exit into liquidity. Selling at a blow-off top, for example, is selling into a buying frenzy! "Buy the rumor, sell the news" also suggests the benefits of selling when everyone starts buying. Of course, not all the exits in an exit strategy can be of a kind that takes advantage of exiting into liquidity.

Conclusion

A complete exit strategy makes coordinated, simultaneous use of a variety of exit types to achieve the goals of effective money management and profit taking. Every trader must employ some kind of catastrophe and money management stop. It is also advisable to use a trailing stop to lock in profits when the market is moving in the trade's favor. A risk- or volatility-based exit is useful for closing positions before a stop gets hit—getting out with the market still moving in a favorable direction, or at least not against the trade, means getting out quickly and with less slippage.

TESTING EXIT STRATEGIES

In the next few chapters, a variety of exit strategies are tested. In contrast to entries, where an individual entry could be tested on its own, exits need company. An entire exit strategy must be tested even if, for purposes of scientific study, only one element at a time is altered to explore the effects. The reason for this involves the fact that an exit must be achieved in some fashion to complete a trade. If an entry is not signaled now, one will always come along later. This is not so with an exit, where exposure to market risk can become unlimited over time, should one not be signaled. Consider, for example, a money management stop with no other exit. Are looser stops, or perhaps the absence of any money management stop, better than tight ones? The first test determines the consequences of using a very loose stop. If the *no-stop* condition was the first tested, there would be no trades to use to evaluate money management stops; i.e., there would only be an entry to a trade from which an exit would never occur. With a loose stop, if the market goes in favor of the trade, perhaps the trade would be held for years or never exited, leading to the same problem as the no-stop condition. These examples illustrate why exits must be tested as parts of complete, even if simple, strategies, e.g., a stop combined with a time limit exit.

For the aforementioned reasons, all the tests conducted in Chapter 13 employ a basic exit strategy, specifically, the standard exit strategy (and a modification thereof) used throughout the study of entries; this will provide a kind of baseline. In Chapters 14 and 15, several significant variations on, and additions too, the standard exit will be tested. More effective stops and profit targets, which attempt to lock in profit without cutting it short, are examined in Chapter 14. In Chapter 15, techniques developed in the section on entries are brought into the standard exit strategy as additional components, specifically, as signal exits. Moreover, an attempt will be made to evolve some of the elements in the exit strategy. To test these various exit strategies in a manner that allows comparisons to be made, a set of standard entry models is needed.

STANDARD ENTRIES FOR TESTING EXITS

When studying entries, it was necessary to employ a standard, consistent exit methodology. Likewise, the investigation of exits requires the use of a standard entry method, a rather shocking one, i.e., the *random entry model*. It works this way: The market is entered at random times and in random directions. As in all previous chapters, the number of contracts bought or sold on any entry is selected to create a trade that has an effective dollar volatility equal to two contracts of the S&P 500 at the end of 1998. Due to the need to avoid ambiguity when carrying out simulations using end-of-day data, the entries used in the tests of the various exit strategies are restricted to the open. If entry takes place only at the open, it will be possible to achieve unambiguous simulations with exits that take place on intrabar limits and stops. Unambiguous simulations involving such orders would otherwise not be possible without using tick-by-tick data. As previously, the standard portfolio and test platform will be used.

The Random Entry Model

To obtain the random entries, a pseudo–random number generator (RNG) is used to determine both when the trades are entered and whether those trades are long or short. This approach is being taken for a number of reasons. First of all, a uniform way of testing exits is needed. Different types of entry systems have their own unique characteristics that affect the ways in which different exits and/or stops behave. For example, if an entry system forecasts exact market turning points, a very tight money management stop can be used that might even improve the system. However, with more typical entries, that might not be the case. Therefore, it is preferable to take the kinds of entries that might be typical of a bad system, or a system that is slightly tradable but not very good, to see how much improvement can be had by use of a good exit. Obviously, a great entry system makes everything easier and reduces the need to find perfect exits. An entry system that stays fixed over the exploration of the different types of exits allows determination of the degree to which profitability can be improved (or losses reduced) by effective money management and exit strategies.

Second, random entries help ensure that the system contains a number of bad trades, which are needed to test the mettle of any exit strategy. After all, the whole idea of a good exit strategy is to cut all the bad trades quickly before they do damage and to preserve and grow the good trades. With a really good exit strategy, it is reasonable to assume that bad trades will be exited before large losses are incurred and that profit will be made from the good trades. This relates to the popular notion that if losses are cut short, the profits will come, regardless of the system. The studies that follow put the truth of this axiom to the test.

Last, the approach provides an entry model that has a reasonably large, fixed number of trades. The sample consists of all kinds of trades, many bad ones and some good ones (by accident or chance). Under such circumstances, the overall performance of the system is expected to be due exclusively to the exits.

Generating the Random Entries. The random entry model generates a long series of numbers (composed of +1s, −1s, and 0s), each of which corresponds to a trading day. The numbers represent whether, for any given date, a long entry signal ($+1$), a short entry signal (-1), or no entry signal at all (0) should be generated. For example, the random entry system might generate a -1 on October 29, 1997, which means that there is a signal to enter a short trade at the open on that date.

The RNG used to implement the random entry strategy is the one described as *ran2* in *Numerical Recipes in C* (Press et al., 1992). The period of this RNG is greater than 2 multiplied by 10^{18}. It is by far a better RNG than those normally found in the run-time libraries that usually come with a programming language. Signals are generated based on random numbers from this generator. On each bar, a uniformly distributed random number between 0 and 1 is obtained from the RNG. If the random number is less than 0.025, a short signal is generated. The probability of a short being generated on any bar is 0.025; i.e., a short signal should occur every 40 bars, on average. If the random number is greater than 0.975, a long signal is issued; these signals also should occur, on average, every 40 bars. In other words, on average, a long or a short trading signal should occur every 20 bars. The limit and stop prices are calculated in the usual way. Orders are placed in the usual manner.

CHAPTER 13

The Standard Exit Strategy

The standard exit strategy (SES) was used throughout the tests of entry methods. Basically, the SES employs a money management stop, a profit target limit, and a market order for exit after a specified amount of time. The examination of this strategy provides a baseline against which variations and more complex exit strategies (studied in the next two chapters) may be judged. The SES is being investigated using the random entry technique discussed in the "Introduction" to Part III.

WHAT IS THE STANDARD EXIT STRATEGY?

Although the *standard exit strategy* is basic and minimal, it does incorporate elements that are essential to any exit strategy: profit taking, risk control, and time exposure restraint. The profit-taking aspect of the SES is done through a profit target limit order that closes out a trade when it has become sufficiently profitable. The risk control aspect of the SES is accomplished using a simple money management stop that serves to close out a losing position with a manageable loss. The time exposure restraint is achieved with a market order, posted after a certain amount of time has elapsed. It closes out a languishing trade that has hit neither the money management stop nor the profit target.

CHARACTERISTICS OF THE STANDARD EXIT

The standard exit was intended to be simply a minimal exit for use when testing various entry strategies. As such it is not necessarily a very good exit. Unlike an optimal exit strategy, the standard exit is unable to hold onto sustained trends and ride them to the end. In addition, a profit can be developed and then lost. The reason is that the SES has no way of locking in any proportion of paper profit that may develop. A good exit strategy would, almost certainly, have some method of doing this. After having made a substantial paper profit, who would want to find it quickly vanish as the market reverses its course? The fixed time limit also contributes to the inability of the SES to hold onto long, sustained moves, but it was a desirable feature when testing entry strategies. Finally, the SES lacks any means of attempting to exit a languishing trade at the best possible price, as might be done, e.g., by using a shrinking profit target.

On the positive side, the SES does have the basics required of any exit strategy. Through its money management stop, the SES has a means of getting out of a bad trade with a limited loss. The limit order or profit target allows the SES to close a trade that turned substantially profitable. Using the time limit exit, the SES can exit a trade that simply does not move. These three features make the standard exit definitely better than a random exit or a simple exit after a fixed number of bars.

PURPOSE OF TESTING THE SES

A major reason for testing the SES is to be able to make comparisons between it and the other exit strategies that will be tested. The SES will serve as a good pivot point or baseline, having been used in the study of entries. An additional benefit that is quite important and useful is derived from these tests. The SES will be tested with a *random entry*, providing a random entry baseline against which the various real entries (tested in Part II) may be compared. The tests in this chapter, therefore, provide baselines for both the previous chapters and those that follow. An additional reason for doing these tests is to determine how much was lost by restricting the SES to the close in earlier tests. In some of the tests below, the restriction to the close will be lifted, an action that should improve the overall performance of the SES.

Four tests will be conducted. The first three tests examine the SES in the form that was used in all the earlier chapters; i.e., entries will be taken at the open, on a stop, or on a limit, and exits will take place only on the close. The remaining test will study the SES in a way that permits stop and limit exits to take place inside the bar, lifting the restriction of the exit to the close; the entry in this test will only take place on the open, to avoid the kinds of ambiguity mentioned in the previous chapter.

TESTS OF THE ORIGINAL SES

To test the original SES, the random entry method is used (described in the "Introduction" to Part III). The exits are the usual standard exits (with exit restricted on the close) that were used throughout the study of entries. The rules for the SES are as follows: If, at the close, the market is more than some multiple (the money management stop parameter) of the 50-bar average true range below the entry price, then exit; this is the money management stop. If the price at the close is greater than some other multiple (the profit target limit parameter) of the same average true range above the entry price, then exit; this is the profit target limit. These rules are for long positions, and the exit is restricted to the close. For short positions, the placement of the thresholds are reversed, with the money management exit placed above the entry price and the profit target exit placed below. If, after 10 days, neither the money management stop nor profit target limit has been hit, close out the trade with a market-at-close order. The code that follows implements these rules, as well as the random entry. There are three tests, one for each type of entry order (at open, on limit, and on stop). The standard software test platform and portfolio are used.

```
static void Model (float *parms, float *dt, float *opn, float *hi,
float *lo, float *cls, float *vol, float *oi, float *dlrv, int nb,
TRDSIM &ts, float *eqcls) {

    // Implements the random entry model with the standard exit
    // File = x19mod01.c
    // parms   - vector [1..MAXPRM] of parameters
    // dt      - vector [1..nb] of dates in YYMMDD form
    // opn     - vector [1..nb] of opening prices
    // hi      - vector [1..nb] of high prices
    // lo      - vector [1..nb] of low prices
    // cls     - vector [1..nb] of closing prices
    // vol     - vector [1..nb] of volumes
    // oi      - vector [1..nb] of open interest numbers
    // dlrv    - vector [1..nb] of average dollar volatilities
    // nb      - number of bars in data series or vectors
    // ts      - trading simulator class instance
    // eqcls   - vector [1..nb] of closing equity levels

    // declare local scratch variables
    static int rc, cb, ncontracts, maxhold, ordertype, signal;
    static float mmstp, ptlim, stpprice, limprice, tmp;
    static float exitatr[MAXBAR+1], rnum;
    static int ranseed;
    static long iseed;

    // copy parameters to local variables for clearer reference
    ranseed   = parms[8];  // used to select random seed
    ordertype = parms[9];  // entry: 1=open, 2=limit, 3=stop
    maxhold   = 10;        // maximum holding period
```

```
ptlim    = 4;           // profit target in volatility units
mmstp    = 1;           // stop loss in volatility units

// perform whole-series calculations
AvgTrueRangeS(exitatr,hi,lo,cls,50,nb);      // ATR for exit

// seed the random number generator
// ... we want a different seed for each tradeable
iseed = -(ranseed + 10 * ts.model());
rnum = ran2(&iseed);

// step through bars (days) to simulate actual trading
for(cb = 1; cb <= nb; cb++) {

   // take no trades before the in-sample period
   // ... same as TradeStation's MaxBarsBack setting
   if(dt[cb] < IS_DATE) { eqcls[cb] = 0.0; continue; }

   // execute any pending orders and save closing equity
   rc = ts.update(opn[cb], hi[cb], lo[cb], cls[cb], cb);
   if(rc != 0) nrerror("Trade buffer overflow");
   eqcls[cb] = ts.currentequity(EQ_CLOSETOTAL);

   // calculate number of contracts to trade
   // ... we want to trade the dollar volatility equivalent
   // ... of 2 new S&P-500 contracts as of 12/31/98
   ncontracts = RoundToInteger(5673.0 / dlrv[cb]);
   if(ncontracts < 1) ncontracts = 1;

   // avoid placing orders on possibly limit-locked days
   if(hi[cb+1] == lo[cb+1]) continue;

   // generate entry signals, stop prices and limit prices
   signal = 0;
   rnum = ran2(&iseed);                      // random number 0...1
   if(rnum < 0.025) signal = -1;      // random short entry
   else if(rnum > 0.975) signal = 1;  // random long entry
   limprice = 0.5 * (hi[cb] + lo[cb]);
   stpprice = cls[cb] + 0.5 * signal * exitatr[cb];

   // enter trades using specified order type
   if(ts.position() <= 0 && signal == 1) {
      switch(ordertype) { // select desired order type
         case 1: ts.buyopen('1', ncontracts); break;
```

```
         case 2: ts.buylimit('2', limprice, ncontracts); break;
         case 3: ts.buystop('3', stpprice, ncontracts); break;
         default: nrerror("Invalid buy order selected");
      }
   }
   else if(ts.position() >= 0 && signal == -1) {
      switch(ordertype) { // select desired order type
         case 1: ts.sellopen('4', ncontracts); break;
         case 2: ts.selllimit('5', limprice, ncontracts); break;
         case 3: ts.sellstop('6', stpprice, ncontracts); break;
         default: nrerror("Invalid sell order selected");
      }
   }

   // instruct simulator to employ standard exit strategy
   tmp = exitatr[cb];
   ts.stdexitcls(`X', ptlim*tmp, mmstp*tmp, maxhold);

   } // process next bar
}
```

The code is similar to that presented in earlier chapters. Only the generation of the entry signals has changed. Entry signals are now issued using a pseudo–random number generator (RNG). Before entering the loop that steps through bars to simulate the process of trading, the RNG is initialized with a unique seed. The initialization seed is determined by the market number and by a parameter (*ranseed*). By changing the parameter, a totally different sequence of random entries is generated. The exact seed values are irrelevant in that, for every seed, a unique series will be generated because the period of the RNG is extremely large.

The RNG used is the one described as *ran2* in *Numerical Recipes in C* (Press et al., 1992). The period of this RNG is greater than 2 multiplied by 10^{18}. This RNG is by far better than those that normally come as part of a programming language library. Inside the loop, where trading actually takes place, signals are generated based on random numbers. The steps are very simple. On each bar, a uniformly distributed random number between 0 and 1 is obtained from the RNG. If the random number is less than 0.025, a short signal is generated. The probability of a short being generated on any bar is 0.025; i.e., a short signal should occur every 40 bars, on average. If the random number is greater than 0.975, a long signal is issued; these signals should also occur, on average, every 40 bars. In other words, on average, a long or a short trading signal should occur every 20 bars. The limit and stop prices are calculated in the usual way. Orders are placed and exits specified in the usual manner.

The steps that are used to conduct each of the three tests are as follows: On the in-sample data and for each entry order type, 10 distinct series of random entries are generated and traded. The best of those sequences are then examined on the verification or out-of-sample data. The process mimics that of optimizing a parameter in a real system by stepping it from, e.g., 1 to 10; here the parameter simply selects a totally different series of random entries for each value.

Test Results

Tables 13-1, 13-2, and 13-3 present the portfolio performance that resulted from trading random entries with the standard exit strategy. Each of the numbers in the column *RAND* represents a seed modifier (*ranseed*) that causes the RNG to generate a different sequence of random entries. *NET* = the total net profit, in thousands of dollars. *NETL* = the total net profit for the longs. *NETS* = the total net profit for the shorts. *PFAC* = the profit factor. *ROA%* = the annualized return on account. *ARRR* = the annualized risk-reward ratio. *PROB* = the statistical significance or probability. *DRAW* = the drawdown, in thousands of dollars. *TRDS* = the number of trades. *WIN%* = the percentage of wins. *AVTR* = the average trade, in dollars. *TRDB* = the average bars per trade, rounded to the nearest integer. *VER* = the performance for the random sequence that provided the best in-sample performance when this sequence is continued and then tested on the verification sample. *AVG* = the average in-sample value of the numbers in rows 1 through 10. *STDEV* = the standard deviation for the in-sample performance data shown in rows 1 through 10.

Test 1: SES with Random Entries at the Open.   This system did not perform very well in-sample. The average trade, over all 10 randomizations, lost $2,243, with a

TABLE   13-1

Results for the Standard Exit with Random Entries at the Open

RAND	NET	NETL	NETS	PFAC	ROA%	ARRR	PROB	DRAW	TRDS	WIN%	AVTR	TRDB
1	-6835	-2142	-4692	0.81	-10.3	-1.65	1.0000	6798	3946	38	-1732	6
2	-8873	-2585	-6287	0.76	-10.3	-2.16	1.0000	8864	3961	37	-2240	6
3	-9030	-3066	-5964	0.75	-10.2	-2.31	1.0000	9110	3903	37	-2313	6
4	-10513	-3828	-6684	0.71	-10.2	-2.70	1.0000	10532	3931	36	-2674	6
5	-9662	-2621	-7041	0.74	-10.2	-2.40	1.0000	9679	3878	37	-2491	6
6	-10014	-3659	-6355	0.73	-10.3	-2.46	1.0000	10009	3863	36	-2592	6
7	-9484	-2991	-6492	0.73	-10.1	-2.45	1.0000	9626	3875	36	-2447	6
8	-8346	-2719	-5627	0.76	-10.1	-2.09	1.0000	8493	3782	37	-2207	6
9	-8539	-3574	-4964	0.76	-10.0	-2.10	1.0000	8797	3912	37	-2182	6
10	-7693	-961	-6731	0.79	-10.0	-1.92	1.0000	7918	3985	38	-1930	6
VER	-3152	-1446	-1706	0.80	-22.6	-1.81	0.9999	3312	1692	37	-1863	6
AVG	-8376	-2690	-5686	0.76	-11.3	-2.19	1.0000	8467	3703	36.91	-2243	6
STDEV	2024	900	1510	0.03	3.8	0.31	0.0000	1995	669	0.70	304	0

TABLE 13-2

Results for the Standard Exit with Random Entries on a Limit

RAND	NET	NETL	NETS	PFAC	ROA%	ARRR	PROB	DRAW	TRDS	WIN%	AVTR	TRDB
1	-4712	-1510	-3202	0.83	-10.3	-1.33	1.0000	4695	3040	40	-1550	7
2	-5191	-1156	-4034	0.81	-10.3	-1.44	1.0000	5166	3127	39	-1660	7
3	-5152	-1451	-3700	0.81	-10.0	-1.51	1.0000	5264	3040	39	-1694	7
4	-6885	-2052	-4832	0.76	-10.0	-1.97	1.0000	7033	3082	38	-2234	6
5	-6163	-1147	-5016	0.78	-10.0	-1.68	1.0000	6345	3067	38	-2009	6
6	-7061	-2391	-4670	0.75	-10.2	-2.02	1.0000	7090	3039	38	-2323	7
7	-6253	-2036	-4216	0.77	-10.2	-1.86	1.0000	6258	3010	39	-2077	7
8	-4789	-1672	-3117	0.82	-9.6	-1.39	1.0000	5110	2968	40	-1613	7
9	-4639	-1767	-2871	0.83	-9.8	-1.30	1.0000	4868	3067	39	-1512	6
10	-4738	82	-4821	0.83	-10.0	-1.34	1.0000	4846	3162	39	-1498	6
VER	-3988	-1615	-2372	0.69	-22.0	-2.56	1.0000	4315	1305	37	-3056	6
AVG	-5416	-1520	-3896	0.79	-11.1	-1.67	1.0000	5545	2901	38.73	-1930	6.55
STDEV	1012	651	906	0.04	3.6	0.39	0.0000	967	532	0.90	477	0.52

TABLE 13-3

Results for the Standard Exit with Random Entries on a Stop

RAND	NET	NETL	NETS	PFAC	ROA%	ARRR	PROB	DRAW	TRDS	WIN%	AVTR	TRDB
1	-3589	-1057	-2532	0.78	-9.7	-1.20	0.9999	3793	1647	36	-2179	7
2	-3710	-1369	-2341	0.76	-9.9	-1.33	1.0000	3854	1634	37	-2270	7
3	-3296	-1179	-2116	0.79	-9.7	-1.23	0.9999	3495	1634	36	-2017	7
4	-4312	-1405	-2907	0.73	-10.0	-1.55	1.0000	4402	1640	35	-2629	7
5	-3578	-1537	-2040	0.78	-10.0	-1.28	1.0000	3672	1633	36	-2191	7
6	-3308	-1078	-2229	0.79	-9.0	-1.17	0.9999	3779	1598	37	-2070	7
7	-3701	-897	-2803	0.76	-9.5	-1.32	1.0000	4002	1554	35	-2381	7
8	-2065	-1119	-945	0.86	-8.3	-0.72	0.9880	2552	1590	38	-1298	7
9	-3422	-1627	-1795	0.77	-9.5	-1.28	1.0000	3713	1574	37	-2174	7
10	-2744	441	-3186	0.82	-9.6	-0.95	0.9984	2946	1591	38	-1725	7
VER	-1087	42	-1129	0.84	-18.0	-0.84	0.9585	1438	728	35	-1493	7
AVG	-3165	-980	-2184	0.79	-10.3	-1.17	0.9950	3422	1529	36.36	-2039	7.00
STDEV	898	649	699	0.04	2.6	0.24	0.0126	826	268	1.12	391	0.00

standard deviation of $304. In terms of average dollars-per-trade, the less attractive systems that were tested when studying entries were on par with the results for the current system. In fact, some of them performed significantly worse than chance. The percentage of wins was very stable, with the average at 36.91% and a standard deviation of only 0.7%. The total number of trades taken per commodity, over the 10-year in-sample period, was 3,703, about the number it should be, given the probability of taking a random entry on any bar.

Out-of-sample, performance was within the expected range, consistent with in-sample performance. The percentage of wins was 37%, very close to that for in-sample results. The average loss per trade was $1,883, which is within 1 standard deviation of the in-sample estimate. Obviously, the standard exit was unable to pull a profit out of trades entered randomly.

Test 2: SES with Random Entries on Limit.   Table 13-2 is identical to Table 13-1, except that it shows portfolio behavior for the standard exit with random entries taken on a limit order. In-sample, the average loss per trade of $1,930 was somewhat less, demonstrating the effect of the limit order in reducing transaction costs. The standard deviation was somewhat higher: $477. The percentage of winning trades (38.73%) was just under 2% better, due to the better prices achieved with a limit entry. As was anticipated, other than such small changes as those described, nothing else in Table 13-2 is of any great interest.

Out-of-sample, the system lost $3,056 per trade, just over 2 standard deviations worse than in-sample behavior. For whatever reason, the limit order may have had some real effect with random entries, making the system perform more poorly in recent years. The percentage of wins was also slightly worse, i.e., 37%, just under 2 standard deviations below in-sample behavior, but on par with entry at the open.

Test 3: SES with Random Entries on Stop.   Table 13-3 contains information about the portfolio behavior for the standard exit when trades were entered randomly on a stop. In terms of dollars-per-trade, in-sample performance was between that of the other two orders, with a loss per trade of $2,039. The standard deviation was $391. The percentage of wins was lower, 36.36%, with a standard deviation of 1.12%. The lower percentage of wins probably reflects the poorer entry prices achieved using the stop.

Out-of-sample, the average trade and percentage of wins were within 2 standard deviations plus or minus the in-sample figures, demonstrating that out-of-sample performance was within the statistically expected range and fundamentally no different from in-sample performance.

The performance figures in Tables 13-1 through 13-3 provide a baseline (in the form of means and standard deviations) that can serve as a yardstick when evaluating the entries studied in Part II of this book. For this purpose the $TRD and WIN% figures are the best ones to use since they are not influenced by the number of trades taken by a system.

Market-by-Market Performance for SES with Random Entries at Open.   In Table 13-4, the behavior of the standard exit with random entries taken at the open is broken down by market and by sample. The particular randomization used was the one that produced the best in-sample performance (in terms of annualized risk-to-reward ratio) in Test 1. The leftmost column (*SYM*) contains the commodity

TABLE 13-4

Market-by-Market Results for the Standard Exit with Random Entries at the Open

SYM	IN-SAMPLE RESULTS						OUT-OF-SAMPLE RESULTS					
	NETL	NETS	ROA%	AVTR	WIN%	TRDS	NETL	NETS	ROA%	AVTR	WIN%	TRDS
SP	-44	-211	-7.9	-2483	41	103	11	-136	-11.1	-2314	33	54
YX	54	-66	-0.4	-98	40	121	162	-61	23.5	2150	46	47
US	-67	-278	-8.9	-3267	38	106	57	-141	-10.6	-1961	41	43
TB	-271	4	-7.8	-3109	40	86	-78	-255	-16.9	-6410	34	52
TY	-204	-207	-9.2	-3709	36	111	27	-262	-16.2	-4271	32	55
BP	65	-105	-2.7	-385	41	103	-36	-70	-12.7	-2366	44	45
DM	272	-30	25.9	2575	45	94	-106	-129	-23.5	-5033	27	47
SF	111	-217	-3.9	-934	39	114	-128	-128	-22.4	-6259	29	41
JY	260	-150	4.8	897	44	123	-131	175	9.1	770	41	58
CD	-52	-127	-6.5	-1954	38	92	-116	35	-6.0	-1468	30	55
ED	-390	-239	-10.3	-5578	33	113	-60	-78	-12.3	-3384	36	41
CL	-222	-9	-5.9	-1914	36	121	50	2	10.4	1095	37	48
HO	-132	-199	-6.0	-3024	36	110	-121	-134	-22.5	-5570	26	46
HU	60	-206	-3.3	-1279	41	114	-17	0	-5.0	-380	43	46
GC	-36	-199	-7.7	-2313	35	102	37	215	62.9	5770	50	44
SI	-381	-202	-9.8	-4822	34	121	-186	-42	-19.5	-3958	32	58
PL	130	-48	4.2	640	50	128	-183	-157	-22.1	-7109	27	48
PA	-137	-20	-5.5	-1491	37	106	206	-74	25.6	3145	54	42
FC	72	49	5.0	1030	43	118	-160	107	-10.8	-1126	40	47
LC	-14	-129	-6.9	-1309	38	110	-14	-47	-6.6	-1434	30	43
LH	192	-101	3.1	928	47	98	149	-4	20.5	3796	44	38
PB	-283	-143	-8.7	-4064	29	105	-89	-141	-16.0	-4211	32	55
S	-157	-187	-7.6	-3316	35	104	149	-20	28.6	3800	47	34
SM	-56	-49	-3.7	-1095	40	97	50	14	16.3	1268	50	52
BO	-152	-31	-8.0	-1754	40	105	-90	8	-15.6	-1586	38	52
C	-190	60	-6.6	-1244	38	104	-225	14	-22.1	-4482	31	47
O	-295	-19	-9.8	-3185	35	99	-148	-7	-23.1	-3000	36	52
W	-230	-447	-9.9	-5794	27	117	-137	38	-10.6	-2372	30	42
KW	-143	-198	-8.5	-2625	39	130	-219	-89	-23.0	-6716	32	46
MW	138	-178	-1.4	-334	40	118	20	-20	-0.1	-6	44	36
KC	-141	-10	-3.7	-1437	35	106	38	0	6.1	1047	52	36
CC	-141	14	-5.3	-1207	37	105	-117	-40	-19.5	-4051	33	39
SB	-246	-270	-9.3	-4455	35	116	-80	-108	-15.2	-3503	37	54
JO	1	-137	-5.3	-1022	39	133	71	-16	10.4	1214	42	45
CT	34	-224	-6.5	-1826	35	104	-52	-112	-20.6	-3293	40	50
LB	457	-170	8.9	2631	45	109	22	-33	-2.7	-208	37	54
AVG	-59	-130	-4.0	-1731	38	110	-40	-47	-4.8	-1734	38	47
STDEV	190	109	7.0	2027	5	11	111	98	19.4	3238	8	6

symbol. The remaining columns contain information about various aspects of performance, both in-sample and out-of-sample. *NETL* and *NETS* are the net profits for long and short positions (respectively), in thousands of dollars. *ROA%* = the annualized return-on-account. *AVTR* = the average dollars profit or loss per trade. *WIN%* = the percentage of winning trades. *TRDS* = the number of trades taken. The last two rows (*AVG* and *STDEV*) show the averages and standard deviations (respectively) across all markets for the various performance figures.

In-sample, the British Pound, the Japanese Yen, Feeder Cattle, Live Hogs, and Lumber were the only markets that had positive returns. Only the Deutschemark had a strong return on account at 25.9% annualized. Out-of-sample, the NYFE, the Japanese Yen, Light Crude, COMEX Gold, Palladium, Live Hogs, Soybeans, Soybean Meal, Coffee, and Orange Juice had positive returns. Only the Japanese Yen and Live Hogs were profitable in both samples. The random entry system was among the least consistent systems of those examined in the study of entries.

The average trade, across all markets, lost $1,731 in-sample and $1,734 out-of-sample. Long trades lost less than shorts, a finding observed many times. In-sample, all the currencies, except the Canadian Dollar and Eurodollars, were profitable on the long side. These are trendy markets, and therefore, such profitability is likely due to the behavior of the standard exit, not to chance factors involved in the random entries.

The analysis of the standard exit with random entries taken using various entry orders should serve well as a baseline of comparison for both the real, non-random entries (studied in earlier chapters) and the more sophisticated exits (to be studied in subsequent chapters).

TESTS OF THE MODIFIED SES

The next test involves changing the SES a bit, thus producing the *modified standard exit strategy* (MSES). The SES is made more realistic by allowing the money management stop and profit target limit to function inside the bar, not merely at the close. To avoid ambiguities in the simulation when using end-of-day data, all entries are now restricted to the open. This allows complete freedom to explore a wide range of exit strategies. Other than lifting the restriction to the close, the MSES is identical to the original SES used when testing entries. The rules for the MSES are as follows: Upon entry, set up an exit stop below (long positions) or above (short positions) the entry price and an exit limit above (long) or below (short) the entry price. Place the exit stop some multiple (the money management stop parameter) of the average true range away from the entry price. Place the exit limit some other multiple (the profit target parameter) of the average true range away from the entry price. Exit on the close after 10 days have elapsed if neither the money management stop nor the profit target limit has yet closed out the trade. A 50-bar average true range is used in these rules. The code below implements random entries at the open together with the modified standard exit strategy.

```
static void Model (float *parms, float *dt, float *opn, float *hi,
float *lo, float *cls, float *vol, float *oi, float *dlrv, int nb,
TRDSIM &ts, float *eqcls) {
```

```
// Implements random entries with modified standard exit
// File = x19mod02.c
// parms    - vector [1..MAXPRM] of parameters
// dt       - vector [1..nb] of dates in YYMMDD form
// opn      - vector [1..nb] of opening prices
// hi       - vector [1..nb] of high prices
// lo       - vector [1..nb] of low prices
// cls      - vector [1..nb] of closing prices
// vol      - vector [1..nb] of volumes
// oi       - vector [1..nb] of open interest numbers
// dlrv     - vector [1..nb] of average dollar volatilities
// nb       - number of bars in data series or vectors
// ts       - trading simulator class instance
// eqcls    - vector [1..nb] of closing equity levels

// declare local scratch variables
static int rc, cb, ncontracts, maxhold, signal, ranseed;
static float mmstp, ptlim, limprice, stpprice;
static int entryposted, entrybar;
static float exitatr[MAXBAR+1], rnum, entryprice;
static long iseed;

// copy parameters to local variables for clearer reference
ranseed = parms[8];   // used to select random seed
maxhold = 10;         // maximum holding period in days
ptlim   = 4.0;        // profit target limit in atr units
mmstp   = 1.0;        // money mgmt stop in atr units

// perform whole-series calculations
AvgTrueRangeS(exitatr,hi,lo,cls,50,nb); // ATR for exit

// seed the random number generator
// ... use a different seed for each tradeable
// ... ts.model() returns a market index (SP=1, YX=2, ...)
iseed = -(ranseed + 10 * ts.model());
rnum = ran2(&iseed);

// step through bars (days) to simulate actual trading
for(cb = 1; cb <= nb; cb++) {

   // take no trades before the in-sample period
   // ... same as TradeStation's MaxBarsBack setting
   if(dt[cb] < IS_DATE) { eqcls[cb] = 0.0; continue; }

   // execute any pending orders and save closing equity
   rc = ts.update(opn[cb], hi[cb], lo[cb], cls[cb], cb);
   if(rc != 0) nrerror("Trade buffer overflow");
   eqcls[cb] = ts.currentequity(EQ_CLOSETOTAL);
```

```
// calculate number of contracts to trade
// ... we want to trade the dollar volatility equivalent
// ... of 2 new S&P-500 contracts as of 12/31/98
ncontracts = RoundToInteger(5673.0 / dlrv[cb]);
if(ncontracts < 1) ncontracts = 1;

// avoid placing orders on possibly limit-locked days
if(hi[cb+1] == lo[cb+1]) continue;

// generate "standard" random entry signals
signal = 0;
rnum = ran2(&iseed); // random number between 0 and 1
if(rnum < 0.025) signal = -1;      // random short entry
else if(rnum > 0.975) signal = 1;  // random long entry

// enter trades on the open
entryposted = 0;
if(ts.position() <= 0 && signal == 1) {
    ts.buyopen('1', ncontracts);
    entryposted = 1;
    entryprice = opn[cb+1];
    entrybar = cb + 1;
}
else if(ts.position() >= 0 && signal == -1) {
    ts.sellopen('2', ncontracts);
    entryposted = -1;
    entryprice = opn[cb+1];
    entrybar = cb + 1;
 }

// exit trades using the modified standard exit
if(entryposted > 0) {
    // initialization and exits for longs on entry day
    limprice = entryprice + ptlim * exitatr[cb];
    stpprice = entryprice - mmstp * exitatr[cb];
    ts.exitlonglimit('A', limprice);
    ts.exitlongstop('B', stpprice);
}
else if(entryposted < 0) {
    // initialization and exits for shorts on entry day
    limprice = entryprice - ptlim * exitatr[cb];
    stpprice = entryprice + mmstp * exitatr[cb];
    ts.exitshortlimit('C', limprice);
    ts.exitshortstop('D', stpprice);
}
else {
```

```
                    // exits for after the entry day
                    if(ts.position() > 0) { // longs
                       ts.exitlonglimit('F', limprice);
                       ts.exitlongstop('G', stpprice);
                       if(cb-entrybar >= maxhold) ts.exitlongclose(`E');
                    }
                    else if(ts.position() < 0) { // shorts
                       ts.exitshortlimit('I', limprice);
                       ts.exitshortstop('J', stpprice);
                       if(cb-entrybar >= maxhold) ts.exitshortclose('H');
                    }
                 }
              } // process next bar
        }
```

The code used to run the current test is identical to the code used for the ear-lier test, except for changes required by the modified exit strategy. A trade is entered on a random signal that is generated as discussed earlier. However, buying and selling occur only on the open. In addition, information is recorded about entry activity, i.e., whether an entry (long, short, or none) was posted on the cur-rent bar (*entryposted*), the price (*entryprice*) at which the entry took place (if one was posted), and the bar on which it took place (*entrybar*). This data is required in computing the exits. The exits are then generated. If an entry is posted for the next bar (i.e., if the market is entered long or short at the open of the next bar), a prof-it target and a stop loss are also posted for that bar. For the longs, the stop loss, or money management stop, is set at the entry price minus a parameter that is multi-plied by the average true range. The limit price for the profit target is set as the entry price plus another parameter that is multiplied by the average true range. If, on the current bar, a short entry is posted for the next open, then orders are also posted to exit the resulting short position on a limit or a stop. The limit and stop are calculated in a manner similar to that for the longs, except the directions are flipped around. If a given bar is not an entry bar, a check is made to determine whether there is an existing position after the close of the bar. If there is, two orders (possibly three) are posted: the money management stop and profit target limit orders, using the stop and limit prices calculated on the bar the entry was ini-tially posted; and if the trade has been held for more than *maxhold* bars, an order to exit on the close is also posted.

TEST RESULTS

Test 4: MSES with Random Entries at Open.   Table 13-5, which has the same format as Tables 13-1 through 13-3, provides data on the portfolio performance of the modified standard exit strategy with trades entered randomly at the open. In-sample, the average trade lost $1,702, with a standard deviation of $365. The percentage of wins was 31.73%, with a standard deviation of 1.10%. The average trade lost less than it did in the tests of the original, unmodified SES. The reduction in the loss on the average trade was undoubtedly caused by the ability of the MSES to more quickly escape from bad trades, cutting losses short. The more rapid and frequent escapes also explain the decline in the percentage of winning trades. There were fewer wins, but the average loss per trade was smaller, an interesting combination. Overall, the MSES should be regarded as an improvement on the unmodified standard exit.

Out-of-sample, the average trade lost $836. Statistically, this was significantly better than the in-sample performance. It seems that, in more recent years, this exit provided a greater improvement than it did in earlier years. The markets may be more demanding than they were in the past of the ability to close out bad trades quickly. Other figures in Table 13-5 indicate a similar pattern of changes.

Market-by-Market Results for MSES with Random Entries at Open.   Table 13-6 contains the market-by-market results for the MSES with the best set of random entries taken at the open. The best set was chosen from the randomizations shown in Table 13-5. The Swiss Franc, Light Crude, Heating Oil, COMEX Gold, and Live Cattle had positive returns both in- and out-of-sample. For some markets, the MSES was able to pull consistent profits out of randomly entered trades! Many more markets were profitable in both samples than when the unmodified SES was

TABLE 13-5

Results for the Modified Standard Exit with Random Entries at the Open

RAND	NET	NETL	NETS	PFAC	ROA%	ARRR	PROB	DRAW	TRDS	WIN%	AVTR	TRDB
1	-6334	-2058	-4276	0.81	-10.3	-1.69	1.0000	6294	3983	33	-1590	6
2	-6258	-1603	-4654	0.81	-10.0	-1.68	1.0000	6391	3982	31	-1571	6
3	-7606	-2075	-5530	0.77	-10.2	-2.14	1.0000	7646	3939	31	-1931	6
4	-7645	-2426	-5219	0.77	-9.8	-2.09	1.0000	7989	3980	31	-1921	6
5	-8243	-2625	-5618	0.76	-10.1	-2.23	1.0000	8393	3899	31	-2114	6
6	-7706	-2260	-5445	0.77	-10.0	-2.06	1.0000	7902	3917	31	-1967	6
7	-7728	-2278	-5449	0.77	-10.0	-2.15	1.0000	7912	3898	31	-1982	6
8	-6591	-1966	-4625	0.80	-10.2	-1.80	1.0000	6609	3811	31	-1729	6
9	-6861	-2580	-4280	0.79	-9.9	-1.85	1.0000	7114	3932	32	-1745	6
10	-5306	-344	-4961	0.84	-9.5	-1.43	1.0000	5749	3973	33	-1335	6
VER	-1444	175	-1620	0.90	-21.9	-0.85	0.9598	1570	1728	34	-836	6
AVG	-6520	-1822	-4698	0.80	-11.1	-1.82	0.9963	6688	3731	31.73	-1702	6
STDEV	1891	914	1133	0.04	3.6	0.41	0.0121	1897	666	1.10	365	0

used, again a sure sign that the more responsive, modified exit is better. As usual, and across both samples, the long side was more profitable (lost less) than the short side. Surprisingly, out-of-sample, the long side actually turned a very small whole-portfolio profit with this exit strategy; it is, however, nothing one would want to trade.

TABLE 13-6

Market-by-Market Results for the Modified Standard Exit
with Random Entries at the Open

SYM	IN-SAMPLE RESULTS						OUT-OF-SAMPLE RESULTS					
	NETL	NETS	ROA%	AVTR	WIN%	TRDS	NETL	NETS	ROA%	AVTR	WIN%	TRDS
SP	216	-187	2.0	256	32	113	26	-155	-17.3	-2639	30	49
YX	82	-44	1.8	321	40	116	112	-118	-1.1	-148	36	44
US	-69	-171	-7.3	-2171	34	111	15	-106	-10.0	-1652	30	55
TB	-95	-262	-8.8	-3191	35	112	-81	-272	-23.8	-7223	28	49
TY	-124	-210	-8.5	-3281	29	102	-87	-111	-19.1	-5101	30	39
BP	-26	25	-0.1	-12	34	119	31	30	9.4	1254	36	49
DM	188	-218	-1.3	-281	34	106	60	9	14.2	1492	42	47
SF	127	0	4.6	1229	38	104	64	-32	6.7	617	40	52
JY	155	-131	1.2	244	37	97	-56	36	-2.7	-415	34	49
CD	54	-193	-5.8	-1203	32	116	-163	30	-12.3	-2516	30	53
ED	-100	-335	-9.4	-4226	33	103	-138	-247	-22.0	-7022	34	55
CL	66	-19	3.4	430	42	110	82	55	32.0	2462	35	56
HO	257	-5	13.2	2276	42	111	-35	72	5.0	933	41	39
HU	-38	0	-2.3	-328	35	118	195	-193	0.5	32	38	55
GC	200	131	18.5	2806	43	118	-53	174	26.3	2823	41	43
SI	-176	-160	-6.6	-3368	29	100	-95	-5	-13.3	-2352	30	43
PL	-234	-302	-10.0	-5415	26	99	126	5	26.6	2549	42	52
PA	-238	-272	-8.1	-4333	30	118	62	-57	0.7	96	35	51
FC	-33	-283	-9.3	-2331	28	136	-6	-113	-14.6	-2502	33	48
LC	261	-54	11.5	1989	36	104	85	-50	6.0	747	41	48
LH	8	-193	-6.2	-1581	33	117	-42	-8	-11.0	-925	29	55
PB	18	-60	-2.9	-415	37	102	129	-157	-3.9	-569	33	48
S	-8	-11	-0.7	-176	37	113	-82	-217	-21.3	-5270	22	57
SM	-43	-222	-7.0	-2858	30	93	83	-92	-2.4	-227	32	43
BO	46	-64	-1.1	-154	35	114	97	154	94.3	7182	51	35
C	-285	-357	-9.9	-5952	25	108	171	-109	8.9	1161	41	53
O	-290	-225	-8.9	-4871	26	106	6	-94	-7.7	-1892	32	46
W	14	-89	-3.0	-714	35	105	-80	33	-4.9	-910	29	51
KW	45	-141	-3.1	-869	31	111	-61	72	2.5	286	35	39
MW	-269	-451	-8.8	-5953	20	121	-45	-141	-20.2	-4082	23	46
KC	-10	-44	-3.0	-484	31	114	41	-43	-0.4	-47	23	55
CC	-188	-83	-9.0	-2520	32	108	-87	26	-9.5	-1132	38	54
SB	-77	-13	-4.1	-810	36	112	-28	26	-0.4	-29	37	54
JO	73	-27	2.8	358	38	128	-84	9	-10.3	-1764	34	43
CT	54	-133	-3.2	-727	36	108	28	-18	1.9	269	31	38
LB	96	-146	-1.4	-498	32	100	-11	-10	-3.4	-620	28	35
AVG	-10	-137	-2.5	-1356	33	110	5	-45	0.1	-754	34	48
STDEV	151	126	6.7	2253	5	9	88	104	21.0	2773	6	6

CONCLUSION

The results clearly demonstrate that many of the entry strategies tested in earlier chapters using the SES were no better than random entries. Sometimes they were worse. The results also indicate that the SES is not a great exit strategy. The MSES, which simply lifts the restriction of the exit to the close, performed much better and even managed to pull a small profit out-of-sample on the long side. The MSES should still be considered a minimalist exit strategy, but the results support the contention that a really good exit strategy is, more than anything else, the key to successful trading. If the findings from this and previous studies are correct, it should be possible to find an exit strategy that can actually extract substantial profits from randomly entered trades, at least in some markets. Such an exit strategy would substantiate what many great traders have said: An experienced trader, skilled in money management, can make a profit even with a bad system, while a novice trader, unskilled in money management, can lose everything trading a great system (*system*, in this context, usually referring to an entry model). In all the remaining tests in this book, the MSES will replace the original, unmodified exit strategy (SES).

WHAT HAVE WE LEARNED?

- A good exit strategy is extremely important. It can even pull profits from randomly entered trades! Think of what it could do for trades entered on the basis of something better than the toss of the die.
- Even simple modifications can make a big difference, as evidenced by the results above where slight changes proved effective.
- When combined with the suboptimal SES, many of the entry strategies tested in the previous section of this book can be seen to perform no better than the random one. Some even did worse! Of course, a few performed dramatically better than did the random entry model.

CHAPTER 14

Improvements on the Standard Exit

In continuation of the endeavor to improve upon the standard exit strategy (SES) and develop a good exit, a number of modifications are explored. In the previous chapter, it was demonstrated that the exit strategy can have a substantial impact on the overall performance of a trading system. To make it more compatible with the kinds of exit strategies examined in this and the next chapter, the original SES (used in the study of entries) was changed and became the modified SES (or MSES): While maintaining consistency, the restriction of exiting at the close was removed. It was no longer necessary to restrict the exit to the close, because in the study of exits, entries are restricted to the open. In previous chapters, entries were not restricted to the open. Therefore, to avoid ambiguity in the simulations, it was necessary to restrict exits to the close. The MSES represents a kind of baseline, minimalist exit that can serve as a standard for comparing better exit methods, as well as provide some consistency and comparability with the unmodified SES. In this chapter, variations, both small and large, of the MSES are explored in an attempt to find a better exit strategy.

PURPOSE OF THE TESTS

When specifying the original SES (as well as when modifying it so that inside-the-bar stops and limits could be used), specifications for the tightness of the money management stop and closeness of the profit target were arbitrary and fixed. For long entries, the money management stop was placed at 1 average true range unit below the entry price, while the profit target was placed 4 average true range units above the entry price. For short entries, the placements were reversed. The intention was to place a stop fairly close in so that losing trades would quickly be taken out, while placing the profit target far enough away so profits would not be cut short on trades that were favorable. The first test below examines the performance of the stop and profit target when the arbitrary settings are adjusted.

The second set of tests involves replacing the fixed money management stop in the MSES with a more dynamic stop. The minimalist MSES lacks many desirable characteristics. One of the features any good trader wants in an exit is the ability to lock in at least some of the paper profit that develops in the course of a successful trade, i.e., to avoid having to watch profitable trades turn into losers. Locking in some of the profit can be accomplished using a trailing stop: Instead of having a money management stop placed a fixed distance from the entry price, the stop moves toward current prices as the trade becomes profitable. As prices move in the trade's favor, the stop moves in along with them, locking in a proportion of the developing profits. Should the market reverse, the trade will not be closed out at a loss, as might have been the case with the fixed stop, but at a profit, if the moving stop has gone into positive territory. There are several strategies for the placement and relocation of a stop designed to prevent winning trades from turning into losers and to lock in as much of the unrealized profit as possible. The second set of tests explores such strategies.

Originally, the profit target in the MSES (and SES) was implemented as a limit order with a fixed placement. In the third set of tests, the fixed profit target is, like the stop in the previous tests, replaced with something more dynamic. It would be desirable if the profit target could also move in toward the prices, especially in languishing trades. This would enable the trader to exit at a better price, perhaps even with a small profit, in the absence of strong, favorable movement. Exiting the market on spikes or noise should lead to more profitable trades than simply exiting on a time constraint or waiting for the money management stop to be hit. At the same time, the trader does not want the profit target to cut profits short. A profit target that is too close might provide a higher percentage of winning trades, but it will also significantly limit the size of the profits. In all likelihood, it will cause the overall strategy to perform less well. It should be advantageous to make the profit target dynamic in the same way that the stop was made dynamic, i.e., to place the profit target far away from the market at the beginning of the trade, or when the market is steadily moving in a favorable direction. In this way, it would not be necessary to settle for a small profit on a potentially very profitable trade; the trader could "let profits run." Conversely, in trades that are languishing, or when the market is exhibiting blow-off behavior, the profit target could be made to move in tight to close out the trade, and to do so at the best possible price, before the market has a chance to reverse. Modifications of the profit target limit order placement are studied below.

Finally, the time limit exit from the MSES model is adjusted and tested on the assumption that, with effective dynamic stops and profit targets, a short time limit is no longer so necessary. Trades will be exited quickly by other means if they are languishing, but will be held for as long as possible if favorable movement is occurring. The intention is to let profits develop and not be cut short simply because of an order to exit on an arbitrary time limit.

TESTS OF THE FIXED STOP AND PROFIT TARGET

The MSES makes use of a fixed stop and profit target that do not change their placements during a trade. Originally, the parameters for the placement of these stops were somewhat arbitrary and certainly not optimal. What happens when these parameters are stepped through a range of values in search of an optimal combination?

In this test, the money management stop parameter is stepped from 0.5 to 3.5 in increments of 0.5. The profit target limit parameter is also stepped from 0.5 to 5 in increments of 0.5. The profit target parameter is simply the multiple of the average true range used in placing the profit target limit. Likewise, the money management stop parameter is the multiple of the average true range used for placing the money management stop.

```
float *lo, float *cls, float *vol, float *oi, float *dlrv, int nb,
TRDSIM &ts, float *eqcls) {

    // Implements random entries with variations on the
    // modified standard exit. This model tests the
    // MSE using variations in its parameters.
    // File = x20mod01.c
    // parms    - vector [1..MAXPRM] of parameters
    // dt       - vector [1..nb] of dates in YYMMDD form
    // opn      - vector [1..nb] of opening prices
    // hi       - vector [1..nb] of high prices
    // lo       - vector [1..nb] of low prices
    // cls      - vector [1..nb] of closing prices
    // vol      - vector [1..nb] of volumes
    // oi       - vector [1..nb] of open interest numbers
    // dlrv     - vector [1..nb] of average dollar volatilities
    // nb       - number of bars in data series or vectors
    // ts       - trading simulator class instance
    // eqcls    - vector [1..nb] of closing equity levels

    // declare local scratch variables
    static int rc, cb, ncontracts, maxhold, signal, ranseed;
    static float mmstp, ptlim, limprice, stpprice;
    static int entryposted, entrybar;
    static float exitatr[MAXBAR+1], rnum, entryprice;
    static long iseed;
```

```
// copy parameters to local variables for clearer reference
ptlim = parms[1];      // profit target limit in atr units
mmstp = parms[2];      // money mgmt stop in atr units
maxhold = parms[3];    // maximum holding period in days
ranseed = parms[8];    // used to select random seed

// perform whole-series calculations
AvgTrueRangeS(exitatr,hi,lo,cls,50,nb);            // ATR for exit

// seed the random number generator
// ... use a different seed for each tradeable
// ... ts.model() returns a market index (SP=1, YX=2, ...)
iseed = -(ranseed + 10 * ts.model());
rnum = ran2(&iseed);

// step through bars (days) to simulate actual trading
for(cb = 1; cb <= nb; cb++) {

    // take no trades before the in-sample period
    // ... same as TradeStation's MaxBarsBack setting
    if(dt[cb] < IS_DATE) { eqcls[cb] = 0.0; continue; }

    // execute any pending orders and save closing equity
    rc = ts.update(opn[cb], hi[cb], lo[cb], cls[cb], cb);
    if(rc != 0) nrerror("Trade buffer overflow");
    eqcls[cb] = ts.currentequity(EQ_CLOSETOTAL);

    // calculate number of contracts to trade
    // ... we want to trade the dollar volatility equivalent
    // ... of 2 new S&P-500 contracts as of 12/31/98
    ncontracts = RoundToInteger(5673.0 / dlrv[cb]);
    if(ncontracts < 1) ncontracts = 1;

    // avoid placing orders on possibly limit-locked days
    if(hi[cb+1] == lo[cb+1]) continue;

    // generate "standard" random entry signals
    signal = 0;
    rnum = ran2(&iseed);
    if(rnum < 0.025) signal = -1;    // random short entry
    // random short entry               // random long entry
    else if(rnum > 0.975) signal = 1;

    // enter trades on the open
    entryposted = 0;
    if(ts.position() <= 0 && signal == 1) {
        ts.buyopen('1', ncontracts);
        entryposted = 1;
```

```
            entryprice = opn[cb+1];
            entrybar = cb + 1;
        }
        else if(ts.position() >= 0 && signal == -1) {
            ts.sellopen('2', ncontracts);
            entryposted = -1;
            entryprice = opn[cb+1];
            entrybar = cb + 1;
        }

        // exit trades using the modified standard exit
        if(entryposted > 0) {
            // initialization and exits for longs on entry day
            limprice = entryprice + ptlim * exitatr[cb];
            stpprice = entryprice - mmstp * exitatr[cb];
            ts.exitlonglimit('A', limprice);
            ts.exitlongstop('B', stpprice);
        }
        else if(entryposted < 0) {
            // initialization and exits for shorts on entry day
            limprice = entryprice - ptlim * exitatr[cb];
            stpprice = entryprice + mmstp * exitatr[cb];
            ts.exitshortlimit('C', limprice);
            ts.exitshortstop('D', stpprice);
        }
        else {
            // exits for after the entry day
            if(ts.position() > 0) {           // longs
                ts.exitlonglimit('F', limprice);
                ts.exitlongstop('G', stpprice);
                if(cb-entrybar >= maxhold) ts.exitlongclose('E');
            }
            else if(ts.position() < 0) { // shorts
                ts.exitshortlimit('I', limprice);
                ts.exitshortstop('J', stpprice);
                if(cb-entrybar >= maxhold) ts.exitshortclose('H');
            }
        }
    } // process next bar
}
```

The code implements the standard random entry at the open and the modified standard exit strategy. The rules for the exit are as follows: A limit order exit is placed a certain number of true range units above (long) or below (short) the entry price. The number of true range units that the limit order is placed away from the entry price is specified by the parameter *ptlim*. Besides the profit target limit, an exit stop is placed a specified number of average true range units below (long) or above (short) the entry price. The parameter *mmstp* determines the number of true range units that the stop is placed away from the entry price. Finally, *maxhold* is a parameter that specifies the maximum time any position is held. If they were not closed out earlier by the profit target limit or money management stop, all trades will be closed out with an exit at the close after *maxhold* days or bars have elapsed since entry. In the test, *maxhold* is fixed at a value of 10, the same value used throughout the tests in this book.

Table 14-1 shows the annualized risk-to-reward ratio (*ARRR*), the percentage of winning trades (*WIN%*), and the average trade profit or loss (*AVTR*), for every combination of money management stop and profit target limit parameter settings. At the right of the table, the *AVG* or average values (average taken over all money management stop parameters) for all the performance figures are presented for each profit target limit parameter value. At the bottom of the table, the *AVG* or averages (taken over all profit target limit parameters) for each of the money management stops are shown.

A number of things are immediately apparent in the results. As the profit target limit got tighter, the percentage of winning trades increased; this was expected. A tight profit target has a greater chance of being hit and of pulling a small profit out of the market. However, the increased percentage of winning trades with tighter profit targets was not sufficient to overcome the effects of cutting profits short on trades that had the potential to yield greater profits. Looser profit targets performed better than tight ones. For most of the profit target limits, there was an optimal placement for the money management stop, between a value of 1.0 and 2.0 average true range units away from the entry price. As the stop got looser, the percentage of winning trades increased, but the other performance figures worsened. As it got tighter, the percentage of winning trades declined along with the other measures of performance.

The overall optimal performance, in terms of both annualized risk-to-reward ratio and average trade, was with a profit target limit of 4.5 and a money management stop of 1.5. As deviation from the optimal combination occurred, the annualized risk-to-reward ratio increased, as did the average loss per trade. There was relatively little interaction between placement of the profit target and the money management stop. The values that were optimal for one varied only slightly as the parameter controlling the other was adjusted. Another almost equally good combination of parameters was 1.5 and 4 (profit target and stop, respectively). This provided a very slightly better average trade and a trivially worse annualized risk-to-reward ratio. It is interesting that the arbitrarily assigned values came fairly close to the optimal values, appearing only one cell away from the optimal cells in Table 14-1. The optimal values, however, provided 6% more winning trades than the arbitrary values of 4 (profit target) and 1 (stop).

TABLE 14-1

In-Sample Portfolio Performance with Modified Standard Exit and Random Entry as a Function of Profit Target Limit (Left) and Money Management Stop (Top) Parameters

PTLIM	\ MMSTP	0.5	1.0	1.5	2.0	2.5	3.0	3.5	AVG
0.5	ARRR	-7.37	-5.25	-4.32	-3.65	-3.47	-3.45	-3.54	-4.44
	WIN%	46	62	69	73	75	75	76	68
	AVTR	-2232	-2131	-2094	-2022	-2085	-2210	-2364	-2163
1.0	ARRR	-4.70	-3.15	-2.62	-2.35	-2.43	-2.53	-2.55	-2.90
	WIN%	34	49	57	60	62	62	63	55
	AVTR	-1922	-1771	-1749	-1778	-1974	-2159	-2278	-1947
1.5	ARRR	-3.75	-2.49	-2.16	-2.02	-2.09	-2.17	-2.16	-2.41
	WIN%	27	41	48	52	53	54	54	47
	AVTR	-1861	-1709	-1736	-1812	-1983	-2147	-2221	-1924
2.0	ARRR	-3.56	-2.36	-2.07	-1.99	-2.05	-2.11	-2.07	-2.32
	WIN%	22	36	43	46	48	49	49	42
	AVTR	-2011	-1816	-1844	-1951	-2117	-2261	-2288	-2041
2.5	ARRR	-3.22	-2.17	-1.86	-1.80	-1.91	-1.98	-1.93	-2.12
	WIN%	21	34	41	44	46	46	47	40
	AVTR	-1980	-1809	-1786	-1882	-2083	-2236	-2248	-2003
3.0	ARRR	-2.99	-2.02	-1.70	-1.69	-1.81	-1.89	-1.87	-2.00
	WIN%	20	33	40	43	45	46	46	39
	AVTR	-1960	-1779	-1722	-1844	-2057	-2226	-2259	-1978
3.5	ARRR	-2.86	-1.93	-1.63	-1.63	-1.75	-1.83	-1.81	-1.92
	WIN%	19	33	40	43	45	45	46	39
	AVTR	-1949	-1757	-1689	-1806	-2030	-2190	-2226	-1950
4.0	ARRR	-2.61	-1.69	-1.47	-1.50	-1.62	-1.69	-1.68	-1.75
	WIN%	19	33	39	43	44	45	46	38
	AVTR	-1846	-1590	-1568	-1712	-1922	-2068	-2108	-1831
4.5	ARRR	-2.54	-1.66	-1.46	-1.48	-1.60	-1.68	-1.67	-1.73
	WIN%	19	32	39	43	44	45	45	38
	AVTR	-1824	-1590	-1581	-1714	-1933	-2077	-2109	-1833
5.0	ARRR	-2.53	-1.66	-1.46	-1.46	-1.57	-1.64	-1.62	-1.71
	WIN%	19	32	39	42	44	45	45	38
	AVTR	-1847	-1613	-1604	-1704	-1917	-2058	-2082	-1832
AVG	ARRR	-3.61	-2.44	-2.08	-1.96	-2.03	-2.10	-2.09	-2.33
	WIN%	25	39	46	49	51	51	52	44
	AVTR	-1943	-1757	-1737	-1823	-2010	-2163	-2218	-1950

The percentage of wins for the optimal solution was 39%. When the numbers were examined in relationship to those for a profit target limit of 0.5 (with the same stop), 69% (instead of 39%) winning trades resulted, but with a much worse risk-to-reward ratio and average trade. This clearly shows the importance of letting profits run or, at least, not cutting them short.

No combinations of parameters yielded profitable results. Given that this is a minimalist exit strategy, and that random entries were being used, such an outcome was expected. Nevertheless, the performance of the exit strategy across different parameter combinations can be compared.

Conclusion

Profits should not be cut short even though a higher percentage of winning trades might be gained. Doing so may make the average trade a larger loser or smaller winner. In addition, there appears to be an optimal placement for a fixed money management stop. Too wide a stop increases the percentage of wins. However, it also increases the overall loss. Too tight a stop keeps the individual losses small, but drastically cuts the percentage of winning trades, again resulting in worse overall performance. An optimal value provides a moderate percentage of winning trades and the best performance. In this case, the optimal distance to place the money management stop away from the entry price was 1.5 average true range units. With some entry systems, the optimal placement might be much closer.

TESTS OF DYNAMIC STOPS

In this group of tests, the fixed money management stop of the MSES is replaced with what will; it is hoped, be a much better stop. The placement of the stop is dynamically adjusted. The goal is to capture as much unrealized profit as possible, while not turning potentially profitable trades into losing ones, as might happen with an overly tight, fixed stop.

There are many ways to adjust the stop so that it follows or trails the market, locking in some of the profit that develops in the course of a trade. One popular method is, for long positions, to place the stop for the next bar at the lowest of the lows of the current and previous bars. The stop is only placed at progressively higher levels, never lower levels. For short positions, the stop is placed at the highest of the current bar's and previous bar's highs. It is only allowed to move down, never up. This simple methodology is examined in the first test.

The second test is of a dynamic stop that mimics the fixed stop used in the MSES. The stop is adjusted up (long) or down (short) based on the current price minus (long) or plus (short) a multiple of the average true range. Unlike the stop used in the MSES, where the placement was fixed, the placement revisions of this stop are based on current market value. The revised placements may only occur in one direction: up for long positions, down for short ones. The intention is to keep the stop a similar statistical distance from the best current price achieved at each stage of the trade, just as it was from the original entry price. The stop for long positions is calculated as follows: (1) Subtract from the entry price a parameter (*mmstp*) multiplied by the average true range (the result is the stop for the next bar). (2) On the next bar, subtract from the current price another parameter (*stpa*) multiplied by the average true range. (3) If the stop resulting from the calculations in Step 2 is greater than the current stop, then replace the current stop with the resultant stop; otherwise the stop remains unchanged. (4) Repeat Steps 2 and 3 for each successive bar. In the stop for short positions, the multiples of the average true range are added to the market prices and the stops are ratcheted down.

The third test involves a more sophisticated approach. For long positions, the stop is initialized a certain number of average true range units below the entry price, as usual. The stop is then moved up an amount that is determined by how far the current prices are above the stop's current value. For short positions, the initialization occurs above the entry price, and the stop is moved down to an extent determined by how far the current prices are below it. The stop initially moves in quickly, losing momentum as it reaches the vicinity of the current price level. This method involves nothing more than a kind of offset exponential moving average (EMA), except that the moving average is initialized in a special way on entry to the trade and is only allowed to move in one direction; i.e., the stop is never pulled further away from the market, only closer. The stop for long positions is calculated as follows: (1) Initialize the stop to be used on the entry bar by subtracting from the entry price a parameter (*mmstp*) multiplied by the average true range. (2) At the next bar, subtract from the high a parameter (*stpa*) multiplied by the average true range; then subtract the current placement of the stop, and finally multiply by another parameter (*stpb*). (3) If the resultant number from Step 2 is greater than zero, then add that number to the value of the current stop; otherwise the stop remains unaltered. (4) Repeat Steps 2 and 3 for each successive bar. In the stop for short positions, the multiples of the average true range are added to the market prices and only corrections that are negative are added to the stop prices.

```
static void Model (float *parms, float *dt, float *opn, float *hi,
float *lo, float *cls, float *vol, float *oi, float *dlrv, int nb,
TRDSIM &ts, float *eqcls) {

    // Implements random entry tests of the standard exit
    // strategy modified to use "dynamic" stops.
    // File = x20mod02.c
    // parms   - vector [1..MAXPRM] of parameters
    // dt      - vector [1..nb] of dates in YYMMDD form
    // opn     - vector [1..nb] of opening prices
```

```
// hi      - vector [1..nb] of high prices
// lo      - vector [1..nb] of low prices
// cls     - vector [1..nb] of closing prices
// vol     - vector [1..nb] of volumes
// oi      - vector [1..nb] of open interest numbers
// dlrv    - vector [1..nb] of average dollar volatilities
// nb      - number of bars in data series or vectors
// ts      - trading simulator class instance
// eqcls   - vector [1..nb] of closing equity levels

// declare local scratch variables
static int rc, cb, ncontracts, maxhold, signal, ranseed;
static float stpa, stpb, mmstp, ptlim, limprice, stpprice;
static int entryposted, entrybar, modeltype;
static float exitatr[MAXBAR+1], rnum, entryprice, tmp, atr;
static long iseed;

// copy parameters to local variables for clearer reference
mmstp     = parms[1]; // used to set the initial stop
stpa      = parms[2]; // additional stop parameter
stpb      = parms[3]; // additional stop parameter
ptlim     = parms[6]; // profit target limit in atr units
modeltype = parms[7]; // type of dynamic stop to use
maxhold   = parms[8]; // maximum holding period in days
ranseed   = parms[9]; // used to select random seed

// perform whole-series calculations
AvgTrueRangeS(exitatr,hi,lo,cls,50,nb);      // ATR for exit

// seed the random number generator
// ... use a different seed for each tradeable
// ... ts.model() returns a market index (SP=1, YX=2, ...)
iseed = -(ranseed + 10 * ts.model());
rnum = ran2(&iseed);

// step through bars (days) to simulate actual trading
for(cb = 1; cb <= nb; cb++) {

    // take no trades before the in-sample period
    // ... same as TradeStation's MaxBarsBack setting
    if(dt[cb] < IS_DATE) { eqcls[cb] = 0.0; continue; }

    // execute any pending orders and save closing equity
    rc = ts.update(opn[cb], hi[cb], lo[cb], cls[cb], cb);
    if(rc != 0) nrerror("Trade buffer overflow");
    eqcls[cb] = ts.currentequity(EQ_CLOSETOTAL);
```

```
// calculate number of contracts to trade
// ... we want to trade the dollar volatility equivalent
// ... of 2 new S&P-500 contracts as of 12/31/98
ncontracts = RoundToInteger(5673.0 / dlrv[cb]);
if(ncontracts < 1) ncontracts = 1;

// avoid placing orders on possibly limit-locked days
if(hi[cb+1] == lo[cb+1]) continue;

// generate "standard" random entry signals
signal = 0;
rnum = ran2(&iseed);
if(rnum < 0.025) signal = -1;      // random short entry
else if(rnum > 0.975) signal = 1; // random long entry

// enter trades on the open
entryposted = 0;
if(ts.position() <= 0 && signal == 1) {
    ts.buyopen('1', ncontracts);
    entryposted = 1;
    entryprice = opn[cb+1];
    entrybar = cb + 1;
}
else if(ts.position() >= 0 && signal == -1) {
    ts.sellopen('2', ncontracts);
    entryposted = -1;
    entryprice = opn[cb+1];
    entrybar = cb + 1;
}

// exit trades using basic exit with improved stops
atr = exitatr[cb];
if(entryposted > 0) {
    // initialization and exits for longs on entry day
    switch(modeltype) {
      case 1:
       limprice = entryprice + ptlim * atr;
       stpprice = min (Lowest(lo, 2, cb),
           entryprice - mmstp * atr);
       break;
      case 2:
      case 3:
       limprice = entryprice + ptlim * atr;
       stpprice = entryprice - mmstp * atr;
       break;
```

```
            default: nrerror("Invalid modeltype");
        }
        ts.exitlonglimit('A', limprice);
        ts.exitlongstop('B', stpprice);
    }
    else if(entryposted < 0) {
        // initialization and exits for shorts on entry day
        switch(modeltype) {
          case 1:
            limprice = entryprice - ptlim * atr;
            stpprice = max (Highest(hi, 2, cb),
                entryprice + mmstp * atr);
            break;
          case 2:
          case 3:
            limprice = entryprice - ptlim * atr;
            stpprice = entryprice + mmstp * atr;
            break;
          default: nrerror("Invalid modeltype");
        }
        ts.exitshortlimit('C', limprice);
        ts.exitshortstop('D', stpprice);
    }
    else {
        // exits for after the entry day
        if(ts.position() > 0) { // longs
            switch(modeltype) {
              case 1:
                stpprice = max(stpprice, Lowest(lo,2,cb));
                break;
              case 2:
                stpprice = max(stpprice, cls[cb]-stpa*atr);
                break;
              case 3:
                tmp = (hi[cb] - stpa * atr) - stpprice;
                if(tmp > 0.0) stpprice += stpb * tmp;
                break;
            }
            ts.exitlonglimit('F', limprice);
            ts.exitlongstop('G', stpprice);
            if(cb-entrybar >= maxhold) ts.exitlongclose('E');
        }
        else if(ts.position() < 0) { // shorts
            switch(modeltype) {
              case 1:
                stpprice = min(stpprice, Highest(hi,2,cb));
```

```
                        break;
                    case 2:
                        stpprice = min(stpprice, cls[cb]+stpa*atr);
                        break;
                    case 3:
                        tmp = (lo[cb] + stpa * atr) - stpprice;
                        if(tmp < 0.0) stpprice += stpb * tmp;
                        break;
                }
                ts.exitshortlimit('I', limprice);
                ts.exitshortstop('J', stpprice);
                if(cb-entrybar >= maxhold) ts.exitshortclose('H');
            }
        }
    } // process next bar
}
```

The code above implements the MSES with the original fixed stop replaced with one of the three more responsive, dynamic stops. The parameter *modeltype* selects the stop, and depending on which is to be tested, up to three other controlling parameters are set and adjusted. For the two-bar highest-high/lowest-low (HHLL) stop, the parameter (*mmstp*) is the multiple of the average true range that is added to or subtracted from the entry price to obtain the stop price for the entry bar. The stop price on the entry bar is set to either the lowest low of the last two bars or the entry price plus or minus the specified multiple of the average true range, whichever is further away from the current market price. For the other two kinds of stops (ATR-based and MEMA), the stop price on the entry bar is initialized to the usual value, i.e., the entry price minus (long) or plus (short) the money management stop parameter (*mmstp*) multiplied by the average true range.

On each bar after the entry bar, the stop price is adjusted. The adjustment used depends on the particular type of stop being employed, as selected by the *modeltype* parameter. For the HHLL stop, the highest high or lowest low is calculated according to whether the position is short or long (respectively). If the result of the calculation is closer to the current market price than the current stop price is, then the current stop price is replaced with the new value. For the next model (dynamic ATR-based stop), a second money management stop parameter (*stpa*) is multiplied by the average true range. Then the resultant number is subtracted from (long) or added to (short) the current closing price. If the resultant number is closer to the market than the current value of the stop price, the stop price is replaced with that number and, therefore, moved in closer to the market. For the third type of stop (MEMA), a stop parameter (*stpa*) is multiplied by the average true range, and then subtracted from the current high (longs) or added to the current low (shorts) as a kind of offset. The stop price is then subtracted from the resultant number. The result of this last calculation is placed in a variable (*tmp*). The stop price is updated on successive bars by adding *tmp* multiplied by another parameter (*stpb*, a correction rate coefficient) to the existing stop price. The current stop price is adjusted, however, only if the adjustment will move the stop closer to the current price level. The computations are identical to those used when calculating an exponential moving average (EMA). The only difference is that, in a standard exponential moving average, the stop price would be corrected regardless of whether the correction was up or down and there would be no offset involved. In this model, *stpb* determines the effective length of an exponential moving average that can only move in one direction, in toward the prices.

Test of Highest-High/Lowest-Low Stop

In this test (*modeltype* = 1), the initial money management stop parameter controls the maximum degree of the stop's tightness on the first bar. It is stepped from 0.5 to 3.5 in increments of 0.5.

Each row in Table 14-2 presents data on the in-sample performance of each of the values through which the parameter was stepped (*INSTP*). The last row describes the behavior of the model with the best parameter value (as found in the stepping process) retested on the out-of-sample data. Table 14-2 may be interpreted in the same way as the other optimization tables presented in this book; in the table, *DRAW* represents drawdown, in thousands of dollars.

This stop appears to have been consistently too tight, as evidenced by a decreased percentage of winning trades when compared with the baseline MSES model. In the previous test, the best solution (*mmstp* parameter 1.5, *ptlim* parameter 4.5) had 39% wins, had a risk-to-reward ratio of −1.46, and lost an average of $1,581 per trade. In the current test, the best solution has only 28% of the trades winning in-sample and 29% out-of-sample. Many potentially profitable trades (some of the trades that would have been profitable with the basic MSES, using an optimal fixed stop) were converted to small losses. The tightness of this stop is also demonstrated by the total number of bars the average trade was held (4), compared with the usual 6 to 8 bars. The average risk-to-reward ratio (−2.52 in-sample and −2.38 out-of-sample) and the average loss per trade ($1,864 in-sample, $1,818 out-of-sample) have also significantly worsened when compared with the optimal fixed stop. The 2-bar HHLL stop is obviously no great shakes, and one would be better served using a fixed, optimally placed stop, like that which forms part of the MSES when used with optimized parameters, such as those discovered and shown in the test results in Table 14-1.

Test of the Dynamic ATR-Based Stop

In this model, the two parameters (represented in the code as *mmstp* and *stpa*) are multipliers for the average true range. They are used when calculating placement of the stop on the entry bar and later bars, respectively. The entry bar stop parameter

TABLE 14-2

Portfolio Performance for the 2-Bar Highest-High/Lowest-Low Trailing
Stop with the Optimal Fixed Profit Target Found in Table 14-1

IN-SAMPLE											
INSTP	NET	NETL	NETS	PFAC	ROA%	ARRR	PROB	DRAW	TRDS	WIN%	AVTR	TRDB
0.50	-7957	-3534	-4423	0.67	-10.3	-2.71	1.000	7951	4210	25	-1890	3
1.00	-7719	-3333	-4386	0.70	-10.3	-2.54	1.000	7711	4187	27	-1843	4
1.50	-7792	-3353	-4438	0.70	-10.3	-2.53	1.000	7778	4178	28	-1865	4
2.00	-7857	-3343	-4514	0.70	-10.3	-2.54	1.000	7839	4172	28	-1883	4
2.50	**-7775**	**-3297**	**-4478**	**0.70**	**-10.3**	**-2.52**	**1.000**	**7756**	**4171**	**28**	**-1864**	**4**
3.00	-7745	-3257	-4487	0.70	-10.3	-2.52	1.000	7727	4171	28	-1857	4
3.50	-7754	-3262	-4492	0.70	-10.3	-2.52	1.000	7736	4171	28	-1859	4
OUT-OF-SAMPLE											
2.50	-3259	-1511	-1748	0.71	-22.4	-2.38	1.000	3450	1793	29	-1818	4

(*FIRST* in Table 14-3) and the parameter for the stop after the entry bar (*LATER*) are
both stepped from 0.5 to 3.5 in increments of 0.5.

As with the previous tests of stops, the parameters had a gradual effect on
performance and did not interact with one another to any great extent. An examination of the average performance for each value of the entry bar stop parameter
reveals that the best results, in terms of risk-to-reward ratio, were obtained when
that parameter was set to 2. For the parameter that applied to later bars, the best
average result was achieved with values of either 2 or 2.5. For individual combinations of parameters, a *FIRST* parameter of 2 and a *LATER* parameter of 2.5 produced the best overall performance, with the least bad risk-to-reward ratio and
nearly the smallest loss per trade. This stop model was marginally better than the
optimal fixed stop, used as a baseline, that had a risk-to-reward ratio of -1.46, as
opposed to -1.40 in the current case. As in Table 14-1, the best solution is shown
in boldface type. The percentage of winning trades (42%) was also marginally better than that for the optimal fixed stop (39%).

Test of the MEMA Dynamic Stop

There are three parameters in this model: the initial money management stop parameter, which sets the stop for the first bar; the ATR offset parameter (*ATRO* in
Table 14-4); and the correction or adaptation rate coefficient (*COEFF*), which
determines the relative rate at which the stop pulls in to the market or, equivalently,
the speed of the *modified exponential moving average* underlying this model. All
three parameters are optimized with an extensive search.

Table 14-4 shows portfolio performance only as a function of the ATR offset
and the adaptation rate coefficient, the most important parameters of the model.
The initial stop parameter was fixed at 2.5, which was the parameter value of the
optimal solution.

TABLE 14-3

Portfolio Performance as a Function of First-Bar and Later-
Bar Stop Parameters Using the Dynamic ATR-Based Stop-
Loss Model

FIRST \	LATER	0.50	1.00	1.50	2.00	2.50	3.00	3.50	AVG
0.50	ARRR	-3.48	-2.95	-2.75	-2.61	-2.53	-2.54	-2.54	-2.77
	WIN%	26	23	20	20	19	19	19	21
	AVTR	-1846	-1869	-1873	-1847	-1808	-1820	-1820	-1840
1.00	ARRR	-2.89	-2.16	-1.85	-1.65	-1.60	-1.67	-1.66	-1.93
	WIN%	32	32	31	32	32	32	32	32
	AVTR	-1813	-1743	-1652	-1558	-1528	-1601	-1595	-1641
1.50	ARRR	-2.86	-1.88	-1.60	-1.49	-1.43	-1.53	-1.46	-1.75
	WIN%	33	34	36	37	39	39	39	37
	AVTR	-1865	-1641	-1588	-1567	-1532	-1659	-1583	-1634
2.00	ARRR	-2.83	-1.69	-1.43	-1.42	**-1.40**	-1.56	-1.51	-1.69
	WIN%	34	35	37	40	42	42	42	39
	AVTR	-1868	-1493	-1467	-1558	**-1586**	-1784	-1741	-1642
2.50	ARRR	-2.76	-1.67	-1.45	-1.46	-1.50	-1.64	-1.60	-1.73
	WIN%	34	35	38	40	43	43	44	40
	AVTR	-1832	-1486	-1503	-1629	-1742	-1947	-1914	-1722
3.00	ARRR	-2.76	-1.68	-1.49	-1.50	-1.57	-1.77	-1.73	-1.79
	WIN%	34	35	38	41	43	44	44	40
	AVTR	-1837	-1498	-1543	-1691	-1853	-2129	-2125	-1811
3.50	ARRR	-2.76	-1.69	-1.51	-1.51	-1.60	-1.85	-1.78	-1.81
	WIN%	34	35	38	41	43	44	45	40
	AVTR	-1838	-1506	-1564	-1708	-1908	-2250	-2218	-1856
AVG	ARRR	-2.91	-1.96	-1.73	-1.66	-1.66	-1.79	-1.75	-1.92
	WIN%	32	33	34	36	37	38	38	35
	AVTR	-1843	-1605	-1599	-1651	-1708	-1884	-1857	-1735

Again, the model responded in a well-behaved manner to changes in the parameter values. There was some interaction between parameter values. This was
expected because the faster the moving average (or adaptation rate), the greater the
average true range offset must be to keep the stop a reasonable distance from the
prices and achieve good performance. The best overall portfolio performance (the
boldfaced results in Table 14-4) occurred with an ATR offset of 1 and an adaptation
rate coefficient of 0.3 (about a 5-bar EMA). Finally, here is a stop that performed
better than those tested previously. The risk-to-reward ratio rose (−1.36), as did the
percentage of winning trades (37%) and the average trade in dollars (−$1,407).

TEST OF THE PROFIT TARGET

This test is the best stop thus far produced: The MEMA stop had an initial money
management parameter of 2.5, an average true range offset of 1, and an adaptation

rate coefficient of 0.30. In the original MEMA test above (the results reported in Table 14-4), the optimal fixed profit target was used. In the current test, the optimal fixed profit target is replaced with a *shrinking profit target*, i.e., one that starts out far away from the market and then pulls in toward the market, becoming tighter over time. The intention is to try to pull profit out of languishing trades by exiting with a limit order on market noise, while not cutting profits short early in the course of favorably disposed trades. The approach used when constructing the shrinking

TABLE 14-4

Portfolio Performance of the EMA-Like Dynamic Stop as a Function of the ATR Offset and Adaptation Rate Coefficient with an Initial Stop Parameter of 2.5 ATR Units

ATRO \	COEFF	0.10	0.20	0.30	0.40	0.50	AVG
0.00	ARRR	-1.49	-1.56	-2.34	-2.57	-3.01	-2.19
	WIN%	38	36	35	35	35	36
	AVTR	-1636	-1517	-1929	-1912	-2003	-1799
0.50	ARRR	-1.42	-1.42	-1.78	-2.29	-2.42	-1.87
	WIN%	40	36	35	35	35	36
	AVTR	-1619	-1478	-1672	-1918	-1876	-1713
1.00	ARRR	-1.41	-1.5	-1.36	-1.54	-1.85	-1.53
	WIN%	42	38	37	36	35	38
	AVTR	-1621	-1629	-1407	-1508	-1676	-1568
1.50	ARRR	-1.54	-1.41	-1.43	-1.45	-1.48	-1.46
	WIN%	43	40	39	38	38	40
	AVTR	-1794	-1607	-1563	-1542	-1540	-1609
2.00	ARRR	-1.62	-1.55	-1.39	-1.47	-1.42	-1.49
	WIN%	43	42	41	40	40	41
	AVTR	-1925	-1806	-1593	-1646	-1565	-1707
2.50	ARRR	-1.59	-1.63	-1.56	-1.56	-1.56	-1.58
	WIN%	44	43	43	42	42	43
	AVTR	-1909	-1924	-1841	-1824	-1806	-1861
3.00	ARRR	-1.55	-1.57	-1.54	-1.56	-1.58	-1.56
	WIN%	44	44	44	44	43	44
	AVTR	-1870	-1880	-1836	-1849	-1872	-1861
AVG	ARRR	-1.52	-1.52	-1.63	-1.78	-1.90	-1.67
	WIN%	42	40	39	39	38	40
	AVTR	-1768	-1692	-1692	-1743	-1763	-1731

profit target is very similar to the one used when constructing the MEMA stop. An exponential moving average is initialized in an unusual way; i.e., the running sum is set to the entry price plus (long) or minus (short) some multiple (*ptlim*) of the average true range. In this way, the profit target limit begins just as the fixed profit target limit began. After the first bar, the price at which the limit is set is adjusted in exactly the same way that an exponential moving average is adjusted as new bars arrive: The distance between the current limit price and the current close is multiplied by a parameter (*ptga*). The resultant number is then subtracted from the current limit price to give the new limit price, pulling the limit price in tighter to the current close. In contrast to the case with the stop, the limit price is allowed to move in either direction, although it is unlikely to do so because the limit order will take the trade out whenever prices move to the other side of its current placement. The second parameter (*ptga*) controls the speed of the moving average, i.e., the shrinkage rate. The rules are identical to those in the test of the MEMA stop above, except as they relate to the profit target limit on bars after the first bar.

```
// exit trades using basic exit with improved stops
// and profit targets
atr = exitatr[cb];
if(entryposted > 0) {
    // initialization and exits for longs on entry day
    switch(modeltype) {
      case 1:
        limprice = entryprice + ptlim * atr;
        stpprice = min (Lowest(lo, 2, cb),
            entryprice - mmstp * atr);
        break;
      case 2:
      case 3:
      case 4:
        limprice = entryprice + ptlim * atr;
        stpprice = entryprice - mmstp * atr;
        break;
      default: nrerror("Invalid modeltype");
    }
    ts.exitlonglimit('A', limprice);
    ts.exitlongstop('B', stpprice);

}
else if(entryposted < 0) {
    // initialization and exits for shorts on entry day
    switch(modeltype) {
      case 1:
        limprice = entryprice - ptlim * atr;
```

```
           stpprice = max (Highest(hi, 2, cb),
               entryprice + mmstp * atr);
          break;
        case 2:
        case 3:
        case 4:
         limprice = entryprice - ptlim * atr;
         stpprice = entryprice + mmstp * atr;
         break;
        default: nrerror("Invalid modeltype");
      }
      ts.exitshortlimit('C', limprice);
      ts.exitshortstop('D', stpprice);
  }
  else {
      // exits for after the entry day
      if(ts.position() > 0) { // longs
          switch(modeltype) {
            case 1:
               stpprice = max(stpprice, Lowest(lo,2,cb));
               break;
            case 2:
               stpprice = max(stpprice, cls[cb]-stpa*atr);
               break;
            case 3:
               tmp = (hi[cb] - stpa * atr) - stpprice;
               if(tmp > 0.0) stpprice += stpb * tmp;
               break;
            case 4:
               tmp = (hi[cb] - stpa * atr) - stpprice;
               if(tmp > 0.0) stpprice += stpb * tmp;
               limprice = limprice - ptga*(limprice-cls[cb]);
               break;
          }
          ts.exitlonglimit('F', limprice);
          ts.exitlongstop('G', stpprice);
          if(cb-entrybar >= maxhold) ts.exitlongclose('E');
      }
      else if(ts.position() < 0) { // shorts
          switch(modeltype) {
            case 1:
               stpprice = min(stpprice, Highest(hi,2,cb));
               break;
            case 2:
               stpprice = min(stpprice, cls[cb]+stpa*atr);
               break;
```

```
      case 3:
        tmp = (lo[cb] + stpa * atr) - stpprice;
        if(tmp < 0.0) stpprice += stpb * tmp;
        break;
      case 4:
        tmp = (lo[cb] + stpa * atr) - stpprice;
        if(tmp < 0.0) stpprice += stpb * tmp;
        limprice = limprice + ptga*(cls[cb]-limprice);
        break;
    }
    ts.exitshortlimit('I', limprice);
    ts.exitshortstop('J', stpprice);
    if(cb-entrybar >= maxhold) ts.exitshortclose('H');
  }
}
```

The code fragment above shows the implementation of the shrinking limit, along with the MEMA stop reported in Table 14-4.

Table 14-5 provides information on the portfolio performance as the initial profit target limit (*ptlim* in the code, *INIT* in the table) and the shrinkage coefficient (*ptga* in the code, *COEFF* in the table) are varied. The parameter that controlled the initial placement of the profit target, in average true range units away from the price, was stepped from 2 to 6 in increments of 0.5. The shrinkage coefficient was stepped from 0.05 to 0.4 in increments of 0.05. The best combination of parameters produced a solution that was an improvement over the fixed profit target limit. The risk-to-reward ratio became -1.32, the percentage of winning trades remained the same at 37%, but the average loss per trades was less at $1,325. Again, the model was well behaved with respect to variations in the parameters. The results indicate that care has to be taken with profit targets: They tend to prematurely close trades that have large profit potential. As can be seen in Table 14-5, as the initial profit target placement became tighter and tighter, the percentage of winning trades dramatically increased, as more and more trades hit the profit target and were closed out with a small profit. On the down side, the risk-to-reward ratio and the average worsened, demonstrating that the increased percentage of winning trades could not compensate for the curtailment of profits that resulted from the tight profit target. Sometimes it is better to have no profit target at all than to have an excessively tight one. The same was true for the shrinkage rate. Profit targets that too quickly moved into the market tended to close trades early, thereby cutting profits short.

TEST OF THE EXTENDED TIME LIMIT

In all the tests conducted so far, a position was held for only a maximum of 10 days. Any position that still existed—that had not previously been closed out by

TABLE 14-5

Portfolio Performance as a Function of the Initial Profit Target Limit Placement and the Shrinkage Coefficient

INIT \	COEFF	0.05	0.10	0.15	0.20	0.25	0.30	0.35	0.40	AVG
2.00	ARRR	-2.03	-2.19	-2.31	-2.42	-2.46	-2.64	-2.62	-2.72	-2.42
	WIN%	42	46	50	52	53	53	54	53	50
	AVTR	-1686	-1738	-1782	-1802	-1756	-1819	-1737	-1734	-1757
2.50	ARRR	-1.76	-2.13	-2.24	-2.30	-2.49	-2.56	-2.61	-2.66	-2.34
	WIN%	39	41	45	48	50	51	51	51	47
	AVTR	-1560	-1800	-1826	-1817	-1899	-1888	-1837	-1812	-1805
3.00	ARRR	-1.63	-1.80	-2.13	-2.21	-2.36	-2.54	-2.59	-2.58	-2.23
	WIN%	38	39	42	46	48	49	49	50	45
	AVTR	-1510	-1604	-1815	-1817	-1882	-1941	-1926	-1829	-1791
3.50	ARRR	-1.58	-1.69	-1.97	-2.15	-2.19	-2.38	-2.57	-2.52	-2.13
	WIN%	37	38	40	43	46	47	48	49	44
	AVTR	-1513	-1547	-1724	-1822	-1788	-1887	-1958	-1862	-1763
4.00	ARRR	-1.51	-1.59	-1.76	-2.07	-2.19	-2.25	-2.47	-2.58	-2.05
	WIN%	37	38	39	42	44	47	47	48	43
	AVTR	-1485	-1502	-1594	-1795	-1845	-1829	-1940	-1963	-1744
4.50	ARRR	-1.36	-1.53	-1.70	-2.07	-2.12	-2.19	-2.38	-2.51	-1.98
	WIN%	37	37	38	40	43	46	46	47	42
	AVTR	-1363	-1484	-1572	-1828	-1817	-1816	-1900	-1945	-1716
5.00	ARRR	-1.41	-1.38	-1.59	-1.85	-2.04	-2.20	-2.32	-2.52	-1.91
	WIN%	37	37	38	40	42	44	46	46	41
	AVTR	-1437	-1363	-1498	-1665	-1766	-1856	-1884	-1981	-1681
5.50	ARRR	-1.37	**-1.32**	-1.45	-1.75	-1.99	-2.18	-2.23	-2.49	-1.85
	WIN%	37	**37**	38	39	42	44	45	46	41
	AVTR	-1419	**-1325**	-1391	-1595	-1745	-1855	-1839	-1979	-1644
6.00	ARRR	-1.39	-1.36	-1.38	-1.63	-1.99	-2.07	-2.22	-2.46	-1.81
	WIN%	37	37	38	39	41	43	45	45	41
	AVTR	-1448	-1372	-1350	-1508	-1772	-1776	-1856	-1977	-1632
AVG	ARRR	-1.56	-1.67	-1.84	-2.05	-2.20	-2.33	-2.45	-2.56	-2.08
	WIN%	38	39	41	43	45	47	48	48	44
	AVTR	-1491	-1526	-1617	-1739	-1808	-1852	-1875	-1898	-1726

the stop or profit target—was closed out after 10 days, regardless of its profitability. In this test, an exit strategy that uses an adaptive MEMA stop, with optimal parameters and a shrinking profit target, is examined. The only difference between the test reported in Table 14-6 and the one reported in Table 14-5 is in the extension of the maximum time a trade may be held, from 10 to 30 days. The initial profit target limit is reoptimized by stepping it from 5 to 7 in increments of 0.5. Likewise, the shrinkage rate coefficient is stepped from 0.05 to 0.4 in increments of 0.05. The code is the same as for the previous test. Only the setting of the max-hold parameter, which controls the maximum time a trade may be held, is changed.

The best performance was achieved with an initial target parameter of 5.5 and a shrinkage coefficient of 0.1. The average risk-to-reward ratio went from −1.32 to −1.22. The percentage of wins remained the same, but the average trade lost only $1,236, rather than $1,325 in the previous test. Extension of the time limit improved results, but not dramatically. Most trades were closed out well before the time limit expired; i.e., the average trade only lasted between 6 and 10 bars (days).

MARKET-BY-MARKET RESULTS FOR THE BEST EXIT

Table 14-7 reports on performance broken down by market for the best exit strategy discovered in these tests, i.e., the one that used the MEMA stop and the shrinking profit target and in which the time limit was extended to 30 days. Both in- and out-of-sample results are presented, and consistency between the two can

TABLE 14-6

Portfolio Performance as a Function of the Initial Profit Target Limit Setting and the Shrinkage Coefficient When the Trade Limit Is Increased to 30 Days

INIT \	COEFF	0.05	0.10	0.15	0.20	0.25	0.30	0.35	0.40	AVG
5.00	ARRR	-1.31	-1.31	-1.57	-1.84	-2.04	-2.20	-2.32	-2.52	-1.89
	WIN%	36	37	38	40	42	44	46	46	41
	AVTR	-1380	-1303	-1486	-1662	-1766	-1856	-1884	-1981	-1665
5.50	ARRR	-1.27	**-1.22**	-1.42	-1.75	-1.98	-2.18	-2.23	-2.49	-1.82
	WIN%	36	**37**	38	39	42	44	45	46	41
	AVTR	-1353	**-1236**	-1372	-1599	-1741	-1856	-1839	-1979	-1622
6.00	ARRR	-1.28	-1.24	-1.36	-1.62	-1.98	-2.07	-2.22	-2.46	-1.78
	WIN%	36	37	37	39	41	43	45	45	40
	AVTR	-1378	-1274	-1336	-1502	-1767	-1776	-1856	-1977	-1608
6.50	ARRR	-1.25	-1.27	-1.31	-1.53	-1.91	-2.03	-2.18	-2.36	-1.73
	WIN%	36	37	37	39	40	42	44	45	40
	AVTR	-1368	-1320	-1307	-1443	-1712	-1770	-1841	-1919	-1585
7.00	ARRR	-1.25	-1.29	-1.33	-1.40	-1.77	-2.01	-2.11	-2.30	-1.68
	WIN%	36	37	37	38	40	42	44	45	40
	AVTR	-1375	-1362	-1339	-1346	-1623	-1769	-1790	-1896	-1563
AVG	ARRR	-1.27	-1.27	-1.40	-1.63	-1.94	-2.10	-2.21	-2.43	-1.78
	WIN%	36	37	37	39	41	43	45	45	40
	AVTR	-1371	-1299	-1368	-1510	-1722	-1805	-1842	-1950	-1608

be seen.

In both samples, profits for the NYFE occurred on the long side, but not on the short. Substantial profits occurred in both samples for Feeder Cattle—for long and short positions in-sample, but only for short positions out-of-sample. Live Hogs were profitable in both samples for both long and short positions. The Deutschemark and Japanese Yen showed profits in-sample on the long side, but had overall losses out-of-sample. The only exception was a small profit in the Japanese Yen on the short side, but it was not enough to overcome the losses on the long side. Lumber was strongly profitable on the long side in-sample, but only

TABLE 14-7

Performance Broken Down by Market for Best Exit Strategy with EMA-Like Stop, Shrinking Profit Target, and Trade Time Limit Extended to 30 Days

SYM	IN-SAMPLE						OUT-OF-SAMPLE					
	NETL	NETS	ROA%	AVTR	WIN%	TRDS	NETL	NETS	ROA%	AVTR	WIN%	TRDS
SP	-13	-66	-5.1	-792	41	100	-34	-102	-13.1	-2444	35	56
YX	122	-134	-0.6	-96	38	121	24	-36	-2.8	-263	40	47
US	105	-273	-5.7	-1580	36	106	-28	-139	-19.9	-3918	34	43
TB	-175	-25	-7.1	-2388	36	84	-105	-263	-20.8	-6953	26	53
TY	-148	-227	-9.2	-3486	34	108	-5	-233	-19.0	-4335	29	55
BP	0	-157	-7.8	-1500	37	105	-29	-45	-9.9	-1767	40	42
DM	274	-22	24.7	2731	44	92	-123	-92	-22.7	-4677	26	46
SF	125	-190	-2.8	-578	36	112	-112	-147	-22.3	-6491	20	40
JY	215	-33	8.1	1504	42	121	-156	95	-8.5	-1080	40	57
CD	-20	-239	-7.4	-2861	29	91	-67	72	0.5	101	36	55
ED	-367	-166	-9.3	-4813	33	111	90	-180	-8.4	-2327	41	39
CL	-136	59	-4.4	-662	34	116	112	-57	12.5	1124	36	49
HO	-178	-339	-8.4	-4749	33	109	-95	-111	-22.6	-4492	32	46
HU	30	-89	-1.6	-529	39	113	84	56	50.2	3187	47	44
GC	-51	-38	-4.3	-869	32	104	-69	302	58.0	5540	52	42
SI	-174	-194	-10.2	-3078	35	120	-84	-48	-16.3	-2333	35	57
PL	108	-170	-2.6	-474	43	131	-126	-110	-22.9	-4828	30	49
PA	-64	-88	-6.9	-1545	38	99	185	-39	32.0	3573	56	41
FC	196	50	10.9	2150	44	115	-41	194	43.1	3394	46	45
LC	-44	-165	-7.3	-1905	36	110	-115	-56	-14.3	-4010	30	43
LH	256	1	15.5	2662	46	97	150	23	31.9	4463	51	39
PB	-283	-42	-7.8	-3104	33	105	-70	-144	-17.2	-3913	34	55
S	-136	-188	-7.3	-3241	30	100	147	-36	31.6	3384	48	33
SM	-80	-85	-6.2	-1786	35	93	102	-3	23.1	1861	49	53
BO	-172	110	-4.6	-611	39	102	-93	63	-6.1	-567	30	53
C	-205	32	-7.4	-1698	36	102	-166	1	-18.7	-3456	31	48
O	-214	90	-5.6	-1311	36	94	-98	0	-16.2	-1976	36	50
W	-16	-328	-9.6	-2920	31	118	-172	46	-12.5	-3244	28	39
KW	-63	-182	-6.0	-1937	37	127	-121	-105	-20.2	-4452	33	51
MW	-27	-94	-5.4	-1072	38	113	9	-52	-10.9	-1229	45	35
KC	-192	136	-1.8	-541	33	104	37	22	12.4	1710	40	35
CC	-94	-20	-6.4	-1066	34	108	-95	-31	-19.8	-3427	29	37
SB	-110	-235	-10.1	-3146	37	110	-59	-46	-12.9	-2040	36	52
JO	-51	17	-1.7	-263	41	131	59	-81	-3.7	-477	40	45
CT	39	-205	-5.9	-1643	33	101	-100	-123	-22.6	-4781	36	47
LB	514	-255	7.9	2374	44	109	39	-130	-12.5	-1691	38	54

had a very small profit on the long side out-of-sample. The two most outstanding performers were Feeder Cattle and Live Hogs which, even despite the random entries, could actually be traded. In-sample, there was a 10.9% annualized return for Feeder Cattle and a 15.5% return for Live Hogs. Out-of-sample, the returns were 43.1% and 31.9%, respectively. There were more profitable results out-of-sample than in-sample, but this could easily have been due to the smaller sample and fewer trades taken in the out-of-sample period.

CONCLUSION

Exits do make a big difference. By improving the risk management and profit target elements in an exit strategy, losses can be cut and the risk-to-reward ratio can be enhanced. The improvements in the tests above, however, were not as good as expected. For example, although the best exit did appear capable of pulling profits from random trades taken in two markets, no profits were obtained on the portfolio, which is somewhat inconsistent with our earlier experiences (Katz and McCormick, March 1998, April 1998) in which profitable systems were achieved with random entries on the S&P 500. In those studies, exits were tuned to the market under examination, rather than keeping parameters constant across an entire portfolio as done in the investigations above. This difference may account for the poorer results in the current set of tests. In general, better results can be obtained (albeit with much greater risk of curve-fitting and over-optimization) by tuning the various components of a trading model to the specific characteristics of an individual market. It should also be kept in mind that the tests conducted here were fairly harsh with respect to transaction costs. For some markets (e.g., the S&P 500), commissions are almost negligible in terms of its typical dollar volatility, and only slippage is a factor. However, in many smaller markets, great numbers of contracts would have to be traded, causing the issue of commissions to become a very significant consideration. In our earlier study, little or no transaction costs were assumed, and a market in which the commission component would be fairly small (i.e., the S&P 500) was examined. This factor may also have contributed to the difference in findings.

When compared with the standard exit strategy used in the tests of entry methods, which lost an average of $2,243 per trade and had a standard deviation of $304, the best exit strategy thus far developed reduced the loss per trade to $1,236, representing a reduction in loss per trade of over 44%. The reduction is substantial enough that many of the better (albeit losing) entry models would probably show overall profitability if they were combined with the best exit strategy.

WHAT HAVE WE LEARNED?

- Exits can make a substantial difference in overall performance. The attempts described in this chapter have yielded an extra $1,000 per trade over the standard exit strategy used in tests of entry models.
- Just as with entries, finding a good exit is like searching for a tiny island of inefficiency in a sea of efficient market behavior. While such islands are there, they are difficult to find.

CHAPTER 15

ADDING AI TO EXITS

In this chapter, the modified standard exit strategy (MSES) is explored with the addition of elements based on neural networks and genetics. In Chapter 11, neural network forecasters were developed for use in generating entries. One of the particular neural forecasters (the time-reversed Slow %K net) attempted to predict whether tomorrow's prices would be near the low or high end of the range of prices that would occur over the next several days. This network can be added to an exit strategy: If the net suggests that the market is near the top of its near-future range and a long position is being held, it would probably be a good idea to exit before the market begins to move down. Likewise, if the net forecasts a rising market while a short position is being held, the trade should be exited before the market begins to rise.

The first test conducted below explores the use of the time-reversed Slow %K network (developed when studying entries) as an additional element to our modified standard exit strategy. The net, which generates what might be called a *signal exit*, cannot be used on its own for exiting because it will not always close out a trade. This network was designed to provide entry signals. When it generates a signal, the market is likely to behave in some expected manner. However, the absence of a signal does not mean that the market will not do something significant. When a position is being held, at some point an exit has to be taken, and that action cannot be postponed until a significant event is finally predicted. The MSES, in this case, guarantees that all trades have some money management protection and are exited after a given amount of time. The neural net, however, can possibly improve the strategy by occasionally triggering an exit when a predicted move against the trade is expected. In this way, the net may turn a certain proportion of losing trades into winners.

The second batch of tests (one for the long side, one for the short) involves the use of a genetic algorithm to evolve a set of rules to generate a signal exit. The rules are used in a manner similar to the way the net is used, i.e., to generate additional exits, within the context of the MSES, when the market is likely to reverse. The rule templates and rule-generating methodology are the same as those used in Chapter 12, where evolved rules generated entries. In the current tests, rules are evolved to generate additional exits within the context of the MSES. The rules are used as signal exits. The additional exits will, it is hoped, improve profitability by turning some losses into wins and by killing other trades before they become larger losses.

More sophisticated exits can be developed using the techniques described above. Although not explored in this chapter, a neural network could be evolved to produce outputs in the form of placements for stops and limits, as well as for immediate, outright exits. Genetically evolved rules could also be employed in this manner.

When used in the context of entries, neural networks proved to be fairly good forecasters. In-sample, incredible profits were produced due to the accurate predictions. Out-of-sample, the nets yielded much better than chance results (albeit not very profitable on the whole portfolio). Real predictive ability was demonstrated. Using such forecasts to exit trades before the market reverses should improve system performance, even if only by eliminating a small percentage of bad trades. The same applies to the genetically evolved rules. However, when the rules that produced entry signals for rare event trades are applied to exits, great improvement in exit performance should not be expected. Given the nature of the rules, only a small number of signals are likely to be generated, which means that only small numbers of trades will be affected. If only a few of the large number of trades that will be taken are improved, only a small overall benefit will be evidenced. Since the rules are being reevolved for the tests below, more instances of exit opportunities may be found than were discovered for entry opportunities.

TEST METHODOLOGY FOR THE NEURAL EXIT COMPONENT

The larger of the two best neural networks, trained to predict the time-reversed Slow %K, are used. The preprocessing and forecast-generating logic are identical to those discussed in Chapter 11. A series of predictions are generated using the 18-14-4-1 net (18 first-layer neurons, 14 neurons in first middle layer, 4 in the second middle layer, and 1 output). The MSES is also used. Along with the exits provided by the MSES, an additional exit condition is being added: If the predicted reverse Slow %K is greater than some threshold, indicating that the market is high relative to its near-future price range, any long position is exited. Likewise, if the net's prediction indicates that the market is near the low of its near-future price range, by being below 100 minus the previous threshold, any short position is exited. Exits triggered by the neural net forecasts are taken at the close of the bar.

```
static void Model (float *parms, float *dt, float *opn, float *hi,
float *lo, float *cls, float *vol, float *oi, float *dlrv, int nb,
TRDSIM &ts, float *eqcls) {

    // Implements random entries with modified standard exit
    // enhanced with an additional "signal exit" based on
    // a neural forecatser for the reverse Slow %K.
    // File = x21mod01.c
    // parms   - vector [1..MAXPRM] of parameters
    // dt      - vector [1..nb] of dates in YYMMDD form
    // opn     - vector [1..nb] of opening prices
    // hi      - vector [1..nb] of high prices
    // lo      - vector [1..nb] of low prices
    // cls     - vector [1..nb] of closing prices
    // vol     - vector [1..nb] of volumes
    // oi      - vector [1..nb] of open interest numbers
    // dlrv    - vector [1..nb] of average dollar volatilities
    // nb      - number of bars in data series or vectors
    // ts      - trading simulator class instance
    // eqcls   - vector [1..nb] of closing equity levels

    // declare local scratch variables
    static int rc, cb, ncontracts, maxhold, signal, ranseed;
    static float mmstp, ptlim, limprice, stpprice, entryprice;
    static int entryposted, entrybar;
    static float exitatr[MAXBAR+1], prd[MAXBAR+1], rnum, thresh;
    static long iseed;

    // copy parameters to local variables for clearer reference
    thresh = parms[1];    // neural output threshold
    ranseed = parms[2];   // used to select random seed
    maxhold = 10;       // maximum holding period in days
    ptlim = 4.5;        // profit target limit in atr units
    mmstp = 1.5;        // money mgmt stop in atr units

    // perform whole-series calculations
    AvgTrueRangeS(exitatr,hi,lo,cls,50,nb);       // ATR for exit
    NeuralForecast(prd, cls, nb);           // forecasts

    // seed the random number generator
    // ... use a different seed for each tradeable
    // ... ts.model() returns a market index (SP=1, YX=2, ...)
    iseed = -(ranseed + 10 * ts.model());
    rnum = ran2(&iseed);

    // step through bars (days) to simulate actual trading
    for(cb = 1; cb <= nb; cb++) {
```

```
// take no trades before the in-sample period
// ... same as TradeStation's MaxBarsBack setting
if(dt[cb] < IS_DATE) { eqcls[cb] = 0.0; continue; }

// execute any pending orders and save closing equity
rc = ts.update(opn[cb], hi[cb], lo[cb], cls[cb], cb);
if(rc != 0) nrerror("Trade buffer overflow");
eqcls[cb] = ts.currentequity(EQ_CLOSETOTAL);

// calculate number of contracts to trade
// ... we want to trade the dollar volatility equivalent
// ... of 2 new S&P-500 contracts as of 12/31/98
ncontracts = RoundToInteger(5673.0 / dlrv[cb]);
if(ncontracts < 1) ncontracts = 1;

// avoid placing orders on possibly limit-locked days
if(hi[cb+1] == lo[cb+1]) continue;

// generate "standard" random entry signals
signal = 0;
rnum = ran2(&iseed);
if(rnum < 0.025) signal = -1; // random short
else if(rnum > 0.975) signal = 1; // random long

// enter trades on the open
entryposted = 0;
if(ts.position() <= 0 && signal == 1) {
    ts.buyopen('1', ncontracts);
    entryposted = 1;
    entryprice = opn[cb+1];
    entrybar = cb + 1;
}
else if(ts.position() >= 0 && signal == -1) {
    ts.sellopen('2', ncontracts);
    entryposted = -1;
    entryprice = opn[cb+1];
    entrybar = cb + 1;
}

// exit trades using the modified standard exit
// strategy along with the neural signal exit
if(entryposted > 0) {
    // initialization and exits for longs on entry day
    limprice = entryprice + ptlim * exitatr[cb];
    stpprice = entryprice - mmstp * exitatr[cb];
    ts.exitlonglimit('A', limprice);
```

```
                 ts.exitlongstop('B', stpprice);
                 if(prd[cb] > thresh) ts.exitlongclose('C');
         }
         else if(entryposted < 0) {
                 // initialization and exits for shorts on entry day
                 limprice = entryprice - ptlim * exitatr[cb];
                 stpprice = entryprice + mmstp * exitatr[cb];
                 ts.exitshortlimit('D', limprice);
                 ts.exitshortstop('E', stpprice);
                 if(prd[cb] < 100.0-thresh) ts.exitshortclose('F');
         }
         else {
                 // exits for after the entry day
                 if(ts.position() > 0) { // longs
                   ts.exitlonglimit('G', limprice);
                   ts.exitlongstop('H', stpprice);
                   if(cb-entrybar >= maxhold ||
                      prd[cb] > thresh) ts.exitlongclose('I');
                 }
                 else if(ts.position() < 0) { // shorts
                   ts.exitshortlimit('J', limprice);
                   ts.exitshortstop('K', stpprice);
                   if(cb-entrybar >= maxhold ||
                      prd[cb] < 100.0-thresh) ts.exitshortclose('L');
                 }
         }
     } // process next bar
}
```

The code fragment above implements the logic of the exit strategy. The parameters *ptlim* and *mmstp* are set to 4.5 and 1.5, respectively; these are the values that gave the best overall portfolio performance (see Table 14-1, Chapter 14). The thresh parameter, i.e., the threshold used to generate exits based on the neural forecasts, is optimized. The logic of the additional exit can be seen in the "if" statements that compare the prediction of the network with the threshold and that post an exit at close order based on the comparison. The parameter *thresh* is stepped from 50 to 80 in increments of 2.

RESULTS OF THE NEURAL EXIT TEST

Baseline Results

Table 15-1 contains data on the baseline behavior of the MSES. The threshold was set high enough to prevent any net-based exits from occurring. The numbers in this table are the same as those reported in Chapter 14 (Table 14-1) for an optimal fixed stop and profit target. The abbreviations in Table 15-1 may be interpreted as follows: *SAMP* = whether the test was on the training or verification sample (*IN* or *OUT*); *NETL* = the total net profit on long trades, in thousands of dollars; *NETS* = the total net profit on short trades, in thousands of dollars; *PFAC* = the profit factor; *ROA%* = the annualized return-on-account; *ARRR* = the annualized risk-to-reward ratio; *PROB* = the associated probability or statistical significance; *TRDS* = the number of trades taken across all commodities in the portfolio; *WIN%* = the percentage of winning trades; *AVTR* = the average profit/loss per trade; and *TRDB* = the average number of bars or days a trade was held.

There was great consistency between in- and out-of-sample performance: The average trade lost $1,581 in-sample and $1,580 out-of-sample; both samples had 39% winning trades; and the risk-to-reward ratios were −1.46 in-sample and −1.45 out-of-sample.

Neural Exit Portfolio Results

Table 15-2 is the standard optimization table. It shows the in-sample portfolio performance for every threshold examined and the out-of-sample results for the threshold that was the best performer during the in-sample period.

In-sample, an improvement in overall results was obtained from the use of the additional neural network exit. The average trade responded to the threshold in a consistent manner. A threshold of 54 produced the best results, with an average trade losing $832. There were 41% wins and an annualized risk-to-reward ratio of −0.87. The numbers represent a dramatic improvement over those for the baseline presented in Table 15-1. Out-of-sample, however, no improvement was evident: Performance was not too different from that of the optimal MSES without the neural signal element. In the tests conducted using the neural net for entries, performance deteriorated very significantly when moving from in-sample to out-of-sample data. The same thing appears to have happened in the current test, where the same net was used as an element in an exit strategy.

TABLE 15-1

Baseline Performance Data for the Modified Standard Exit Strategy to Be Used When Evaluating the Addition of a Neural Forecaster Signal Exit

SAMP	NETL	NETS	PFAC	ROA%	ARRR	PROB	TRDS	WIN%	AVTR	TRDB
IN	-1976	-4073	0.83	-10.3	-1.46	1.0000	3826	39	-1581	8
OUT	-974	-1632	0.84	-21.6	-1.45	0.9985	1649	39	-1580	8

TABLE 15-2

Portfolio Performance of the Modified Standard Exit Strategy with an Added Neural Signal Exit Evaluated over a Range of Threshold Parameter Values

SAMP	THR	NETL	NETS	PFAC	ROA%	ARRR	PROB	TRDS	WIN%	AVTR	TRDB
IN	50	-1881	-4185	0.73	-10.3	-2.22	1.0000	4282	37	-1416	3
IN	52	-901	-3130	0.86	-10.4	-1.12	0.9998	4030	40	-1000	5
IN	54	-439	-2855	0.89	-10.0	-0.87	0.9966	3956	41	-832	6
IN	56	-482	-3073	0.89	-10.3	-0.91	0.9977	3918	41	-907	7
IN	58	-600	-3040	0.89	-10.3	-0.91	0.9978	3886	41	-936	7
IN	60	-854	-3131	0.88	-10.4	-0.98	0.9989	3864	41	-1031	7
IN	62	-1294	-3379	0.87	-10.3	-1.14	0.9998	3854	40	-1212	7
IN	64	-1533	-3466	0.86	-10.4	-1.21	0.9999	3847	40	-1299	7
IN	66	-1729	-3665	0.85	-10.4	-1.30	1.0000	3837	40	-1405	7
IN	68	-1915	-3882	0.84	-10.3	-1.40	1.0000	3832	39	-1513	8
IN	70	-1959	-3955	0.84	-10.3	-1.42	1.0000	3830	39	-1544	8
IN	72	-1966	-3994	0.84	-10.3	-1.44	1.0000	3829	39	-1556	8
IN	74	-1976	-4010	0.84	-10.3	-1.44	1.0000	3828	39	-1563	8
IN	76	-1976	-3986	0.84	-10.3	-1.44	1.0000	3827	39	-1557	8
IN	78	-1976	-4011	0.84	-10.3	-1.44	1.0000	3827	39	-1564	8
IN	80	-1976	-4047	0.83	-10.3	-1.45	1.0000	3826	39	-1574	8
OUT	54	-1291	-1432	0.81	-22.3	-1.68	0.9997	1710	39	-1592	6

Neural Exit Market-by-Market Results

Table 15-3 shows the performance data for the portfolio, broken down by market, for the optimal MSES with the added neural signal exit. The results are for the composite exit with the best threshold value (54) found in the optimization presented in Table 15-2.

Live Hogs was the only market that was substantially profitable in both samples. A number of markets (e.g., the Deutschemark and Japanese Yen) showed strong profitability in-sample that was not evident out-of-sample. On the long side, the NYFE and Unleaded Gasoline were profitable in both samples. This could easily be a statistical artifact since, in-sample, a large number of markets had profitable performance on the long side.

TEST METHODOLOGY FOR THE GENETIC EXIT COMPONENT

Since it is almost certain that different rules are required for the long side, as opposed to the short side, two tests are run. In the first test, random entries are generated for long positions using the standard random entry strategy. Any short trades generated are simply not taken. Rules are genetically evolved for inclusion in the MSES for the long positions. In the second test, only short entries are taken. Any long entries generated by the random entry strategy are ignored. An attempt is made to evolve rules that work well as additional elements to the MSES for the short side.

TABLE 15-3

Market-by-Market Performance for the Modified Standard Exit with a
Neural Signal Addition Using Random Entries

SYM	IN-SAMPLE						OUT-OF-SAMPLE					
	NETL	NETS	ROA%	AVTR	WIN%	TRDS	NETL	NETS	ROA%	AVTR	WIN%	TRDS
SP	116	-215	-4.2	-948	43	104	0	-97	-12.1	-1765	40	55
YX	150	-220	-2.7	-583	42	120	126	-27	23.7	2158	47	46
US	40	-97	-2.4	-532	46	107	-17	-68	-16.4	-2001	46	43
TB	-22	-75	-3.8	-1152	44	85	-104	-214	-19.3	-5912	29	54
TY	0	-161	-6.5	-1434	40	113	-4	-220	-18.1	-4020	35	56
BP	158	-143	1.2	147	43	100	-51	14	-7.6	-807	40	45
DM	260	-15	23.9	2501	47	98	-47	-56	-14.4	-2198	40	47
SF	-4	-150	-7.7	-1415	37	110	-156	-68	-23.2	-5367	30	42
JY	346	57	41.9	3304	54	122	-50	21	-5.2	-494	43	57
CD	85	-177	-3.6	-984	39	94	-57	20	-3.5	-603	37	61
ED	-416	-183	-9.9	-5260	36	114	-67	-143	-13.7	-4919	34	43
CL	-79	61	-0.9	-151	37	122	117	17	40.7	2870	40	47
HO	-103	-314	-8.6	-3793	37	110	-138	-137	-22.9	-5885	27	47
HU	125	-158	-1.0	-282	45	118	81	-15	20.4	1429	45	46
GC	-55	-30	-4.7	-814	39	105	31	233	84.4	6027	54	44
SI	-321	-120	-9.0	-3742	37	118	-171	55	-14.9	-2038	33	57
PL	-54	-67	-3.9	-920	48	133	-168	-160	-21.8	-6845	29	48
PA	-20	-23	-1.7	-423	42	104	102	-63	9.0	882	50	44
FC	135	104	11.5	1996	48	120	-133	110	-3.8	-498	42	45
LC	38	-106	-4.2	-620	37	110	-46	-74	-11.5	-2815	27	43
LH	191	128	15.6	3295	51	97	13	157	46.1	4602	54	37
PB	-216	-112	-8.6	-3104	33	106	-137	-202	-20.8	-5962	29	57
S	-1	-138	-4.4	-1292	45	108	107	-90	4.4	445	42	38
SM	-1	17	0.7	158	49	97	129	5	33.8	2503	53	54
BO	-246	90	-6.8	-1469	40	106	-50	47	-0.9	-69	40	54
C	-186	142	-3.5	-429	37	103	-215	-117	-22.7	-6792	28	49
O	-213	-93	-9.8	-3137	36	98	-128	-5	-21.5	-2565	26	52
W	-88	-257	-10.0	-2979	32	116	-110	16	-10.2	-2336	42	40
KW	-78	-126	-6.9	-1585	41	129	-128	-87	-22.9	-4495	33	48
MW	-11	14	0.2	30	38	114	80	-37	10.6	1227	45	35
KC	-171	-60	-5.2	-2106	34	110	90	5	21.3	2740	48	35
CC	-99	-19	-5.5	-1089	36	109	-120	-20	-19.2	-3622	38	39
SB	-209	-146	-9.7	-3211	36	111	-51	-50	-12.7	-1952	42	52
JO	-70	-70	-4.3	-1048	40	135	56	-11	9.9	971	47	46
CT	160	-90	4.4	696	42	101	-53	-52	-19.2	-2117	44	50
LB	425	-91	12.1	3057	48	109	-18	-113	-14.2	-2445	37	54

```
static void Model (float *parms, float *dt, float *opn, float *hi,
float *lo, float *cls, float *vol, float *oi, float *dlrv, int nb,
TRDSIM &ts, float *eqcls) {

    // Implements random entries with modified standard exit
    // enhanced with an additional genetically-evolved
    // "signal exit". File = x21mod01.c
    // parms    - vector [1..MAXPRM] of parameters
    // dt       - vector [1..nb] of dates in YYMMDD form
    // opn      - vector [1..nb] of opening prices
```

```
// hi      - vector [1..nb] of high prices
// lo      - vector [1..nb] of low prices
// cls     - vector [1..nb] of closing prices
// vol     - vector [1..nb] of volumes
// oi      - vector [1..nb] of open interest numbers
// dlrv    - vector [1..nb] of average dollar volatilities
// nb      - number of bars in data series or vectors
// ts      - trading simulator class instance
// eqcls   - vector [1..nb] of closing equity levels

// declare local scratch variables
static int rc, cb, ncontracts, maxhold, signal, ranseed;
static float mmstp, ptlim, limprice, stpprice, entryprice;
static int entryposted, entrybar, exitsignal, modeltype;
static int rule1[MAXBAR+1], rule2[MAXBAR+1], rule3[MAXBAR+1];
static float exitatr[MAXBAR+1], rnum, thresh;
static long iseed;

// copy parameters to local variables for clearer reference
ranseed = parms[14];    // used to select random seed
modeltype = parms[15];  // 1=longs, 2=shorts
maxhold = 10;           // maximum holding period in days
ptlim = 4.5;            // profit target limit in atr units
mmstp = 1.5;            // money mgmt stop in atr units

// perform whole-series calculations including rules
AvgTrueRangeS(exitatr,hi,lo,cls,50,nb);        // ATR for exit
Rules (opn, hi, lo, cls, vol, oi, exitatr, nb,
    parms[1], parms[2], parms[3], parms[4], rule1);
Rules (opn, hi, lo, cls, vol, oi, exitatr, nb,
    parms[5], parms[6], parms[7], parms[8], rule2);
Rules (opn, hi, lo, cls, vol, oi, exitatr, nb,
    parms[9], parms[10], parms[11], parms[12], rule3);

// seed the random number generator
// ... use a different seed for each tradeable
// ... ts.model() returns a market index (SP=1, YX=2, ...)
iseed = -(ranseed + 10 * ts.model());
rnum = ran2(&iseed);

// step through bars (days) to simulate actual trading
for(cb = 1; cb <= nb; cb++) {

    // take no trades before the in-sample period
    // ... same as TradeStation's MaxBarsBack setting
    if(dt[cb] < IS_DATE) { eqcls[cb] = 0.0; continue; }
```

```
// execute any pending orders and save closing equity
rc = ts.update(opn[cb], hi[cb], lo[cb], cls[cb], cb);
if(rc != 0) nrerror("Trade buffer overflow");
eqcls[cb] = ts.currentequity(EQ_CLOSETOTAL);

// calculate number of contracts to trade
// ... we want to trade the dollar volatility equivalent
// ... of 2 new S&P-500 contracts as of 12/31/98
ncontracts = RoundToInteger(5673.0 / dlrv[cb]);
if(ncontracts < 1) ncontracts = 1;

// avoid placing orders on possibly limit-locked days
if(hi[cb+1] == lo[cb+1]) continue;

// generate "standard" random entry signals
signal = 0;
rnum = ran2(&iseed);
if(rnum < 0.025 &&
    modeltype == 2) signal = -1; // random short
else if(rnum > 0.975 &&
    modeltype == 1) signal = 1; // random long

// enter trades on the open
entryposted = 0;
if(ts.position() <= 0 && signal == 1) {
    ts.buyopen(`1', ncontracts);
    entryposted = 1;
    entryprice = opn[cb+1];
    entrybar = cb + 1;
}
else if(ts.position() >= 0 && signal == -1) {
    ts.sellopen(`2', ncontracts);
    entryposted = -1;
    entryprice = opn[cb+1];
    entrybar = cb + 1;
}

// exit trades using the modified standard exit
// strategy along with the neural signal exit
exitsignal = rule1[cb] && rule2[cb] && rule3[cb];
if(entryposted > 0) {
    // initialization and exits for longs on entry day
    limprice = entryprice + ptlim * exitatr[cb];
    stpprice = entryprice - mmstp * exitatr[cb];
    ts.exitlonglimit(`A', limprice);
```

```
                ts.exitlongstop('B', stpprice);
                if(exitsignal) ts.exitlongclose('C');
        }
        else if(entryposted < 0) {
                // initialization and exits for shorts on entry day
                limprice = entryprice - ptlim * exitatr[cb];
                stpprice = entryprice + mmstp * exitatr[cb];
                ts.exitshortlimit('D', limprice);
                ts.exitshortstop('E', stpprice);
                if(exitsignal) ts.exitshortclose('F');
        }
        else {
                // exits for after the entry day
                if(ts.position() > 0) { // longs
                        ts.exitlonglimit('G', limprice);
                        ts.exitlongstop('H', stpprice);
                        if(cb-entrybar >= maxhold ||
                                exitsignal) ts.exitlongclose('I');
                }
                else if(ts.position() < 0) { // shorts
                        ts.exitshortlimit('J', limprice);
                        ts.exitshortstop('K', stpprice);
                        if(cb-entrybar >= maxhold ||
                                exitsignal) ts.exitshortclose('L');
                }
        }
    } // process next bar
}
```

The code above shows the logic of both the entries and exits. The *modeltype* parameter controls whether the longs or shorts are tested. Parameters *ptlim* and *mmstp* are for the profit target and stop (respectively). They are fixed at the same optimal values used in the neural network test earlier. Each of the three rules is calculated as a series of *TRUE/FALSE* values, and if all three rules are TRUE, a rule-based exit signal (*exitsig*) is generated. In the exit code, "if" clauses have been added. For example, an exit at the close is generated *if* an exit signal is produced by all three rules being *TRUE* (*exitsig = TRUE*). The evolution of rules for the long and short sides follow the same steps as in the chapter on genetics, in which similar rules were evolved for use in entries. The same 12 parameter chromosomes, broken into three genes (each specifying a rule), are employed, and there is no change in that logic in the current test. Rules for the short side and for the long side are produced by allowing 2,500 generations to pass (2,500 runs using OptEvolve). The top 10 solutions for the longs and for the shorts are then tested on both the in-sample and out-of-sample data.

Top 10 Solutions with Baseline Exit

Table 15-4 shows the top 10 solutions found for the long side and for the short side. In the table, *LINE* = the line or generation number; *PROB* = the probability or statistical significance (the decimal point is omitted but implied in the formatting of these numbers); *$TRD* = the average dollars-per-trade; *TRDS* = the total number of trades taken; *PFAC* = the profit factor; and *AROA* = the annualized return-on-account.

The best solution for the longs was discovered in the 845 generation of the evolutionary process. For the short side, it was in the 1,253 generation. In contrast to the situation when rules were evolved for use in an entry model, none of the solutions were profitable. However, Table 15-5 shows that when genetically evolved rule-based exits were added, substantial improvement over the baseline was achieved.

The rules in Table 15-4 were translated into plain language. The rules for exiting a long position were as follows: If the close on the current bar is greater

TABLE 15-4

Top 10 Solutions from the Evolutionary Process
for Longs and for Shorts

LONG SOLUTIONS					
LINE	PROB	$TRD	TRDS	PFAC	AROA
845	706728	-324	1972	0.96	-4.9
1752	712448	-350	1947	0.96	-4.4
1804	737793	-354	1994	0.96	-5.0
1464	728199	-379	1944	0.96	-5.0
1755	729060	-382	1934	0.96	-5.1
1591	761321	-384	1999	0.96	-4.5
1584	733418	-394	1925	0.96	-4.8
637	750316	-397	1974	0.96	-5.2
1810	739410	-399	1944	0.96	-5.0
1850	742540	-399	1938	0.96	-5.3
SHORT SOLUTIONS					
LINE	PROB	$TRD	TRDS	PFAC	AROA
1253	999842	-1645	1959	0.78	-10.2
1758	999695	-1646	1943	0.80	-10.1
1183	998990	-1717	1885	0.81	-10.1
1379	999639	-1755	1920	0.79	-9.9
1129	999211	-1756	1885	0.81	-10.1
472	999161	-1757	1885	0.81	-10.2
1833	999161	-1757	1885	0.81	-10.2
1816	999834	-1764	1932	0.79	-10.3
1881	998851	-1764	1869	0.82	-9.9
1427	999581	-1767	1916	0.80	-10.0

than a 12-bar exponential moving average (EMA) of the closes, but is less than a 49-bar EMA of the closes, and the current bar represents a 6-bar new high, then exit the long trade. The rules seem to be searching for a situation in which the longer trend is down, but a short-term retracement against the trend has occurred and has reached a point where completion of the retracement is likely and the longer-term downward trend will resume—a sensible point to exit a long position. The rules for the short side suggest that an exit should occur if the close on the current bar is greater than the 16-bar EMA of the closes and a 22-bar simple moving average of the closes, and if the MACD is sloping down. The specific MACD used employs a 6-bar EMA for its faster moving average and a 10-bar EMA for its slower moving average. The idea encapsulated in these rules seems to be that it is wise to close out short positions if the market, when smoothed, still appears to be moving down, but the most recent close broke above two moving averages, indicating the market may be starting a new trend up.

Results of Rule-Based Exits for Longs and Shorts

Table 15-5 presents the performance data for best of the top 10 solutions (longs and shorts) for the MSES with the addition of genetically evolved, rule-based signal exits. Trades were entered randomly. The table is broken down into results for long positions and results for short positions. It is further broken down by sample and test. Sample (*IN* or *OUT*) and test may be *BSLN* (when the rules were not used) or *RULE* (when the rules were used).

On the long side, in-sample, the addition of the genetically evolved rule-based exit substantially reduced the loss on the average trade from a baseline of $688 to $324. The percentage of winning trades increased from 41 to 43%. The annualized risk-to-

TABLE 15-5

Performance of the Modified Standard Exit Strategy with an Added Genetically Evolved Rule-Based Signal Exit When Trades Are Entered Randomly

LONG POSITIONS												
TEST	SAMP	NET	NETL	NETS	PFAC	ROA%	ARRR	PROB	TRDS	WIN%	AVTR	TRDB
BSLN	IN	-1324	-1324	0	0.93	-7.3	-0.35	0.8628	1923	41	-688	8
RULE	IN	-640	-640	0	0.96	-4.9	-0.17	0.7067	1972	43	-324	7
BSLN	OUT	-942	-942	0	0.89	-13.2	-0.61	0.8938	830	39	-1135	8
RULE	OUT	-845	-845	0	0.89	-15.6	-0.60	0.8903	854	41	-990	7
SHORT POSITIONS												
TEST	SAMP	NET	NETL	NETS	PFAC	ROA%	ARRR	PROB	TRDS	WIN%	AVTR	TRDB
BSLN	IN	-3850	0	-3850	0.80	-9.9	-1.09	0.9997	1847	37	-2084	8
RULE	IN	-3223	0	-3223	0.78	-10.3	-1.15	0.9998	1959	37	-1645	6
BSLN	OUT	-1497	0	-1497	0.82	-20.4	-1.02	0.9818	792	38	-1890	8
RULE	OUT	-889	0	-889	0.86	-18.2	-0.73	0.9325	841	40	-1058	6

reward ratio improved from −0.35 to −0.17. Out-of-sample, the benefit of the genet-ically evolved rule-based signal exit was maintained, but not quite as dramatically. The loss on the average trade was cut from $1,135 to $990. The percentage of winning trades increased from 39 to 41%. The risk-to-reward ratio improved slightly from −0.61 to −0.60. Overall, adding the genetically evolved rule-based element to the exit strategy worked. In contrast to the neural exit, the benefit was maintained out-of-sam-ple, suggesting that curve-fitting and over-optimization were not major issues.

On the short side, similar benefits were observed in both samples. In-sample, the addition of the genetically evolved rule-based element reduced the loss on the average trade from a baseline of $2,084 to $1,645. The percentage of winning trades remained unchanged. Paradoxically, the annualized risk-to-reward ratio worsened somewhat, going from −1.09 to −1.15. Out-of-sample, the loss on the average trade dropped substantially, from $1,890 in the baseline test to $1,058, when the rule element was active. The percentage of winning trades rose from 38 to 40%, and the annualized risk-to-reward ratio improved, from −1.02 to −0.73. Again, the addition of the genetically evolved rule-based signal exit to the MSES worked and continued to work out-of-sample.

Market-by-Market Results of Rule-Based Exits for Longs

Table 15-6 contains information regarding the market-by-market performance of the MSES for the long side, with the added rule-based signal exit. Several markets showed profitability in both samples: the NYFE, Light Crude, Unleaded Gasoline, and Live Hogs. Other markets were profitable in-sample, but lost heavily out-of-sample (and vice versa). The consistency between in-sample and out-of-sample results was not high.

Market-by-Market Results of Rule-Based Exits for Shorts

Table 15-7 shows the same market-by-market breakdown as in Table 15-6, but only the short side is represented. More consistency was evident between in-sam-ple and out-of-sample performances for the short side than for the long. Most notably profitable in both samples was the Japanese Yen. Light Crude, Unleaded Gasoline, Feeder Cattle, Live Hogs, Soybean Meal, and Coffee were also prof-itable in both samples.

CONCLUSION

Several important points were demonstrated by the above tests. First, neural net-works hold up less well in out-of-sample tests than do genetically evolved rule-based solutions. This is no doubt a result of the greater number of parameters

TABLE 15-6

Market-by-Market Performance of the Modified Standard Exit with an Added Genetically Evolved Rule-based Signal Exit When Tested Using Random Long Trade Entries

SYM	NETL	PFAC	ROA%	AVTR	WIN%	TRDS	NETL	PFAC	ROA%	AVTR	WIN%	TRDS
SP	124	1.36	14.1	2599	50	48	-20	0.92	-4.0	-956	33	21
YX	128	1.26	8.2	2301	44	56	178	2.12	56.9	7769	60	23
US	-39	0.91	-2.6	-725	46	54	34	1.18	8.7	1457	50	24
TB	-186	0.67	-7.6	-3524	39	53	33	1.11	5.6	1344	52	25
TY	-56	0.91	-3.7	-912	41	62	36	1.14	9.8	1442	52	25
BP	63	1.16	5.6	1246	45	51	-127	0.31	-19.3	-6057	33	21
DM	257	1.74	34.5	5259	51	49	-70	0.66	-19.4	-3065	43	23
SF	50	1.12	4.7	980	42	52	-146	0.14	-21.2	-9794	13	15
JY	159	1.31	16.6	2417	46	66	-44	0.83	-7.6	-1519	37	29
CD	6	1.02	0.4	132	50	50	-184	0.55	-14.7	-5260	31	35
ED	-481	0.45	-10.1	-8294	34	58	-158	0.47	-14.7	-6872	43	23
CL	29	1.05	1.3	497	45	60	230	2.71	64.9	10040	56	23
HO	-107	0.80	-4.9	-1927	42	56	-155	0.27	-20.0	-8633	11	18
HU	154	1.32	8.5	2963	46	52	109	1.63	32.4	4562	54	24
GC	-122	0.75	-5.1	-2506	44	49	-20	0.92	-3.0	-848	45	24
SI	-232	0.64	-7.8	-3742	38	62	-83	0.74	-9.3	-3214	34	26
PL	50	1.09	2.6	715	51	70	-190	0.38	-20.4	-8270	30	23
PA	-116	0.76	-6.4	-2166	38	54	221	3.40	76.0	13036	70	17
FC	209	1.52	14.7	3944	50	53	-114	0.58	-17.1	-4089	39	28
LC	17	1.04	1.1	341	44	52	-55	0.77	-8.5	-1980	39	28
LH	154	1.33	11.3	3025	54	51	211	3.77	133.6	13223	75	16
PB	-176	0.64	-8.5	-3599	36	49	-120	0.60	-12.7	-4004	36	30
S	-81	0.82	-3.0	-1447	41	56	49	1.50	27.6	2595	52	19
SM	-70	0.82	-2.8	-1446	36	49	228	3.39	116.8	9946	69	23
BO	-240	0.48	-8.4	-5238	32	46	-61	0.78	-12.1	-2052	33	30
C	-143	0.76	-5.0	-2702	33	53	-172	0.40	-17.4	-6630	26	26
O	-188	0.64	-10.3	-3853	34	49	-164	0.42	-18.4	-5674	20	29
W	-101	0.83	-5.6	-1814	41	56	-158	0.44	-18.7	-6872	30	23
KW	39	1.07	2.3	639	50	61	-158	0.50	-19.2	-5470	31	29
MW	85	1.15	5.9	1350	46	63	-17	0.90	-4.6	-850	40	20
KC	-150	0.70	-4.4	-2784	38	54	147	2.97	56.8	7774	57	19
CC	-60	0.86	-3.9	-1139	41	53	-115	0.25	-22.1	-7202	25	16
SB	-19	0.95	-1.9	-350	47	55	0	1.00	0.0	0	52	21
JO	-132	0.77	-5.2	-2077	39	64	106	1.93	54.1	5073	66	21
CT	159	1.40	17.6	3390	46	47	-61	0.75	-16.6	-2282	37	27
LB	378	1.80	24.1	6410	50	59	-35	0.87	-7.6	-1167	40	30

involved in the neural network model, as compared with the rule-based models being used. In other words, the effects of curve-fitting were damaging to the neural network solution. Also discovered was the fact that the addition of a sophisticated signal exit, whether based on a neural net or a set of genetically evolved entry rules, can greatly improve an exit strategy. When the more robust, genetically evolved rules were applied, the performance benefits obtained persisted in out-of-sample evaluations.

The neural network and the rule templates (but not the actual rules) that were used in developing the signal exits were originally developed for inclusion in an

TABLE 15-7

Market-by-Market Performance of the Modified Standard Exit with an Added Genetically Evolved Rule-Based Signal Exit When Tested Using Random Short Trade Entries

SYM	NETS	PFAC	ROA%	AVTR	WIN%	TRDS	NETS	PFAC	ROA%	AVTR	WIN%	TRDS
SP	-187	0.58	-7.5	-3126	33	60	-191	0.41	-19.8	-5640	29	34
YX	-310	0.40	-9.0	-4770	35	65	-17	0.91	-4.2	-748	30	23
US	-85	0.77	-6.0	-1554	40	55	-41	0.75	-11.0	-2175	36	19
TB	-162	0.56	-8.4	-5073	37	32	-119	0.48	-23.4	-4283	28	28
TY	-138	0.67	-7.9	-2769	34	50	-243	0.22	-21.6	-7862	25	31
BP	-106	0.71	-6.0	-2052	36	52	-69	0.69	-11.1	-3030	39	23
DM	-104	0.72	-9.0	-2263	39	46	-53	0.72	-12.9	-2143	44	25
SF	-101	0.75	-8.0	-1663	39	61	42	1.28	17.1	1473	58	29
JY	138	1.50	13.1	2473	46	56	141	1.88	59.8	5251	51	27
CD	-157	0.57	-6.8	-3660	25	43	-62	0.78	-11.2	-2415	34	26
ED	-417	0.36	-10.1	-7458	23	56	-180	0.17	-22.9	-9515	21	19
CL	87	1.24	8.1	1482	37	59	10	1.07	3.8	403	40	27
HO	-264	0.51	-7.7	-4725	32	56	-7	0.97	-1.3	-246	48	29
HU	14	1.03	0.7	238	39	61	61	1.46	22.4	2661	56	23
GC	-177	0.64	-10.3	-3107	31	57	252	4.44	148.2	13288	73	19
SI	-64	0.86	-3.4	-1129	40	57	70	1.32	28.5	2438	48	29
PL	-104	0.76	-5.4	-1776	44	59	-158	0.45	-21.1	-6617	33	24
PA	-64	0.80	-5.4	-1286	42	50	7	1.07	2.2	306	48	25
FC	34	1.09	2.2	534	41	65	90	1.79	32.7	6043	60	15
LC	-158	0.64	-8.5	-2827	33	56	-35	0.76	-5.9	-2081	23	17
LH	38	1.13	2.4	870	40	44	126	2.46	54.7	6654	57	19
PB	27	1.07	1.6	505	38	54	-166	0.44	-19.5	-6177	40	27
S	-292	0.37	-9.2	-5848	34	50	-119	0.28	-17.1	-7945	33	15
SM	16	1.06	1.4	376	48	43	32	1.17	9.8	1028	37	32
BO	-26	0.94	-2.0	-439	40	61	-11	0.93	-2.9	-558	35	20
C	-29	0.93	-1.3	-598	34	50	30	1.28	13.5	1445	52	21
O	-53	0.86	-3.5	-1112	35	48	0	1.00	0.0	3	37	24
W	-197	0.60	-10.1	-3188	35	62	33	1.38	13.1	2223	53	15
KW	-45	0.91	-2.3	-667	33	68	23	1.15	6.5	1231	31	19
MW	-45	0.90	-2.2	-864	37	53	-79	0.44	-17.8	-5645	35	14
KC	84	1.27	6.7	1723	46	49	4	1.05	1.8	316	40	15
CC	-17	0.95	-1.1	-327	42	54	26	1.27	7.3	1182	45	22
SB	-157	0.65	-8.0	-2588	36	61	-94	0.64	-10.7	-2963	21	32
JO	-55	0.89	-4.3	-830	37	67	-68	0.64	-16.4	-2759	40	25
CT	-30	0.91	-2.5	-593	42	52	-42	0.71	-12.8	-1850	47	23
LB	-106	0.74	-5.0	-2257	40	47	-80	0.63	-22.1	-3100	34	26

entry model. When the rules were used in an entry model, it was acceptable for them to generate rare event trades. In an exit strategy, however, rules that fire more frequently would be more desirable. There is every indication that a set of rule templates (and ways of combining the rules to obtain signals), specifically designed for use in an exit strategy, would provide much better results than those obtained here. The same should be true for neural networks.

WHAT HAVE WE LEARNED?

- Curve-fitting can be bad not only when building entries, but also when building exits.
- Sophisticated technologies, including genetic algorithms, can be effectively used to improve an exit strategy.
- Even crude efforts to improve exits, such as those carried out here, can enhance profits by several hundred dollars per trade.

Conclusion

A long road has been traveled since beginning the study of entry and exit strategies. Sometimes the trip has been tedious and discouraging; at other times, stimulating and surprising. As usual after extended journeys, the questions "What knowledge has been gained?" and "How may that knowledge be applied?" beg to be answered. The first question will be addressed by a successively more detailed examination of the results: going from discoveries made about the portfolio performance of entire classes of models, to more specific model-order combinations, down to an inspection of individual markets and how they are best traded.

The perspectives taken in the following discussions of what has been achieved are analogous to views from an airplane flying at night. At first, the plane is at a very high altitude: All that can be seen when looking down are large patches of darkness (classes of models that are ineffective or lose) and some patches of light (classes of models that, overall, work fairly well or, at least, perform better than chance). This view provides a basic idea of which models are, overall, viable relative to the entire portfolio of tradables.

The plane then descends. More detail is seen. It becomes evident that the brightest spots are often formed by clusters of light having various luminosities (model-order combinations that are, to one extent or another, profitable). Occasionally the dark patches also contain small isolated points of brightness (successful model-order combinations amid approaches that usually are ineffective). At this level, a number of dim areas can be seen as well (model-order combinations that are not profitable, but that have better than chance performance that could be enhanced if combined with a good exit).

Finally, landing is imminent. It is possible to look inside the bright spots and see their detail, i.e., the individual markets the various model-order combinations trade best. The second question above can now be addressed: By identifying the consistently profitable (across samples) model-order combinations and the markets best traded by them, a good portfolio trading strategy can be developed. At this time, it will become clear that out of all the studies performed during the long trip, enough has been learned to assemble a lucrative portfolio of systems and tradables. By way of demonstration, such a portfolio will be compiled and run with the standard exit strategy.

THE BIG PICTURE

For this perspective, each class of entry model (e.g., all trend-following moving average models, all breakouts, all small neural networks) was examined in its entirety. All the tests for each model type were averaged. Out-of-sample and in-sample performances were separately evaluated.

By far the best out-of-sample performer was the genetic model: Out of all the models, it was the only one that showed a substantial profit when averaged over all the different tests. The profit per trade was $3,271.

Next best, in terms of out-of-sample behavior over all tests, were the small neural networks. The neural network models were broken down into those for small and large nets because curve-fitting appeared to be a serious issue, especially affecting large nets. The breakdown was a natural and easy one to accomplish because, in the tests, each model was tested with one small and one large network. Out-of-sample, all the small neural networks taken together averaged a loss of $860 per trade. This indicates a significantly better than chance entry in that random entries produced an average loss of over $2,000, with a standard deviation of slightly under $400.

Going down in quality, the next best overall approach involved seasonality. Altogether, all tests of seasonality models showed an average loss of $966 per trade.

Three of the moving average models (crossover, slope, and support/resistance) followed the performance of seasonality. These models, when averaged across tests, lost around $1,500 per trade, which is close to the $2,100-per-trade loss expected when using random entries. In other words, the moving average models were only marginally better than random.

All the remaining models tested provided entries that were very close to random. Cycles were actually worse than random.

In-sample, the genetic models ($12,533 per trade), all the neural network models (small, $8,940, and large, $13,082), and the breakouts ($1,537) traded profitably. Out-of-sample, the genetic models continued to be profitable, the nets were better than chance (although there was significant shrinkage in their performance due to curve-fitting), and the breakouts deteriorated to chance (optimization cannot be a factor in this case).

The next best performers in-sample were the support/resistance moving average models ($300 loss per trade) and the seasonality models ($671 loss per trade).

Further down the ladder of best-to-worst performers were the lunar and solar models, which lost $1,076 and $1,067, respectively. Losses in the $1,300 to $1,700 range were observed for the moving average models. The oscillator and cycle models exhibited losses of over $2,000 per trade; when taken as a whole, these models were no better than chance.

It is interesting that the genetic model and the small neural network models were the ones that held up out of sample. Such models offer great opportunities for curve-fitting and tend to fail in out-of-sample tests and real trading. Seasonality, which is only rarely the topic of articles, also exhibited potential. On the other hand, the most popular methods (e.g., moving average, oscillator, and cycle models) performed the worst, trading badly both in- and out-of-sample. The breakout models are noteworthy in the sense that, taken as a group, they worked well in the past; but, due to increased market efficiency, have since deteriorated to the point where they currently perform no better than chance.

Table C-1 contains the annualized return-on-account (the first line of each model-order combination) and average dollars-per-trade (the second line of each model-order combination) data for all the tests (all model and order combinations) conducted for entry models using the standard exit strategy. The data presented are for portfolio performance as a whole. The model descriptions (leftmost column) are the same as used elsewhere in this book. The last six lines of the table contain data that can be used as a baseline against which the various entry models can be compared. The baseline data are derived from using the random entry strategy with the unmodified standard exit strategy. *Mean ROA%* is the average return on account over several sets of random entries; *StdDev ROA%* is the standard deviation of the return-on-account. *Mean $TRD* is the average dollars-per-trade over several sets of random entries; and *StdDev $TRD* is the standard deviation of the dollars-per-trade.

Breakout models had the unique characteristic of being consistently profitable in-sample across almost every model-order combination tested. Except for the volatility breakouts, these models performed much better than chance, albeit not profitably, out-of-sample; i.e., the loss per trade was under $1,000, sometimes under $300 (the average loss to be expected was around $2,000 with random entries). In other words, the breakouts, taken together, were better than random. However, out-of-sample, the volatility breakouts did much worse than chance: With at-open and on-stop orders, the model lost more than $5,000 per trade, as though the market's current behavior is precisely designed to make these systems costly to trade.

The trend-following moving average models (crossover and slope) all performed slightly better than chance in-sample: They all lost rather heavily, but the losses were almost always less than $2,000. None of the systems, however, did very well. Out-of-sample, the picture was somewhat more variable, but had the same flavor: Most of the models were somewhat better than chance, and one or two were much better than chance (but still not profitable).

TABLE C-1

Summary of Portfolio for All Entry Models Tested with All Order Types

	In-sample			Out-of-sample			Average	Average
	Open	Limit	Stop	Open	Limit	Stop	In	Out
Close-only	-1	33		-14	-10		16	-12
channel breakout	-60	1066		-671	-299		503	-485
HHLL breakout	1	36	9	-16	-2	-15	15	-11
	82	1558	430	-912	-72	-798	690	-594
Volatility breakout	27	48	12	-20	-17	-23	29	-20
	4675	3616	931	-7371	-2094	-5272	3074	-4912
Volatility breakout		53			-15		53	-15
longs only		4100			-1640		4100	-1640
Volatility breakout		36			18		36	18
currencies only		3977			2106		3977	2106
Volatility breakout		68			-20		68	-20
with ADX filter		4570			-2415		4570	-2415
SMA	-9	-8	-7	-23	-21	-20	-8	-21
Cross	-1765	-926	-1045	-1628	-1213	-1337	-1245	-1393
EMA	-9	-7	-9	-20	-22	-20	-9	-21
Cross	-1570	-705	-1534	-1269	-1755	-1223	-1270	-1416
FWTMA	-9	-8	-9	-22	-18	-23	-9	-21
Cross	-1666	-890	-1720	-1984	-1265	-2715	-1425	-1988
AMA	-10	-7	-8	-22	-19	-24	-8	-22
Cross	-1942	-769	-1731	-1798	-1071	-2350	-1481	-1740
SMA	-10	-9	-10	-22	-19	-24	-9	-22
Slope	-1667	-906	-1076	-1083	-615	-2528	-1216	-1409
EMA	-10	-10	-9	-23	-20	-21	-9	-21
Slope	-2137	-1629	-1289	-1714	-1096	-1199	-1685	-1336
FWTMA	-10	-9	-8	-23	-19	-3	-9	-15
Slope	-1842	-1365	-1203	-1647	-1561	-91	-1470	-1100
AMA	-10	-10	-9	-23	-23	-23	-9	-23
Slope	-2353	-1531	-1603	-1872	-1391	-2002	-1829	-1755
SMA-CC	-10	-10	-10	-23	-21	-21	-10	-21
	-2220	-1630	-1120	-3221	-1917	-1731	-1657	-2290
EMA-CC	-10	-10	-9	-23	-23	-23	-10	-23

TABLE C-1

(Continued)

		-2350	-1905	-1171	-2471	-2214	-3128	-1809	-2604
FWTMA-CC		-10	-9	-9	-21	-17	-20	-9	-19
		-2405	-1869	-1246	-1821	-971	-1343	-1840	-1378
AMA-CC		-10	-10	-9	-23	-23	-21	-10	-22
		-1865	-1488	-1033	-2222	-2254	-1604	-1462	-2027
SMA-SR		-10	-10	4	-20	-17	15	-5	-8
		-1099	-844	227	-1962	-1512	482	-572	-997
EMA-SR		0	0	0	0	0	0	0	0
		0	0	0	0	0	0	0	0
FWTMA-SR		-8	-3	9	-13	-14	-22	-1	-16
		-841	-261	1015	-1444	-1087	-3566	-29	-2032
AMA-SR		0	0	0	0	0	0	0	0
		0	0	0	0	0	0	0	0
Stochastic ob/os		-10	-10	-10	-24	-24	-23	-10	-23
		-3672	-2228	-2586	-3130	-2504	-2650	-2829	-2761
RSI ob / os		-10	-10	-10	-21	-18	-21	-10	-20
		-7073	-4093	-6878	-3537	-1978	-3824	-6015	-3113
Stochastic signal line		-10	-10	-10	-24	-23	-24	-10	-23
		-2656	-1813	-2026	-2324	-1330	-1968	-2165	-1874
MACD signal line		-10	-10	-8	-22	-21	-19	-9	-21
		-1808	-1210	-1476	-1259	-1434	-533	-1498	-1075
Stochastic divergence		-10	-10	-10	-22	-21	-20	-10	-21
		-3245	-2443	-3008	-3259	-3182	-2179	-2899	-2873
RSI divergence		-10	-9	-7	-22	-19	-20	-9	-20
		-2278	-1529	-1309	-3065	-3400	-2935	-1705	-3133
MACD divergence		26	12	27	2	20	-5	22	5
		1393	1250	2062	140	985	-589	1568	179
Seasonal crossover		-10	-4	-1	-6	-2	8	-5	0
		-1127	-424	-179	-300	-56	576	-577	73
Seasonal momentum		-9	-7	3	-14	-14	-16	-4	-15
		-1069	-757	275	-952	-785	-1750	-517	-1162
Crossover with confirmation		-10	-7	6	-14	-21	20	-4	-5
		-1195	-832	846	-1512	-3408	1677	-394	-1081
Crossover with		-10	-9	-2	-20	-23	1	-7	-14

TABLE C-1

(Continued)

conf. + inver.	-1669	-1696	-229	-2545	-2642	95	-1198	-1697
Lunar	-9	-6	-6	-14	-10	-10	-7	-12
crossover	-1287	-406	-686	-894	-643	-702	-793	-746
Lunar	-10	-10	-8	-15	-20	-8	-9	-14
momentum	-2410	-1560	-1288	-1316	-1942	-372	-1753	-1210
Crossover with	-8	-7	2	-21	-21	-19	-4	-20
confirm	-1251	-655	234	-3465	-3896	-2449	-557	-3270
Crossover with	-9	-10	-8	-21	-21	-20	-9	-21
conf. & inv.	-1546	-1078	-998	-2937	-3203	-2995	-1207	-3045
Solar breakout	-9	-9	0	-22	-22	-14	-6	-19
	-1631	-1519	-52	-2284	-2956	-1329	-1067	-2190
Cycle top / bot	-10	-10	-8	-23	-23	-15	-9	-20
	-1329	-1037	-1245	-3741	-3551	-944	-1204	-2745
Reverse Slow %K	193	182	154	-3	-3	3	176	-1
18-6-1 net	6917	7879	6764	-233	-331	362	7187	-67
Reverse Slow %K	535	547	329	-18	-17	-16	470	-17
18-14-4-1 net	7080	8203	6304	-1214	-961	-1154	7196	-1110
Turning Point Long	311	308	237	-17	-16	-11	285	-15
18-10-1 net	9316	9373	10630	-2327	-2197	-2868	9773	-2464
Turning Point Long	768	742	469	-13	-13	-2	660	-9
18-20-6-1 net	18588	18569	15392	-2001	-1886	-518	17516	-1468
Turning Point Short	207	209	175	12	8	-6	197	5
18-10-1 net	8448	8701	12553	580	405	-1138	9901	-51
Turning Point Short	602	604	387	-19	-20	-22	531	-21
18-20-6-1	18550	18905	6320	-5314	-5163	-2076	14592	-4184
Long Genetic	82	66	42	63	88	12	63	54
	17264	14846	16247	10231	14920	4246	16119	9799
Short Genetic	55	17	23	-10	-11	-13	32	-11
	11929	7424	7493	-2711	-3351	-3704	8949	-3255
Baseline (Random)								
Mean ROA%	-11.3	-11.1	-10.3	-22.6	-22.0	-18.0	-10.9	-20.9
StdDev ROA%	3.8	3.6	2.6				3.3	
Mean $TRD	-2243	-1930	-2039	-1863	-3056	-1493	-2071	-2137
StdDev $TRD	304	477	391				391	

The countertrend moving average models were more variable than the trend-following ones. Many of them showed much smaller losses or even small profits, in-sample. A similar picture was seen out-of-sample, especially with the simple moving average support/resistance model.

Except for the MACD divergence model, which behaved differently from the others, oscillators performed very poorly. There was a lot of variability, but on the whole, these models gave per-trade profits that were worse than expected by chance both in-sample and out-of-sample. The RSI overbought/oversold model was the worst of them all. In both samples, it provided staggering losses that were (statistically) significantly worse than those that would have been achieved with a random entry.

The seasonal models, on the whole, were clearly better than chance. Although only one of these models actually provided profits in both samples, two of them were profitable out-of-sample, and several had only very small losses (much less than would be expected by chance using random entries) across samples.

The basic lunar model had mixed findings. Most of the in-sample results were slightly positive when compared with chance (the random entry), but not profitable. The basic crossover model, however, was decidedly biased above chance in both samples.

Although the solar models performed slightly better than chance in-sample, they were mixed and variable out-of-sample. This was also true for the cycle models. However, the cycle models, when using entry at open or on limit, actually performed significantly worse in recent years than a random entry. As with breakouts, the findings are not due to optimization; significant curve-fitting was only detected with the genetic and neural network models. Because of the tremendous sample involved in the portfolio, the optimization of one or two parameters, necessary for most models (other than the genetic and neural ones), had minimal curve-fitting effect.

Surprisingly, the neural network models showed a fairly consistent bias to perform better than chance out-of-sample. In-sample, of course, performance was stellar across all tests. There was shrinkage (evidence of curve-fitting), but the shrinkage was not complete, leaving some predictive utility in the out-of-sample data.

The results for the genetically evolved rules were the best. In-sample, performance was excellent. Out-of-sample, performance was exceptional for models involving long positions.

Summary

Many of the models described as significantly better than chance (i.e., better than what would be produced by a random entry) would likely become profitable if coupled with a better exit strategy. In Part III, it was evident that when tested with random entries, the use of a good exit could bolster profits (or cut losses) by about $1,000 per trade. This means that, with a good exit, some of the entry models that had losses of several hundred dollars could be brought into positive, profitable territory.

As mentioned above, the journey was a long one, sometimes tedious and discouraging. However, this bird's-eye view revealed that a lot of potentially profitable entry models were indeed discovered. There were also a number of surprises: Despite terrible reputations and dangerous tendencies toward curve-fitting, the neural network and genetic models were the best performers when tested with data that was not used in training or evolving. Another surprise was that some of the most popular trading approaches, e.g., moving-average crossovers and oscillator-based strategies, turned out to be among the worst, with few exceptions. The results of the cycle models were also revealing: Because of their theoretical elegance, better—if not ideal—performance was expected. However, perhaps due to their popularity, poor performance was observed even though the implementation was a solid, mathematical one.

POINTS OF LIGHT

The portfolio performance of each model was examined for each of the three order types (at open, on limit, and on stop). Out-of-sample and in-sample performances were separately evaluated.

The out-of-sample performance was, by far, the best for the long-side genetic models. Entry at open was especially noteworthy, with a 64.2% in-sample return and 41.0% out-of-sample. The same model was also profitable with entry on limit and on stop, yielding very high dollars-per-trade profits, although small numbers of trades (easily increased with more elaborate models of this kind).

In terms of out-of-sample performance, the next best specific model-order combination was the seasonal crossover with confirmation using entry on stop. Like the long genetic models, this one was significantly profitable in both sampling periods: in-sample, $846 per trade, with a 7.4% return; out-of-sample, $1,677 per trade, with a 9.5% return. Other seasonal models also did okay, with out-of-sample profits being made using the simple seasonal crossover model.

Next down the list was the short turning-point model that used the small 16-10-1 network. This model was profitable in both samples across all orders: out-of-sample, at open, a 9.3% annualized return, with $580 per trade; in-sample, a 35.2% return and $8,448 per trade profit.

While still on the subject of neural networks, the reverse Slow %K model was a profitable performer, especially when a stop order was used. Out-of-sample, the annualized return was 6.1%, with $362 per trade. In-sample, there was a 22.5% return, with a $6,764-per-trade profit. Note the large shrinkage from in-sample to out-of-sample for these models: While this is evidence of curve-fitting, enough real curves were caught for profits to be made in the verification sample.

Another model that produced profits in both samples was the MACD divergence model, especially with entry on limit. This model had a 6.1% annualized return, out-of-sample, and a $985-per-trade profit. In-sample, the figures were a 6.7% return and a $1,250 profit per trade.

Finally, among the models that were profitable in both samples was the simple moving-average support/resistance model with entry on stop: It took 6.4% out of the market, with $482 per trade, out-of-sample; and $5.8%, with $227 per trade, in-sample.

Almost all other models lost money out-of-sample, and often in-sample, as well. The only exception was the volatility breakout model restricted to the currencies, which performed fairly well. Out-of-sample, it had an 8.5% return and made $2,106 per trade. In sample, it had a 12.4% return, with $3,977 profit per trade.

Summary

Even though most of the other model-order combinations lost out-of-sample, in many cases, the losses were much less than would be expected with a totally random entry. In a number of instances, however, they were worse.

It seems evident that there are a number of models that, although not ideal and in need of further development, do yield profitable trading that holds up in a verification sample and yields reasonable statistics.

LOOKING INTO THE LIGHT

Until this point, only tests and models that operate on the whole portfolio have been discussed. In the course of the tests, many observations were made regarding the performance of specific models when trading individual markets. A recurrent observation was that certain models seem to trade certain markets well, while other models trade them poorly. Some markets just seem to be difficult to trade, regardless of model. There is no doubt that by selecting a number of the better models, and then selecting markets that these models trade well, a portfolio of systems to trade a portfolio of markets could be assembled. Therefore, good system-market combinations were selected from among the tests conducted in this book. No optimization of model parameters was performed.

A portfolio was assembled on the basis of in-sample statistical significance. The intention was to find one good model-order combination for each of the markets in the portfolio. If there were several potential models for a given market, the additional ones were discarded based on such things as model complexity (the more complex the model, the less it was trusted), mediocre portfolio performance, and other similar factors. The specific model-order combinations spanned the entire spectrum of models and orders tested, with various oscillators, moving averages, lunar and solar models, and seasonal and neural network models being represented; genetic models, however, were not included. In the current tests, the particular genetic models that were evolved only traded rare events. For those in-sample markets that performed well, there were generally no out-of-sample trades. The profitable out-of-sample behavior was achieved on almost a totally different

FIGURE C-1

Equity Growth for Multiple-System and Market Portfolio

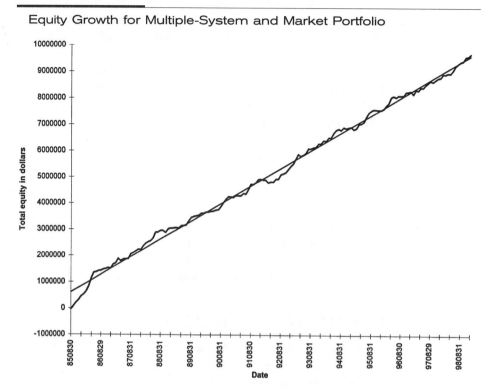

set of markets than the in-sample behavior of the model. This does not mean that the out-of-sample performance was bad while the in-sample performance was good, but rather that most markets simply did not trade in one sample if they did in the other. The low number of trades observed with the genetic models was due to the specific nature of the particular rule templates and the ways in which the individual rules were combined to obtain buy and sell signals. With some changes in the rule templates, especially in the number of rules used and in how they are combined, the pattern of rare event trading can be entirely altered.

There were times when the preferred kind of model was not available for a given market. In such cases, models were examined that performed poorly on a whole-portfolio basis, but that did trade one or two difficult markets acceptably. For example, the RSI overbought/oversold model with entry on limit was a poor performer on a portfolio-wide basis. However, this model traded Gold and Silver reasonably well. It pulled returns of 27.3 and 3.9%, annualized, on the in-sample data, with average trades of $9,446 and $4,164, respectively. Out-of-sample, the system pulled 23.6% out of the Gold and 51.7% out of the Silver markets, with average trades yielding $12,194 and $24,890, respectively.

One of the large neural networks that appeared to be highly over-optimized was used for the three wheat markets—markets that did not trade at a statistically significant level with any of the other models. The large, long-side, turning-point network with entry on limit, however, had high statistical significance when trading each of the wheats, pulling more than 40% annually from each, and more than $15,000 per trade. The amazing thing is that, out-of-sample, despite the size of the net and the degree of curve-fitting seen on its portfolio performance, the model pulled in no less than 24%, with $5,000 per trade, from each of the wheats.

The cycle model, which worked well on hardly any market, did trade the S&P 500 profitably—returning 15.3%, with an average in-sample trade of $4,613, and 21.4% with $4,698-per-trade profit out-of-sample. It should be noted that a cycle model was found to trade the S&P-500 successfully in the tests reported in our earlier study (Katz and McCormick, May 1997).

Once each market was paired with a good model-order combination, the performance data were analyzed, both in- and out-of-sample, for each of the markets. An equity curve was prepared that covered both periods (see Figure C-1). Returns and statistical significance were calculated for the multiple-model portfolio, both in-sample and out-of-sample. It was surprising to discover that the out-of-sample performance data revealed a return-on-account of 625% annualized! A manifestation of the Holy Grail? Because model-market combinations were selected on the basis of their in-sample statistical significance, the 544% annualized in-sample return was not unexpected. The probability of obtaining an in-sample profit as large as that is less than 1 in 3,000,000,000,000,000,000 (i.e., 3×10^{18}). Even if massive amounts of optimization, with tests of tens of thousands of combinations, took place, the results would still be extremely significant, in a statistical sense. Out-of-sample, the probability of finding a risk-to-reward ratio or annualized return as good as that observed is less than 1 in 40 million. Again, even corrected for extensive optimization, the results would still be of extreme statistical significance. In fact, no out-of-sample optimization took place. In-sample, the systems were only optimized on the entire portfolio. Model parameters were never adjusted for the selected markets on which the models were to be traded. And only the minimal standard exit strategy was used. Performance could be very substantially improved using the best of the exits found in Part III.

These findings demonstrate that while most systems do not work and most tests show losses, a sufficiently extensive search (as conducted in this book) can discover enough that do work to put together a portfolio trading strategy capable of producing nothing less than stellar results.

COMPANION SOFTWARE AVAILABLE

We invite all readers to visit our website at **www.scientific-consultants.com** or to e-mail us at **katz@scientific-consultants.com**.

Those who wish to replicate and expand on our research may obtain a *free* copy of the C-Trader Toolkit (the software required to run the code presented in this book) from our website at **www.scientific-consultants.com**. A CD-ROM is also available for the nominal cost of $59.00. It contains the following:

- Complete code for every method tested in this book

- Commodities data from Pinnacle

- Spreadsheets containing all optimization data, market-by-market analyses, equity curves, figures, and tables

- The C-Trader Toolkit, which includes the C++ Trading Simulator, OptEvolve (the genetic optimizer), the Portfolio Simulation Shell, and related manuals

Name _____ Company _____
Address _____
City _____ State _____ Zip _____
Country _____ Country code _____
Phone: home (___)_____ office (___)_____
Fax (___)_____ E-mail _____

Please send me the companion CD-ROM: $59.00 × _____ copies $ _____

Numerical Recipes in C (994 page book) $54.95 × _____ copies $ _____

Numerical Recipes in C software IBM disks: $39.95 × _____ copies $ _____

Shipping & handling: CD only: add $3.50 per copy US, $7.50 outside US $ _____

Shipping & handling: *Numerical Recipes*: add $12 US, $35 outside US $ _____

Sales tax (NYS residents add ___% for your county _____) $ _____

TOTAL $ _____

CHECK ONE: ___ Enclosed is my check or money order (U.S. only)
                    __ Charge my Visa/Mastercard/AmEx account (fill in information below)

    account # _____ expiration _____

    signature _____

E-mail your order (**katz@scientific-consultants.com**), or mail, phone, or fax it to:

SCIENTIFIC CONSULTANT SERVICES, INC.   **Phone & fax:**
20 Stagecoach Road, Selden, New York 11784   631-696-3333

References and Suggested Reading

Alexander, Colin (June 1993). "Trade with Moving Averages." *Technical Analysis of Stocks and Commodities,* pp. 67–71.

Appel, Gerald (1990). *The Advanced Moving Average Convergence-Divergence Trading Method.* Videotape and manual distributed by Signalert Corportion, New York (516-829-6444).

Barrie, Scott (September 1996). "The COT Index." *Technical Analysis of Stocks and Commodities,* pp. 16–36.

Barrie, Scott (October 1996). "Pork Bellies and the COT Index." *Technical Analysis of Stocks and Commodities,* pp. 79–92.

Bernstein, Jake (1995). *Trade Your Way to Riches.* MBH Commodity Advisors, Inc. (1-800-457-0825), 1995.

Blau, William (January 1993). "Stochastic Momentum." *Technical Analysis of Stocks and Commodities,* pp. 26–35.

Burke, Gibbons (May 1993). "Good Trading a Matter of Breeding?" *Futures Magazine,* pp. 26–329.

Center for Solar and Space Research, Yale University (1997). *Sunspot Predictions.* Release distributed by Virtual Publishing Company.

Chande, Tushar S. (March 1992). "Adapting Moving Averages to Market Volatility." *Technical Analysis of Stocks and Commodities,* pp. 46–53.

Davies, D. W. (June 1993). "Cyclical Channel Analysis and the Commodity Channel Index." *Technical Analysis of Stocks and Commodities,* pp. 38–45.

Davis, Lawrence (Ed.) (1991). *Handbook of Genetic Algorithms.* New York: Van Nostrand Reinhold.

Ehlers, John (March 1989). "Moving Averages and Smoothing Filters." *Technical Analysis of Stocks and Commodities,* pp. 42–46.

Gauquelin, H., Gauquelin, R., and Eysenck, S. B. G. (1979). "Personality and Position of the Planets at Birth: An Empirical Study." *British Journal of Social and Clinical Psychology,* Vol. 18, pp. 71–75.

Goedde, Richard (March 1997). "Timing a Stock Using the Regression Oscillator." *Technical Analysis of Stocks and Commodities,* pp. 54–60.

Hannula, Hans (November 1991). "The Seasonal Cycle." *Technical Analysis of Stocks and Commodities,* pp. 65–68.

Hoel, Paul G. (1966). *Elementary Statistics,* 2d ed., New York: John Wiley & Sons.

Holland, John (1975). *Adaptation in Natural and Artificial Systems.* Ann Arbor: The University of Michigan Press.

Jurik, Mark (1999). "Finding the Best Data." *Computerized Trading,* Mark Jurik (Ed.). New York: New York Institute of Finance/Prentice Hall, pp. 355–382.

Katz, Jeffrey Owen (April 1992). "Developing Neural Network Forecasters for Trading." *Technical Analysis of Stocks and Commodities,* pp. 58–68.

Katz, Jeffrey Owen, and McCormick, Donna L. (1990). *Calendar Effects Chart.* New York: Scientific Consultant Services.

Katz, Jeffrey Owen, and McCormick, Donna L. (March/April 1993). "Vendor's Forum: The Evolution of N-TRAIN." *PCAI,* pp. 44–46.

Katz, Jeffrey Owen, and McCormick, Donna L. (1994). "Neural Networks: Some Advice to Beginners." *Trader's Catalog and Resource Guide,* Vol. II, No. 4, p. 36.

Katz, Jeffrey Owen, and McCormick, Donna L. (July/August 1994). "Neurogenetics and Its Use in Trading System Development." *NeuroVe\$t Journal,* pp. 8–11.

Katz, Jeffrey Owen, and McCormick, Donna L. (1995a). "Introduction to Artificial Intelligence: Basics of Expert Systems, Fuzzy Logic, Neural Networks, and Genetic Algorithms." *Virtual Trading,* J. Lederman and R. A. Klein (Eds.). Chicago: Probus Publishing, pp. 3–34.

Katz, Jeffrey Owen, and McCormick, Donna L. (1995b). "Neural Networks in Trading." *Virtual Trading,* J. Lederman and R. A. Klein (Eds.). Chicago: Probus Publishing, pp. 35–64.

Katz, Jeffrey Owen, and McCormick, Donna L. (November 1996). "On Developing Trading Systems." *Technical Analysis of Stocks and Commodities,* pp. 46–60.

Katz, Jeffrey Owen, and McCormick, Donna L. (December 1996). "A Rule-Based Approach to Trading." *Technical Analysis of Stocks and Commodities,* pp. 22–34.

Katz, Jeffrey Owen, and McCormick, Donna L. (January 1997). "Developing Systems with a Rule-Based Approach." *Technical Analysis of Stocks and Commodities,* pp. 38–52.

Katz, Jeffrey Owen, and McCormick, Donna L. (February 1997). "Genetic Algorithms and Rule-Based Systems." *Technical Analysis of Stocks and Commodities,* pp. 46–60.

Katz, Jeffrey Owen, and McCormick, Donna L. (April 1997). "Seasonality and Trading." *Technical Analysis of Stocks and Commodities,* pp. 50–61.

Katz, Jeffrey Owen, and McCormick, Donna L. (May 1997). "Cycles and Trading Systems." *Technical Analysis of Stocks and Commodities,* pp. 38–46.

Katz, Jeffrey Owen, and McCormick, Donna L. (June 1997). "Lunar Cycles and Trading." *Technical Analysis of Stocks and Commodities,* pp. 38–46.

Katz, Jeffrey Owen, and McCormick, Donna L. (July 1997). "Evaluating Trading Systems with Statistics." *Technical Analysis of Stocks and Commodities,* pp. 50–61.

Katz, Jeffrey Owen, and McCormick, Donna L. (August 1997). "Using Statistics with Trading Systems." *Technical Analysis of Stocks and Commodities,* pp. 32–38.

Katz, Jeffrey Owen, and McCormick, Donna L. (September 1997). "Sunspots and Market Activity." *Technical Analysis of Stocks and Commodities,* pp. 46–54.

Katz, Jeffrey Owen, and McCormick, Donna L. (November 1997). "Adding the Human Element to Neural Nets." *Technical Analysis of Stocks and Commodities,* pp. 52–64.

Katz, Jeffrey Owen, and McCormick, Donna L. (February 1998). "Exits, Stops and Strategy." *Technical Analysis of Stocks and Commodities,* pp. 32–40.

Katz, Jeffrey Owen, and McCormick, Donna L. (March 1998). "Testing Exit Strategies." *Technical Analysis of Stocks and Commodities,* pp. 35–42.

Katz, Jeffrey Owen, and McCormick, Donna L. (April 1998). "Using Trailing Stops in Exit Strategies." *Technical Analysis of Stocks and Commodities,* pp. 86–92.

Katz, Jeffrey Owen, and McCormick, Donna L. (May 1998). "Using Barrier Stops in Exit Strategies." *Technical Analysis of Stocks and Commodities,* pp. 63–89.

Katz, Jeffrey Owen, and McCormick, Donna L. (July 1998). "Barrier Stops and Trendlines." *Technical Analysis of Stocks and Commodities,* pp. 44–49.

Katz, Jeffrey Owen, and McCormick, Donna L. (1999). "Case Study: Building an Advanced Trading System." *Computerized Trading,* Mark Jurik (Ed.). New York: New York Institute of Finance/Prentice Hall, pp. 317–344.

Katz, Jeffrey Owen, and McCormick, Donna L. (February 1999). "Trading Stocks with a Cyclical System." *Technical Analysis of Stocks and Commodities,* pp. 36–42.

Katz, Jeffrey Owen, and Rohlf, F. James (April 1975). "Primary Product Functionplane: An Oblique Rotation to Simple Structure." *Journal of Multivariate Behavioral Research*, Vol. 10, pp. 219–232.

Knight, Sheldon (September 1999). "How Clean Is Your End-of-Day Data?" *Futures Magazine*, p. 64.

Krutsinger, Joe (1994). *The Trading Systems Toolkit,* Chicago: Probus Publishing.

Lederman, J., and Klein, R. A. (Eds.). (1995). *Virtual Trading.* Chicago: Probus Publishing.

Lupo, Louis M. (December 1994). "Trading Markets with Stochastics." *Technical Analysis of Stocks and Commodities,* pp. 38–49.

Marder, Kevin (1999). "Financial Data Sources." *Computerized Trading,* Mark Jurik (Ed.). New York: New York Institute of Finance/Prentice Hall, pp. 345–354.

Masters, Timothy (1995). *Neural, Novel & Hybrid Algorithms for Time Series Prediction.* New York: John Wiley & Sons.

Mayo, J., White, O., and Eysenck, H. J. (1978). "An Empirical Study of the Relation between Astrological Factors and Personality." *The Journal of Social Psychology,* Vol. 105, pp. 229–236.

McWhorter, W. Lawson (January 1994). "Price/Oscillator Divergences." *Technical Analysis of Stocks and Commodities,* pp. 95–98.

Meibahr, Stuart (December 1992). "Multiple Length Stochastics." *Technical Analysis of Stocks and Commodities,* pp. 26–32.

Meyers, Dennis (May 1997). "Walk Forward with the Bond XAU Fund System." *Technical Analysis of Stocks and Commodities,* pp. 16–25.

Montgomery, Douglas C., and Peck, Elizabeth A. (1982). *Introduction to Linear Regression Analysis.* New York: John Wiley & Sons.

Mulloy, Patrick G. (February 1994). "Smoothing Data with Less Lag." *Technical Analysis of Stocks and Commodities,* pp. 58–70.

Murphy, John J. (1991). *Intermarket Technical Analysis: Trading Strategies for the Global Stock, Bond, Commodity and Currency Markets.* New York: John Wiley & Sons.

Myers, Raymond H. (1986). *Classical and Modern Regression with Applications.* Boston: Duxbury Press.

Oliver, Jim (March 1994). "Finding Decision Rules with Genetic Algorithms." *AI Expert,* pp. 32–39.

Pardo, Robert (1992). *Design, Testing, and Optimization of Trading Systems.* New York: John Wiley & Sons.

Press, W.H., Flannery, B.P., Teukulsky, S.A., and Vetterling, W.T. (1986). *Numerical Recipes: The Art of Scientific Computing.* Cambridge, England: Cambridge University Press.

Press, W. H., Teukolsky, S. A., Vetterling, W. T., and Flannery, B. P. (1992). *Numerical Recipes in C.* Cambridge, England: Cambridge University Press.

Price, Kenneth, and Storm, Rainer (April 1997). "Differential Evolution." *Dr. Dobbs Journal,* pp. 18–24.

Ruggiero, Murray A., Jr. (April 1994). "Getting the Lag Out." *Futures Magazine,* pp. 46–48.

Ruggiero, Murray A., Jr. (October 1996). "Trend-Following Systems: The Next Generation." *Futures Magazine.*

Ruggiero, Murray A., Jr. (1997). *Cybernetic Trading.* New York: John Wiley & Sons.

Ruggiero, Murray A., Jr. (May 1998). "Unholy Search for the Grail." *Futures Magazine.*

Schwager, Jack (October 1992). "Selecting the Best Futures for Computer Testing." *Technical Analysis of Stocks and Commodities,* pp. 65–71.

Sharpe, William F. (Fall 1994). "The Sharpe Ratio." *Journal of Portfolio Management.*

Space Science Institute (1996). "A Magnetic Storm Rips through Earth's Atmosphere." A news release on their web site: www@www-ssi.colorado.edu.

Star, Barbara (July 1993). "RSI Variations." *Technical Analysis of Stocks and Commodities*, pp. 54–60.

Stendahl, David (1999). "Evaluating Trading Performance." *Computerized Trading.* New Jersey: New York Institute of Finance/Prentice Hall, pp. 137–162.

Sweeney, John (1993). "Where to Put Your Stops." *Technical Analysis of Stocks and Commodities* (Bonus Issue), pp. 30–32.

Sweeney, John (April 1998). "Applying Moving Averages." *Technical Analysis of Stocks and Commodities,* pp. 48–50.

Tilley, D.L. (September 1998). "Moving Averages with Resistance and Support." *Technical Analysis of Stocks and Commodities,* pp. 62–87.

Trippi, Robert R., and Turban, Efraim (Eds.) (1993). *Neural Networks in Finance and Investing.* Chicago: Probus Publishing.

White, Adam (April 1993). "Filtering Breakouts." *Technical Analysis of Stocks and Commodities,* pp. 30–41.

Wilder, J. Welles (1978). *New Concepts in Technical Trading Systems.* Trend Research.

Williams, Larry (1979). *How I Made One Million Dollars Last Year Trading Commodities.* New York: Windsor Books.

Yuret, Deniz, and de la Maza, Michael (June 1994). "A Genetic Algorithm System for Predicting the OEX." *Technical Analysis of Stocks and Commodities,* pp. 58–64.

INDEX

Adaptation in Natural and Artificial Systems (Holland), 257
Adaptive moving averages, 111, 112
ADX trend filter:
    breakout models, 102–104
    moving average models, 131
AI (*see* Genetic algorithms, Neural networks)
Alexander, Colin, 113
All-past-years technique, 158
Analysis, 39
Analytic optimizers, 39, 40, 48
Annealing, 38
Annualized risk-to-reward ratio (ARRR), 15, 60
Appel, Gerald, 133
Artificial intelligence (*see* Genetic algorithms,
    Neural networks)
Astrology, 179
    (*See also* Lunar and solar rhythms)
Author's conclusions, 353–363
Average directional movement index (*see* ADX trend filter)
Average true range, 86

Back-adjustment, 3, 4
Bad curve-fitting, 54
Band-pass filter, 207
Barrier exits, 287
Barron's, 12
Bars, 109
Basic crossover model:
    lunar activity, 191–194
    seasonality, 166–170
Basic momentum model:
    lunar activity, 194, 195
    seasonality, 170, 171
Bernstein, Jake, 154
Best exit strategy (market-by-market results), 330–332
Best possible solution to a problem, 30
Beta weights, 55
Blau, William, 134
Bonneville Market Information (BMI), 11
Borland, 24, 25
Bottom turning-point model, 243, 249, 250
Bouncing tick, 25
Breakout models, 74, 83–108
    ADX trend filter, 102–104
    analysis by market, 106, 107

Breakout models (*Cont.*):
    breakout types, 104
    channel breakouts, 86–97
    characteristics of breakouts, 84, 85
    close only channel breakouts, 86–92
    currencies only, 101, 102
    entry orders, 104–106
    highest high/lowest low breakouts, 92–97
    interactions, 106
    lessons learned, 107, 108
    long positions only, 100, 101
    restrictions/filters, 106
    summary of results, 104–107
    testing, 85–104
    types of breakouts, 83, 84
    volatility breakout variations, 100–104
    volatility breakouts, 97–100
Bressert, 203
Brute force optimizers, 32–34, 47
Burke, Gibbons, 257
Butterworth filters, 206, 207

C++, 14, 15, 24–26, 46
C++ Builder, 26
C++ Genetic Optimizer, 49
C-Trader toolkit, 14, 15, 19, 27, 36, 99, 114, 214
Calendar effects chart, 154
Catastrophe stop, 288
CCI (commodities channel index), 135, 136
CD-ROM, 364
Centered smoothing, 155, 181
Central limit theorem, 61, 68
Chande, Tushar S., 110–112
Channel breakouts, 86–97
Chromosome, 258
Clipping, 164
Close only channel breakouts, 86–92
Code listings:
    cycle-based entries, 214–219
    dynamic stops, 317–321
    genetic algorithms, 262–268
    genetic exit strategy, 342–345
    lunar activity, 183–189
    moving average models, 115–118
    MSES, 302–305

Code listings (*Cont.*):
  neural exit strategy, 337–339
  neural networks, 233–237
  oscillator-based entries, 140–143
  profit target (fixed stop), 311–313
  reverse slow %K model, 233–237
  seasonality, 159–163
  shrinkage profit target, 326–328
  standard exit strategy (SES), 295–297
  turning-point models, 241, 242
Commodities channel index (CCI), 135, 136
Commodities pricing data, 3, 4
Commodities Systems Incorporated (CSI), 11
Companion software available, 364
Computerized Trading (Jurik), 227
Conclusions, 353–363
Confidence interval, 60
Confirmation-and-inversion model:
  lunar activity, 182, 196
  seasonality, 156, 173
Constant-investment model, 81
Continuous contract, 3
Contrarian crossover model, 125
Contrarian trading, 289
Correlational statistics, 52
Cost function, 30
Counter-trend moving average entry models, 113, 114,
  125–130
CRITBINOM function, 60
Critical threshold exits, 283
Crossover:
  genetic algorithms, 258, 259
  lunar activity, 181, 182
  seasonality, 155, 156
  (*See also* Basic crossover model)
Crossover-with-confirmation model:
  lunar activity, 182, 195, 196
  seasonality, 156, 171–173
CSI (Commodities Systems Incorporated), 11
C-Trader toolkit, 14, 15, 19, 27, 36, 99, 114, 214
Cumulative t-distribution, 58, 59
Curve-fitting:
  bad, 54
  good, 54
  neural networks, 230, 255
  optimization, and 54–57
Cycle, 203
Cycle-based entries, 76, 203–226
  Butterworth filters, 206, 207
  characteristics, 213, 214
  code testing, 214–219
  filter banks, 204–213

Cycle-based entries (*Cont.*):
  generating cycle entries using filter banks, 213
  lessons learned, 226
  maximum entropy, 203, 204
  test methodology, 214–220
  test results, 220–224
  wavelet-based filters, 207–213
  (*See also* Seasonality)
Cycle Trader, 203

Data, 3–12
  quality, 6–11
  sources/vendors, 11, 12
  time frames, 5, 6
  types, 3, 4
Data Broadcasting Corporation (DBC), 11
Data-checking utility, 7–10
Data errors, 7
Data points, 109
Data quality, 6–11
Data smoother, 110
Data Transmission Network (DTN), 11
Davies, D.W., 135
Davis, Lawrence, 47, 257
DBC (Data Broadcasting Corporation), 11
de la Maza, Michael, 257
Degrees of freedom, 42, 55
Delphi, 24–26
Design, Testing and Optimization of Trading Systems
  (Pardo), 48
Detail reports, 19–22
Dewey, Edward R., 180
Differential evolution, 47
Directional movement index, 85
  (*See also* ADX trend filter)
Divergence, 75, 136, 137, 148
Divergence models, 148–150
Divergengine, 137
Dollar volatility equalization, 78–81
DTN (Data Transmission Network), 11
Dynamic ATR-based stop, 322, 323
Dynamic stops, 316–324

Easy Language, 14, 15, 22, 24, 25, 33, 140
8-minute cycle, 76
Ehlers, 203
Ehlers, John, 110, 134
End-of-day pricing data, 4
Endogenous, 76
Entry methods, 71–280
  breakout models, 83–108
  cycles and rhythms, 203–226

Entry methods (*Cont.*):
  dollar volatility equalization, 78–81
  genetic algorithms, 257–280
  good entry, 71
  introduction, 71–82
  lunar/solar phenomena, 179–202
  moving average models, 109–132
  neural networks, 227–256
  orders used in entries, 72–74
  oscillators, 133–152
  seasonality, 153–177
  standard portfolio, 81, 82
  standardized exits, 77, 78
Equis International, 25, 47
Evolutionary model building
    (*see* Genetic algorithms)
Evolver, 47, 49
Excalibur, 47, 48
Exit strategies, 281–351
  barrier exits, 287
  best exit strategy (market-by-market results),
    330–332
  contrarian trading, 289
  critical threshold exits, 283
  dynamic ATR-based stop, 322, 323
  dynamic stops, 316–324
  extended time limit, 328
  fixed stop/profit target, 311–316
  genetic components, 341–348
  gunning, 288
  highest high/lowest low stop, 322
  importance, 281, 282
  improvements on standard exit, 309–333
  MEMA dynamic stop, 323, 324
  modified standard exit strategy (MSES), 302–307
  money management exits, 283, 284
  neural networks, 336–341
  profit target exits, 285, 286, 311–316, 324–328
  protective stops, 288, 289
  random entry model, 291, 292
  shrinking profit target, 324–328
  signal exits, 287, 288
  slippage, 289
  standard exit strategy (SES), 293–302
  time-based exits, 286
  trailing exits, 284, 285
  volatility exits, 287
Exogenous, 76
Exponential moving average, 111, 112
Extended time limit (exit strategies), 328
Eysenck, H.J., 179
Eysenck, S.B.G., 180

Feed-forward neural networks, 228, 229
Filter banks, 204–213
Filters, 205
Fitness, 30
Fitness function, 30, 66
Fixed money management exit, 282
Flannery, B.P., 48, 49, 297
FM Labs, 26
Front-month contracts, 3
Front-weighted triangular moving average, 111
Futures, 133
FutureSource-Bridge, 11
Futures Truth, 47

GAs (*see* Genetic algorithms)
Gauquelin, H., 180
Gauquelin, R., 180
Gene, 258
Generalization, 56
GENESIS, 47
Genesis Financial Data Services, 11
Genetic algorithms, 77, 257–280
  code listing, 262–268
  evolving an entry model, 259–261
  exit strategies, 341–348
  lessons learned, 279, 280
  market-by-market test results, 274–276
  reference material, 257
  rule templates, 258, 260, 261
  rules for long entry, 277, 278
  rules for short entry, 278, 279
  solutions evolved for long entries, 270, 271
  solutions evolved for short entries, 271
  standard portfolio - test results, 272, 273
  terminology, 258
  test methodology, 261–269
  test results, 269–279
  what are they, 257, 258
Genetic operators, 258
Genetic Optimizer (C++), 49
Genetic optimizers, 35–38, 47–49
Genetic search, 259
Genetically evolved exits, 341–348
Genetically evolved systems, 66
Goedde, Richard, 133
Good curve-fitting, 54
Good entry, 71
Grefenstette, John, 47
Gunning, 288

Handbook of Genetic Algorithms (Davis), 47
Hannula, Hans, 154

HHLL breakouts, 92–97
HHLL stop, 322
High-pass Butterworth filter, 206
Highest high/lowest low breakouts, 92–97
Highest high/lowest low stop, 322
Histograms, 22, 23
Holland, John, 257

Implicit optimizers, 31
IMSL, 25, 26, 48
Individual contract data, 3
Inferential statistics (*see* Statistics)
Information sources:
  data, 11, 12
  optimizers, 48, 49
International Mathematics and Statistics Library (IMSL),
    25, 26, 48
Intraday pricing data, 4
Inversions, 156, 182
  (*See also* Confirmation-and-inversion model)
Investor's Business Daily, 12

Jackknife, 158
January effect, 154
Jurik, Mark, 11, 227, 232

Katz, Jeffrey Owen, 57, 76, 77, 154, 170, 181, 197, 199,
    202, 204, 227, 252, 257, 258, 262, 332, 363
Klein, R.A., 227
Knight, Sheldon, 11

Lag, 110
Lane's stochastic, 135
Leave-one-out method, 158
Lederman, J., 227
Limit orders, 72, 73
Linear band-pass filters, 134
Linear programming, 40, 41
Low-pass Butterworth filter, 206
Low-pass filter, 110
Lunar and solar rhythms, 75, 76, 179–202
  basic crossover model, 191–194
  basic momentum model, 194, 195
  code listing, 183–189
  crossover model with confirmation, 195, 196
  crossover model with confirmation and
      inversions, 196
  generating lunar entries, 181, 182
  lessons learned, 201, 202
  solar activity, 197–201
  summary analyses, 196, 197
  sunspots, 180

Lunar and solar rhythms (*Cont.*):
  test methodology, 183–190
  test results, 190–197
Lunar momentum series, 181
Lupo, Louis M., 134

MACD, 134
MACD divergence models, 150
MACD Histogram (MACD-H), 134
MACD signal lines models, 148
Marder, Kevin, 11
Market orders, 72, 73
Masters, Timothy, 48, 49
MathWorks, The, 48
Mating, 258
MATLAB, 48
Maximum entropy (MEM), 203, 204
Maximum entropy spectral analysis (MESA), 203
Mayo, J., 179
McCormick, Donna L., 57, 76, 77, 154, 170, 181, 197, 199,
    202, 204, 227, 252, 257, 258, 262, 332, 363
McWhorter, W. Lawson, 136
Mean, 58
Mean squared deviation, 58
Meibahr, Stuart, 135, 139
MEM, 204
MEMA dynamic stop, 323, 324
MESA, 203
MESA96, 76
MetaStock, 25, 47
Metasystems, 15, 26
Modified exponential moving average (MEMA), 323, 324
Modified standard exit strategy (MSES), 302–307
Momentum, 133, 155, 181
  (*See also* Basic momentum model)
Money management, 282
Money management exits, 283, 284
Money management stop, 78
Monte Carlo simulations, 67
Morelet wavelet, 207, 208
Moving average, 109
Moving average convergence divergence oscillator
    (MACD), 134
Moving average crossover, 113
Moving average models, 74, 109–132
  ADX trend filters, 131
  code listing, 115–118
  counter-trend models, 113, 114, 125–130
  equity curves, 130
  lag, 110, 111
  lessons learned, 131, 132
  moving average, defined, 109

Moving average models (*Cont.*):
    orders used, 114
    purpose of moving average, 110
    test methodology, 114–119
    trend-following models, 112–114, 119–125
    types of moving averages, 111, 112
MSES, 302–307
Mulloy, Patrick G., 110
Multiple correlation coefficient, 56
Multiple regression, 67
Mutation, 258
Myers, Raymond H., 67

N-TRAIN, 238
NAG (Numerical Algorithms Group), 26, 48
NAG library, 25, 48
National Climatic Data Center (NCDC), 11
National Geophysical Data Center (NGDC), 11
Net profit, 66
Nets (*see* Neural networks)
Neural exit components, 336–341
Neural networks, 77, 227–256
    bottom turning-point model, 243, 249, 250
    conclusion, 252–255
    code listing, 233–237
    curve-fitting, 230, 255
    exit strategies, 336–341
    feed-forward networks, 228, 229
    forecasting, and, 230, 231
    lessons learned, 255, 256
    reference material, 227
    summary analyses, 252
    time-reverse Slow %K model, 231–240, 246–249
    top turning-point model, 244, 250–252
    trading, and, 229, 230
    trading results, 244–252
    turning-point models, 240–244, 249–252
    what are they, 228, 229
Neural Networks in Finance and Investing
    (Trippi/Turban), 227
Neural, Novel & Hybrid Algorithms for Time Series
    Prediction (Masters), 48
NexTurn, 227
Noise spike, 7
Nonparametric statistics, 52
Normalization, 164
N-TRAIN, 238
Numerical Algorithms Group (NAG), 26, 48
Numerical Algorithms Group (NAG) library, 25, 48
Numerical Recipes, 26
Numerical Recipes in C (Press), 48, 49, 59,
    292, 297

Numerical Recipes in Fortran (Press), 48
Numerical Recipes library, 25

Object Pascal, 24–26, 46
Omega Research, 14, 47
OptEvolve, 47, 259, 345
Optimal f, 81
Optimization, 29, 54
Optimizers, 29–49
    alternatives to traditional optimization, 45, 46
    analytic, 39, 40
    brute force, 32–34
    choosing the right one, 48, 49
    failure of, 41–43
    genetic, 35–38
    how used, 30, 31
    implicit, 31
    linear programming, 40, 41
    parameters, 43–45
    sample size, 41–44
    simulated annealing, 38, 39
    sources of tools/information, 47, 48
    steepest ascent, and, 39
    success of, 43–45
    types, 31–41
    user-guided optimization, 34, 35
    verification, 43, 45
    what they do, 29, 30
Oscillator, 133–136
Oscillator-based entries, 74, 75, 133–152
    characteristics, 138, 139
    code listing, 140–143
    divergence models, 148–150
    generating entries, 136–138
    lessons learned, 152
    MACD divergence models, 150
    MACD signal line models, 148
    orders used, 138
    oscillator, described, 133
    overbought/oversold models, 144–147
    RSI divergence models, 149, 150
    RSI overbought/oversold models, 147
    signal line models, 147, 148
    stochastic divergence models, 149
    stochastic overbought/oversold models, 145, 146
    stochastic signal line models, 147
    summary table of results, 150–152
    test methodology, 139–144
    test results, 144–150
    types of oscillators, 134–136
Out-of-sample, 53
Out-of-sample testing, 67, 68

Outliers, 7
Overbought/oversold models, 144–147
Overextension, 133

Paired-associate learning, 228
Palisade Corporation, 47, 49
Parameters, 30
Pardo, Robert, 48
Pinnacle Data Corporation, 7, 9, 11, 82
Planetary influences (*see* Lunar and solar rhythms)
Plasmode, 213
Population, 53
Press, W.H., 48, 49, 297
Price, Kenneth, 47
Profit target exits, 285, 286
    fixed stop, 311–316
    shrinking coefficient, 324–328
Program code (*see* Code listings)
Prophet Financial Systems, 11
ProQuest, 12
Protective stops, 288, 289

Quadrature mirror filters, 208
Quotations, 4

Random entry model, 291, 292
Random number generator (RNG), 291, 292
Random sample, 61
Reference material, 365–368
Relative strength index (RSI), 135
Representative sample, 44
Resonance, 205
Resonating filter, 205
Reverse Slow %K model, 231–240, 246–249, 336–341
Risk-to-reward ratio, annualized, 15
RNG, 291, 292
RSI (relative strength index), 135
RSI divergence models, 149, 150
RSI overbought/oversold models, 147
Ruggiero, Murray A., Jr., 204, 213
Ruggiero Associates, 47, 48, 203
Rule induction, 259
Rule templates, 258, 260, 261
Rules, 30
Runs test, 52

Sample, 53
Sample standard deviation, 58
Sampling, 53, 54
Schwager, Jack, 4, 82
Scientific Consultant Services, 14, 26, 47, 49, 99, 203, 227,
    239, 258, 259, 364

Seasonal momentum series, 155
Seasonality, 75, 153–177
    basic crossover model, 166–170
    basic momentum model, 170, 171
    characteristics of seasonal entries, 156, 157
    code listing, 159–163
    crossover model with confirmation, 171–173
    crossover model with confirmation and inversions, 173
    generating seasonal entries, 155, 156
    lessons learned, 177
    orders used, 157
    summary analyses, 174–176
    test methodology, 158–166
    test results, 166–176
    what is it, 153–155
Selection, 258
Self-adaptive systems, 46
Serial correlation, 62, 67
Serial dependence, 61, 62
SES, 293–302
Settlement price, 4
Sharpe, William F., 15
Sharpe ratio, 15
Shrinkage, 44, 55, 56
Shrinkage correction formula, 42
Shrinkage-correlated multiple correlations, 56
Shrinking profit target, 324–328
Signal exit, 287, 288, 335
Signal line, 75, 136, 147
Signal line models, 147, 148
Simple moving average, 109, 111
Simple trendline breakout, 83
Simulated annealing, 38, 39, 48
Simulators, 13–27
    capacity, 24
    choosing the right one, 26
    output, 15–22
    performance, 22–25
    performance summary reports, 15–19
    power, 24, 25
    reliability, 25, 26
    speed, 22, 24
    trade-by-trade reports, 19–22
    types, 13–15
    used in book, 26, 27
Slippage, 72, 289
Slow %K, 156
    (*See also* Time-reversed Slow %K model)
Software availability (Scientific Consultant Services), 362
Solar activity, 197–201
    (*See also* Lunar and solar rhythms)
Solution, 29

Solver, 48, 49
Sources of information/tools:
  data, 11, 12
  optimizers, 48, 49
Spreadsheets, 22
Standard deviation, 58
Standard deviation of the mean, 58
Standard exit strategy (SES), 293–302
Standardized portfolio, 81, 82
Star, Barbara, 135
Statistics, 51–69
  central limit theorem, 61, 68
  correlational, 52
  CRITBINOM function, 60
  example (evaluating in-sample tests), 62–65
  example (evaluating out-of-sample tests), 58–62,
    65, 66
  genetically evolved systems, 66
  Monte Carlo simulations, 67
  multiple regression, 67
  optimization/curve-fitting, 54–57
  out-of-sample testing, 67, 68
  population, 53
  serial dependence, 61
  sample size/representativeness, 57
  sampling, 53, 54
  shrinkage correction, 56
  t-statistic, 66
  t-tests, 51, 58
  violations of assumptions, 52
  walk-forward testing, 68
  why used, 52
Steepest ascent optimization, 39
Stendahl, David, 19
Stochastic divergence models, 149
Stochastic hook, 138
Stochastic oscillator, 134–136
Stochastic overbought/oversold models, 145, 146
Stochastic signal line models, 147
Stop orders, 72, 73
Stops (see Exit strategies)
Storm, Rainer, 47
Suggested reading, 365–368
Summary of conclusions, 353–363
Sunspots, 180
  (See also Lunar and solar rhythms)
SuperCharts, 47
Supervised learning, 228
Sweeney, John, 22, 113

T-statistic, 66
T-tests, 51, 58

Technical Analysis of Stocks and Commodities, 74, 109,
    133, 139, 227
Technical Tools, 11
Teukolsky, S.A., 48, 49, 297
3-day cycle, 76
Tick, 5
Tick Data, 11
Tick volume, 4
Tilley, D.L., 113
Time-based exits, 286
Time-reversed Slow %K model, 231–240, 246–249,
    336–341
Time series, 109
Time window, 109
Tools of the trade, 1–69
  data, 3–12
  introduction, 1, 2
  optimizers, 29–49
  simulators, 13–37
  sources of information, 11, 12
  statistics, 51–69
Top turning-point model, 244, 250–252
Trade-by-trade reports, 19–22
TradeCycles, 76, 203
TradeStation, 14, 15, 19, 32, 33, 37, 47, 48, 88, 111, 139,
    140, 258
Trading simulators (see Simulators)
Trailing exits, 284, 285
Training fact set, 231
Trend filters (ADX), 102–104, 131
Trend-following moving average entry models, 112–114,
    119–125
Trippi, Robert R., 227
TS-Evolve, 47, 48, 258
Turban, Efraim, 227
Turning-point models, 240–244,
    249–252

Unsupervised learning, 228

Vetterling, W.T., 48, 49, 297
VIDYA, 112
Virtual Trading, 227, 257
Visual Basic, 24, 26, 46
Visual Basic for Applications, 22
Visual C++, 26
Visual Numerics, Inc., 48
Volatility bands, 83
Volatility breakout variations, 100–104
Volatility breakouts, 97–100
Volatility exits, 287
Volatility units, 78

Walk-forward optimization, 46
Walk-forward testing, 46, 68
Wall Street Journal, 12
Wavelet-based filters, 207–213
Wavelet theory, 207
Weighted moving average, 111

White, Adam, 203
White, O., 179
Wilder, J. Welles, 85, 103
Williams, Larry, 180, 260

Yuret, Deniz, 257